SOLOMON
ISLANDS

PAPUA
NEW GUINEA

20:30
12:00

21:00
12:00

AF239249

Torres-Strait

4073 ▲

Iron Range

Gulf of
Carpentaria

Cooktown ○

Cairns ●

▲
1611

Coral Sea

Forsayth ○

Flinders

Townsville ●

Great Barrier Reef

rritory

ALIA

Mackay ○

Queensland

Great Dividing Range

Rockhampton ○

c   k

Diamantina

Cooper Creek

Lake
Eyre

Quilpie ○

Toowoomba ○

Brisbane ■
Gold Coast ●

ustralia   Marree ○

Cunnamulla ○

New South Wales

Kempsey ○

Broken
Hill ○

Darling

Newcastle ●

Mildura ○

Murrumbidgee

Blue Mountains

Great Dividing Range

Sydney ■
Rockdale ●
Wollongong ●

Adelaide ■

Murray

Canberra ●
Australian Capital
Territory

Victoria

Great Dividing Range

▲ 2230
Mount
Kosciusko

Pacific

Ballarat ○

Geelong ● Melbourne ■

Bass Strait

Ocean

Tasman Sea

P

Tasmania

Hobart ●

0 100 200 300 400 500 km

Camden Market

Textbook 5

Für Klasse 9

Diesterweg

Camden Market 5

Herausgegeben von:
Otfried Börner, StD a.D. und
Dr. phil. h.c. Christoph Edelhoff, StD a.D.,
Vorsitzender THE ENGLISH ACADEMY

Erarbeitet von:
Ruth Barker, Deborah Berger, Verena Büter,
Lorcan Flynn, Ulrike Handke, Isabel Kombartzky
und Sylvia Redlich
sowie: Viola Beyer-Kessling, Ingrid Gebhard,
Pamela Hanus, Pat Jüngst und Sylvia Wauer
Unter Mitwirkung der Redaktion:
Lisa Fast, Julia Mohm, Dr. Philippa Söldenwagner
und Henriette Vahle

Fachliche Beratung:
Sigrid Boinski, Elke Dreyer, Petra Günther,
Grit Machut, Ada Quade, Annette Schade,
Claudia Stammwitz und Gabriele Uplawski

**Zusatzmaterialien
zum vorliegenden Schülerbuch**
• Workbook 5 mit Audio-CD für Schüler
  (Best.-Nr. 978-3-425-72831-5)
• Workbook 5
  (Best.-Nr. 978-3-425-72817-9)
• Audio-CD für Schüler 5
  (Best.-Nr. 978-3-425-72859-9)

Lehrer-Materialien
• Audio-CD 5 für Lehrer
  (Best.-Nr. 978-3-425-72871-1)
• Teacher's Manual 5 inkl. Copymaster
  und Workbook-Lösungsheft
  (Best.-Nr. 978-3-425-72897-1)
• Lehrer-Software 5
  (Best.-Nr. 978-3-425-72839-1)
• Vorschläge für Lernerfolgskontrollen 5
  mit CD-ROM
  (Best.-Nr. 978-3-425-72867-4)

© 2009 Bildungshaus Schulbuchverlage
Westermann Schroedel Diesterweg Schöningh Winklers GmbH, Braunschweig
www.diesterweg.de

Druck A^8 / Jahr 2017
Alle Drucke der Serie A sind im Unterricht parallel verwendbar.

Redaktion: Lisa Fast, Julia Mohm, Dr. Philippa Söldenwagner, Henriette Vahle
Herstellung: Sandra Grünberg
Illustrationen: Ulf Marckwort, Kassel
Umschlaggestaltung: blum design und kommunikation, Hamburg
Satz: Bock Mediengestaltung, Hannover
Vokabelanhang: Lea Gonsior
Druck und Bindung: westermann druck GmbH, Braunschweig

ISBN 978-3-425-**72807**-0

Welcome to Camden Market 5!

Liebe Schülerinnen und Schüler,

Camden Market 5 erwartet euch in diesem Jahr mit vielen interessanten Themen. So werdet ihr gleich zu Beginn eine Menge über Australien, das Land *down under*, erfahren.
Ihr könnt euch in diesem Band auch einen Einblick in die Arbeitswelt verschaffen und lernt, was es mit Soft Skills auf sich hat.
Mit dem Thema Freundschaft und dem Zusammenleben mit Menschen aus anderen Kulturen werdet ihr euch ebenfalls beschäftigen. Extrem wird es dann im Bereich des Sports und der ungewöhnlichen Looks, bei denen auch Tattoos und Piercings eine Rolle spielen.
Habt ihr immer schon mal wissen wollen, wie ihr euch ernähren müsst, um topfit zu sein? Liegt euch der Umweltschutz am Herzen? Bei *Camden Market 5* seid ihr richtig.

Natürlich findet ihr auch in Band 5 viele Hinweise und Materialien, die euch beim Lernen helfen, wie z. B. das *dictionary* im hinteren Teil des Buches.

In den Kapiteln geben euch die Symbole in der Randspalte wichtige Hinweise.

- Achtet auf die Tipps – sie helfen euch beim Lösen der Aufgaben oder geben wichtige Informationen.

  tip
  For more information …

- Auf den *Toolbox*-Seiten findet ihr nützliche Arbeitstechniken, z. B. für die Besprechung von Filmen, das Schreiben von Briefen, für Diskussionen und vieles mehr.

  How to …
  listen

- In den *wordbanks* findet ihr die wichtigsten Wörter zu einem Thema.

  wordbank
  statistics **A**

- Bei Fragen zur Grammatik könnt ihr die Erklärungen im *LiF*-Teil zu Hilfe nehmen.

  LiF
  10

- Vergesst nicht, eure eigenen Texte und Produkte im Portfolio-Ordner abzuheften. Füllt auch die Portfolio-Fragebögen im Workbook aus; sie zeigen euch eure Fortschritte.

  portfolio

Have fun with Camden Market 5!

Inhalt

Inhalt

R = *revision* (Wiederholung)

Inhalt

Inhalt

R = *revision* (Wiederholung)

Inhalt

Die Symbole

 **CD**
Dieser Hörtext ist auf der CD für Lehrer und auf der CD für Schüler.

 **CD**
Dieser Hörtext ist nur auf der CD für Lehrer.

 **LiF 9**
Hierzu gibt es eine Erklärung im Grammatik-Teil *Language in Focus*.

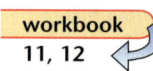 **workbook 11, 12**
Im Workbook gibt es weitere Übungen.

 **portfolio**
Diese Arbeit kannst du in deinem Portfolio-Ordner abheften.

 **How to ...** write
Auf den *How to*-Seiten findest du Techniken, die dir beim Englischlernen helfen.

 **tip** You can ...
Tipps oder Hilfen

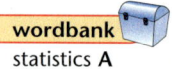 **wordbank** statistics **A**
In den *wordbanks* sind die wichtigsten Wörter zu einem Thema zusammengefasst.

Schwierige Texte und Aufgaben im *MORE*-Teil

Der Aufbau

Der Basis-Teil erfüllt die Grundanforderungen für Klasse 9. Hier werden alle Kompetenzen trainiert.

MORE M6-M8
Verknüpfungsmöglichkeit mit dem *MORE*-Teil

Der *MORE*-Teil bietet Zusatzmaterial zur Differenzierung für mittleres und höheres Niveau.

How to-Seiten vermitteln Lern- und Arbeitstechniken, *wordbanks* stellen thematischen Wortschatz zur Verfügung.

Optionales Zusatzmaterial:
Reading is fun – Lesestoff ergänzend zu jedem *Theme*.

Diese Arbeitsanweisungen findest du in Camden Market:

Act out the dialogue.	Spielt den Dialog nach.
Add notes to your grid.	Ergänze deine Tabelle.
Collect phrases/arguments/information/…	Sammle Redewendungen/Argumente/ Informationen/…
Compare your findings with a partner's.	Vergleiche deine Ergebnisse mit denen eines Partners/einer Partnerin.
Complete the sentences.	Vervollständige die Sätze.
Describe what is happening.	Beschreibe, was passiert.
Find a headline for each paragraph.	Finde eine Überschrift für jeden Absatz.
Find the words that match …	Finde Wörter, die zu … passen.
Find out …	Finde heraus …
Finish the statements/dialogues.	Schreibe die Aussagen/Dialoge zu Ende.
Give each other feedback.	Gebt einander Feedback.
Listen to the song/story/dialogue.	Höre dir das Lied/die Geschichte/den Dialog an.
Listen and take notes.	Höre zu und mache dir Notizen.
Look at the examples/pictures/…	Sieh dir die Beispiele/Bilder/… an.
Make a mindmap/list/fact file/…	Erstelle ein Wortnetz/eine Liste/einen Steckbrief/…
Make up a story.	Denke dir eine Geschichte aus.
Match the pictures/sounds with the texts.	Ordne die Bilder/Geräusche den Texten zu.
Practise your talk/presentation first.	Probe deine Rede/Präsentation zuerst.
Present your findings in class.	Präsentiere der Klasse deine Ergebnisse.
Put the sentences/pictures/events/… in the right order.	Bringe die Sätze/Bilder/Ereignisse/… in die richtige Reihenfolge.
Prepare a short talk/an interview/…	Bereite eine kurze Rede/ein Interview/… vor.
Read the text/article/brochure.	Lies den Text/Artikel/die Broschüre.
Swap your report with a partner.	Tausche deinen Bericht mit einem Partner/einer Partnerin.
Take notes (in a grid).	Mache dir Notizen (in einer Tabelle).
Take turns.	Wechselt euch ab.
Talk to a partner about …	Sprich mit einem Partner/einer Partnerin über …
Watch the film.	Sieh dir den Film an.
Work with a partner/in groups.	Arbeite mit einem Partner/einer Partnerin/ in einer Gruppe.
Write a letter/story/poem/…	Schreibe einen Brief/eine Geschichte/ein Gedicht/…
Write down words/phrases/reasons/…	Schreibe Wörter/Ausdrücke/Gründe/… auf.

Diese Sätze helfen dir, wenn du am Computer arbeitest:

Surf the Internet for information on …	Suche im Internet nach Informationen über …
Can I print it out/download it?	Kann ich das ausdrucken/herunterladen?
I've already saved it.	Ich habe es schon gespeichert.
The computer has crashed.	Der Computer ist abgestürzt.
What's your email address?	Wie ist deine E-Mail Adresse?
You can click on this link.	Du kannst diesen Link anklicken.

The Englis

1 **Look at the pictures and the map. What do YOU think:**

- Where do the teenagers come from?
- What do they have in common?

Helô! Rhiannon dwi. Dw i'n byw yng Nghymru.

Rhiannon, 17

Hi! My name is Henry.

Henry, 18

Jambo! Jina langa ni Zuberi.

Zuberi, 15

English-speaking countries
- mother-tongue use
- official or semi-official use

- ● capital
- ○ city

0   2000   4000 km

NORTH AMERICA

CANADA

UNITED STATES

Anchorage
Vancouver
Winnipeg
Ottawa   Montreal
Chicago   New York
San Francisco   Washington, D.C.
Los Angeles
Miami

Bermuda Is. (UK)

BAHAMAS
Puerto Rico (USA)
JAMAICA   ST. KITTS AND NEVIS
BELIZE   Kingston   ANTIGUA AND BARBUDA
ST. VINCENT AND   DOMINICA
THE GRENADINES   ST. LUCIA
    BARBADOS
    GRENADA
    TRINIDAD AND TOBAGO
GUYANA   Georgetown

Pacific Ocean

SOUTH AMERICA

Atlantic Ocean

Falkland Is. (UK)

EUROPE

UNITED KINGDOM
IRELAND
Dublin   London
Wales

MALTA   CYP

AFRICA

GAMBIA
SIERRA   Abuja
LEONE   Accra   NIGERIA
Freetown   Yaoundé
Monrovia   GHANA   CAMEROON
LIBERIA
    Ka
    RWAN
    Kig

    Lusa
    ZAMBIA
    Ha
NAMIBIA   BOTS
Windhoek   Gabor

    Pret
LESOT

    REPUB
Cape Town   SOUTH

speaking world

G'day mate! My name's Pete.

Pete, 15

Mera naam Gita hai. Mai bharat se hu.

Gita, 16

Ni hao! Wo jiao An.

An, 19

2 You are going to listen to the six teenagers. First make a grid.

CD

a) Listen and note down where the teenagers come from. Were you right in number 1?

b) Listen again. What languages do the teenagers speak? Complete your grid.

name	where from?	languages
Henry		
Rhiannon		
...		

How to ...
listen

Swahili • English • Hindi • Welsh • French • Japanese • Patois • Mandarin Chinese

3 On which continents are these countries? Work with a partner and play 'True or false'. Take turns.

True or false? Bangladesh is in Australia.

False. It's in Asia.

True or false? …

True./False. It's in …

1 Ghana is in South America.
2 Sri Lanka is in Africa.
3 Malta is in Europe.

4 Uganda is in Africa.
5 …

4 Find out more about countries where English is spoken. Form six groups. Each group chooses one country. Use books and the Internet to find information on:

- the continent the country is in
- the languages spoken there
- its capital
- its history
- other interesting information

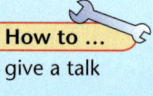
How to …
give a talk

Present your results in class.

 PEOPLE & PLACES

The English-speaking world

English is spoken in many places all over the world. It is the first language (mother tongue) of about 325 million people in the United Kingdom, the United States, Canada, Australia, New Zealand, Ireland and parts of the Caribbean.

More than 350 million people have English as their second language. In countries where many different languages are spoken people need one official language for schools and universities, in business and in government. But at home these people normally use their mother tongue. This happens in India, Kenya, Singapore and many other countries that belong to the Commonwealth because English is the one common language spoken in these countries.

The Commonwealth, also known as the Commonwealth of Nations, is a group of about 50 countries.

The Queen of Britain, Elizabeth II, is the head of the Commonwealth. Most of the members used to be British colonies, but they are now independent states. Some are still very poor, others are better off.

The Commonwealth countries work together to support each other and to deal with the problems of the world.

In almost every other part of the world people speak English when they can't understand each other's mother tongue. For example, a German tourist in Sweden can talk to the Swedes in English. About 750 million people speak English as a foreign language – and you are one of them!

tip
Learn more about the Commonwealth at www.the commonwealth. org

12

DOWN UNDER

In this Theme …

- you will learn a lot about Australia.
- you will talk about population statistics.
- you will make a fact file about an Australian animal.
- you will find out about the Aborigines' history and culture.
- you can read about the Great Barrier Reef.
- you will have the chance to give a presentation about Australia.

1 Australia – a land 'down under' 👂 👄

a) Look at the pictures and listen to the sounds.
   What comes to your mind when you think of Australia?

When
I think of Australia,
I think of …

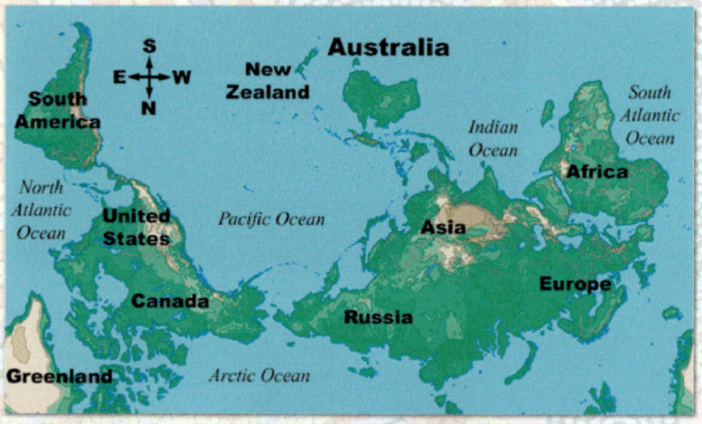

workbook
1-4

CD

14

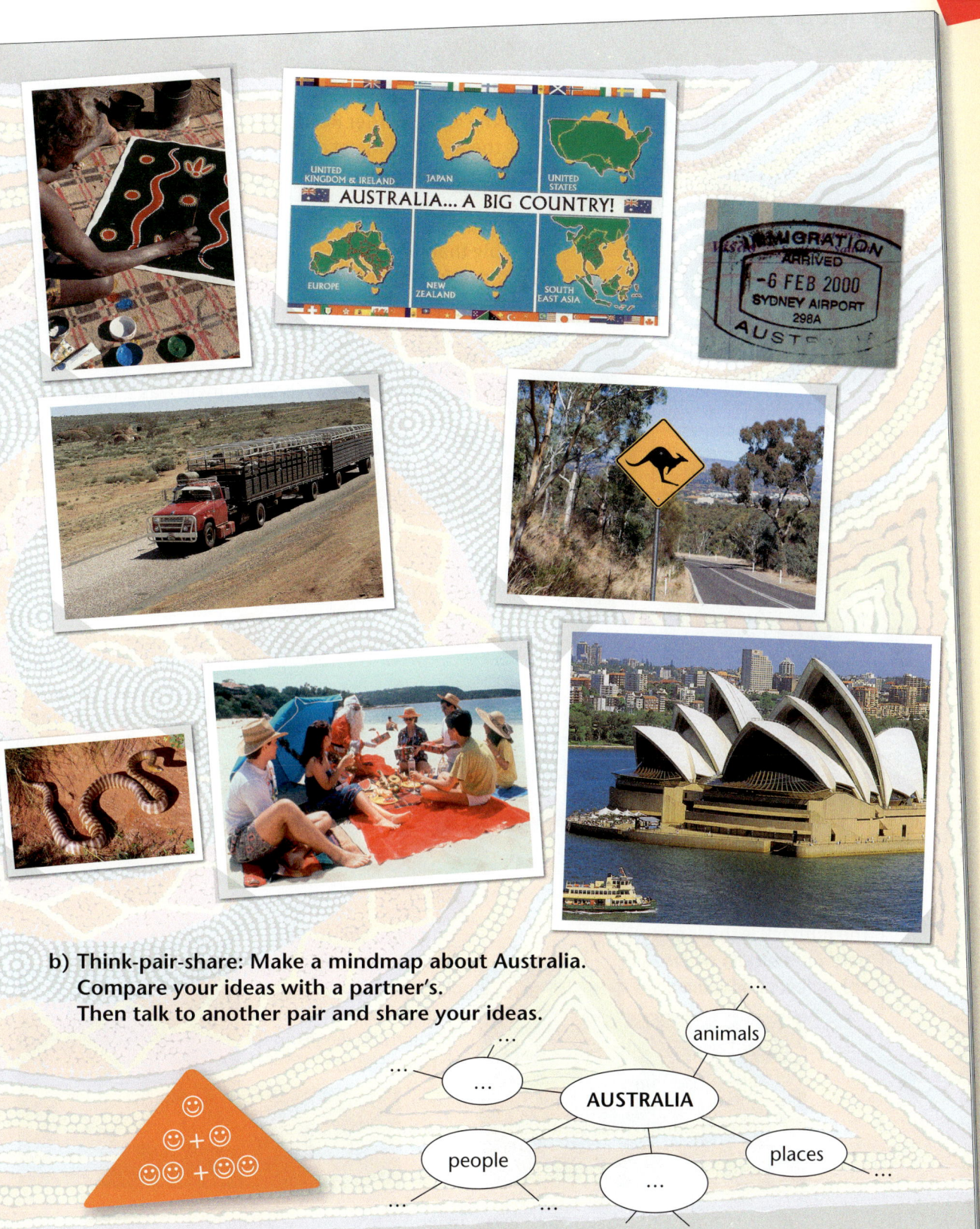

AUSTRALIA... A BIG COUNTRY!

b) **Think-pair-share: Make a mindmap about Australia.**
Compare your ideas with a partner's.
Then talk to another pair and share your ideas.

...   animals
...
...   AUSTRALIA
people   places
          ...   ...
...   ...
     ...   ...

2 Facts about Australia 👓

a) Here are some facts about Australia. Match the pictures with the texts.

MORE
M1-M3
Great Barrier Reef

A

7 The Great Barrier Reef is the world's largest coral reef system, with over 2,900 individual reefs and 900 islands. It is so big that it can even be seen from outer space.

B

1 The first people who settled in Australia came from Asia more than 40,000 years ago. Later the Europeans called them 'Aborigines'.

C

5 Steve Irwin was a famous Australian film-maker and animal lover. He was called the 'Crocodile Hunter'. He was 44 years old when he was killed by a stingray in the Great Barrier Reef.

D

4 Uluru or Ayers Rock, as the Europeans called it, is a holy place for the Aborigines.

E

3 The first 'immigrants' were 160,000 prisoners from Great Britain who were brought to Australia between 1788 and 1868. In the 20th century people from all over the world came to Australia.

2 The outback is the 'empty part' of Australia where only a few people live.

6 In 1770 the British captain James Cook arrived in Australia and declared that Australia was British from now on.

F

G

workbook
5

b) Look at your mindmap from 1b) again and add new information.

3 If I had the chance ...

What would YOU like to see and do if you had the chance to visit Australia?

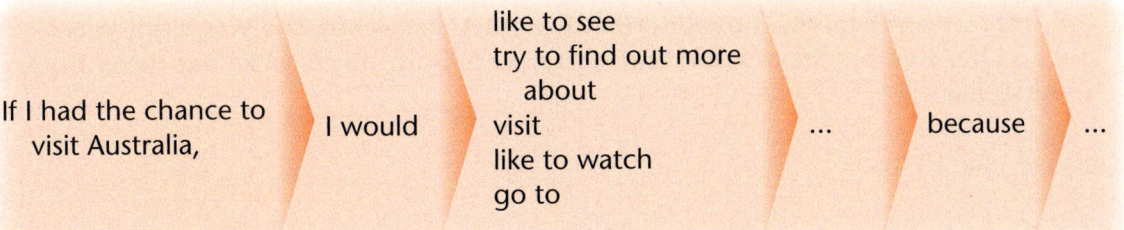

| If I had the chance to visit Australia, | I would | like to see / try to find out more about / visit / like to watch / go to / ... | ... | because | ... |

tip
Look at pages 14-16 for ideas.

LiF
12

workbook
6

4 All kinds of Australians

Australia has got a population of about 21 million people. About 500,000 of them are Aborigines. Five million of the people who live in Australia weren't born there. The immigrants come from 200 different countries. There are many Greeks living in Melbourne. Only Athens has got more Greeks than Melbourne.

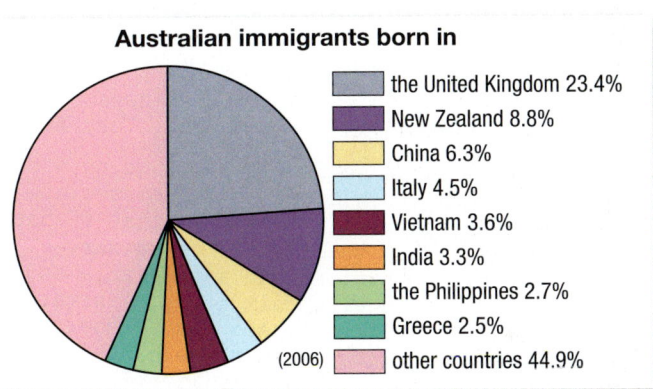

Australian immigrants born in
- the United Kingdom 23.4%
- New Zealand 8.8%
- China 6.3%
- Italy 4.5%
- Vietnam 3.6%
- India 3.3%
- the Philippines 2.7%
- Greece 2.5%
- other countries 44.9%

(2006)

a) Read the figures and say them aloud.

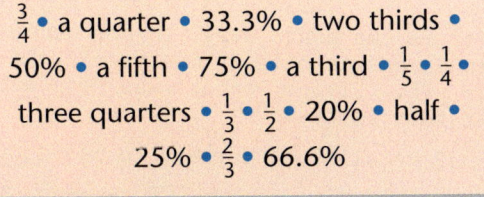

$\frac{3}{4}$ • a quarter • 33.3% • two thirds • 50% • a fifth • 75% • a third • $\frac{1}{5}$ • $\frac{1}{4}$ • three quarters • $\frac{1}{3}$ • $\frac{1}{2}$ • 20% • half • 25% • $\frac{2}{3}$ • 66.6%

You write	You say
50%	fifty per cent
$\frac{3}{4}$	three quarters
33.3%	thirty-three point three per cent

wordbank
statistics A

b) Which figures and words go together?

50% = $\frac{1}{2}$ = half

33.3% = ... = ...

c) Now talk about the statistics.

3.3% of Australian immigrants were born in India.

Almost a quarter of Australian immigrants come from ...

LiF
1, 15

workbook
7

5 The outback 👓 👄

a) **Look at the photos in the email. What do you think life is like in the outback?**

b) **Now read this email from Natasha, 16, to her cousin Mike, who is 22 and lives in the UK. Natasha's family moved to Bandya, Australia, when she was eight years old and her two brothers, Jason and Harry, were born there. Mike has never been to Australia.**

How to ...
read

Subject: Re: Hi there!

Hi Mike,

How are you? Thanks for the email! Well, everything is really different here in Western Australia. It's the outback and it's really empty. I'm sending you a picture, so that you can see what I mean … I like it, but there aren't many people! I miss having friends in my neighbourhood. It can be really hot – it was 46°C in January. Yeah, Christmas is in summer, as you probably know. I love that! On Christmas Day we usually have a barbecue or 'barbie' as it is called here. ;-) And then in July it was -4°C, but no snow … Oh, by the way, in the photo you can see Harry and me decorating the Christmas tree. He is nearly two years old and we're all very fond of playing with him!

We have about 8,000 sheep. Well, I guess I should say 'had'. We've got a real problem with dingoes at the moment. They killed about 100 of our sheep. :-(

You asked me about school. Well, I go to a boarding school in Perth, about 900 kilometres away from home. My classmates are all right, but sometimes they make fun of me and call me a 'pommy' – that's what Australians like to call people from Britain. That really gets on my nerves! Before Perth I "went" to 'SOA' – 'School of the Air'. I had a timetable and listened to the 30-min lessons over the radio. I could also talk to my classmates but I couldn't see their faces. For Jason it's different. All his teachers and the other kids in his class have a webcam on their computers so he can see them all! That's good, but he can't do his schoolwork in his pyjamas, like I did! :-D

You can't do much travelling because everything's so far away. I hate travelling in the car for so long, but I love going by plane. My parents bought me a jeep, which I'm allowed to drive. It's really cool, but I'm afraid of driving it at the moment. I need more practice! :-/

It can be a problem that the nearest doctor is two hours away. In emergencies there are the 'Flying Doctors'. Once, when Jason was only 14 months old, he drank something which was really dangerous. The 'Flying Doctor' was here after about two hours but Mum and Dad thought it took forever.

So, when exactly are you coming to visit us? We all look forward to seeing you in Bandya!

CU! Natasha

PS Lots of love from Mum, Dad, Jason and Harry!

c) **What did you already know?**
What information is new to you?

> It's surprising that …

> I've already heard about …

d) **Put the headlines in the right order.**
(Be careful: There are more headlines than you need.)

> Needing a doctor • A dingo problem •
> Great distances • Summer in December •
> A car accident • Our dogs •
> School life in the outback

e) **Read the email again.**
Natasha has different feelings about life in the outback.

Example: **She enjoys celebrating Christmas in summer.**

She	likes	(have) friends in the neighbourhood.
	misses	(travel) by car.
	loves	(see) her cousin Mike.
	doesn't like	(celebrate) Christmas in summer.
	enjoys	(live) in the outback.
	is fond of	(drive) a jeep.
	hates	(go) by plane.
	is afraid of	(play) with her little brother Harry.
	looks forward to	(be) called a 'pommy' by her classmates.

LiF
19

f) **What would or wouldn't YOU like, hate, … doing in the outback?**

workbook
8-11

6 On his way to the outback

Mike has decided to visit Natasha and her family during his Christmas holidays. Now he is on his way to Bandya. In Kalgoorlie, halfway between Perth and Bandya, Mike tries the Gold Dust Backpackers Hostel.

CD

a) **Listen to Mike talking to the receptionist.**
Write down the numbers of the phrases you hear.

1. I'd like to book a room.

2. Is that per room or per bed?

3. We have private rooms and mixed dorms.

4. A private room is 50 AUD.

5. Would you like a single or a double room?

6. Is breakfast included?

7. I just need your signature here, please.

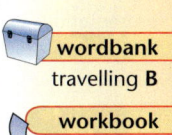
How to …
listen

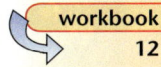
wordbank
travelling **B**

workbook
12

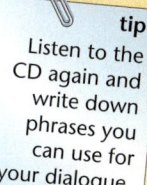
tip
Listen to the CD again and write down phrases you can use for your dialogue.

b) **Explain these words:**
receptionist • mixed dorm •
AUD • signature

c) **Role-play: Work with a partner and make up a scene at the youth hostel. One of you is the receptionist, the other one is the guest. Act out your scene to the class.**

1

CD

7 Things to see – things to do 👂 👄

a) The next morning Mike meets a young backpacker in the breakfast room. Listen to Mike and Ben. Which of these cities and places do they talk about?

> Canberra • Sydney • Melbourne • Uluru/Ayers Rock •
> Blue Mountains • Great Barrier Reef • Alice Springs •
> Brisbane • Cairns • Kalgoorlie • Perth

north-west **NORTH** north-east
WEST — **EAST**
south-west **SOUTH** south-east

b) Find these cities and places on the map at the front of your book. Describe where they are.

workbook 13

> Melbourne is in the south-east of Australia.

> ... is in the eastern part of ...

8 Dingo and company 👂

CD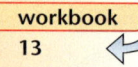

In Perth Mike visited the famous Perth Zoo. Now he is talking to Ben about typical Australian animals.

Listen and match the pictures with the correct names. Give reasons for your choice.

> I think picture number 1 is a ... because it looks like a .../ has got ...

> platypus • wallaby • dingo • wombat • koala • emu

1

2

3

4

9 YOUR fact file: Australian animals 👓 ✏️

MORE M4 YOUR presentation

a) Make a fact file about a typical Australian animal.

- Go to Perth Zoo's homepage: www.perthzoo.wa.gov.au
- Choose an Australian animal that you want to present in your fact file.

tip
Try to find a photo of your animal for your fact file.

b) Search for information on:

- what it looks like (size, weight, ...)
- what it eats
- where it lives
- what is special about it (colour, fur, paws, ...)
- ...

Then put the information in your fact file.

portfolio

c) Have a class exhibition with all the fact files.

AGILE WALLABY

SIZE: 85–120 cm long
WEIGHT: 15–27 kg
FOOD: Grass, leaves, fruit, roots
AREA: Northern Australia

SPECIAL INFORMATION: Has big feet and small paws like a kangaroo; makes a sound like 'tch, tch, tch' when it doesn't like something.

10 Aboriginal songs

Listen to some parts of three different songs.
What is the music like? How do you like the music?

> sad • happy • fast • funny • aggressive • great
> • slow • strange • relaxing • too loud • …

I think the music of the first/second/ … song is …

I can understand a few words, for example …

I like/don't like the rhythm/instruments in song number … because …

11 Dreamtime stories

Aborigines believe that the world and everything on it was made by 'ancestor spirits'. These spirits arrived a very long time ago, some from the sky, some from across the water, and some from the ground. Aborigines call this period of time the 'Dreamtime'. This Dreamtime story, told by a singer of the famous band 'Yothu Yindi', tells how the sun and stars were made.

a) Listen to the Dreamtime story and read along.
Which of the pictures fits the story best?
Give reasons.

A long time ago
it was very, very dark. It was
always night. An emu and a crane
started to fight over the emu's eggs.
The emu cracked the eggs. The crane
kicked the eggs up into the sky. There was
an explosion. The yellow yolk of the eggs
became the sun. The pieces of eggshell
became the stars. And from then on,
the world was full of light and
warmth.

tip
You can read another Dreamtime story on page 125.

b) Now listen to another Dreamtime story.
Write down words you understand.
Then draw a picture that matches the story.

 CD

 CD

12 About a family

a) Read the story of an Aboriginal woman called Jennifer.

CD

MORE
M5-M9
Rabbit-Proof
Fence

My grandmother, Rebecca, was born in 1890. She lived with her tribal people in the Kempsey area. Rebecca was the youngest of a big family. One day, when she was about five years old, some religious people came. They thought she was a pretty little girl. Anyway, they took her to live with them.

They didn't look after Rebecca well. At the age of fourteen she had a baby, my mother Grace, and later three other girls: Esther, Violet and May. She married my grandfather Laurie and, at the age of twenty-three, she died of tuberculosis.

Grandfather took the four girls to live with their aunt and uncle. Grandfather worked and supported the girls.

One day a policeman came. He told my grandfather that the girls had to go to Cootamundra Home. There they would be trained to get a job for when they were older. If grandfather didn't sign the papers, he would go to prison and never come out. This was about 1915.

My mother and Esther were sent to Cootamundra. Violet and May were sent to the babies' home at Rockdale. Grace and Esther never saw their sister Violet again. She died of tuberculosis at Waterfall Hospital within two years.

Cootamundra in those days was very strict and cruel. The home was overcrowded. Girls were coming and going all the time. They were taught reading, writing and arithmetic. They all had to learn to clean, wash clothes and cook.

Auntie Esther was a big girl for her age, so she was sent out to work as a cook when she was twelve. Mum, who was smaller, was sent out as a children's nurse at fourteen. She had to look after four young children, one of them only a baby, for 24 hours a day.

This was not the end of the story. Like her grandmother and her mother, Jennifer was forced to leave her family and live in Cootamundra when she was eleven years old. This happened in 1952 and Jennifer only went back to her family five years later.

b) The text is about six women from one family. Write down their names first and then add notes about their lives.

LiF
15

c) Use your notes to talk about the six women.

Rebecca was born in 1890. Grace, Esther and Jennifer were sent to ...

Rebecca:
- born in 1890
- when she was five, some people took her away from her family
- ...
Grace:
- ...

workbook
14-16

d) How does the text make you feel?

I feel ...
I think it's not fair ...
I don't understand why ...

In my opinion, ...
I'm surprised/shocked that ...
I believe ...

PEOPLE & PLACES

Aborigines

About 50,000 years ago the islands in the north of Australia were much nearer to the islands of New Guinea. The people moved about from island to island in canoes or on rafts. But about 8,000 years ago, at the end of the last ice age, the sea divided the islands of Australia and New Guinea. Australia was now a continent, not attached to any other land. The Aborigines, who probably came from South-East Asia to Australia, were left on the new continent.

The Aborigines lived off the land and hunted, picked berries and fished. Each group of Aborigines lived together and spoke their own language. There were up to 600 different languages. The Aborigines had and still have legends and stories about how the land and the first people were made. Today they call this the 'Dreamtime'.

When the first British settlers arrived in 1788, there were between 300,000 and 1 million Aborigines. But a hundred years later, their number had dropped to under 100,000. Fights with the white settlers,

disease and alcohol were the reasons. Their land was taken from them and they had to move to places where they could not farm or live in their traditional way.

Between 1869 and 1969 about 100,000 Aboriginal children were taken away from their families to turn them into "good" Australians by educating them "properly". Today these children are called the 'Stolen Generations'. Now there are about 500,000 native Australians but most of them are very poor. Things are getting better slowly: The Australian government plans to compensate them for losing their family lands. Aboriginal schools now teach the traditional culture. In February 2008 the Australian government apologized to the 'Stolen Generations'.

workbook
17-18

13 Choose an activity

- **What can you find out about the history of the Aborigines? Make a timeline with dates and events.**

tip
Look at the People & Places box for information.

- **What do you know about didgeridoos? Search for information in books or on the Internet about this instrument. Find out, for example:**
  - where it comes from
  - who plays it
  - why it is called 'didgeridoo'

  Report your findings to the class.

- **What would you like to ask an Australian Aborigine your age? Write an email or a letter to him/her with your questions. Think about:**
  - free time
  - traditions
  - history
  - religion
  - music
  - family
  - ...

Subject: Some questions

Hi Sam,
My name is ... I have read a few things about Aboriginal history and art but I've got a few more questions. Would you mind answering them? For example, I would like to know ...
...
Thank you very much!
Best wishes,
...

**How to ...**
write a letter

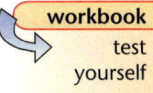**portfolio**

workbook
test yourself

MORE

M1 A World Heritage Site

a) Read the text and find a title for each paragraph. Compare your ideas with a partner's.

How to …
read

tip
km² =
square
kilometres

Hundreds of brilliant colours, 14,000 kinds of life – all coming together in a fascinating area off the coast of Queensland in north-east Australia: That is the Great Barrier Reef, often simply called GBR. The Great Barrier Reef is 2,000 kilometres long and includes 900 islands. It is the world's biggest single structure made by living organisms, which are known as coral polyps. Polyps are tiny animals which join up to form colonies. Each polyp lives inside a hard shell called coral. Millions of corals make up the reef. This "underwater city" is so large (344,400 km²) that it can be seen from outer space.

It's not only the size of the area that is impressive. It's the thousands of different kinds of sea life living together. The corals are constantly taking on new forms to get more light. There are worms that look like they are dancing. Millions of colourful, unusual and beautiful fish, including the parrotfish and the clownfish, live in the reef.

The GBR isn't just ideal for fish; it supports a wide range of life. Turtles are born there and hatch from their eggs after several weeks. Then they swim into the sea but female sea turtles return after about 30 years to lay their own eggs. Sharks, whales, dolphins, snakes and even frogs call the reef their home. Many large colonies of birds nest on the islands of the Great Barrier Reef.

Because the GBR is so special, it was declared a World Heritage Site in 1981.

However, many tourists still seem to think they own the reef. Australia quickly noticed the large interest and started offering tours in glass-bottomed boats, fishing tours, scuba diving and even helicopter flights over the Great Barrier Reef. Because of this the water is getting dirtier and the corals can't grow properly. The natural balance of life under the sea has been disturbed by overfishing and souvenir divers.

To preserve this immense beauty, Australians now try to work with nature instead of destroying it.

workbook
M1

b) Now sort the information about the Great Barrier Reef in a grid like this:

location	size	animals	activities	other interesting facts
…	…	- coral polyps - …	…	…

How to …
give a talk

c) Prepare a short talk about the Great Barrier Reef and present it in class.

M2 The GBR – a special place

a) Look at these two pictures of corals. What do you think happened to the white corals? Talk to your partner.

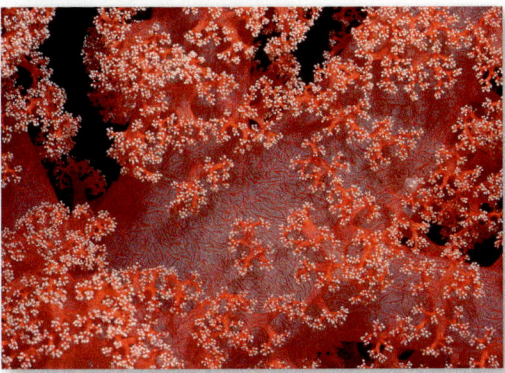 

b) Now read what Brian, a young Australian, says about the corals. Were your guesses in a) correct?

A friend of mine is a member of Reef Relief. It's an organization which helps to protect the Great Barrier Reef. It was founded at Key West in the USA but now they work for coral reefs all over the world.

My friend told me about how global warming affects the Great Barrier Reef and the whole ecosystem along the coast. Corals need tiny animals – the zooxanthellae – that live on and inside them. These animals are food for the corals and give them their colour. Different corals like different zooxanthellae and have different colours. When the temperature goes up, the corals are stressed and spit out these little helpers. The result is that the corals lose their colour and die. Because they look white after this process, it's called 'coral bleaching'. I've seen it myself when scuba diving. It really looks terrible. Some scientists say the Great Barrier Reef could be dead in thirty years. Others say it might survive. After hearing this, I joined Reef Relief in order to help to protect the ocean I love so much.

c) Read the text again. Work with a partner and ask and answer questions. Take turns.

Ask your partner …

1 … what 'Reef Relief' does.
2 … where it was founded.
3 … what zooxanthellae are.
4 … why they are important for corals.
5 … what happens when the ocean temperature goes up.

What does 'Reef Relief' do?

It helps to protect the Great Barrier Reef.

d) Which area that YOU know should be protected? What can YOU do to protect it? In class, form a double circle and tell each other your ideas.

CD

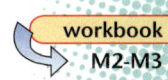
LiF
18

workbook
M2-M3

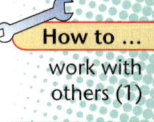
How to …
work with others (1)

MORE

workbook
M4–M5

M3 Slip-slop-slap

Lena and her younger brother Leo are visiting their Australian aunt Claire in Cairns, a city close to the Great Barrier Reef. They've booked a one-day boat trip to the reef. On the boat, Lena and Leo notice everyone putting on hats. Claire takes one out, too.

How to ...
help out in English

a) Read the dialogue. What does Lena say to her aunt Claire? What does she say to Leo? Write the sentences into your exercise book.

Slip on a shirt
Slop on sunscreen
Slap on a hat
It isn't "just" skin cancer. It's a killer.

Claire: Don't you have hats?
Leo: Wie bitte?
Lena: Claire will wissen ...
Leo: Wieso brauchen wir Hüte?
Lena: Claire, Leo wants to know ...
Claire: It's time to slip-slop-slap. It's the time of day when we wear hats and put on sunscreen.
Lena: Das klingt ja lustig. Um diese Zeit ...
Leo: Warum sollte man das machen?
Lena: He asked ...

Claire: Australia and New Zealand have a big problem with the ozone hole. The sun can be really bad for your skin.
Lena: Sie sagt, dass ...
Leo: Ist das wirklich so wichtig?
Lena: Leo, du nervst! Claire, now he wants to know ...
Claire: Australia and New Zealand have the highest rates of skin cancer in the world. Everyone has to be very careful here.
Lena: Australien und ...
Leo: Oh nein! Wo kriegen wir denn jetzt Hüte her?
Claire: I understand that. Don't worry – I've got some for you, too!

CD

b) Now listen to the CD. Compare your sentences with what Lena really said.

c) Work in groups of three and read or act out the scene.

M4 Project: YOUR presentation of Australia

Work in groups. Agree on a topic from this Theme that you find interesting.

1 PLAN IT In your group think about:

- Where can you get information and pictures (books, the Internet, ...)?
- Who is going to do what for your presentation?

2 DO IT Collect information and take notes. Then decide:

- What do you want to present?
- How do you want to present it?
- Who is going to present what?

3 CHECK IT Check your presentation:

- Are the photos, statistics, maps, ... big enough for the class to see them?
- Are the texts correct?

How to ...
give a talk

4 PRESENT IT

portfolio

- Practise your presentation first, then present it to the class.

- immigration to Australia
- School of the Air
- Flying Doctors
- Aboriginal art
- slip-slop-slap
- an Australian city
- ...

M5 Rabbit-Proof Fence

a) Look at the pictures from the Australian film 'Rabbit-Proof Fence', which is based on a true story. What do you think happens in the film?

b) Read this summary of the film. Were you right in a)?

'Rabbit-Proof Fence' is set in Australia in 1931. It tells the story of three girls, sisters Molly and Daisy and their cousin Gracie, who are taken away from their parents by the government. They are brought to Moore River Native Settlement, over 2,000 kilometres away from their home. There they are forced to go to school and to be trained as servants.

The girls despise Moore River and want to return to their families. Led by Molly – at 15 the oldest of the girls – they flee from the settlement and start to walk the long distance home.

To get there they follow the "rabbit-proof fence" – originally built to keep rabbits out of Western Australia – for more than 2,400 kilometres. The walk takes them nine weeks. During their journey the girls are followed by a white man from the government called A.O. Neville and a black tracker. Their task is to bring the girls back to the settlement. They are able to lead Gracie away from the other two girls and capture her. She is taken back to Moore River, but the sisters Molly and Daisy manage to return home.

workbook
M6

c) Find words in the text which mean the same as the words below.

the space between people or places

catch

escape

hate

a person who looks for other people or animals

are able to

d) People who were taken to places like Moore River are called the 'Stolen Generations'. Name three things they had to leave behind.

M6 What if ...?

The sisters Molly and Daisy managed to find their way back home.
Imagine: What would have happened if things had gone differently for them?
Finish the sentences.

Example: If the children had not escaped, they wouldn't have seen their parents again for years.

LiF
13

If the fence had not been there to guide them, ...
If the authorities had managed to find the sisters, ...
If Molly and Daisy had not found their way back home, ...

workbook
M7

If the children had never been taken away from their parents, ...

M7 Moving pictures

a) Watch the film. How would you describe the atmosphere? These words might help you. Maybe you can guess the meaning of some of them before you look them up in a dictionary.

How to ...
watch

sad • dreamlike • dramatic • exciting • touching • mysterious • magical • gloomy • happy • ...

b) Did you like the film? Say why or why not.

workbook
M8-M9

c) What, in YOUR opinion, is the message of the film? Talk about your ideas in class.

M8 Choose an activity

- Write a poem about 'Rabbit-Proof Fence'.

- Think of a different title for the film. Present your title to the class and explain why you have chosen it.

- Your e-pal from England asks you about the film. Write an email telling him/her what you liked or didn't like about it.

STOLEN
BRAVE GIRLS
THE LONG FENCE
SHOWS THEM THEIR WAY
FREEDOM!

- Find out about the author of the book (Doris Pilkington, Aboriginal name: Nugi Garimara) on which the film 'Rabbit-Proof Fence' is based. Use the Internet and write a short portrait of her.

portfolio

M9 **Prime minister says sorry to Stolen Generations** 👓

MORE

In February 2008 the Australian prime minister, Kevin Rudd, officially apologized for the wrongs that had been done to Aborigines. As thousands of Australians listened, he especially said sorry to the 'Stolen Generations', the Aboriginal children who were taken from their families between 1869 and 1969. It took the Australian government almost 40 years to apologize for this period in Australia's history.

a) Read this part of Kevin Rudd's speech. What are the things he apologizes for?

Today we honour the indigenous peoples of this land, the oldest continuing cultures in human history. We reflect on their past mistreatment.

We reflect in particular on the mistreatment of those who were Stolen Generations – this blemished chapter in our national history.

The time has now come for the nation to turn a new page – a new page in Australia's history by righting the wrongs of the past and so moving forward with confidence to the future. We apologise for the laws and policies of successive parliaments and governments that have inflicted profound grief, suffering and loss on these our fellow Australians.

We apologise especially for the removal of Aboriginal and Torres Strait Islander children from their families, their communities and their country.

For the pain, suffering and hurt of these Stolen Generations, their descendants and for their families left behind, we say sorry.

To the mothers and the fathers, the brothers and the sisters, for the breaking up of families and communities, we say sorry.

And for the indignity and degradation thus inflicted on a proud people and a proud culture, we say sorry.

We the parliament of Australia respectfully request that this apology be received in the spirit in which it is offered as part of the healing of the nation. For the future we take heart; resolving that this new page in the history of our great continent can now be written.

We today take this first step by acknowledging the past and laying claim to a future that embraces all Australians.

A future where this parliament resolves that the injustices of the past must never, never happen again. (...)

b) Why does he say the words 'we say sorry' not only once but over and over again?

c) Why do you think it took so long to make this apology?

CD

tip
Don't panic: You don't have to understand every word.

tip
In Britain and Australia 'apologize' is sometimes spelt with an 's'.

workbook
M10

Check it out!

Did you get it all?

tip
You can quiz your partner!

- How many people live in Australia?
- Who were the first people in Australia?
- What is Uluru?
- Who arrived in Australia in 1770?
- What killed Steve Irwin?
- What do these Australian words mean: 'barbie', 'pommy'?
- What is the money in Australia called?
- What are the wild dogs that live in Australia called?
- Which animal looks very much like a kangaroo?

Good to know ...

There's nowhere I can have a quiet nap!

Australia is home to many poisonous spiders. That's why people should always shake out their shoes before putting them on in case there are spiders hiding in them.

Did you know that ...

... there are more sheep than people in Australia?

... Australians are crazy about sports?

What are the favourite sports in Australia?

... Australia is the only state that is a country, a continent and an island?

... Kylie Minogue is one of the most successful female singers in the world?

In which Australian city was Kylie born?

... Australia has three different time zones?

It's 9am in Germany. What's the time in Australia?

... in Australia spring begins in September?

... Australians sometimes say g'day instead of hello?

... 95% of Australians live on 1% of the land?

Find more typical Australian words and phrases.

... the ten most poisonous snakes in the world live in Australia?

MIXED FEELINGS

In this Theme …

- you will talk about what friends do together.
- you will read about difficulties in a friendship.
- you will learn about the rights and responsibilities of teenagers in other countries.
- you can find out about a youth project about tolerance.
- you will get the chance to discuss the pros and cons of teen courts.

1 True friends 👄 👂

a) Look at the pictures. What are the friends doing?

LiF
2

b) What might the people in the pictures be saying? Choose a picture and write a speech bubble. Can your partner guess which picture or person you chose?

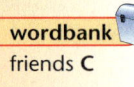
wordbank
friends **C**

tip
B.F.F. =
best friends
forever

True Friend

We sign our cards and letters B.F.F.
You've got a million ways to make me laugh
You're looking out for me
You've got my back
It's so good to have you around

You know the secrets I could never tell
And when I'm quiet you break through my shell
Don't feel the need to do a rebel yell
'cause you keep my feet on the ground

Chorus:

You're a true friend
You're here till the end
You pull me aside when something ain't right
Talk with me now and into the night
Till it's alright again
You're a true friend

Words and Music: Jeannie Lurie

CD c) Listen to the song 'True Friend'. How do you like the song?

workbook
1-2
 d) Now read the lyrics of the song.
Which phrases match the pictures in a)?

> I think line two matches picture number … because …

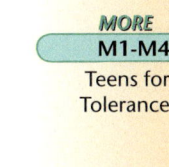

2 Summer break 👓 👄

a) Look at the pictures. They tell the story of two girls, Emily and Leyla. What do you think happens?

workbook
3

MORE
M1-M4
Teens for
Tolerance

b) Now read Emily's blog. Were your guesses in a) correct?

How to ...
read

www.thinespace.com/emmy123sso-calledlife

7 July, 5:29pm

The two boys were outside our school again today. Leyla thinks their uniforms are from that expensive Bales College. We walked past them and heard them say they would be in the park again at the weekend. 😎

Add comment

11 July, 8:11pm

Leyla and I were in the park when Nigel and Darren (that's their names) came and just sat down next to us. They are both SEVENTEEN and they thought we were too. 😎

Add comment

16 July, 6:04pm

Why are parents so intolerant??? My mother wants us to spend the whole summer with her family in Ireland for the 10th time or so. I am going to miss Leyla's 15th birthday and she is going to miss mine. It is so unfair!!! Wait till I'm 16. Mum won't be able to force me to go with her then. Leyla's parents are taking her to Pakistan again. Boring!!! Leyla and I exchanged presents and promised not to open them before our birthdays. I got Leyla a really cool hat. I am looking forward to seeing her with it after the summer holidays.

Add comment

www.thinespace.com/emmy123sso-calledlife

2 September, 5:45pm

Oh my God!!! First day back and Leyla arrived at school wearing a headscarf! I was dying to ask her why but the other Muslim girls in the class didn't leave us alone for a minute. Three of them have always worn really traditional Muslim clothes but I never paid much attention to them before. And they never paid much attention to Leyla. Now they are all best friends.

Add comment

4 September, 6:26pm

I am beginning to feel like the odd one out. Talking to Muna, Maryam, Nadia and Leyla is more or less the same as it is with other girls and they are all very nice. But they look so different from the rest of us. In a way I even feel sorry for them. Everybody we walked past seemed to look at them in a strange way. Or is it my imagination?

Add comment

tip
The word 'hijab' is pronounced hɪˈdʒaːb.

5 September, 7:21pm

I finally got Leyla alone today. I asked her straight out if her parents made her wear the hijab (that's what she calls the headscarf). I was really angry with her answer. She said that all "Westerners" believed that Muslim women had no will of their own. She said that nobody was forcing her to wear the hijab. She wants people to know she is a Muslim and she doesn't want to be a "sex object" for men. I mean, who does she think she is calling "Westerner"? She grew up on Shuttleworth Road like me. And she didn't mind being a "sex object" when she thought Nigel was a real cutie!

Add comment

8 September, 9:33pm

I hope this is just a phase Leyla is going through. I phoned to ask her to go for a walk in the park. I was hoping we might see Nigel and Darren. Leyla arrived at my place wearing her headscarf and a horrible dress that looked like a sack on her. I told her we couldn't go walking in the park if she looked like my grandmother. I was only joking but she got really angry and went home. My parents said she had a right to dress the way she wanted to and that I should tell her I was sorry for offending her. On the one hand they are right, but on the other hand it's not fair that they make it sound as if it is all MY fault.

Add comment

15 September, 5:52pm

I wonder how Leyla feels. I'd love to ask her but I'm afraid of saying the wrong things. I've never been afraid of saying anything to Leyla before. The worst thing is she is not unfriendly to me. All in all, she seems like a different person. We haven't laughed together for weeks. I miss that most.

Add comment

c) Put the events in the right order. What word do you get? (Be careful: Some sentences don't belong to the story.)

- **S** Emily and Leyla stopped laughing together.
- **R** Emily went to Ireland for the summer holidays.
- **E** Leyla suddenly started hanging out with the other Muslim girls in her class.
- **A** Because of Leyla, Nigel and Darren didn't want to talk to Emily anymore.
- **I** Emily was surprised when Leyla came back to school wearing a headscarf.
- **F** Nigel and Darren met the girls in the park.
- **D** Emily's parents said that Leyla could dress any way she liked.
- **J** Leyla told Emily that Muna was her best friend now.
- **N** Leyla got angry when Emily told her that she didn't like Leyla's clothes.

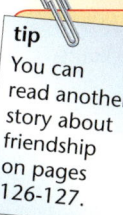
tip
You can read another story about friendship on pages 126-127.

d) What do you think Emily should do? Write a comment to her last entry and give her some advice.

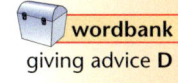
wordbank
giving advice D

3 Different views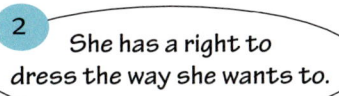

a) Who said these things? Match the statements with the right person.

1 Nobody is forcing me to wear the hijab.

Emily

Leyla

Emily's parents

workbook
4

2 She has a right to dress the way she wants to.

3 All Westerners believe that Muslim women have no will of their own.

4 Do your parents make you wear the hijab?

5 We can't go walking in the park if you look like my grandmother.

Example: **Statement number 1 was said by Leyla.**

b) Now find the sentences in the blog that match the statements in a). Write down both sentences in your exercise book. Look at the example for help.

LiF
17

Example: **Leyla said: "Nobody is forcing me to wear the hijab."**
Emily wrote in her blog: She said that nobody was forcing her to wear the hijab.

4 Choose an activity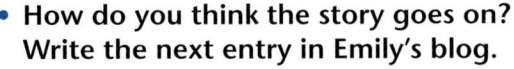

- **How do you think the story goes on?** Write the next entry in Emily's blog.

17 September, 8:16pm
Yesterday at school Leyla invited me home. First I thought ...

workbook
5

- **Work with a partner. Write a dialogue between Emily and Leyla that matches the blog entry from 8 September. Then act out the scene.**

How to ...
talk

- **Leyla wears a hijab to show that she is Muslim. What other pieces of clothing show that someone belongs to a certain group?** Work with a partner and collect ideas.
Example: **Rappers usually wear baggy trousers.** Present your findings to the class.

portfolio

5 Knowing your rights and responsibilities

a) Read about some important teenage rights and responsibilities in three countries.

MORE
M5-M7
teen courts

Britain:

At **5** you have to go to school.

At **10** you are responsible for crimes you commit (but in Scotland the age is eight).

At **14** you can have a part-time job (with some restrictions).

At **16** you can leave school.
you must have your own passport.
you can get married with your parents' permission.

At **17** you can drive a car.

At **18** you can vote.
you can change your name.
you can get a tattoo.
you are allowed to go to a club.
you can buy alcohol.
you can buy fireworks.

Some things are different in the USA:

At **6** you have to go to school in California.

At **15** you have to stay at home after 9pm in some cities.

At **18** you have to serve as a juror if you are chosen.

At **21** you are allowed to buy alcohol.

And there are differences in Australia, too:

At **15** you can leave school.

At **16** you can drive a car in some parts of Australia.

At **18** it is your responsibility to vote at all elections.

At **18** you can buy alcohol.

At **ANY AGE** you have to wear a helmet at all times when riding a bike.

LiF
14

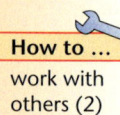
How to ...
work with others (2)

b) What are YOUR rights and responsibilities? Write down two or three facts that you know. Then walk around the classroom and ask your classmates about their facts. Give one of your facts to each classmate you talk to and take one from everyone you talk to.

c) Go through all the facts, then get together in small groups and talk about them. Present your results to the class. You can also make a classroom poster about teenage rights and responsibilities in Germany.

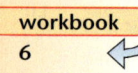
workbook
6

6 Get the message?

a) Describe what is happening in the cartoon. Use these questions for help:

> Who? • Where? • What?

LiF
6, 10

b) What do you think happened before this scene? What is going to happen next?

c) What would YOU say or do if you were the woman in the cartoon?

"Really, Kevin! You'll ruin your teeth!"

PEOPLE & PLACES

Binge drinking

In Britain excessive drinking is becoming a big problem. Especially girls or young women – a group who used to drink less than men – have started drinking too much alcohol.

When someone drinks a lot of alcohol in a short time, this is known as 'binge drinking'. UK teens are the third worst binge drinkers in the EU. A study has shown that 44% of 18 to 24-year-olds are regular binge drinkers. It is common to see many young people out on a Friday or Saturday night clubbing. This is when the most alcohol is consumed, and ambulances are often needed for those who go too far with their drinking.

But UK teens are not the only ones drinking too much. In Germany almost 20,000 teenagers end up in hospital with alcohol poisoning every year after excessive 'Kampftrinken'.

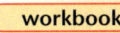
workbook
7

7 Underage clubbing

a) Are there special music events for people under 18 in your area? If so, have you been to one of them?

b) Now read about Sam. Why did he start an underage club in London?

At 16, Sam Kilcoyne is a hero to London's teens. When he was 14 years old, he wanted to see his favourite band in concert. But the doormen didn't let him in. Because rules about selling alcohol to people under 18 have become stricter in Britain, Sam wasn't allowed to enter a place where alcohol was sold. So Sam decided to do something. The solution was Underage Club, a new night club for teenagers only, without alcohol or drugs, just good music. His club nights for 14 to 18-year-olds became so very popular that fans wanted more. The Guardian newspaper even called Sam a "rising star". Now, when he's not studying for school, Sam organises the Club and the Underage Festival – the world's first festival for teens only. There's always cool music but no parents or alcohol.

tip
In Britain a 'Disko' is called 'disco' but more often 'club'.

workbook
8

8 Teenagers in clubs?

a) Listen to the discussion. Who do you think is talking?

b) Listen again. Write down reasons why teenagers should or should not be allowed into regular clubs.

c) What's YOUR opinion? Add your arguments to the grid from b). Then write a text and say what you think.

pros	cons
- dance to good music	

CD

How to …
write your opinion

9 The virtual world

This is a page from a brochure written for British children and teenagers. Explain to someone who doesn't speak English what it is about.

How to ...
help out in
English

Staying safe online

- It is your responsibility never to give out personal information online. If you're in a chat room, watch what you say about where you live, the school you go to, or your email address.

- Never tell anyone your password, only your parents.

- If someone sends a mean or threatening message, don't answer. Save it or print it out and show it to an adult.

- Never open emails from someone you don't know or from someone you know is a bully.

- Don't put anything online that you wouldn't want your classmates to see, even in an email.

- Don't send a message when you're angry. Before clicking "send", ask yourself how you would feel if someone sent it to you.

- Help kids who are bullied online by not joining in and showing bullying messages to an adult.

- Always be as polite online as you are in real life.

10 I was a cyberbully

a) What comes to your mind when you read the word 'cyberbully'? What do you think a cyberbully does? Brainstorm with a partner.

workbook
9-10

b) Read Nick's text and find out if you were right in a).

CD

I heard about a lot of things my friends were doing online that were really mean. I never thought I would do anything like that. One day my friend Jamie showed me a website he was making. On it was a list of girls from our school. He gave the guys we knew the access code to the website so they could rate the girls – a kind of of 'hot or not' website. I thought it was pretty funny so I rated them, too. We had a good time and I thought that was the end of it.

The next day everyone at school was talking about the website. Jamie had sent it out for the whole school to see. A few girls had been crying – no wonder I thought. The comments about them on the website weren't very nice. I felt bad but I felt even worse when I came home that night.

It turned out the guys thought it would be funny to put my little sister Paula on the site, too. She was crying when I got home and wouldn't even look at me. I would never have said those things to someone directly. I didn't even mean them, I thought it was just a joke between friends.

Now Jamie is suspended from school and they might kick me out, too. Once you put something online, it's not private anymore. People can use it in ways you never even thought about. I learned that the hard way. I wish I'd never seen that stupid website.

2

c) How would you express these phrases from the text in German?

> really mean • pretty funny • rate someone •
> learn something the hard way • suspend someone

d) Find out who ...

1 ... made a website. 2 ... gave others the access code.
3 ... rated the girls. 4 ... was talking about the website the next day.
5 ... had been crying. 6 ... didn't look at her brother.
7 ... was suspended from school. 8 ... wished he had never seen that website.

e) Have you heard other stories about cyberbullying? Tell the class about them.

11 Calling the helpline

a) What would YOU do if you were being cyberbullied?

b) If you are being cyberbullied, you can call a helpline. You are going to listen to Nick's sister Paula and another teenager calling the helpline 'Kids Help Phone'. Copy the grid, then listen and take notes.

CD

How to ...
listen

	Paula	Bruce
What did the cyberbullies do?		
What advice does the helpline give?		

c) Did you get all the information? Work with a partner and compare your notes.

d) Do you agree with the lady from the helpline? Say why or why not.

12 Choose an activity

• Design an anti-cyberbullying poster.

• What rights and responsibilities did teenagers have 50 years ago? Ask people who were young in the 1950s and '60s and report your findings to the class.

tip
You can use your notes from 5b).

• If you had the power to change the laws that were made to protect young people, which laws would you change? Would you add new ones? Write a short text and give reasons.

• Design a leaflet for your own underage club. Think about:

  – location
  – music
  – food and drink
  – entrance fee
  – ...

portfolio

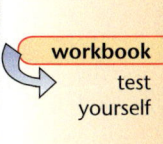
workbook
test
yourself

39

2

MORE

Mixed feelings: Living together

M1 Difficult times

How to ...
read

a) Read the newspaper articles and take notes in a grid.

1,300 CARS BURNT AS PARIS RACE RIOT GROWS

11 July 2005
France was hit by new race violence last night after 1,300 vehicles were torched by angry mobs.

AFTER THE RACIST ATTACKS IN MÜGELN

Germany Wonders How to Stop the Neo-Nazis

The Mügeln incident of 2007 was the first in a new wave of violent, racially motivated attacks on immigrants in Germany.

RACE RIOTS SET FIRE TO BRADFORD

8 July 2001
People in Bradford are cleaning up after one of the worst riots in Britain for years. Police have promised to find all the people – mainly groups of Asian and white youths – who were in the riots. About 1,000 youths threw stones, bottles and petrol bombs at the police.

	Who?	What?	When?
Mügeln			**2007**
Paris	**angry mobs**		
Bradford			

workbook
M1-M2

b) Use your grid and tell somebody who hasn't read the articles what happened in Mügeln, Paris and Bradford.

M2 Teens for Tolerance

The youth project 'Teens for Tolerance' started after the riots in Bradford. It wants to teach young people from different cultures about each other.

CD

a) Listen to John and Adeela talking about their work for 'Teens for Tolerance'. Who is a team leader? Who is a member?

How to ...
read

b) Now read the texts. Were you right in a)?

I come from Leeds, where the group Teens for Tolerance was founded. I thought the group was a brilliant idea because I was shocked by the riots here in the north, and because I realised I didn't know much about other people myself. There are parts of Leeds I never go to because white people just don't go there. I wanted to get to know the people from these areas.

In the beginning I only went to special events that Teens for Tolerance organised, like football games or parties. I met a lot of nice people there and now I have friends all over Leeds.

I became a regular member of Teens for Tolerance about a year ago. I think it is important to keep the group going even though nothing really bad has happened in the last few years. Now I go to meetings once a week and help with the organization. And I hope that many other teenagers get the chance to become part of this group and find friends from different backgrounds.

workbook
M3-M4

40

I started going to the Teens for Tolerance group in Bradford. Some time ago there were a lot of race riots in the north of England and especially in Bradford. The people who started the group thought that it would help if young people understood each other better so that they could all accept one another.

Now I work as a team leader for the organization. It can be stressful sometimes, organising events like football matches or repairing community centres. But it's also fun and everyone learns to work with people with whom they wouldn't normally work.

For me, this is a really important idea. I go to Feversham College, which is a secondary school for Muslim girls but I don't want people to think that I am different to them. I go to the school because of my parents and because my religion is part of who I am, but I'm also just a normal teenage girl.

c) Look at the texts from b) again and say why John and Adeela joined 'Teens for Tolerance'.

John (and) Adeela	want(s) would like	the group other teenagers all parts of Leeds people	to get the chance to find friends from different backgrounds. to think that she is just a normal teenage girl. to keep going. to understand and accept each other. to be open for everyone.

LiF
20

M3 A teacher's view

Mr Turnbell is a teacher at a school in Leeds, and was one of the people who brought 'Teens for Tolerance' into schools. He has worked with both John and Adeela.

Listen to Mr Turnbell. Which statement fits to what he says?

1 The work is very stressful for the children.
2 Mr Turnbell hopes to finish the project in three months' time.
3 Mr Turnbell is happy that so many schools want to take part in the project.

workbook
M5

CD

How to …
listen

M4 Choose an activity

- **Find out from how many different countries the pupils in your school come from. Do a survey and present the results.**

- **Talking to people and understanding them is important for tolerance. Think of people or groups you have never talked to (e. g. other people from your school, homeless people, …). How could you change that? Make a list of activities you could start.**

- **Can you imagine a youth project on tolerance in YOUR area? What would you like to change? How could you do it?**

workbook
M6

portfolio

M5 **Teen courts**

a) Read this article about a way of dealing with young offenders in America. Do you know if there is anything similar in Germany?

TEEN COURTS

Young people help young people

Teen courts started more than 20 years ago. Today, over 1,250 can be found all over America. These courts are for teenagers who have committed small crimes and have been caught for the first time.

The idea behind the teen courts is that teenagers may be helped more if they are punished by other teenagers and not by adults. This is why the judge, jury, prosecutor and lawyers in the teen courts are all teenagers.

Years ago, teenagers who committed a crime had to appear before a traditional juvenile court. With a criminal record it was then difficult for them to find a job.

Now young criminals get a second chance. If they admit that they have done wrong – and if it happened for the first time – they can appear before a teen court. The judge and the lawyers are all young people who learned how to do the job in training courses.

> **tip**
> 'Sentence' has two different meanings. What are they?

b) Which of these people can or can't appear before a teen court? Say why or why not.

- Kevin, 18, was seen drinking beer in a public park. He got caught the third time.
- Katie, 22, drove at 75 miles per hour where she was only allowed to drive 60 miles per hour.
- Pete, 16, threatened a classmate on the phone and in a chat room for three months.

c) Look at the sentences given by the teen courts. Can you think of two more? Then rank them from light to hard.

> **workbook**
> M7

d) Work with a partner and compare your rankings. Are they similar?

M6 **Short sentences**

Make these sentences shorter. Example:
Teenagers who are caught by the police for the first time can appear before a teen court.

> **LiF**
> 26

Teenagers caught by the police for the first time can appear before a teen court.

1 The judge, jury and lawyers who are working for the teen court are all teenagers.
2 Some of the sentences that are passed by a teen court are letters of apology or community services.
3 A young person who is found drinking alcohol in public places will be sent to an alcohol class.

> **workbook**
> M8

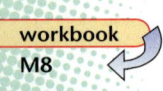

4 The teenagers who are serving as jurors were often offenders themselves.

Other sentences can be, for example:
- paying back stolen money
- making an apology
- doing community service
- writing an essay

Many of the young offenders must take part in a program to help change their behavior, for example anti-alcohol or anti-aggression training.

The courts are a success. Statistics show that only 13% of teenagers who appear before a teen court commit another offence. If they do, they are sent to a traditional juvenile court. The other 87% have learned a lesson and often, after they have served on a jury and taken part in a training course, become judges or lawyers in the teen courts so that they can help others.

Among the offences are:
- stealing or shoplifting (less than $100)
- smoking in public places
- drinking alcohol
- driving offences or
- bullying

Sometimes there are teenagers in the jury who were criminals themselves. Serving as juror can be a sentence.

M7 YOUR discussion about teen courts

a) Get together in three groups:

- Group one thinks teen courts are a good idea.
- Group two thinks teen courts are a bad idea.
- Group three listens to the arguments and takes notes.

b) In each group prepare for the discussion:

- In group one, collect arguments for teen courts.
- In group two, collect arguments against teen courts.
- In group three, get your pens and paper ready; think about the best way to take notes during the discussion.

c) Now have a discussion about teen courts:

- Make sure group one and two take turns when presenting their arguments.
- Every group should get an equal amount of time to express their opinions.

d) At the end of the discussion group three decides:
Which group had the best arguments?

How to ...
discuss

workbook
M9

43

2 Check it out!

Did you get it all?

tip
You can quiz your partner!

- Who wrote the song 'True Friend'?
- What is a 'hijab'?
- What is the address of Emily's blog?
- Where did Leyla go for the summer holidays?
- At what age are you allowed to buy alcohol in the USA?
- Who started an underage club?
- How would you translate 'binge drinking'?
- On which page can you find a 'mouse-surfer'?

Good to know ...

People from different cultures have different ways of saying hello – some shake hands and some kiss or bow. It depends on how close they want to get to strangers. Always be careful not to get too close to people, you might make them feel uncomfortable.

Did you know that ...

... there are over 300 languages spoken in London?

List the five most widely-spoken languages in the world.

... there are 350,000 underage drinkers in Britain?

... 'netiquette' means good behaviour on the Internet?

... Anti-Bullying Week takes place in the UK every year?

Find out more about Anti-Bullying Week on the Internet.

... at the end of 2007 there were more than 112 million blogs on the Internet?

How many people in your class write blogs?

... Amsterdam is the city with the most different nationalities in the world? People from 177 different states live in Amsterdam.

Find out how many nationalities there are in the world.

... the Underage Festival takes place every year in Victoria Park, London?

... Feversham College in Bradford was voted best secondary school in Britain in 2005?

EXPRESS YOURSELF!

In this Theme …

- you will talk about different kinds of exciting sports.
- you will read about street skateboarding.
- you will find out how young people express themselves.
- you can create a class folder about youth groups.
- you can find out about an interesting expedition.

1 Getting active

a) How many sports can you write down in one minute?

b) Compare your ideas with a partner. Who has got the most sports? Then talk to another pair and share your results. Add the new sports to your list.

2 Exciting sports

a) Match each picture with the correct sport.

wordbank
sports E

> BMX biking • kickboxing • skydiving • free climbing • kitesurfing • parkour • freestyle football • whitewater rafting • bungee jumping • caving

A · B · C · F · D · E

b) Have you ever tried any of these or other sports?
Ask your partner about it.

tip
Look at your list of sports from number 1.

Have you ever done/ played ...?

Yes, I have. It was ... / No, I haven't.

Would you like to try ...?

When/Where did you do/ play ...?

I did/played it in ... last ... It was ...

Yes, I would. I think it's ... / No, I wouldn't because ...

LiF
3, 6

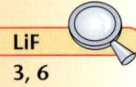

workbook
1-2

3 It's great!

a) Look at the sports in the box in number 2 again and listen to the people on the CD. Which sports are they talking about? Write them down.

b) Listen again. Write down the words that helped you find the right sport.

sport	keywords
kickboxing	kick

CD

How to …
listen

workbook
3

4 Adventure courses

a) Look at the leaflet for adventure courses in Australia and the USA and find the English words for:

> Wildnis • Fähigkeiten • entwickeln • Erfahrung • Verantwortung • Schlitten

CHALLENGE YOURSELF. CHANGE YOUR WORLD. OUTWARD BOUND™.

OUTWARD BOUND

Since 1941 Outward Bound™ has offered active learning expeditions for young people. Instructors take groups of teenagers and young adults on expeditions into the wilderness where they learn all sorts of skills they need in their everyday life. Outward Bound™ wants to help people see and develop their abilities to care for themselves, others and the world around them. Here are two examples of courses you can do:

The Adventure Course – 8 days (Australia)

How about eight days of exciting activities such as hiking, rock climbing, bush cooking, rafting or canoeing? The Adventure Course is a fun wilderness experience for any young person who wants to "go bush" with other kids the same age, learn new skills and try new activities. It is also about learning to take responsibility for yourself – and have a lot of fun at the same time!

Dog sledding & skiing – 8 days (USA)

Interested in a weeklong dog sledding expedition? We travel by ski and dog sled across snow-covered lakes. You learn to travel in extreme weather, to care for and manage your dog team and to read the ice of frozen lakes. Your instructors will teach you how to stay warm when camping.

b) A friend of yours is interested in the courses but doesn't understand much English. Look at the leaflet and try to answer the questions.

1 'Outward Bound' ist der Name des Veranstalters, oder? Was ist denn das Besondere an 'Outward Bound'?
2 Und wie alt sind die Kursteilnehmer ungefähr?
3 Was kann man in den acht Tagen in Australien alles machen?
4 In den USA kann man Hundeschlitten fahren, richtig? Was genau lernt man in dem Kurs?

How to …
help out in English

workbook
4-5

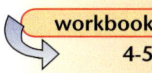

LiF
18

5 Street skateboarding

a) You will read an article about Diego, a teenager from Toronto who does street skateboarding. Look at his picture. What would you like to ask him?

b) Now read the article. Can you find answers to your questions in the text?

How to ...
read

MORE
M2-M5

Jason's journey

"GET OUTTA HERE YOU PUNK!"

"You're destroying the property! I'll call the cops if you don't leave now!" Since I started street skateboarding in Toronto three years ago, I've heard things like that a lot. Most people see street skateboarders as useless troublemakers with no respect for public areas, but I'm just a normal 16-year-old kid who likes to hang out in the city with his friends.

arrested when we tried some tricks on the stairs outside a city building. Although it was late and no one was there, the cops charged us with trespassing and vandalism and we had to pay a fine.

My parents aren't too happy about my hobby because I keep hurting myself. Last year I fell down some stairs and I broke my elbow. I was in a cast for seven weeks, and then when I got better and got back on my board, I broke three bones in my foot when I tried to skate down a rail. That one was bad, the doctor had to put bits of metal and a lot of screws in my foot.

There are lots of skateboarding parks that we could go to, but street skateboarding is cool because you don't have to build a ramp or spend any money to do it. I have much more fun in the city because I like city noises and big buildings.

When I was little, we lived in the country. We moved to Toronto when I was twelve and I immediately started street skateboarding. I really get a thrill when I find good sidewalks, stairs and rails to try new tricks on. Toronto is full of them. It's the biggest city in Canada. You could skate your whole life and there would still be lots of places you haven't been to.

The problem is that street skateboarding is illegal almost everywhere in town. Two months ago some friends and I got

So yeah, street skateboarding is dangerous and can get you arrested, but so what? The feeling I get when I make up a new trick or find a new place to skate makes it all worth it. It gives me a kind of energy that I don't get from any other sport, and I've met all kinds of cool people.

A lot of kids who started skateboarding on the streets have become professional skateboarders. I don't know if I'll ever be good enough to make skateboarding my job, but I don't think I'll ever stop doing it.

c) Choose a headline for each paragraph.

Accidents • The risks are worth it • Getting arrested • I love the city •
A wrong picture of street skateboarders • Street skateboarders becoming professionals •
Toronto – a great place for street skateboarders

d) **Why does Diego prefer street skateboarding to skateboarding? Work with a partner and collect Diego's arguments from the text.**

e) **Do you agree or disagree with Diego? Give reasons.**

workbook 6

6 Diego's experience

a) **Look at the article again and match the sentence parts.**

b) **Put the sentences in the correct order. What word do you get?**

LiF 8

1 Diego had to pay a fine

2 Diego was in a cast for seven weeks

3 Before they moved to Toronto

4 The police charged Diego and his friends with vandalism and trespassing

5 The doctor put bits of metal in Diego's foot

6 Diego started street skateboarding

K after he had broken his elbow.

T although they had not bothered anyone.

S after the cops had arrested him.

R immediately after his family had moved to Toronto.

A Diego's family had lived in the country.

E after he had tried to skate down a rail.

workbook 7-8

7 Choose an activity

• **Work with a partner and prepare an interview with Diego the street skateboarder. Think of six questions you would like to ask him. One of you takes Diego's role and gives the answers. Present your interview to the class.**

 How to … talk

• **Choose a sport YOU find exciting. Find information, then write about:**
  – where you play it   – equipment
  – number of players   – records
  – basic rules   – …

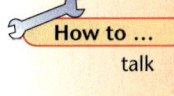 wordbank sports E

• **Create an advert for sports clothes and present it to your class. Find out if they would buy your product. Why? Why not?**

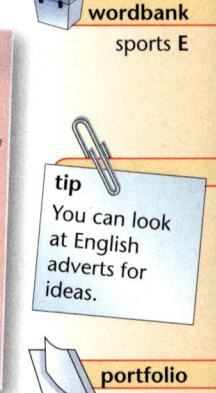

tip You can look at English adverts for ideas.

portfolio

49

3

8 Different people, different looks

a) Look at the photos. Which of these looks do you know? Where have you seen them? What are they called?

b) Which of these looks do or don't you like? Give reasons.

tip
Most of these looks are called the same in English and German.

> tree hugger • biker • punk • hip hopper • emo • rasta • hippie • goth

David

Keiko

Tomasz

Luca

Olivia

Gail & Ed

workbook
9

9 Special looks

CD

a) Listen to two radio interviews with people shown in the photos in number 8. Who are they?

b) Listen again and take notes. Why did they choose this look?

Hyun-Chung

Jerome

Pippa

10 Being different

a) In an Internet forum about different looks, one of the people shown in the photos has written about themselves. Who is it?

I'm 17 years old and I'm from Manchester. Wherever I go people stare at me or shout nasty things. Especially children and old people find me scary. My aunt thinks I might be a little shy and that I like to hide behind my clothes and my make-up. But she is wrong. The truth is that I like to provoke people and make them think.

I always wear dark clothes and a lot of black make-up around my eyes. I'm proud of my long black hair and I enjoy wearing long necklaces.

Two years ago my best friend and I became goths. My parents were shocked at first. They thought I worshipped death and feared I might kill myself. But that's not true. Goths accept death as a part of life. Although I prefer dark clothes, I'm an optimistic person who loves dancing and going out with friends.

b) What do people think when they see him/her? Are they right? Say why/why not.

c) Choose one of the other people shown in the photos.
Use your imagination and write his/her text for the Internet forum.

- Describe his/her look,
- try to imagine his/her free time activities,
- say why he/she chose this look,
- say what his/her personality might be like.

d) Who did other people in your class write about?
Collect all the texts in class and hang them up in your classroom.

CD

workbook
10-12

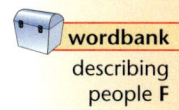
wordbank
describing
people F

tip
Look through the text in a) for phrases you can use in your text.

51

11 Beautiful

a) Listen to the song 'Beautiful' by Christina Aguilera.
How does it make you feel?

CD

b) Now read the lyrics. What is beautiful for Christina Aguilera?
What is beautiful for YOU?

MORE
M7-M8

Christina
Aguilera

Every day is so wonderful, then suddenly, it's hard to breathe
Now and then I get insecure, from all the pain
I'm so ashamed

I am beautiful no matter what they say
Words can't bring me down
I am beautiful in every single way
Yes words can't bring me down
So don't you bring me down today

To all your friends you're delirious
So consumed in all your doom
Trying hard to fill the emptiness, the pieces gone,
Left the puzzle undone, is that the way it is

You're beautiful no matter what
they say
Words can't bring you down
'Cause you are beautiful in every
single way
Yes words can't bring you down
So don't you bring me down
today

No matter what we do
No matter what we say
We're the song inside the tune,
full of beautiful mistakes
And everywhere we go, the sun will always shine
And tomorrow we might awake on the other side

'Cause we are beautiful no matter what they say
Yes words won't bring us down, no
We are beautiful in every single way
Yes words can't bring us down
So don't you bring me down today

workbook
13

c) Is Christina Aguilera right when she says 'Words can't bring you down'?
What do YOU think?

3

🇬🇧 PEOPLE & PLACES

Youth cultures

There are many different types of youth cultures or groups today. Some of them started many years ago, like the teds and the mods. Most of these groups were gone again after a few years.

One well-known group that has not disappeared is the punks. They came up in Britain in the 1970s as a result of 'punk rock', a new type of rock music.

There are still punks today, but now there are many different types. Goth culture started as punk culture, but now has become something very individual.

Goths use lots of make-up and many wear tattoos and/or piercings. They do this either to shock society or just to show people that they are individuals who don't have to do what everyone else is doing.

But tattoos and piercings have existed for thousands of years. At first, they had special meanings, for example religious meanings. Then people had them because they thought it was a sign of beauty and strength. Today everyone has a different reason for getting a tattoo or piercings.

> workbook
> 14

12 Project: YOUR class folder about youth groups ✏️

a) **Work in groups of four and write a description of a youth group from the Theme that you find interesting. What do their members believe in? What do they wear? What music do they listen to? What is special about them?**

> 🔧 How to …
> write

- Collect information on the youth group you have chosen. Try to find pictures, too. Perhaps you can also interview someone.

- Use your information to write a description of this youth group.

- Check your description. Is the English correct?

b) **Now put all the descriptions in a class folder and enjoy reading them.**

> 📄 portfolio

> workbook
> test
> yourself

M1 Useful things on a journey

a) You want to go on a journey around the world – on your own. What do you take with you? Work in groups of four and make a placemat.

b) Decide on the five most useful things and write them down in the middle of the placemat.

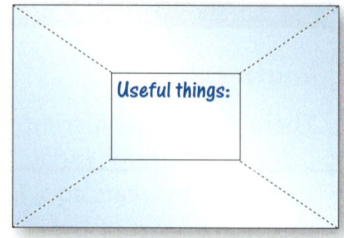

Useful things:

M2 Expedition 360

a) Look at the map which shows the route of an expedition. Why do you think it is called 'Expedition 360'?

How to …
read

b) Read about Jason Lewis and his journey. How did he travel?

Jason Lewis from Dorset in England owned a cleaning company and played music in a band. But he still had a dream: He wanted to travel around the world and be the first to travel by human power alone. Jason was interested in the physical challenge. He also wished to raise people's interest in the environment. So he saved £26,000 to build an 8m wooden pedal boat and to pay for the equipment he needed. When 26-year-old Jason left Greenwich on 12 July 1994, he thought the journey would take him three and a half years. But it took him a lot longer than that – Jason only came home after 13 years!

EXPEDITION 360

THE **FIRST** HUMAN POWERED CIRCUMNAVIGATION OF THE WORLD
1994 – 2007

MOKSHA
PEDAL FOR THE PLANET...

www.expedition360.com

Colorado

… A drunk in his car hit me while I was in-line skating on a road in Colorado. He was 82 years old and also had problems with his eyes. Both my legs were broken and I was in hospital for six weeks. I thought my journey was finished. I needed nine months before I could skate again.

Australia

… I had real problems in the Great Barrier Reef but I finally reached Australia. While my boat was being repaired, thieves stole my equipment that had cost £6,500. So I had to buy new things – a signal light for use in a sea emergency, radios, a lifejacket, a water maker and solar panels.

tip
Learn more about Jason's adventure at www. expedition 360.com

www.expedition360.com

Indonesia

… This part of the journey was the most dangerous so far. First I had to fight really dangerous seas, then a 5m salt water crocodile attacked me and I lost one of my kayak paddles. But I made it to Indonesia. When I arrived in Banda Aceh, I decided to help to rebuild a youth centre that had been hit by the tsunami. We collected $10,000.

The Himalayas

… This is the highest point of my journey – 5,100m in the Himalayas. Great – now it is all downhill to Greenwich, I thought. Suddenly I was attacked by wild dogs. I used a Chinese sausage to escape them. Then my trip nearly came to an end again when my bike broke down. But I was lucky! Two Irish cyclists had some spare parts for me!

Egypt

… I could hardly believe it. While crossing Lake Nasser between Sudan and Egypt, I was arrested by the Egyptian military. They said I was a spy! And my visa ran out at the same time. But I was really lucky. Instead of sending me to prison for 40 years, they let me go again.

c) What difficulties did Jason face? Take notes on these points:

equipment • accidents • nature

d) Find words in the texts that match these definitions:

1 things that you need for doing something
2 the travelling that you do to get from one place to another place
3 a large animal that has short legs, a long body and sharp teeth
4 a rubber or plastic jacket that you wear on a boat

e) How would YOU feel? Finish these statements about Jason's adventure.

It must be wonderful to
I would love to
I think it would be awful to
It wouldn't be my thing to
I would never
My dream would be to

stay …
cycle …
in-line skate …
be alone …
communicate …
swim …
help …
work …
buy …
…

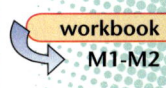
workbook
M1-M2

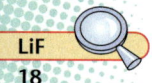
LiF
18

M3 Lots of questions

Work with a partner and ask and answer questions about Jason's trip. Take turns. Ask your partner …

1   … what Jason's dream was.
2   … why Jason went on the trip.
3   … what Jason's job was before the journey.
4   … how much money Jason needed to start his journey.
5   … when and from where Jason left.

6   … how old Jason was when he left and when he returned.
7   … what happened to Jason in Colorado.
8   … which animals Jason had to fight.
9   … where the money went that they collected in Banda Aceh.
10 … why Jason was arrested on Lake Nasser.

M4 An interview with Jason

CD

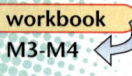
How to …
listen

a) Listen to the interview with Jason after his return. How does Jason feel?

b) Listen again and take notes to answer the questions.

- What things have changed in Britain?
- What things haven't changed?
- What did he miss most about Britain?
- What are Jason's plans?
- What is 'Moksha'?

workbook
M3-M4

c) Did you get all the information? Work with a partner and compare your notes.

M5 More about Jason

LiF
5

a) Be a language expert: Look at these two sentences about Jason in the present perfect. Find out: When do you use *since* and when do you use *for*?

Jason has had contact with people in Banda Aceh for some years now.

Jason has been back in England since October 2007.

Aberdeen

b) Now read more about Jason. Complete the sentences with *since* and *for*.

1   Jason has thought about mini-expeditions for young people **???** a very long time.

2   He has had problems with his legs **???** his accident in Colorado.

3   He has wanted to buy a new bike **???** the old one broke down in the Himalayas.

4   He has made music **???** more than 25 years.

workbook
M5-M6

5   He hasn't slept well **???** a crocodile attacked him.

3
MORE

M6 YOUR adventurous journey

**Imagine YOU went on an adventurous journey.
Make up a story.**

How to ...
write

1 PLAN IT

Collect ideas and make notes:

- Where did you go?
- Why did you go there?
- Did you go alone or with a friend?
- Which things did you take with you?
- What happened on your journey?
- How did you feel?
- ...

2 DO IT

- Write your ideas in sentences and paragraphs.
- Make a first draft.

3 CHECK IT

- Is your story interesting enough for others to read or listen to?
- Is the English correct?
- Swap stories with a partner and give each other feedback on your texts.

4 PRESENT IT

- Make a final copy of your story. If you like, you can add pictures.
- Form small groups and read the stories to each other.
- Collect all the stories and hang them up in your classroom.

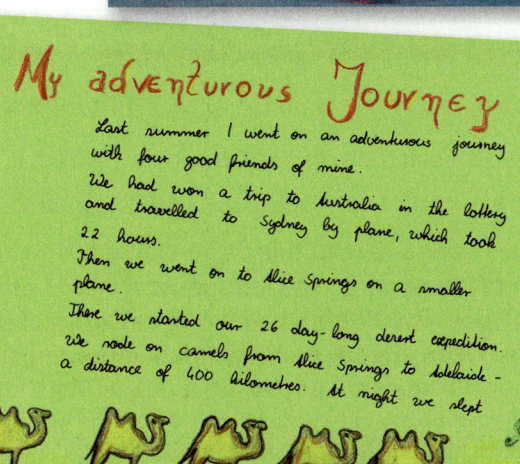

My adventurous Journey

Last summer I went on an adventurous journey
with four good friends of mine.
We had won a trip to Australia in the lottery
and travelled to Sydney by plane, which took
22 hours.
Then we went on to Alice Springs on a smaller
plane.
There we started our 26 day-long desert expedition.
We rode on camels from Alice Springs to Adelaide -
a distance of 400 kilometres. At night we slept

portfolio

MORE

One star, different looks

Look at the photos of Christina Aguilera. How would you describe her different looks? These words might help you:

wordbank
describing
people **F**

crazy • beautiful • cute • glamorous • unusual • wild • normal • unique • scary

1   2   3   4

M8  **Christina Aguilera**

a) **To help you read the article about Christina Aguilera, have a closer look at the words below. Which of the meanings given in the dictionary is the one used in the article? Work with a partner and decide on the best German translation.**

Article: In 1993 Christina **starred** in the Disney Channel's TV show *The New Mickey Mouse Club* although she was only 13!

star I *n* **1.** Stern **2.** Star	**II** *v/tr* **1. to ~ in a film/play** in einem Film/Theaterstück auftreten

Article: Her first album called *Christina Aguilera* **was released** on 24 August 1999 and she became a famous star.

release I *n* **1.** Entlassung **2.** Auslöser **3.** Entspannung, Erleichterung	**II** *v/tr* **1. to ~ sb/an animal** jdn/ein Tier freilassen **2. to ~ sth** etw lösen **3. to ~ a film/CD** einen Film/eine CD herausbringen

b) **Now read this article about Christina Aguilera. Why does she like changing her image?**

Christina Aguilera was born in Staten Island, New York on 18 December 1980. As a child she loved to perform. In 1993 Christina starred in the Disney Channel's TV show *The New Mickey Mouse Club* although she was only 13! Her first album called *Christina Aguilera* was released on 24 August 1999 and she became a famous star.
Christina is famous for her changing image. When her first hit *Genie in a Bottle* was released, she had a very young look – with blonde, straight hair, blue eyes and girly clothes. However, she wasn't really very happy with this image. Therefore, she decided to change what she looked like – so she could be herself. In 2002, when her second album *Stripped* came out, her image was really different.

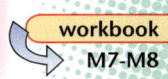

The star got rid of her teenage-pop look and now had braided hair and colourful make-up. During her tour she dyed her hair black. She also had a lot of piercings on her body. The singer explains:
"If I was having a bad day or if something was really getting me down, boy troubles, whatever, I wanted to go out and get a new piercing. It was definitely a release for me. Something that made me feel a little stronger or more empowered because it was something that had to do with me and no one else."
Her hit *Beautiful* won an award. It was very popular because of its message: Everyone is beautiful, no matter who they are or what they look like. Everyone can have their own image and be proud of who they are.
When her next album *Back to Basics* came out in 2006, Christina decided she wanted another new image. She dyed her hair blonde again and now looked like a glamorous Hollywood star from the 1920s! People thought she looked older and more elegant. She liked the change because she felt more like a woman. She wasn't a teenager anymore. Christina has since married and given birth to her son, Max. She will probably soon have a new image for her next album but for now she is enjoying being a mum. In her free time she likes to do 'normal things' like watching movies, shopping and going out with friends. She also likes to give a lot of money to charity.

c) **Read the article again and finish the sentences.**

1 Although she was only 13 years old, Christina …
2 Christina's first album was released in 1999 and she …
3 When her hit *Genie in a Bottle* came out, she …
4 However, she wasn't …
5 Therefore, Chistina decided …
6 She liked looking older and more elegant because she …

d) **Now tell somebody who hasn't read the article what it is about.**

M9 **Choose an activity**

- With a partner choose a star who has also changed his/her image. Find information, then make up an interview or prepare a short talk about him/her.

P!NK

David Beckham

- Find a picture of another famous person. Describe him/her to a group of classmates. Let them draw and guess the star.

- Write a poem about YOUR style.

workbook
M7-M8

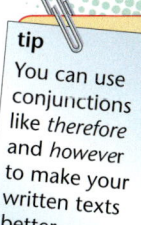
LiF
27

tip
You can use conjunctions like *therefore* and *however* to make your written texts better.

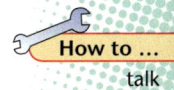
How to …
talk

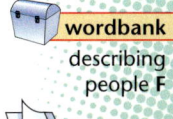
wordbank
describing people F

portfolio

Check it out!

Did you get it all?

tip
You can quiz your partner!

- Name three sports that also created a fashion style.
- What is Diego's hobby?
- Name seven exciting sports.
- Who wears black clothes and a lot of make-up?
- What are the names of four of the youth cultures in this Theme?
- What is Christina Aguilera wearing in the picture on page 52?
- What is the difference between skateboarding and street skateboarding?

Good to know ...

The British are famous for their understatement. Because they don't want to hurt anyone's feelings or bother others with their private problems, they usually play things down. When speaking to a British person, you should remember that it's always better to see the funny side of things.

Did you know that ...

... Camilla Hempleman-Adams, 15, is the youngest British woman to ski to the North Pole?

... Xie Qiuping from China holds the record for the world's longest hair? In 2004 her hair was 5.627m long.

Find out how fast hair can grow.

... kickboxing is a combination of karate and traditional boxing?

... it is impossible to lick your own elbow?

Tell this funny fact to a friend and watch them try it.

... parkour became known worldwide after it appeared in the James Bond film 'Casino Royale' in 2006?

Which other martial arts do you know?

Who plays the role of James Bond in the latest film?

... the word 'punk' originally meant 'something worthless' or 'worthless person'?

FOOD FOR THOUGHT

In this Theme …

- you will talk about healthy food.
- you will find out why junk food is banned in British school canteens.
- you will read about a girl who stopped eating and became very ill.
- you can discuss different food topics.
- you will find out about XXL restaurants.
- you will have the chance to read parts of the book 'Oliver Twist'.

1 Breakfast is ready!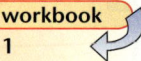

a) **Look at these pictures of different kinds of breakfast. Talk about what you can see. What do you think: Where do people eat these kinds of breakfast?**

workbook
1

olives • cereals • seaweed • tofu • cream cheese • ...

wordbank
food **G**

b) **Which of these kinds of breakfast from a) could be yours? Give reasons.**

c) **Make a survey in class. Ask three classmates what they eat for breakfast. Take notes in a grid like this:**

name	eats what?	why?
Lisa		
Martin		

2 What's in a breakfast?

CD

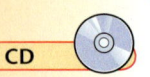

a) **A school magazine interviewed some pupils about their breakfast habits. Listen to three of the interviewed pupils. Add notes to your grid from 1c).**

b) **Look at your grid. Who could you have breakfast with? Why?**

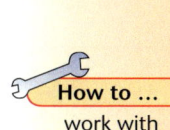

4

3 Healthy eating

a) What do you know about healthy eating?
Work in small groups and talk quietly about
the following questions for a few minutes.
One of you takes notes.

- What type of food should you eat every day?
- How much food should you eat per day?
- Why is it important to eat healthy food?

carbohydrates • calories •
protein • sugary food •
fat-reduced food • vitamins •
minerals • …

How to …
work with
others (3)

wordbank
food **G**

b) Choose a member of your group to present your results to the class.

4 The eatwell plate

a) Look at the pie chart below. It shows what type of food you should eat every day.
Work with a partner and name at least three things from every section. How many
words do you know?

workbook
2–4

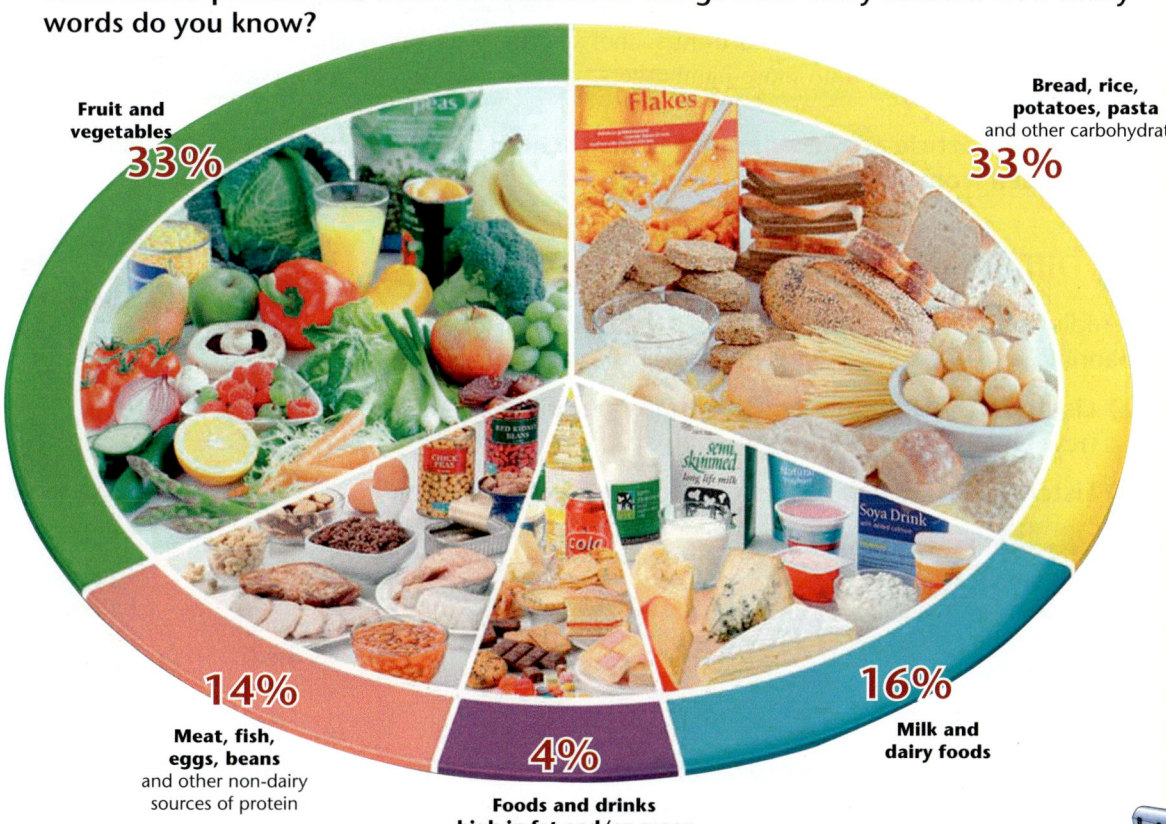

**Fruit and
vegetables**
33%

**Bread, rice,
potatoes, pasta**
and other carbohydrates
33%

**Meat, fish,
eggs, beans**
and other non-dairy
sources of protein
14%

**Foods and drinks
high in fat and/or sugar**
4%

**Milk and
dairy foods**
16%

wordbank
statistics **A**

b) Read the statements. Are they true or false?

1 You should eat
15% more fruit
and vegetables
than meat.

2 33% of your food
should come
from fruit and
vegetables.

3 You should eat
less meat than
dairy foods.

4 You should
drink as many
fizzy drinks as
possible.

tip
Here 'diet'
means
'Nahrung,
Ernährung'
and not 'Diät'.

c) Use the pie chart and put together a perfect diet for one day.

63

5 Food in British school canteens

a) Read the beginning of this newspaper article and find out what junk food is.

Junk food banned in schools

(London)
The government decided that British school canteens will no longer be allowed to sell junk food to pupils. The famous chef Jamie Oliver and others have led a long campaign against school food that makes children overweight and ill. From now on, all food with too much fat, salt or sugar in it will be banned from school canteens. There will be no more hamburgers,

crisps, sweets or fizzy drinks. Pupils will get at least two types of fruit and vegetables with every meal, and chips only twice a week. Machines that sold chocolate and fizzy drinks will now sell milk, water and fruit. There were different reactions to the new law. Some groups think it is a good

b) Read the article again. What did British school canteens sell in the past? What will they sell from now on?

6 Different reactions

A radio station asked some people what they think about banning junk food in school canteens.

a) Listen to the statements. How many people are for the new law and how many are against it?

b) Listen again. Which of these statements can you hear?

> I haven't had a burger since January.

> Children should be allowed to eat what they want.

> I've been a vegetarian for seven years.

> It's a good idea to make sure kids get enough healthy food.

> I don't see the point. Kids will still eat unhealthy food.

c) How good is your memory? Match the sentence parts. What word do you get?

1 My brother hasn't eaten lunch at school — **R** for about three months now.

2 My school canteen hasn't served junk food — **S** for five years because my dad has to get up early.

3 My mother hasn't cooked — **P** since she was 12.

4 Since I was 13 — **C** since he started his diet.

5 My sister hasn't eaten anything but burgers — **S** I have eaten at least three pizzas a week.

6 My parents and I haven't had breakfast together — **I** since my older brother moved out because she doesn't like it.

Sidebar notes:

workbook 4

tip
Be careful of false friends!
chef = *Koch*
boss = *Chef*

MORE
M1–M4
food extremes

CD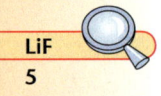

LiF 5

tip
You can listen again to check.

workbook 5–6

PEOPLE & PLACES

Jamie's School Dinners

There are a lot of people in Britain who eat too much unhealthy food. Especially children and teenagers eat the wrong things. They eat a lot of junk food, like chips, burgers and crisps. Studies have shown that one in six English school children is overweight.

Because of this, the famous TV chef Jamie Oliver decided to start a campaign for healthier school dinners. It started in 2005 with a TV documentary called 'Jamie's School Dinners' in which Jamie showed a school dinner lady how to cook fresh, healthy meals and – more important – how to make children like them. All in all, the series was very successful and the British government set new standards for school meals.

Although there was a lot of support for Jamie Oliver's campaign, many pupils did not like the change. They stopped eating at school because they wanted to keep eating junk food. Some parents thought their children shouldn't be forced to eat healthily. At a school in South Yorkshire some mothers even started bringing their children hamburgers and chips, so they wouldn't have to eat the new school menus.

But Jamie is sure that it only takes time to change people's eating habits: "Nobody's expecting to see a massive change over night."

In 2006 Jamie spoke to the mothers in South Yorkshire and they now agree that healthy food is good for their children.

7 Choose an activity

- Should junk food be banned in schools? Collect arguments for and against in a grid. You can listen to number 6 and read the People & Places box again for help with your arguments. Then write a text and say what YOUR opinion is.

- Imagine you want to start a school canteen. What should be sold in your canteen? Write a menu for one week.

- Write a letter or an email to Jamie Oliver and tell him what you think about his school dinners campaign.

- Create your own pie chart about healthy eating with pictures from magazines or flyers. You can look at number 4 for ideas what to include.

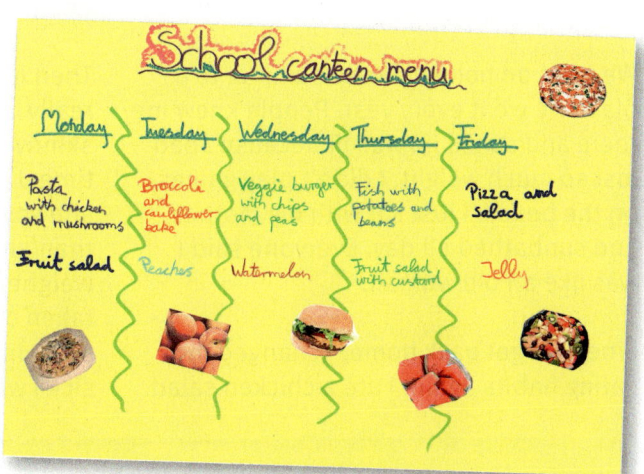

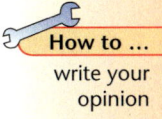

How to …
write your opinion

How to …
write a letter

workbook
7-9

tip
You can contact Jamie Oliver at www.jamieoliver.com

portfolio

4

8 Ella's story

a) The words below are taken from the story of a girl called Ella from York, England. Can you guess what happened to her?

thinner   no breakfast   small lunch   aerobics   eating less

feeling cold   ill   help   hospital   therapy

b) Now work with a partner and talk about your ideas. Then find another pair. Do they share your ideas?

9 In her own words

Some teenagers have problems with eating. Ella is one of them.
She wrote about it in a youth magazine.

How to ...
read

a) Read Ella's story. Do not look up any words. While you're reading take notes on:

- Ella's age at the beginning
- her breakfast at the beginning
- her breakfast after the holidays
- the month when she went to hospital
- her height and weight at age 15
- her weight when she left the hospital

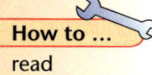

workbook
10-11

MORE
M5-M11
Oliver Twist

I don't know how it started. All I know is that I wanted to be as thin as one of my friends. I wasn't really fat. I was about 14 when I had this idea and I just started eating less and less.

At first I'd just have some fruit for breakfast and a sandwich at lunchtime. Then a very small dinner in the evening. I'd cut everything into very small pieces so that it would take a long time to eat it. After a few weeks I'd just have a slice of melon for breakfast and a boiled egg for lunch. I also started doing aerobics and exercises.

We went on holiday in the summer to a place we went every year. People knew me there and asked if I was ill because I had lost so much weight. I didn't play games on the beach. I just sat with my mother and sunbathed all day. Everyone said I was like an old woman.

When we got back home, I changed my eating habits again. I ate a chicken salad for lunch. But I made it myself. Then my mother wouldn't see that I didn't put any chicken in it! And I stopped eating breakfast. My parents wanted to know what was wrong with me. It was awful for them but I didn't care. We couldn't go to a restaurant because I would just sit and look at the food.

Then it was October and I started to feel really cold. My mother said I was too skinny and that's why I felt cold all the time. I got very angry with her. How could she say I was skinny? I was so much fatter than all my friends. Of course, I really weighed less than them. Anorexia had taken over. I just stopped eating and kept on doing my exercises. I didn't know how sick I was.

66

It was November when my parents brought me to hospital. I was 163cm tall and only weighed 34 kilos. I was now 15. I was so cold and I didn't want any help! But the doctors said that if I didn't start eating now and put on weight, I would be dead within a week or so. The day I arrived, an anorexic girl died. She was also 15 and weighed only 29 kilos. Another boy came back a week later because he wasn't eating anything again and had real problems with his heart. I don't know if he lived.

But still I didn't want to eat and I couldn't eat. Every day I had long talks with the psychologist. She told me that she had had similar problems when she was my age. And then, after a few weeks, I started eating. I had to eat three meals a day, big ones, and three high-calorie snacks, too. It took me two hours to eat a meal and a snack took me an hour. It felt as if I was eating all day. After each meal or snack I had to lie down on my bed for half an hour. I wasn't allowed any exercises. People were nice to me but I was never alone. There was always a psychologist or a therapist. It was hell. I knew that I could die if I stopped eating again. At first, I had real problems with my health but things slowly got better. I was there for seven months.

When I had put on nine kilos, they said I could go home. But I'm still having therapy and this will go on for some years. I hope I'm cured but you never really know.

b) Now read Ella's story again. How do YOU feel about Ella?

I can/can't understand Ella.

I think it's stupid/silly …

It must be difficult …

I feel sorry for her.

…

10 A closer look

a) What can you find out about Ella's illness from the story?
Work with a partner and ask each other about:

- how Ella's illness started
- how other people could tell that Ella was sick
- why she stopped eating

- what Ella is doing now
- how other people reacted
- how Ella felt in hospital

b) Imagine you were one of the following people. What would you do?

LiF
12

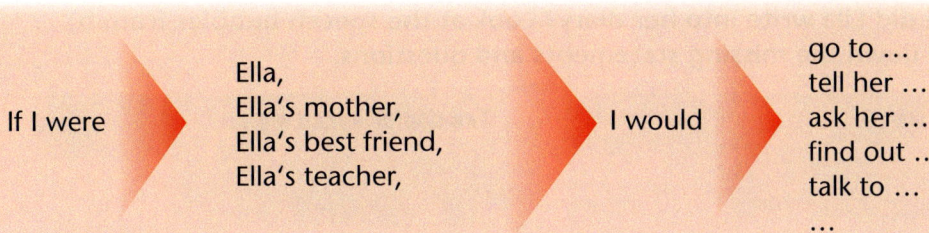

| If I were | Ella, Ella's mother, Ella's best friend, Ella's teacher, | I would | go to … tell her … ask her … find out … talk to … … |

11 Who said what?

a) Look at Ella's story on pages 66-67 again and find out who said or thought what.
Match the sentence parts.

LiF
17

1 People asked	**A** she was like an old woman.
2 Ella thought	**B** she was too skinny.
3 The doctors said	**C** if Ella was ill.
4 Her mother told her	**D** she wanted to be thinner.
5 Everyone said	**E** she would be dead within a week or so.

b) During her time in hospital, Ella kept a diary.
She wrote down how she felt and what she was told by other people.

Look at the speech bubbles and Ella's diary entries.
Match direct and reported speech.

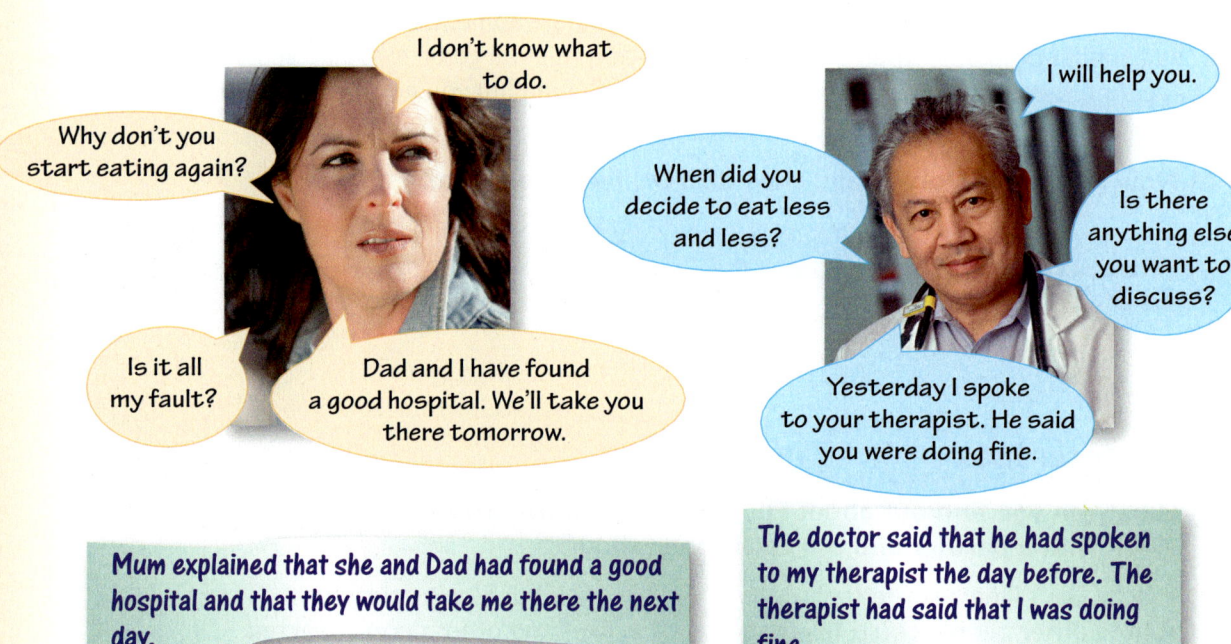

c) What else did Ella write into her diary? Look at the speech bubbles from b)
and write down the missing statements and questions.

d) Be a language expert: Look at the examples of reported speech on this page.
Make a classroom poster about the rules for reported speech.

12 A radio show

a) Listen to the radio show 'Let's talk'.
What is the topic of the show?

b) A friend of yours who doesn't understand
much English is listening, too.
Try to answer his/her questions.

1 Rob hat eine Freundin, richtig?
Was erzählt er von ihr?

2 Was wird denn über Zeitschriften
und das Fernsehen gesagt?

3 Fiona redet doch von Schulen, oder?
Was haben die mit dem Thema zu tun?

4 Warum ruft Peter an?
Hat er Probleme mit seinen Freunden?

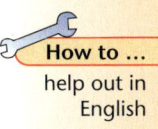
CD

How to ...
help out in
English

workbook
12

13 Through thick and thin: YOUR discussion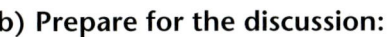

**Choose one of the statements and have
a class discussion:**

- Models have to be thin.
- Looks are not important.
- If children are overweight, it's their
  parents' fault.

a) What's YOUR opinion?
First do a quick survey in class.
Then get together in three groups:

- Group one agrees with the statement.
- Group two disagrees with the statement.
- Group three listens to the arguments
  and takes notes.

How to ...
discuss

b) Prepare for the discussion:

- Collect arguments for or against the statement in your group.
- Group three thinks about the best way to take notes during the discussion
  and finds someone to lead the discussion.

c) Have a discussion in class:

- Present your arguments. Make sure group one and two take turns.

d) At the end of the discussion group three decides:
Which group had the best arguments?

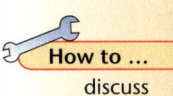

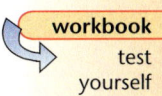
workbook
test
yourself

M1 A lot to eat

Look at the pictures. How do they make you feel? Have you ever seen anything like this?

1

2

3

M2 Too much food?

How to ...
read

a) Read this article from a website about restaurants that serve extra large portions of food. Where can you find them?

workbook
M1

XXL Restaurants

Do you love food? Have you ever finished your dinner and wanted more? Ever dreamed of a place where you could order your favourite meal as a huge portion? Well, in America that dream has come true! American restaurants have always been known for their large portions of food. There are some places, however, where this is taken to the extreme …

XXL restaurants, where the food comes extra, extra large, are now popular in the US. Perhaps the best-known is The Big Texan Steak Ranch in Amarillo, Texas. In this restaurant, hungry guests can eat the largest steak in Texas. This steak, called 'The Texas King', weighs 72oz (2kg) and is the largest meal on the menu. If you can eat the steak within one hour, you get it for free. But only about 8,500 people have managed this, since 1960. If you can't eat your steak

within the hour, it will cost you $72.
Not a fan of steak? Then why not visit The Heart Attack Grill in Arizona? 30 waitresses work here dressed as nurses and they serve large portions of 'flat-line fries': chips that are fried in pure lard. The Grill's 'Jolt Cola' is made with real sugar. And the largest burger on their menu, the

'Quadruple Bypass Burger', has four levels and has over 8,000 calories!! Enough to give anyone a heart attack! And if you weigh over 350lbs (about 160kg), you get every meal for free.
If America is too far away, then have no fear: XXL restaurants are now opening in Germany, too!

tip
oz = ounce
lbs (from Latin 'libra') = pounds

b) What else can you find out from the text? Take notes on:

- names of restaurants
- food served there

LiF
23

c) Work with a partner. Go through the website again and ask and answer questions like these:

> How much does the Texas King weigh?

> How many people have got their steaks for free?

> How much/many …?

M3 XXL food – opinions

a) Read the following Internet forum entries. What do you think? Give each of the comments a number.

> 1 totally agree • 2 agree • 3 disagree • 4 totally disagree

workbook
M2

XTREMEFOOD/comments

Beckiboo_37
Eurgh! I think these restaurants sound disgusting! Who would want to eat so much food at once? It is also unhealthy to eat so much. You wouldn't see me in an XXL restaurant – no way!
Add comment

Steve-6
I personally love my food, and I have a very large appetite! I would love to visit one of these places for an XXL portion! So what if it seems a lot? If someone can eat it all, why does it matter?
Add comment

Maxi
I don't agree with these restaurants at all. OK, so they want to serve people their favourite food – but in such large portions? I think it's awful when people in other countries are starving, with barely enough to survive, and here we are over-eating in places like this. It's just such a waste!
Add comment

***Rachel**
I am a vegetarian, so eating so much meat is my idea of hell! But I think if people enjoy eating more, they should have the option. As long as they eat it all, then it isn't so bad. As long as they don't waste half of it – that really annoys me!
Add comment

---

b) Work with a partner. Share your opinion with him or her.

c) What do YOU think about XXL restaurants? Write your own Internet forum entry.

How to …
write your opinion

M4 Choose an activity

- Have you ever been to an XXL restaurant? Write about your experience.

- Find out more information about an XXL restaurant that interests you and present it to the class.

- Design a pro or an anti-XXL restaurant poster.

- Find statistics about food and health. Present the most interesting facts to the class.

How to …
write

wordbank
food G

portfolio

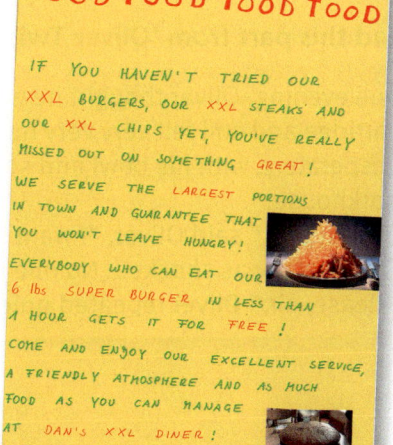

FOOD FOOD FOOD FOOD

IF YOU HAVEN'T TRIED OUR XXL BURGERS, OUR XXL STEAKS AND OUR XXL CHIPS YET, YOU'VE REALLY MISSED OUT ON SOMETHING GREAT! WE SERVE THE LARGEST PORTIONS IN TOWN AND GUARANTEE THAT YOU WON'T LEAVE HUNGRY! EVERYBODY WHO CAN EAT OUR 6 lbs SUPER BURGER IN LESS THAN A HOUR GETS IT FOR FREE! COME AND ENJOY OUR EXCELLENT SERVICE, A FRIENDLY ATMOSPHERE AND AS MUCH FOOD AS YOU CAN MANAGE AT DAN'S XXL DINER!

 **Poor boy**

Today most people in Europe have got enough to eat. But there were times when this was different.

a) Describe this picture from the film 'Oliver Twist'. What do you think is happening?

How to ...
watch

workbook
M3-M4

b) What might the people in the picture be saying or thinking? Choose a person and write a speech or think bubble. Can your partner guess which person you chose?

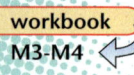 **Oliver Twist**

The novel 'Oliver Twist' was published in the 1830s. Its author, Charles Dickens, wanted to make people aware of the living conditions of poor people in Britain at that time.

Oliver Twist's mother died immediately after his birth and the orphaned boy ended up in a workhouse. British workhouses in the 19th century were terrible places where the poor and homeless had to live.

Read this part from 'Oliver Twist'. What do you learn about Oliver?

One evening, Oliver thought he would go mad with hunger. He had finished his bowl of porridge and still felt very very hungry.
Desperately, with his bowl and spoon in hand, he walked towards the master of the workhouse.
"Please, sir," said Oliver, "I want some more."
The master was shocked. No one had ever dared to ask for more. "What?" he roared.
"Please, sir," Oliver repeated quietly, "I want some more."

M7 **Thrown out** ✏️

a) Oliver's life gets even harder. Look at the pictures and write a caption for each picture.

1

cellar

2

undertaker

3

coffin

4

London 70 miles

b) Now write down the story from the pictures. Then swap stories with a partner and give each other feedback.

c) Read out your story to the class. Which story do you like best? Say why.

d) What do you think happens next?

How to …
write

Oliver Twist

After Tom had dared to ask for more food the master of the workhouse put him into a dark cellar.
Tom didn't know what was going to happen to him and he was very scared.
But after he had been in the cellar for three days the door opened and the master

M8 On his way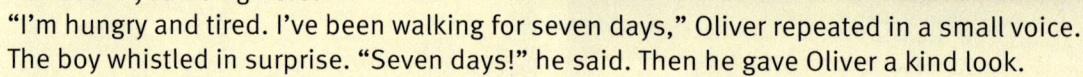

a) Read the next part of the story. Who finds Oliver?

An hour or two passed, and people began appearing in the streets. They saw the dirty and tired orphan who sat on the doorstep, but most of the people looked away and hurried on.

Then suddenly, Oliver felt that someone was staring at him. He looked up and saw a snub-nosed, rough-looking boy standing close by, who looked him up and down with sharp, ugly little eyes.

"Hello!" the boy greeted Oliver happily. "What are you doing here?"

"I'm hungry and tired. I've been walking for seven days," Oliver repeated in a small voice. The boy whistled in surprise. "Seven days!" he said. Then he gave Oliver a kind look. "You'll be wanting something to eat. Don't worry, I'll pay!"

The boy was as good as his word. When Oliver had wolfed down the food which was the first real meal he had had for days, the boy asked: "Going to London?"

"Yes," Oliver told him.

"Got a place where you can stay?"

"No," said Oliver ruefully.

"I suppose you want somewhere that's not too expensive where you can sleep tonight, then?" said the boy.

Oliver nodded. "Yes, I do!"

"I know a nice old gentleman in London who'll give you a bed for nothing – he knows me very well!"

This offer of a free place where he could sleep was just too good to be true Oliver thought, and so he accepted gratefully.

"What's your name?" the boy wanted to know.

Oliver told him.

"Mine's Jack Dawkins – they call me the Artful Dodger!" the boy said proudly.

workbook
M6

b) Were you right in M7 d)?

M9 Who or which?

a) Read the sentences. Then complete them with *who* or *which*.

1 The people ??? were on the streets did not look at Oliver.

2 The boy ??? found Oliver gave him some food.

3 The food ??? the boy bought for Oliver was Oliver's first real meal in days.

4 The town ??? Oliver is going to is called London.

5 A man ??? knows Jack Dawkins will give Oliver a bed for nothing.

b) Be a language expert: Look at the sentences from a) again. Decide where you can leave out the relative pronoun and where you have to add *who* or *which*.

LiF
24

workbook
M7

LiF
25

M10 Lucky pick

The Artful Dodger takes Oliver with him to a house in an old and dirty part of London. For a few weeks Oliver lives here with the Dodger, some other boys and Fagin, the man who looks after them all. Oliver does not yet know that Fagin is a criminal who takes in homeless children and sends them out on the streets to pick pockets. When Oliver is allowed to go out with the Dodger for the first time, he is shocked to discover what his new friends are doing. When they pick the pocket of a gentleman, Mr Brownlow, Oliver is so surprised that he does not run away and is caught and brought to the police.

workbook
M8

a) Listen to what Mr Brownlow tells his friend Mr Clements in the evening. Take notes on:

- what Mr Brownlow was doing when his wallet was stolen
- who told the police that Oliver wasn't the thief
- where Oliver is now
- what Mr Brownlow thinks about Oliver

CD

b) Work with a partner and finish the dialogue. What does Mr Brownlow say? What does his friend say? Make two role cards: one for Mr Brownlow, one for Mr Clements.

c) Act out your dialogue to the class.

> Mr Clements: This boy? Who you found on the streets? The son of a friend of yours? How …
>
> Mr Brownlow: …
>
> Mr Clements: …

tip
If you want to know how Oliver's story ends, you can read the book and watch the film or the musical.

How to …
talk

M11 Project: YOUR research on the time of Oliver Twist

Get together in groups to make a poster, a PowerPoint presentation or a brochure.

1 PLAN IT In your group think about:

- Which topic interests you most?
- Which information do you need to present your topic?
- Where can you get the information?

> crime • clothing in the 1830s • school • Queen Victoria • health and housing • Charles Dickens • …

2 DO IT Collect information and take notes. Then decide:

- What do you want to present?
- How do you want to present it?

Prepare your poster/presentation/brochure.

3 CHECK IT

- Can you make your presentation more interesting?
- Perhaps you could add some photos, a map, …
- Are the texts correct?

How to …
give a talk

4 PRESENT IT

- Practise your talk first, then present your work to the class.

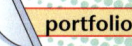
portfolio

4

Check it out!

Did you get it all?

- On which page can you see an English breakfast?
- How much of your daily food should come from fruit and vegetables?
- What has been banned in English school canteens?
- What is Jamie Oliver's job?
- What are the different meanings of 'diet'?
- How much did Ella weigh when she was brought to hospital?
- Who offered Ella help?

Good to know ...

When you're invited to dinner, make sure to always be polite about the food. Never say something is not nice, rather say it is interesting. It is absolutely OK to say so if you don't like something – as long as you're polite.

Did you know that ...

... people have enjoyed eating apples since 6,500 B.C.?

... Germans eat twice as many potatoes as Americans?

Who brought the potato to Europe?

... crisps were invented by a North American Indian called George Crum?

... in the USA pepperoni is the most popular topping for pizza?

... one bee colony can produce 60 to 100 pounds of honey per year?

How many bees does it take to produce a tablespoon of honey?

... it takes about 10 pounds of milk to make one pound of cheese?

... there are over 500 different types of bananas?

Find out what the most popular topping in your class is.

... not all carrots are orange?

Find out some of their names.

... 0.007 calories are consumed while licking a stamp?

76

MAKING A LIVING

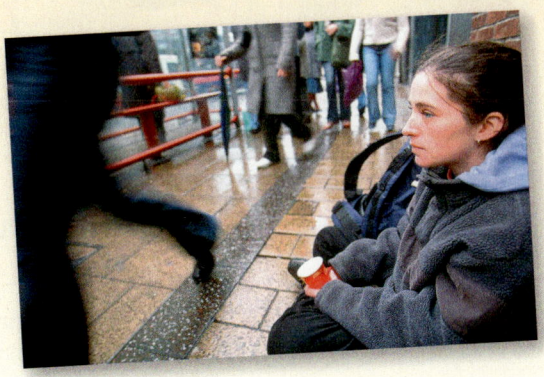

In this Theme …

- you will talk about different jobs and your own job plans.
- you will read about and listen to teenagers and their work experience.
- you will talk about how people spend their money and how not to get into debt.
- you will learn how to fill in an application form for a job abroad.
- you can listen to a job interview and act out an interview yourself.
- you will be able to prepare a short talk about supporting the homeless.

5

CD

1 Job sounds 👂

Listen to the scenes. Which jobs can you hear?

> The first person is a/an …

> The second person …

LiF
21

2 Jobs, jobs, jobs 👄

a) What do you know about these jobs? Collect information in a grid.

receptionist

police officer

shop assistant

social worker

wordbank
jobs **H**

nursery teacher

check-in agent

workbook
1-3

waiter/waitress

builder   nurse

jobs	where	what to do	working hours	should be
scaffolder	outdoors	build scaffolds	eight-hour shifts	strong, good with one's hands

scaffolder

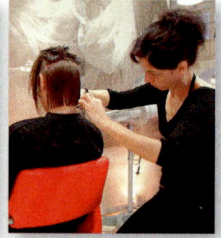
hair stylist

electrician

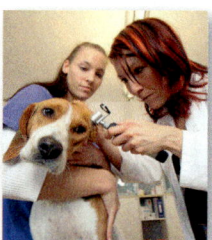
vet's assistant

car mechanic

painter

office administrator

security guard

warehouse worker

b) Work in groups of four. One of you chooses a job from a) and describes it. Can the others guess the job? Take turns.

> He or she works outdoors and … He or she should be strong. …

c) What job will YOU have in five years? How can you get there?

LiF
9

> I will graduate from grade … Then I'll …

> When I'm eighteen, I'll have to do my military service. Afterwards I'll …

> In five years I'll be a car mechanic in …

do my A levels • have a gap year • start training as a/an … •
do military or civilian service •
do volunteer work • do vocational training • go to college

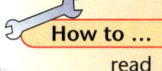

3 Most important skills

a) **What do you think is most important in a job? Look at the examples and make a top five list. Then compare your list with a partner's. Find points you both agree on.**

| You are good at languages. | You are friendly. | You are good at maths. |

| You are polite. | You can talk in front of people. | You are good-looking. |

| You can work in a team. | You can use the Internet. | … |

b) **Now read the website. How would you explain 'soft skills' in German?**

How to …
read

MORE
M1
working
abroad

Good marks aren't everything – score with soft skills!

Not doing well at school? Problems with maths tests? School marks not great? Worried that you won't get a good job? Don't panic! There are more important things than just being a top pupil!

What are soft skills?

Soft skills are those skills that you need in any job you want to do. It is not about having good grades and being a top pupil. It is all about how you work and how you behave.
Are you good in a team? Are you good at listening to others? Are you always polite? Then you have good soft skills. Every boss will love that!

What you need – soft skills!

1 *You are polite.*
2 *You can work in a team.*
3 *You are reliable.*
4 *You have stamina.*
5 *You are flexible.*
6 *You are creative.*
7 *You are communicative.*
8 *You are punctual.*

c) **Read these comments about three teenagers. Which soft skills do they not have?**

| Isaac forgot to bring the pictures and texts for a presentation. Now the group can't go on working. | Nick likes to work on his own. He doesn't share ideas with other members of the group. | Melanie is a very quiet girl. She hardly ever talks or joins in a conversation. |

d) **Look at the list of soft skills from b) again. What are YOUR soft skills?**

Example: **I can work in a team and I like helping people but I'm not very communicative.**

e) **Look at your list from a) again. Would you change it now? Talk about it with your partner.**

workbook
4-5

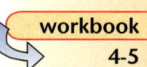

4 Hannah's CV

**a) Look at Hannah's CV.
What does it tell you about her?**

Her surname is …
She speaks …
…

**b) Write your own CV. Swap it
with a partner and give each other
feedback on:**

• layout • spelling • information

Hannah McLeod
51 Brent Street, Hendon, London NW4 2EA
Home: 020 863-48026 ~ Mobile: 0760 111-2314 ~ email: highlander@wub.co.uk

Experience
Summer job with Spade&Shovel, DIY Centre, London

Education
Hendon School, London, 2004-Present
St Mary Primary School, London, 1999-2004

Skills
Excellent teamworking skills
Great communication skills
Wide knowledge of DIY materials

Languages
English, French

References available

5 A new experience

a) Hannah is doing her work experience. Look at the pictures and have a guess:

• Where is Hannah? • What is she doing? • Does she like it?

b) Now read Hannah's email to her friend Lilly. Were you right in a)?

Subject: **I'm working!**

Dear Lilly,

How are you? We're doing our work experience at the moment! Two weeks without
school and that stupid school uniform! I went for a job at our local building centre.
I know a lot about DIY – my boss was quite surprised.
I start at 9 and I've been on time every day so far. The first day was awful.
I cleaned shelves, then cleaned more shelves and then – how surprising – cleaned
more shelves. My jeans looked so dirty at the end of the day. Yuck! Next day
I counted a lot of different articles. Then I had to put the numbers into a portable
computer. Then day 3, I was allowed to help customers. This man came in with a
question about a drill. I was a bit nervous at first, but I felt good because I was able
to help him. But six hours every day is a long time. My feet! I have to do a lot of
writing, too. All kinds of forms and a CV before I started. AND a report at the end.
My teacher is coming in tomorrow. Perhaps I can sell him some tools, haha. OK,
long day tomorrow – I'm off to bed!

Love, Hannah

c) In Hannah's email you learned about her work experience. Read the email again, then copy the mindmap and complete it.

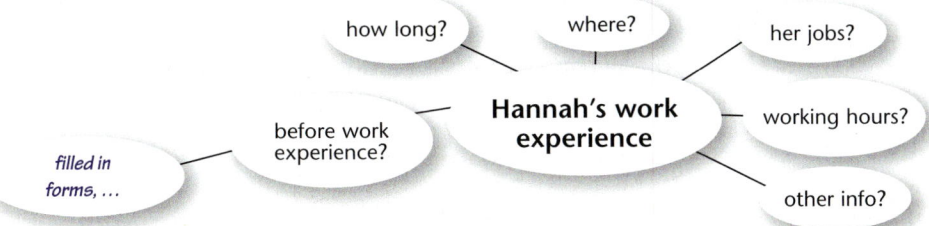

how long? — where? — her jobs?

Hannah's work experience

before work experience? — working hours?

filled in forms, ...

other info?

6 Hannah's interview

How to ...
talk

workbook
7-8

After her work experience Hannah was interviewed for the local newspaper.

Work with a partner. Use your notes from number 5c) and prepare an interview with Hannah. One of you is the reporter, the other takes Hannah's role. Present your interview to the class.

7 Talking about work experience

CD

How to ...
listen

a) What do Hannah's classmates say about their work experience? Read the questions and make a grid. Then listen twice and take notes.

- What are their names?
- Where did they work?
- What were their working hours?
- What did they like about their work?
- What didn't they like?
- What other information can you get?

b) Now choose one person. Use your notes to talk about him/her. Include one piece of false information. Can your classmates find it?

🇬🇧 PEOPLE & PLACES

Training on the job

In Germany there are about 340 jobs for which you need to be trained. Often this training has a practical as well as a theoretical part. After your training you have to take a test. If you pass this test, you are allowed to call yourself – for example – 'Klempner' or 'Elektriker'.

The British system is quite different. You can leave school when you're 16 and start a job immediately. This is called 'training on the job'. But you can also get further qualifications by doing courses.
A lot of these courses are NVQs (National Vocational Qualifications) which are recognized by the state.

8 Ben's report for his language portfolio 👓

After his work experience Ben wrote about it. At first he didn't like his report. Then a classmate helped him to edit his text.

First read Ben's text. Then look at the checklist. Find examples for each point in the text.

My work experience as a car mechanic

did my work experience   *Brent*   *worked*
I ~~worked~~ at the garage in ~~Bent~~ Street. I ~~was~~ there for two weeks.
Normally,   *strong*   *My job was to help*
I wore blue overalls and ~~I wore~~ shoes. ~~I helped~~ the car mechanics. I had to wash the

cars and ~~I had to~~ clean the floors*, too.*
The car mechanics   *Then I often*
I had a morning break at 9 o'clock and a lunch break at 12 o'clock. I had to make tea
I am really interested in   *enjoy*   *learned to*
for the other mechanics. ~~I like~~ cars and working with my hands. I ~~can~~ connect a
even   *, but*
computer to the engine. I can change a tyre. ~~But~~ the boss wouldn't let me do it in the
The boss was
garage. ~~I don't like the boss because he is~~ very unfriendly. He didn't show me new
That is why   *very much.*
things. I didn't like my work experience.

Checklist for texts:

1. Don't begin all your sentences with the same words.
2. Try to use some of these words: **really, normally, often, too,** …
3. Try to connect sentences. Use **and, but, then, because, that is why,** …
4. Use interesting adjectives.
5. Check your spelling.

9 Choose an activity ✏️

How to … write

wordbank jobs H

- **Write a report about a job or work experience you did. Think about:**
  - what kind of job it was
  - when you did it
  - where you did it
  - how long you worked
  - what other information you can give
  - if you liked/didn't like it and why

  Swap your report with a partner. Edit his/her report and give each other feedback.

- **Make a poster or PowerPoint presentation about a job you would like to do.**
  - Collect pictures or photos.
  - Write about skills and soft skills which you need for this job.

  Show your poster or presentation in class.

portfolio

- **Create a job dictionary.**
  Write down jobs YOU find interesting and their definitions.

10 Who wants to be a millionaire?

a) Imagine you had a lot of money. What would you spend it on? Work with a partner and tell each other about things you would like to do or buy.

> If I were really rich, I would go to …

> If I were a millionaire, I would buy …

LiF
12

b) What do YOU think: What is more important than being rich?

> I think being healthy is more important than being rich.

> …

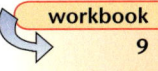
workbook
9

11 Money, money, money

a) Listen to the song 'Money, money, money' by the Swedish band ABBA. What is the singer's problem?

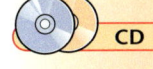
CD

b) Now read the lyrics of the song. How would the singer like to solve her problem?

tip
ain't = isn't

I work all night, I work all day, to pay the bills I have to pay
Ain't it sad
And still there never seems to be a single penny left for me
That's too bad
In my dreams I have a plan
If I got me a wealthy man
I wouldn't have to work at all, I'd fool around and have a ball …

Chorus:
Money, money, money
Must be funny
In the rich man's world
Money, money, money
Always sunny
In the rich man's world
Aha-ahaaa
All the things I could do
If I had a little money
It's a rich man's world

A man like that is hard to find but I can't get him off my mind
Ain't it sad
And if he happens to be free I bet he wouldn't fancy me
That's too bad
So I must leave, I'll have to go
To Las Vegas or Monaco
And win a fortune in a game, my life will never be the same …

c) Do YOU think these are good ways to become rich?
   What other ways can you think of?

12 Teenage spending power

Children and teenagers are important for big companies. Why? Because they have got a lot of money to spend. In the UK children and teenagers make up a large part of the population. In 2007 there were 12.4 million people between the ages of 0 and 19 living in the UK. Teenagers especially have become richer and they can spend more money than ever before.

How to ...
work with
others (1)

How do YOU spend your money? In class, form a double circle and tell each other.

13 Spending your cash

For a study, people were asked about their spending habits.

**a) Read what two of the interviewed people said.
What do they spend or used to spend their money on?**

KENNETH, 65: Well, I started working when I was sixteen and that was the first time I had my own money to spend.
I still lived with my parents at that time and they had never had enough money to give pocket money to my brothers or me.
I had to give some of the money to my parents for rent and food but I could keep the rest. I can still remember what I bought with my first money – a very cheap record player and a Little Richard record. I played it again and again. We always paid cash in those days. Cash machines didn't exist. You took money out of your account if you needed some. I got my first credit card when I was about forty.
I think we had less money than the young today but we also had fewer and less expensive wishes. When I look at my grandchildren's rooms, I often think they only need half of the stuff! I don't think buying or owning things makes you really happy. Friends and a loving family do.

PHOEBE, 19: I had a lot more money to spend as a young teen. I got pocket money from my parents and I had a part-time job at the weekends. I used to buy a lot of clothes, shoes, make-up, DVDs – everything!
The big change came when I got pregnant at 16. My daughter is almost three years old now and the most important person in my life. Her father left me after her birth and I'm trying to take care of the two of us on my own.

I work as a shop assistant and have very little money. I need to pay for my flat, food, clothes, transport and so on. I can't afford to save any money and I try not to use my debit and credit cards too much. I don't want to get into debt! And I'm proud that I work for my money. I can't understand the unemployed. There's this family in my street – both parents out of work and they even seem to like it! At least they're not trying very hard to find jobs.

b) Read Kenneth's statement again. What has changed since he was 16?

workbook
10

c) Read Phoebe's statement again. Why does she prefer to pay cash?

5

14 Money talks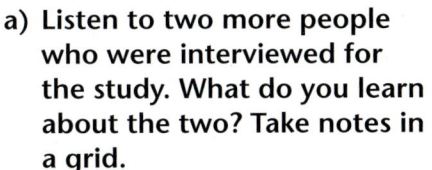

a) Listen to two more people who were interviewed for the study. What do you learn about the two? Take notes in a grid.

name	age	job	lives in	family	spends money on	other info
Susan						
Aiman						

b) Compare your notes with a partner's. Add missing information to your grid.

c) Listen again. Which of the following sentences can you hear?

A I can't understand the unemployed.

B Sometimes I even give money to an organization that helps the homeless.

C The rich get richer.

D The famous are often rich.

E The poor get poorer.

F I don't like the wealthy.

d) Be a language expert: Look at the sentences from c) again. When can you use an adjective as a noun?

CD

workbook
11

MORE
M8–M12
on the streets

LiF
22

15 Money matters

This is a brochure for British teenagers. Explain to someone who doesn't speak English what advice the brochure gives.

How to …
help out in English

Top Tips for Teens!

▶ **Budget!** Write down how much money you get every week/month. Then work out what you can spend. Make sure you leave enough for something unexpected.

▶ **Save!** Try to save the same amount of money every month.

▶ **Aim!** What do you want to save up for? Think about this every time you would like to spend money. Wouldn't it be better to save for the thing you really want?

▶ **Earn!** Think about different ways to earn some extra cash. You could get a part-time job, offer to do little jobs for your family or neighbours, sell things at a car boot sale, etc.

▶ **Think!** Try to think carefully before you buy something. Do you really need it?

▶ **Avoid!** Don't use credit cards and store cards – they often get people into debt. Be in control of your own money.

16 YOUR survey: Money

a) Look at the results of the study on spending habits in the UK. What information does it give you? What do you find interesting or surprising?

Household Spending in the UK 2008 (in %)

Transport	13.4
Recreation and culture	12.5
Housing	11.3
Food	10.5
Clothing	4.8
Education	1.5
Miscellaneous	46.0

b) Do a class survey about YOUR spending habits and create a bar chart out of your findings.

workbook
12-13

wordbank
statistics A

portfolio

workbook
test yourself

M1 Working abroad

a) Read the job adverts. How are these German phrases expressed in the adverts?

How to ...
read

1 Wir kümmern uns um …   3 Wir bieten die Möglichkeit …   5 Bewirb dich bei …
2 Erfahrungen sammeln   4 Die Arbeit besteht darin …

European Work Experience Programme

Work in the UK

We provide the opportunity for nationals from the European Union to work in the UK.
You don't have to worry about anything. We make sure everything is organised before you arrive in England.
We'll sort out a job and a place to live for you.
You can earn up to £5.52 an hour working in fast food chains, restaurants, hotels, pubs or shops in London or at Heathrow or Gatwick Airport.
You will live with a host family or in a house with other young people.
If you are between 16 and 27 years old, flexible and reliable, you can have the time of your life in London. Apply at

www.ewep.com

Animal care in South Africa

The Animal Care Project in South Africa is for anyone who loves animals and wants to gain experience working with them. There are opportunities in South Africa for those who want to look after and care for animals. All you need is to enjoy looking after animals and to want to learn more about them!
You will work with full-time animal carers. You will help with feeding, exercising and rehabilitating the animals. Teamwork skills, being reliable and having stamina are essential.
You will gain many practical skills and develop as a person while living and working in a foreign country.
Find out more and apply at

www.projects-abroad. co.uk

Allanhill Farm, St. Andrews

WE ARE LOOKING FOR FRUIT PICKERS

The work involves picking strawberries and checking fruit for quality.
Payment is on a piecework basis. You will work 6 days a week, so stamina and flexibility are required.
You will live in mobile homes on the farm. In your free time you can watch TV, play sports and discover the beautiful area.
Find out more and apply at

www.allanhill. co.uk/summer.htm

b) Read the adverts again and take notes.

job(s) offered	location(s)	wages	tasks	skills needed
working in restaurants, …				
animal carer				

workbook
M1

wordbank
jobs H

c) Now look at your notes and decide: Which job would YOU like to do? Why?

I think a job as a … would be best for me because …

I've got some experience/I haven't got any experience in …

I would/wouldn't like to have/work …

M2 An application form

When you want to apply for a job, you often have to fill in an application form.

a) Read this application form. What do you learn about the person who filled it in?

workbook
M2

APPLICATION FORM

NAME: Timo   **SURNAME:** Klausen

DATE OF BIRTH: 27/04/1993   **AGE:** 16

MALE ☑   **FEMALE** ☐   **NATIONALITY:** German

ADDRESS:
Glasgower Str. 125, 13349 Berlin, Germany

EMAIL ADDRESS:
timok40@web.de

DO YOU SPEAK ENGLISH?   YES ☑   **NO** ☐

WHICH POSITION ARE YOU APPLYING FOR?
Fruit picker

PLEASE GIVE DETAILS OF PREVIOUS EMPLOYMENT:
No previous employment

WHICH QUALIFICATIONS DO YOU HOLD?
Mittlerer Schulabschluss (graduation from grade 10)

WHY DO YOU WANT TO WORK FOR US?
I want to gain work experience and improve my English.

PLEASE DESCRIBE YOUR EXPERIENCES WITH WORKING IN A TEAM:
I was the leader of a team for the school science project. I organised the work and helped my teammates when they had problems.

PLEASE TELL US ABOUT A DIFFICULT SITUATION EITHER AT WORK OR IN SCHOOL AND HOW YOU RESOLVED IT:
One of my classmates was being bullied and asked for my advice. I told him he should talk to a teacher.

PLEASE TELL US ABOUT YOURSELF (FRIENDS, FAMILY LIFE, AMBITIONS ETC):
I live with my mother, father and two sisters. I have got lots of friends. My favourite subject is English. I want to become a medical technician.

HOBBIES:
Skateboarding, swimming and playing the guitar

WHAT DATE ARE YOU AVAILABLE TO START WORK?
09/07/2010

HOW LONG ARE YOU PLANNING TO STAY?
Four weeks

**b) Read the application form again. Look at the categories below.
Then say which questions belong to each category.**

A Personal details about applicant   B Qualifications
C Soft skills   D Applicant's life and background

MORE

M3 **The first impression counts**

What should or shouldn't you do to make a good first impression at a job interview? Use the pictures for help.

> be prepared • be punctual • be polite • haircut • language • eye contact • clothes • …

> You shouldn't be/have/wear …

> You should be/have/wear …

A

B

workbook
M3

M4 **Be prepared!**

LiF
4

a) Jacob is preparing for a job interview. Find out what he has been doing.

Example: **Jacob has been reading the company's website for two hours.**

read the company's website – for two hours

practise in front of the mirror – over and over again

get advice from a friend on the phone – for an hour

iron his shirt – for at least 30 minutes

look through brochures on job interviews – for quite some time

workbook
M4

b) What else could Jacob do to prepare and make a good impression at a job interview?

5
MORE

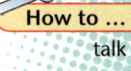 CD

M5 A job interview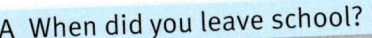

Isabel from Leipzig applied for a job and got an interview on the telephone.

a) **Listen to Isabel's job interview. Which job from M1 did she apply for?**

b) **Now listen again. Which of these questions can be heard during the interview?**

A When did you leave school?

B What are your soft skills?

C Why are you applying for the job?

D What experience would you bring to the job?

E Do you prefer regular working hours?

F How would you describe yourself?

G What interests have you got?

H What are your plans for the future?

c) **Work with a partner. Practise for a telephone interview. Ask each other to spell your names and surnames, the names of your streets and your email addresses.**

M6 YOUR job interview

a) **Work with a partner. One of you is the interviewer, the other one is the applicant. Choose a job from this Theme. The interviewer prepares a list of questions. The applicant prepares a list of reasons why he/she wants the job. Don't forget to talk about soft skills!**

> interviewer:
> applicant:
> I'm good at …
> I have got experience with …

b) **Do the interviews in class. Who gets the job? Why?**

c) **Write a list of suggestions for the people who don't get the job.**

Next time you should/shouldn't/might try to …

How to … talk

wordbank jobs H

workbook M5

M7 Choose an activity

- **Make a poster. Write down ten golden rules for a job applicant.**

- **Imagine you are the boss. Write a job advert for a funny job in Britain or in the USA. Look at the pictures for ideas.**

grape presser

dog carer

Father Christmas

- **Research jobs abroad on the Internet.**
  Think about where you might like to work and what you might like to do. Then try to find information about the place and jobs there online.

 **portfolio**

 No home

a) What comes to your mind when you read the word 'homeless'? Brainstorm with a partner. Then talk to another pair and share your ideas.

portfolio b) Write a poem or an acrostic about 'being homeless'.

 Living on the streets

wordbank
describing
people F

a) Describe the people in the pictures. What do they have in common?

b) What do you think is in their bags?

c) Work with a partner.
Choose a picture and make up
a biography of the homeless person.
Give him/her a name and think of
possible reasons why he/she
has become homeless.

d) How would you react if you walked
past one of these people in the street?
Would you help? How?

M10 Homeless in a big city

CD

a) Listen to Josh, a young homeless man from Hull. He is talking to a social worker. Why does Josh live on the streets?

LiF
4, 22

b) Listen again and take notes to answer the questions.

    1 How long has he been living on the streets?
    2 What does he do all day?
    3 Who has been getting on his nerves?
    4 What does he fear most?
    5 What does he suggest to help the poor and homeless?

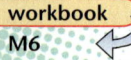
workbook
M6

c) Did you get all the information? Work with a partner and compare your notes.

M11  **Begging**

a) Read the article. What is it about?

1 John Bird – a beggar for 20 years
2 Whether people should give money to the homeless
3 Laws to get people off the streets

Evening Standard

TO BEG OR NOT TO BEG

John Bird, founder of 'The Big Issue', Britain's magazine for the homeless, started a heated discussion yesterday. Mr Bird is well-known for his campaigns supporting the homeless. Now he says that giving money to beggars was "idiotic". In his opinion, cash handouts "murder" especially young people's chances of getting away from the streets and back to a normal life. Mr Bird, who lived on the streets for 20 years himself, argued that living on the streets was made too comfortable for the poor and that it was important to get young runaways off the streets as fast as possible. In his opinion, too many homeless on the streets lead to a lower quality of city life. He said: "By giving the homeless money you are telling them they don't have to find an alternative."

Different reactions to Mr Bird's statements came from the church, the police and charity organizations. Labour MP Glenda Jackson agreed that giving cash to beggars does not solve their problems. "Don't give cash to single persons, give to organizations that support them. People aren't on the streets just because they have nowhere to live. Many have problems with drugs and alcohol and some are mentally ill."
Charity organizations said they were shocked by Bird's views. "People beg for many different reasons. Often this is their only source of income and stopping to give them money won't help, but will make things worse!"
A spokesman for the Church of England said: "There are many better ways to help people, like giving money to projects or charities."

By Wayne Veysey and Laura Burkin

tip
MP = Member of Parliament

b) Read the article again. Who says or thinks what? Write down their names and their arguments.

c) Which arguments do you agree with? Say why.

M12 YOUR talk: Money to beggars?

a) Prepare a two-minute talk about this question: Should people give money to beggars? Make notes on a card. If you don't want to give your own opinion, play the role of a young homeless person, a social worker or a police officer.

b) Practise your talk before you present it to a partner or to the class.

workbook
M7-M8

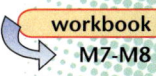
How to …
give a talk

tip
You can also record your talk

5 Check it out!

Did you get it all?

- Where in this Theme can you listen to different job sounds?
- What are soft skills? Name three.
- What does 'CV' mean?
- Where did Ben do his work experience?
- Who sang the song 'Money, money money'?
- How old was Kenneth when he started to work?
- How many people between the ages of 0 and 19 lived in Britain in 2007?

Good to know ...

Applying for a job works differently in different countries. In America, Australia and the UK people do not put a photo on their CV. It is also unusual to include reports from school or university. References from former employers or teachers are much more important.

Did you know that ...

... the average British worker sends 36 emails from the office per day?

... the three favourite jobs for American teenagers are doctor, lawyer and architect?

Find out about dream jobs of people in your class.

... US money isn't made of paper, it's made of cotton and linen?

Find out what the Euro is made of.

... 80% of all millionaires drive second-hand cars?

... 10% of workers in Britain have a second job?

... the oldest coin is over 2,700 years old?

Find out where it was found.

... American Express issued the first credit card in 1958?

Find out the difference between a credit card and a debit card.

... about 250,000 Germans work abroad?

OUR WORLD, OUR FUTURE

In this Theme ...

- you will learn how to act green at home.
- you will answer a questionnaire and find out how 'green' you are.
- you will read and talk about the film 'Wall-E'.
- you can learn about Eco-Schools.
- you can make a plan of action for your school.
- you will talk about different ways of recycling.

1 Using energy at home

a) Which electrical appliances have you got at home?

> television • stereo • fridge • oven • microwave • light bulbs • dishwasher •
> washing machine • heating • …

How to …
work with
others (1)

b) Which of them are really important? Which of them could you live without? In class, form a double circle and tell each other what you think.

workbook
1-2

2 Acting green starts at home

wordbank
environment I

a) Which electrical appliances can you see in the cartoon? What is happening?

LiF
14

b) You want the man in the cartoon to act green. What would you tell him to do?

> You could sort the rubbish.

> …

> You should turn off the lights when you don't need them.

3 Taking action

CD

How to …
listen

a) Listen to Dr Sanjeev Kumar from the organization 'Protect the Planet' telling a British school class how to act green and protect the environment. What is Dr Kumar's most important message?

b) Read the following advice. Then listen again and find out which pieces of advice Dr Kumar gives.

A Don't leave the computer on standby at night.

B If you take a shower instead of a bath, you save energy because you don't have to heat as much water.

MORE
M1-M3
Eco-Schools

C If you sort your rubbish, it can be recycled, so there is less pollution.

D Don't leave the door of the fridge open for too long when you take something out.

E Use energy-saving light bulbs.

F Clean your house with products that aren't dangerous for the environment.

G Turn off lights, computers and other electrical appliances when you aren't using them.

workbook
3-4

H If you buy fruit that isn't wrapped in plastic, you can reduce the amount of rubbish.

I Before you throw things away, ask yourself if they can be repaired or reused.

6

wordbank
environment I

LiF
18

c) Look at the pictures. What else can you do to act green?

1 2 3 4

4 How green are you?

a) Which of the things from number 3 do YOU always/sometimes/never do?

I always …

I sometimes try to …

Unfortunately/To be honest, I never …

b) Now do the questionnaire and test yourself.

How green are you?

Start here: → **What do you do when you're feeling cold at home?** → Turn the heating up a lot, then open the window if it gets too hot.

Put a jumper on.

Turn up the heating a little.

Do you use recycled paper?

Do you turn off the lights when you leave the room? → yes / no

If you see someone throwing rubbish on the street, you … → ask him/her politely to throw it in the right bin.

yes   no

ignore him/her and walk on.

pick it up and throw it away yourself.

How often do you use spray cans?   often

Have you ever volunteered to pick up rubbish in your local park?

What do you do after finishing a bottle of orange juice?

never   sometimes

Recycle the bottle.   Throw the bottle in the bin.

yes   no

Do you take showers or baths?

showers   baths

Well done! You're really very green. Keep up the good work!

You're on the right track, but you could try harder to help the environment.

You could do more to protect our planet. Even small changes in behaviour can help!

workbook
5-7

PEOPLE & PLACES

Stars going green

Many celebrities like Leonardo DiCaprio or Cameron Diaz support green causes. Some of them founded organizations that help the environment, others donate large sums of money. In 2008 film star Vanessa Hudgens took part in the 'Environmental Youth Conference' in Los Angeles. She also supported 'Million Trees LA', a project with the goal of planting and looking after a million trees.

Singers like Jordin Sparks performed at a concert in Washington, D.C. to support 'Earth Day' 2008. 'Earth Day' is a day when people think about the environment. It was started in 1970. More than a billion people celebrate 'Earth Day' each year, and there are lots of celebrations around the world. Former US vice-president Al Gore explored the dangerous effects of global warming on our planet in a documentary called 'An Inconvenient Truth'. The film won an Oscar and Al Gore got the Nobel Peace Prize for this documentary.

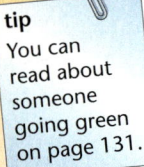

tip
You can read about someone going green on page 131.

5 The three Rs

How to …
help out in English

This is a poster from an environmental group. Explain to someone who doesn't speak English what the 'three Rs' are.

How YOU can Reduce, Reuse and Recycle!

Reducing means…

having fewer new things. This saves you money and reduces pollution and waste going into the environment. Reducing also means choosing things with the least amount of packaging.

Reusing means…

thinking before you throw things away. Can it be used again? Would someone else be able to use it? If you can't reuse it, maybe someone else can. Swap, sell or donate items such as toys, clothing and CDs.

Recycling means…

sorting your waste so it can be turned into new things. Used writing paper, for example, can be made into toilet paper, glass bottles can be cleaned and used again.

6 Choose an activity

How to …
write

• Choose a famous person who works to protect the environment. Write about this person and his/her work. Then present your findings in class. You can use PowerPoint or a flip chart to do this.

wordbank
environment l

• Make a crossword puzzle about the environment for your partner.

portfolio

• Create a poster or a collage about 'Our world, our future'. Show it in class.

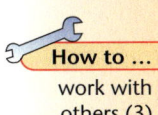

7 In the future

a) What do you think the earth will look like in 800 years? Work in small groups and talk quietly about your ideas for a few minutes. One of you takes notes.

b) Choose a member of your group to present your results to the class.

How to ...
work with
others (3)

8 Wall-E

a) Read this summary of the film 'Wall-E'. Compare your ideas from number 7 to the story of the film. How different from the film were YOUR ideas?

How to ...
read

The animated film 'Wall-E' is set in the year 2815. The humans left earth a long time ago because their environment was so polluted that it was impossible to live there any longer. They went to live on a large spaceship called Axiom.

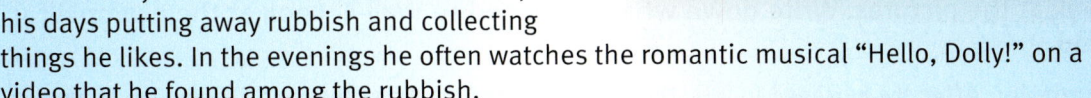

Wall-E is the last of a large army of robots whose job it was to clean up the earth. They were left behind by the humans when they left the planet. All the other robots have broken down and now Wall-E's only friend is a cockroach. Wall-E spends his days putting away rubbish and collecting things he likes. In the evenings he often watches the romantic musical "Hello, Dolly!" on a video that he found among the rubbish.

MORE
M4-M8
recycling

Wall-E's life is not very interesting until one day another robot – EVE – turns up. She is sent by the humans to check out if it is possible for them to return to earth.

Before EVE's arrival Wall-E found a green plant. When EVE sees this plant, she wants to take it back to the Axiom as proof of new life on earth. Wall-E – who has fallen in love with EVE – follows her to the spaceship.

After living on the Axiom for hundreds of years, the humans have become fat and lazy. They don't work and don't even walk anymore. They only sit in moving chairs and watch TV, while all the jobs are being done by robots. But when EVE shows the plant to the captain of the Axiom, he gets active.

Although Auto, the Axiom's autopilot, is programmed to try to keep the humans from returning to earth, Wall-E, EVE and the captain manage to bring the Axiom back to earth after an exciting fight with the autopilot.

The humans from the Axiom are very happy to be back on earth. They have learned that it is important to care for the environment so they start to clean up and plant flowers and trees immediately.

b) Work with a partner and ask and answer questions. Take turns. Ask your partner ...

1 ... who the main characters in the film are.
3 ... why there are no more humans on earth.
5 ... what makes it possible for the humans to return to earth.

2 ... what Wall-E's job is.
4 ... how the humans spend their days on the Axiom.
6 ... what the humans start doing when they are back on earth.

LiF
18

workbook
8-9

9 Cleaning up the earth 👓 👄

a) **Read the summary on page 97 again. Then put the pictures in the right order.**

workbook
10-12

b) **How is Wall-E feeling in the pictures?**

> I think in picture C Wall-E is happy because he is watching his favourite film.

10 Wall-E's story 👄 ✏️

LiF
8

Look at the pictures. Write down what happened to Wall-E. Look at the example for help.

Example: After the humans had left, the robots cleaned up. After they had cleaned up, all the other robots ...

humans • leave   robots • clean up   robots • break down   Wall-E • be all alone for a long time

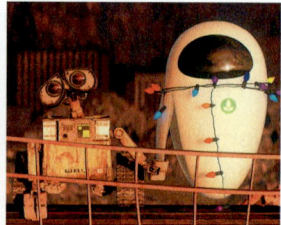

Wall-E • find a living plant   EVE • arrive on earth   Wall-E and EVE • fall in love   Wall-E • follow EVE to the spaceship

11 Seeing it all 👄

How to ...
watch

a) **Watch the film in English. What do/don't you like about it and why?**

b) **How important are sounds for the film? Why?**

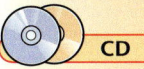 CD

12 Opinions on the film

a) Listen to two friends, Bob and Olivia, who have just watched the film 'Wall-E'. Who liked the film? Who didn't?

b) What did/didn't Bob and Oliva like about the film? Listen again and take notes.

c) Who do you agree with – Bob or Olivia? Give reasons.

13 If only …

What could also have happened?

Example: **If the humans had recycled their waste, it would have been better for the environment.**

If the humans hadn't polluted the earth,	they could (not) have	stayed on earth.
If the other robots hadn't broken down,	they would (not) have	followed her.
If the humans had left the Axiom earlier,	he would (not) have	gone on cleaning.
If Wall-E hadn't fallen in love with EVE,	she would (not) have	died.
If the humans had recycled their waste,	it would (not) have	been better for the environment.
…		…

LiF 13

workbook 13-15

14 Choose an activity

• Write down what YOU think about the film 'Wall-E'. Say what you like/don't like. Give reasons.

How to … write your opinion

• Do you know any other films about saving the environment? Choose one and tell the class about it. Think about:

How to … watch

– the year the film is set in
– the place the film is set in
– what story it tells
– the actors/actresses in the film
– …

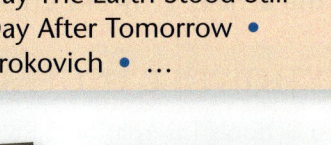
The Day The Earth Stood Still •
The Day After Tomorrow •
Erin Brokovich • …

portfolio

• Make your own Wall-E or EVE. You can use any material you like. What about trying to build one out of rubbish?

workbook test yourself

M1 It's all about global warming

a) Look at the pictures. Then read the explanation from an encyclopedia.

GLOBAL WARMING

The temperature on earth is controlled by the sun. The sun sends sunbeams to our earth. The earth is heated up by these sunbeams. For thousands of years most of the heat went back into the atmosphere, so it didn't become too hot on earth.

But now there are more and more gases like carbon dioxide (CO_2) in the atmosphere. Most of these "greenhouse gases" are produced by cars, factories and homes. The gases stop the heat so that it can't leave the earth's atmosphere anymore.

More and more of the heat is staying in the earth's atmosphere. That is the reason why it is getting warmer and warmer on earth. This is called "global warming" and has bad consequences for everybody.

b) Put the sentences in the correct order.

A The sunbeams make the earth warmer.
B The gases stop the sunbeams.
C Cars, factories and homes produce greenhouse gases.
D The sun sends sunbeams to earth.
E It is getting warmer and warmer on earth.
F The heat can't leave the earth's atmosphere.

workbook
M1-M2

c) What is global warming? Tell somebody who hasn't read the text.

M2 Getting schools active about global warming

How to …
read

a) Read the article. Why did Crickhowell High School become an Eco-School?

CRICKHOWELL HIGH SCHOOL: AN ECO-SCHOOL

Eco-Schools

The Eco-Schools International Programme was developed at the United Nations (UN) Conference on Environment and Development in 1992. Today there are 27,000 Eco-Schools in 43 countries around the world. The aim is to encourage young people and their schools to get active and do useful things to care for and protect the environment.

Crickhowell High School in Wales is one of these Eco-Schools. The pupils and their teachers are proud to take part in the programme. Stories in the media about too much carbon dioxide going into the atmosphere, no water resources, melting ice caps and other environmental problems have motivated them to take action themselves.

The pupils at Crickhowell work on many different topics. One of them is transport. For the summer, walk-to-school-weeks are planned. If pupils live too far away to walk, then they are encouraged to cycle to school. If this is not possible, they are asked to use public transport or share a car.

Good water management is another important topic at this school. Pupils collect rainwater in tanks and use it to water the school gardens. Every week the water usage is checked by some pupils. What's more, Crickhowell has got three water fountains where the pupils can refill their bottles rather than buy new ones.

A third topic is energy. Pupils take weekly readings of the gas and electricity consumption. There are signs around the school about the importance of not wasting energy. Posters created by the pupils tell them, for example, to turn off lights, taps and computers when they aren't needed.

Crickhowell also works on waste minimization. All paper and cardboard used at the school is recycled. Pupils are encouraged to bring their used mobile phones and printer cartridges into school so that they can be recycled to reduce waste.

 **tip**
You can learn more about Eco-Schools at www.eco-schools.org

In order to reduce litter, the school has banned chewing gum. In addition to that, a team of pupils carries out weekly litter picking activities around the school. The litter is sorted into bags of paper and cardboard and another for metals and plastics so that they can be recycled for future use.

By working on these and many other topics, the pupils at Crickhowell have learned a lot about the environment and are proud of what they have done so far. For them it is not as painful as others might think. Their message is clear: Many more Eco-Schools are needed!

b) What is being done at Crickhowell High School to save the environment?

Example: Walk-to-school-weeks are planned. Rainwater is collected ...   ...

 LiF
15

M3 YOUR plan of action

a) Find out what is being done at YOUR school to save the environment. Think about these topics:

> transport • water • energy • waste • ...

b) Then think about what should/could/must still be done at your school. Write down your ideas on a large piece of paper. You can add pictures or drawings.

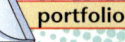 portfolio

c) Present your plan of action to the class. Why not become an Eco-School?

M4 Sorting your rubbish

a) What can you recycle? Give and take: Write down two or three things. Then walk around the classroom and ask several classmates about their ideas.

How to ...
work with others (2)

b) Go through all the ideas, then get together in small groups and talk about them.

c) Where do you put the things on your list? Use the words in the box for help.

paper bank • bottle bank • plastic bottle bank •
can bank • compost bin • non-recyclable waste

Empty cans go to the ...

...

I take bottles to the ...

Old newspapers should be put into ...

M5 Different systems

CD

a) Listen to Nicola and Mareike, her German exchange student. What are they talking about?

How to ...
listen

b) Listen again. How are these materials recycled in London and Hanover? Take notes. Compare them with a partner's.

• cardboard boxes   • batteries   • printer cartridges   • clothes

M6 Message in a bottle

a) Read the comic. Which title do you think fits best?

A The making of plastic   B A bottle's life   C Fizzy drinks

Hey, I'm looking really good. No one would guess that I was made from oil!

Plastic is produced from oil. It can be made into all kinds of things like toys or bottles.

Cool name! And what an interesting colour.

The bottles are sent to different factories. There they are filled with fizzy drinks or ketchup or ...

Whoa! Everything is upside down!

The bottles are taken to shops around the world by ship, plane, train or car. Then they are bought by someone like you!

Ending 1

Hey, don't leave me here! Take me with you!

The bottle is left as rubbish on the beach. Later it is taken out to sea by a wave.

Please, don't eat me. I'm just an old bottle.

The bottle is found by a dolphin who eats it.

I'm sorry. I didn't mean to hurt you.

The plastic makes the dolphin ill. Soon it dies.

Ending 2

The empty bottle is put in a recycling container.

The things from the recycling container are sorted. Then the bottle is sent to a factory where it is cut up into small pieces of plastic.

The pieces of plastic are made even smaller again. Then the plastic is used to make fleece jumpers.

**b) Read the following statements. Then look at the comic again.
Are the statements true or false? Correct the false statements.**

1 Plastic bottles can be made into fleece jumpers.
2 New plastic bottles can be taken to shops by plane only.
3 Dolphins don't have to be protected from eating plastic.
4 If dolphins eat plastic, their health can be damaged.
5 Plastic bottles need to be filled with drinks.
6 Empty bottles shouldn't be left on the beach.

M7 In the end …

a) Which ending of the comic do you think is more likely?
Write a short text and give your opinion.

b) Choose one of the endings of the comic and write the story from the point of view of the bottle. You can start like this:
The people in the factory made me out of oil. I thought I looked pretty good! Then …

M8 Choose an activity

• Choose a product and find out how it can be recycled.
Then draw your own comic about
the product and add speech bubbles.

• What can be done with these old things?
How can they be reused?
Present your ideas to the class.

LiF
16

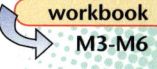
workbook
M3-M6

How to …
write your opinion

How to …
write

tip
You can look at M6 for ideas.

portfolio

103

6 Check it out!

Did you get it all?

- Name five electrical appliances.
- Which organization does Dr Sanjeev Kumar work for?
- Name three things that you can do to save energy.
- What are the three Rs?
- In which year is the film 'Wall-E' set?
- Who or what is EVE?
- What animal is Wall-E's best friend?

Good to know ...

Saving the environment is important all over the world. But people in some countries take the topic more seriously than others. Germany is quite a 'green' country. You should be careful not to be impolite when telling people from other countries to act green.

Did you know that ...

... a plastic yoghurt pot takes 500 years to break down to nothing?

Find out how long a plastic bag takes to break down to nothing.

... 40% of the world population have no electricity?

... about 84% of the things we throw away can be recycled?

... Americans use 2,500,000 plastic bottles every day and most of them are not recycled?

Find out how many plastic bottles are used in your class in one week.

... the amount of energy that is used in rich countries doubles every year?

How much of your rubbish do you put into recycling bins?

... the expression 'global warming' was first used in the 1980s?

... things from other Pixar films can be found in the film 'Wall-E'?

TOOLBOX: HOW TO ... LISTEN

Höre genau hin! – So kannst du mehr verstehen

1 Before you listen – Bevor du eine Höraufgabe bearbeitest

- Sieh dir erst einmal die Bilder oder Überschriften an.
  Überlege: Um was für eine Art Hörtext könnte es sich handeln?
  Zum Beispiel um einen Bericht, eine Geschichte,
  ein (Telefon-)Gespräch, eine Radiosendung oder ein Interview.

- Bevor du den Text hörst, lies die Aufgabenstellung genau.
  Dann weißt du, worauf du beim Hören achten musst.
  Es gibt verschiedene Möglichkeiten, sich Notizen zu Hörtexten zu machen.

sport	keywords
kickboxing	kick
...	...

where? when? ... what? who? **story** why? ... ...

pros	cons
- dance to good music	...

name	eats what?	why?
Lisa	...	...

2 Now listen – Beim Hören

- Beim ersten Hören musst du <u>nicht</u> unbedingt jedes Wort verstehen.
  Versuche herauszufinden, worum es in dem Text eigentlich geht:
    - → Was ist die Situation?
    - → Wer spricht mit wem?
    - → Worüber wird gesprochen?

  Die Hintergrundgeräusche und die Stimmen verraten oft viel, z. B.:
    - → Wo findet das Gespräch statt?
    - → Wie fühlt sich die Sprecherin oder der Sprecher (begeistert, aufgeregt, traurig, ...)?

- Beim zweiten Zuhören machst du dir Notizen – schreibe aber nur Stichworte auf.
  Benutze dabei ein Raster als Hilfe (siehe oben).

3 Did you get it? – Hast du das Wesentliche verstanden?

Vergleiche und vervollständige deine Notizen mit einer Partnerin oder einem Partner,
bevor du sie in der Klasse vorträgst.

Tipp Tipp:

Practice makes perfect! – **Nutze jede Gelegenheit, Englisch zu hören!**
- Mit der Camden Market Schüler-CD kannst du zu Hause dein Hörverstehen trainieren.
- Höre dir englische Musik an und achte auf den Text – was kannst du schon verstehen?

105

TOOLBOX: HOW TO ... WATCH

Filme verstehen

Wenn du dir einen englischsprachigen Film ansiehst, wirst du sicherlich nicht gleich alles verstehen. Die Schauspieler sprechen oft schnell, manchmal undeutlich oder auch mit einem Dialekt. Beim Ansehen der Filme helfen dir die Bilder, die Handlung zu verstehen.

1 **Before you watch – Bevor du dir einen Film ansiehst**

Überlege:
→ Was für eine Art von Film ist es?
→ Worum könnte es in dem Film gehen? Was erwartest du?

> documentary • drama • soap opera • animated film • cartoon • the news
> • sports programme • quiz show • reality show • action film • talk show
> • adventure story • talent show • romance/love story • comedy
> • horror film • science fiction

2 **Look closer – Sieh genau hin**

Bei einem Film spielen Kamera-Einstellungen, Licht und natürlich die Schauspielkunst der Darsteller eine große Rolle. Die Bilder aus einem Film verraten daher viel über die Handlung. Sieh sie dir deshalb genau an:

→ Wer tut was?
→ Was verrät die Kleidung?
→ Welche Gefühle kannst du von den Gesichtern ablesen?
→ Was verrät die Körpersprache?
→ Welche Hinweise gibt dir die Umgebung?
→ Wie würdest du die Stimmung beschreiben?
→ Überlege, worum es in der Szene gehen könnte.

Tipp Tipp: *Practice makes perfect!* – **Trainiere dein Hörsehverstehen!**
• Sieh dir doch mal einen Film, den du schon kennst, auf DVD an. Auf einer DVD kannst du fast immer den englischen Ton (mit oder ohne deutsche Untertitel) einschalten.
  Du kannst aber auch mit englischsprachigen Podcasts üben.
• Wenn du einen Film oder eine Fernsehsendung auf Englisch siehst, helfen dir die Bilder dabei, die Handlung zu verstehen.

3 **Useful phrases – Nützliche Redewendungen**

Wenn du von einem Film erzählen möchtest:

> The film is about ...
> My favourite film is called ...
> The film tells the story of ...
> It describes the life of ...
> The story takes place in ...
> The part of ... is played by ...

So sagst du, was du an einem Film magst oder nicht magst:

> I think Charlie Chaplin did a great job playing
>   the role of ...
> The best scene was when ...
> I really liked the action scenes but I didn't like
>   the music of the film. It was *too* slow.

TOOLBOX: *HOW TO … TALK*

Rollenspiele

Rollenspiele sind eine gute Methode, um dein Englisch zu trainieren.

1 **Before you do the role-play – Vor dem Rollenspiel**

- Denke dich in die Person hinein, die du spielen wirst. Überlege z. B., in was für einer Stimmung die Person ist.
- Mache dir Notizen mit Wörtern und Ausdrücken, die du benutzen möchtest.

2 **Now act out the scene – Spiele die Szene**

- Schlüpfe in die Rolle und benutze Mimik (Gesichtsausdruck) und Gestik (Bewegungen), um deine Rolle überzeugend zu spielen.
  Achte auch bei deinem Partner auf Mimik, Gestik und Tonfall, damit du angemessen reagieren kannst.
- Wenn dir ein Wort nicht einfällt, umschreibe es.
  Du kannst auch deine Hände zu Hilfe nehmen.
- Frage nach, wenn du etwas nicht verstanden hast.
- Versuche, immer deutlich zu sprechen.

Interviews

In einem Interview möchte man vom Interviewpartner etwas erfahren, das man selbst noch nicht weiß. Beachte folgende Punkte, wenn du ein Interview vorbereitest und durchführst:

1 **Prepare questions – Bereite Fragen vor**

- Überlege, was du erfahren möchtest und wie du deinen Interviewpartner ansprichst.
- Formuliere deine Fragen und notiere sie z. B. auf Karteikarten, dann kannst du sie leicht sortieren.
- Vermeide Ja/Nein-Fragen, denn schließlich möchtest du ja möglichst viel von deinem Gesprächspartner erfahren.

2 **Do the interview – Beim Interview**

Stelle dich höflich vor und sage, warum du das Interview machen möchtest:

> Hello, my name is … and I would like to ask you a few questions about …
> I would like to talk to you about … because … My first question is: …

Reagiere auf die Antworten, z. B.:

> That sounds interesting. Could you tell
>   me more about that, please?
> Well, does that mean …?

Bedanke dich für das Interview:

> Thank you very much for talking to me. /
>   Thank you for your time.
> I enjoyed the interview. I hope to see you again.

TOOLBOX: HOW TO … GIVE A TALK

Wenn du etwas vor der Klasse präsentierst

Sicherlich hast du schon häufiger etwas vor der Klasse präsentiert.
Hier findest du noch einmal wichtige Hinweise:

1 Before you talk – Bevor du etwas präsentierst

- Überlege dir eine gute Reihenfolge für das, was du vortragen möchtest.
- Fertige ein Poster oder eine Folie an, um deinen Vortrag anschaulich zu machen. Bilder und Schrift müssen so groß sein, dass jeder im Raum sie sehen und lesen kann. Du kannst aber auch eine PowerPoint Präsentation gestalten.
- Überlege dir kleine Aufgaben für deine Zuhörer, damit sie aufmerksam bleiben. Lass sie z. B. mitgebrachte Speisen oder Instrumente ausprobieren.
- Erstelle außerdem ein Arbeitsblatt für deine Klasse, z. B. einen Lückentext oder ein Quiz. Du kannst sie auch bitten, einen Feedback-Bogen zu deinem Vortrag auszufüllen. So erfährst du, was du demnächst noch besser machen kannst.
- Übe deinen Vortrag vor dem Spiegel, vor Freunden oder deiner Familie – oder nimm deinen Vortrag vorher zur Probe auf einem MP3-Player auf.

2 Now talk – Bei deinem Vortrag

Denke an die drei **T**s:

Touch: Zeige deinen Zuhörern auf einer Folie oder einem Plakat, worüber du gerade sprichst. So wird dein Vortrag für die Klasse interessanter.

Turn: Sieh deine Zuhörer an, wenn du sprichst. Halte immer Blickkontakt.

Talk: Sprich langsam und deutlich. Versuche, frei zu sprechen. Du kannst die wichtigsten Punkte von deinen Notizen oder deinem Poster ablesen.

3 Useful phrases – Nützliche Redewendungen

Diese Sätze kannst du in deinem Kurzvortrag verwenden:

Zu Beginn:

> Good morning. Today I'd like to talk about …
> Hello everybody. My talk is about …

Im Hauptteil:

> The picture shows …
> On my poster you can see …
> It's important …
> Another thing I would like to tell you about is …
> My first/second/next/last point is …

Zum Schluss:

> Finally, I'd like to say …
> Thank you for listening. Have you got any questions?

TOOLBOX: HOW TO … DISCUSS

Wenn du etwas diskutierst

Diskussionen finden täglich über alle möglichen Themen statt. Oft sind solche Diskussionen spontan und ungeplant. Wenn es um ernsthaftere Themen geht, können dir die folgenden Hinweise nützlich sein.

1 **Before you discuss – Bevor du diskutierst**

- Sieh dir das Thema der Diskussion genau an.
  Wie stehst du zu dem Thema? Mache dir Gedanken über mögliche Argumente.
- Stichpunkte und *mindmaps* sind eine gute Hilfe, um nichts Wichtiges zu vergessen.
- Denke auch an Argumente, die gegen deine Meinung sprechen. Überlege dir Antworten auf diese Argumente.

2 **While you discuss – Während du diskutierst**

- Höre genau zu, was die anderen Diskussionsteilnehmer sagen. Stelle sicher, dass du ihre Argumente verstehst.
- Wenn du etwas nicht verstehst, frage höflich nach.
- Äußere deine Meinung. Bleibe dabei immer höflich und freundlich.

> **Tipp Tipp:**
> - Bestimmt einen Diskussionsleiter. Er/Sie sollte darauf achten, dass alle Gesprächsteilnehmer zu Wort kommen können, beim Thema bleiben und die vereinbarte Redezeit einhalten.
> - Bildet eine neutrale Gruppe, die während der Diskussion Notizen macht und nachher Feedback gibt.

3 **Useful phrases – Nützliche Redewendungen**

Wenn du eine Meinung äußern möchtest:

> I think …
> I believe …
> In my opinion, …
> I would say …
> I'm sure …

Wenn du eine Meinung begründen möchtest:

> I think so because …
> Let me give you an example: …
> The reason is …
> Well, it's a fact that …

Wenn du jemandem zustimmen möchtest:

> Yes, that's true.
> I think you're right.
> I agree (with you).
> I think so, too.
> That's a good/important point.

Wenn du jemandem widersprechen möchtest:

> I know, but …
> Sorry, I don't agree with you.
> I don't think so.
> I don't think that's true.

Wenn du nachfragen möchtest:

> Could you say that again, please?
> I don't quite understand what you mean.
> Do you mean that …?
> Can you please explain what you mean?

TOOLBOX: HOW TO … HELP OUT IN ENGLISH

Tipps und Tricks für die Sprachmittlung

Dein Englisch ist jetzt schon so gut, dass du weiterhelfen kannst,
wenn jemand kein Deutsch oder Englisch versteht.
Der englische Begriff *mediation* bedeutet Sprachmittlung.

1 Excuse me, …? – Kannst du helfen?

Du musst nicht Wort für Wort übersetzen.
Es reicht, wenn du den Sinn einer Aussage oder Information wiedergibst.
Das kannst du auch mit deinen eigenen Worten machen.

> … of course I'm sometimes nervous when I sing in front of large crowds. But I really love to sing in Chicago!

> Sie sagt, dass sie manchmal aufgeregt ist vor vielen Leuten, aber sie singt gern in Chicago.

2 Keep it simple – Je einfacher, desto besser

Bei der Sprachmittlung solltest du kurze Sätze benutzen.
Das ist einfacher für dich und für denjenigen, den du informieren willst.

> … und wie ist das so bei euch, wann hast du denn Schulschluss?

> When does school end?

3 In other words – Mit eigenen Worten

Da du in solchen Situationen oft kein Wörterbuch zur Hand hast, kannst du wichtige Wörter auch umschreiben.

> "KiBa"? "Apfelschorle"?! What does that mean?

> Also, KiBa ist ein Gemisch aus Kirsch- und Bananennektar. Und für Apfelschorle mischt man Apfelsaft mit Sprudel.

> "KiBa" is cherry and banana juice. And "Apfelschorle" is apple juice with mineral water.

TOOLBOX: HOW TO … READ

Lesen leicht gemacht!

1 Before you read – Bevor du einen Text liest

Sieh dir zuerst die Bilder und die Überschriften an.

→ Was verrät das Bild?
→ Was erfährst du aus der Überschrift?

Überlege:

→ Um was für einen Text handelt es sich
 (z. B. Zeitungsartikel, Brief, Geschichte, …)?
→ Worum könnte es in dem Text gehen?

2 Now read – Beim Lesen

- Beim ersten Lesen überfliegst du den Text schnell. Du musst nicht jedes Wort
 verstehen. Achte auf die Wörter, die du schon kennst. Sie geben dir Hinweise,
 worum es geht.

- Beim zweiten Lesen kannst du z. B. mit den *wh*-Fragen die wichtigsten
 Informationen herausbekommen:

 Who? What? Where? When? Why?

- Schlüsselwörter (*keywords*) sind
 wichtige Wörter, die dir helfen,
 einen Text zu verstehen.

- Du kannst den Text auch
 Abschnitt für Abschnitt lesen.
 Überlege nach jedem Abschnitt,
 worum es darin geht und finde
 eine passende Überschrift oder
 ein Schlüsselwort.

Who?
What?
Why?
Where?
When?

Steve Irwin was an Australian
television star and wildlife
expert. He became famous after
performing in a documentary
series called The Crocodile
Hunter. This series became very
popular in countries all over the
world.
Irwin wanted to share his excitement about the
natural world, so people would become interested
in animals and especially in protecting endangered
species. He took part in many campaigns to protect
wildlife and even started his own group – Wildlife
Warriors. Together with his wife Terri, he also
owned the Australia Zoo in Queensland. Here he
cared for many animals such as kangaroos,
elephants, snakes, tigers and, of course, crocodiles.
In 2006 Irwin was killed by a stingray while he
was filming at the Great Barrier Reef.

**3 Understanding a text –
Einen Text verstehen**

- Probiere die Tipps aus, wenn du
 einen Text bearbeitest:

Tipp Tipp:

Try to guess the meaning – **Raten erlaubt**
- Manchmal kannst du die Bedeutung von Wörtern, die du nicht kennst, aus dem
 Textzusammenhang erkennen.
- Oft kennst du ein deutsches Wort, das gleich oder ganz ähnlich aussieht, z. B. *series*.
- Überlege, ob du einzelne Bestandteile eines Wortes kennst, z. B. *endangered*.

- Je häufiger du englische Texte liest, desto besser wird dein Leseverstehen. Versuche,
 auch außerhalb der Schule englische Texte zu lesen, die Spaß machen!

TOOLBOX: HOW TO ... WRITE

Schreiben – Schritt für Schritt

1 **Make a draft! – Bevor du anfängst zu schreiben**

Überlege:

Tipp
Auf den Seiten 113-114 erfährst du, wie man auf Englisch einen Brief und eine Meinungsäußerung schreiben kann.

- Welche Art von Text willst du schreiben? Zum Beispiel eine (Fantasie-)Geschichte, einen Sachtext, einen Text über dich, ein Gedicht, einen Brief oder eine E-Mail. Für jede Textsorte sind ganz bestimmte Dinge wichtig, z. B.:

  → Zu einem Brief gehören Datum (*23rd March*), Anrede (*Dear Cheryl*) und Schluss (*Love, Emma*).
  → In eine E-Mail kannst du Emoticons wie :-) :-(;-) einsetzen.
  → Eine Geschichte besteht aus Einleitung, Hauptteil und Schluss. Denke auch an eine Überschrift.

- Sammle Ideen und Wörter zum Thema. Du kannst eine Liste schreiben, deine Ideen in einer *mindmap* sortieren oder dir Notizen zu den *wh*-Fragen machen.

2 **Now write – Beim Schreiben**

Beachte folgende Regeln:

Tipp
Präge dir die Schritte ein:
1. Draft
2. Write
3. Check
4. Publish

→ Beginne nicht alle Sätze mit dem gleichen Wort.
→ Versuche, Wörter wie *really, normally, often, too, ...* zu benutzen.
→ Verbinde Sätze miteinander. Benutze dafür *and, then, because, but, that's why, ...*
→ Finde Adjektive, um Dinge oder Personen zu beschreiben, z. B. *great, fantastic, scary*. Im *G-E dictionary* ab Seite 229 kannst du Wörter nachschlagen. Auch die *wordbanks* ab Seite 116 liefern dir gutes Wortmaterial.

3 **Check it! – So kannst du Fehler aufspüren und verbessern**

- Hast du alles richtig geschrieben? Lies deinen Text noch einmal und schlage Wörter, bei denen du unsicher bist, im *dictionary* nach.

- Tauscht eure Texte untereinander aus und sprecht darüber,
  → was euch an dem Text gefällt,
  → was noch ergänzt werden könnte,
  → was verbessert werden sollte (siehe Punkt 2).

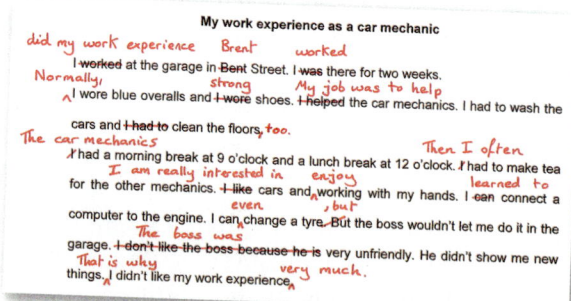

4 **Publish it! – Zeige deinen Text**

Wenn du deinen Text fertig hast, schreibe ihn ins Reine. Du kannst deinen Text präsentieren, indem du ihn z. B. vorliest, aufnimmst, aushängst oder in einem *class book* veröffentlichst. Danach heftest du deinen Text in deiner Portfolio-Mappe ab.

TOOLBOX: HOW TO ... WRITE A LETTER

Einen Brief schreiben

Die Form eines Briefes hängt davon ab, an wen du schreiben willst. Ein Brief an einen Freund/eine Freundin sieht anders aus als ein Brief an eine dir unbekannte Person oder an eine Organisation. Man spricht von persönlichen und formellen Briefen.

1 A personal letter – Ein persönlicher Brief

> **Deine Adresse (ohne deinen Namen) gehört in die rechte obere Ecke.**

Kranzallee 60
14055 Berlin
Germany

2nd March 2009

> **Beginne deinen Brief mit** Dear ...,

> **Fange die erste Zeile mit einem Großbuchstaben an.**

Dear Helen,
Thanks a lot for your letter. It was great to hear about your school trip to France. Did you get a chance to go to Paris?
Yesterday I watched a programme about Australia on TV. I'd really like to go there one day to see Sydney, Uluru (Ayers Rock), the Great Barrier Reef and lots of other places. The animals there are also fascinating. Did you know that there is an animal called wallaby which looks just like a small kangaroo?

Hope to hear from you soon.

Love,
Ella

> **Das Datum folgt unter der Adresse auf der rechten Seite.**

> **So kannst du deinen Brief beenden:**
> Love,
> Yours,
> Best wishes,

> **Am Ende deines Briefes kannst du die andere Person bitten, dir zurückzuschreiben.**

2 A formal letter – Ein formeller Brief

Brentanostraße 2
65187 Wiesbaden
Germany

> **Schreibe den Namen und die Adresse der Organisation oder der Person auf die linke Seite.**

Greenpeace
Canonbury Villas
London N1 2PN
UK

> **Erkläre zu Beginn, warum du den Brief schreibst. Fasse dich dabei kurz.**

23rd April 2009

Dear Sir or Madam,

My class is doing a project on the environment and I would like to have some information about recycling for my project group.
Have you got any leaflets that you could send me? Would it be possible for you to send me the names and addresses of other organizations that could help me?

Thank you very much for your help. I look forward to hearing from you soon.

Yours faithfully,
Oliver Grimm

> **Wenn du den Namen des Empfängers nicht kennst, schreibe** Dear Sir or Madam. **Kennst du den Namen, so beginne mit** Dear Mr/Mrs ...,

> **Sei immer höflich.**

> **Beende den Brief mit** Yours faithfully **(= Mit freundlichen Grüßen/Hochachtungsvoll). Wenn du den Namen des Empfängers jedoch kennst, schreibst du** Yours sincerely **(= Mit freundlichen/herzlichen Grüßen).**

113

TOOLBOX: HOW TO … WRITE YOUR OPINION

Eine kurze Meinungsäußerung schreiben

In einer Meinungsäußerung nimmst du Stellung zu einem bestimmten Thema oder einem Problem, das in einem Text dargestellt ist. Dabei vergleichst du Vor- und Nachteile und begründest deine Meinung.

1 Before you write – Bevor du anfängst zu schreiben

- Notiere die Ideen, die dir zum Thema einfallen. Eine Tabelle mit *pros and cons* oder *examples and reasons* hilft, deine Ideen zu ordnen.
- Mache dir klar, welche Position oder Meinung du vertrittst. Entscheide dich: Bist du dafür? Bist du dagegen? Wenn du dir nicht sicher bist, zähle Beispiele dafür und dagegen auf und wäge sie mit Begründungen gegeneinander ab.

2 Now write – Beim Schreiben

> So kannst du anfangen: Formuliere einen Satz, der das Interesse der Leser weckt und das Thema einleitet.

> Drücke deine Meinung klar aus:
> I think …
> I believe …
> In my opinion, …
> I'm sure …
> Let me give you an example: …

> Wäge deine Argumente gegeneinander ab:
> Some people say … but I think …
> I'm not so sure that …
> On the one hand …,
>   but on the other hand …
> Although …

Today lots of people eat fast food. But the question is: Is fast food good or bad? If you ask me, there are a lot of good and bad things about fast food. Let's start with the good things. Firstly, I think it is good for people who haven't got a lot of time. Secondly, children and teenagers like fast food very much. On the one hand lots of people love fast food because it tastes good, but on the other hand it is not very healthy. It's a fact that fast food has a lot of unhealthy ingredients. So young people should not eat it very often. We all know that you can get fat if you eat too much of it. It is expensive, too.
All in all, I would say that fast food is OK if you don't eat it every day.

> Bringe deine Ideen in eine gute Reihenfolge:
> Firstly, …
> Secondly, …
> Finally, …

> Begründe deine Meinung:
> I think so because …
> The reason is …
> It's a fact that …

> So kannst du enden:
> That's why I think …
> All in all, I would say …

3 Check it! – Überarbeite deinen Text

- Habe ich in der Einleitung verständlich ausgedrückt, worum es geht?
- Zeigt mein Text klar meine Entscheidung pro oder kontra bzw. mein Bemühen, Argumente gegeneinander abzuwägen?
- Habe ich Beispiele mit Begründungen genannt?
- Habe ich einen Schluss formuliert, der meine Meinung klar zum Ausdruck bringt?
- Stimmen Satzbau, Grammatik und Rechtschreibung?

TOOLBOX: *HOW TO … WORK WITH OTHERS*

Verschiedene Arbeitsformen

Ihr kennt bereits einige Methoden, die euch helfen, gut mit anderen zusammenzuarbeiten. Hier werden ein paar weitere Arbeitsformen vorgestellt:

1 Double circle

Ihr bildet in der Klasse zwei einander zugewandte Kreise: einen Innenkreis und einen Außenkreis. Diejenigen von euch, die sich gegenüberstehen oder -sitzen, tauschen sich zu einem vorher bestimmten Thema aus. Danach, z. B. auf ein Signal hin, dreht ihr euch in den beiden Kreisen in entgegengesetzte Richtungen weiter und tauscht euch mit einem neuen Partner/einer neuen Partnerin über das Thema aus. Auf diese Weise erfahrt ihr Ideen und Meinungen von vielen verschiedenen Leuten in der Klasse.

2 Give and take

Jede/r faltet ein leeres Blatt Papier so, dass es aus sechs bis acht gleich großen Feldern besteht. Schreibt zwei bis drei Ideen oder Informationen zu einem Thema in die Felder – eine Idee/Information pro Feld. Anschließend geht ihr im Klassenzimmer umher und befragt eure Mitschüler/innen, um neue Ideen oder Informationen zu sammeln. Pro Mitschüler/in dürft ihr eine neue Idee/Information 'geben' und eine neue Idee/Information 'nehmen', um euer Blatt zu vervollständigen. Seht euch eure Ideen/Infomationen in Ruhe an. Bildet dann kleine Gruppen und besprecht euer Material. Eure Ergebnisse könnt ihr abschließend in der Klasse vorstellen.

3 Buzz groups

Bei dieser Arbeitsform sprecht ihr alle mit leiser Stimme, damit sich die verschiedenen Gruppen nicht gegenseitig stören. *Buzz* heißt summen oder brummen und beschreibt den Geräuschpegel, der dabei im Raum entsteht. In einer *buzz group* diskutieren drei bis fünf Gruppenmitglieder. Ein Gruppenmitglied macht Notizen. Jede Gruppe wählt anschließend einen Sprecher/eine Sprecherin, der/die die Ergebnisse vorträgt.

WORDBANK

A STATISTICS

number   a/one million   a/one thousand   a/one hundred   a/one billion
per cent   total   a/one quarter   a/one third   half
two thirds   population   survey   pie chart   bar chart   ...

What per cent of pupils play football?

tip
You write:
3.3%
You say:
three point three per cent

Nelson School
number of pupils taking part in sports offered (in %)

- 9%
- 4%
- 5%
- 5%
- 27%
- 37%
- 13%

- Rugby
- Cricket
- Football
- Swimming
- Volleyball
- Skiing
- Nothing

It's around 40 per cent.

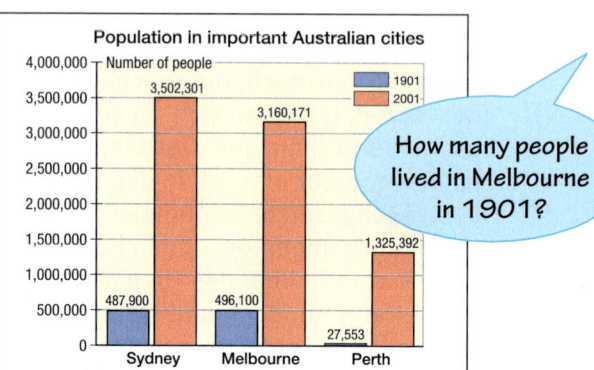

How many people lived in Melbourne in 1901?

About 500,000 people.

Talking about statistics
More than *x* per cent ...
Almost/About one third/ *x* per cent think ...
Most people ...
The statistics clearly show that ...
x people said they ... That's almost one third of the class.
Fewer than *x* per cent/people thought ...
Less than half of the class ...
x per cent of all immigrants are/come from ...

B TRAVELLING

Enjoy your trip!

Have a safe trip!

Getting around

travel by boat   take the train   change trains   go by ship/car
ride a bike   take a tour of a city   ride a motorbike
fly to London   take the underground   walk through the park
buy a ticket for the train   get on/off a bus   take the escalator/lift   ...

Things we do on holiday

visit friends/relatives   stay at a summer camp/youth hostel /hotel   go sightseeing
buy souvenirs   send postcards   go hiking/swimming/...   lie on the beach
speak a foreign language   meet new people   make a reservation   go shopping
visit an exhibition   take pictures of famous sights   enjoy the weather   sit in a coffee shop
have a barbecue   watch people   ask at the tourist information   ...

WORDBANK

Asking for directions
Excuse me, how can I get to …?
Could you tell me the way to …, please?
Could you show it to me on the map, please?

Giving directions
It's the first /second/… street on the right/left.
Turn right/left at the next corner.
Just go across the street, it's on the left/right.
Go straight on.
It's opposite the theatre.

At a youth hostel

Receptionist: Hi. What can I do for you?
Guest: Hello. I'm looking for a room for tonight.
Receptionist: We have private rooms and mixed dorms.
Guest: I'll take a private room, please. How much ist it?
Receptionist: It's 50 AUD. Is that OK?
Guest: Yeah, that's fine. Is breakfast included?
Receptionist: It is. I just need your signature here, please. Your room is on the second floor. Have a good time.
Guest: Thanks a lot. See you later.

Good to know …

In English-speaking countries people are usually very polite, so make sure you say 'excuse me', 'please', 'thank you' and 'sorry' a lot.

117

WORDBANK

C FRIENDS

best friend   boyfriend   classmate   teammate
e-pal   pen-pal   girlfriend   good friend   true friend   …

What friends do

make each other laugh   have time for each other   listen to each other   say sorry
share a secret   talk about problems   give advice to each other   be there for each other
make promises to each other   get along with each other   make new friends
spend time with each other   miss each other   …

Problems

argue with each other	break a promise
be angry at/with each other	talk about someone behind his/her
hurt each other's feelings	back
fight with each other	be intolerant/unfair
pick on each other	offend each other
laugh at each other	…

Good to know …

When meeting an English-speaking friend, be polite, ask questions and don't say that he or she is responsible for things that went wrong.

WORDBANK

D GIVING ADVICE

Why do you think ...?
Why don't you ...?
You could ...
I think it is/was a good idea to ...
I'm not sure about ...
I don't think it is/was such a good idea to ...
If you ask me, I would ...

If I were you, I would ...
You might want to ask him/her if ...
I would ... but maybe you could try to ...
That's a good idea, but maybe you
    could ... instead.
I'm not sure. What about ...?
That's OK. But how about ...?

Girl: I told my mother that I did not want to go on holiday with her
    and she got really angry and I heard her crying.
Boy: She cried? Really? Did you say anything else?
Girl: I told her she was too old to have fun with.
Boy: Ahh.
Girl: But after all it is a fact that she is 45. It is not all my fault.
Boy: Of course, it isn't. Maybe it was the way you told her.
Girl: Yes, right, but what shall I do now? I wonder how she feels.
    I'd love to ask her but I'm afraid to make things worse.
Boy: Why don't you tell her that you are sorry?
Girl: But I'm not sorry about not having to go hiking in Austria.
Boy: Sure. But maybe you could ask her to go somewhere else?
Girl: Hhm ...
Boy: If I were you, I would tell her how I feel.
Girl: What shall I say?
Boy: How about telling her the truth, that you love her but that
    you would like to go camping instead?

Good to know ...

Emily has asked her
German friend Marvin
for advice.

**Many English-speaking people feel that it is rude to tell others what to do and criticize them.
So be careful with phrases like 'You must', 'You have to', 'It is wrong', 'You can't do this', ...**

119

WORDBANK

E SPORTS

You go/do ...
whitewater rafting
skydiving
kitesurfing
bungee jumping
caving
BMX biking
canoeing
dog sledding
rock climbing
skiing
street skateboarding
free climbing
kickboxing
...

Sports can be ...
exciting • fun • great •
dangerous • fantastic •
extreme • interesting •
boring • expensive • crazy
• ...

Would you like to try skydiving?

Yes, I would. I think it's really exciting.

(Street) skateboarding
build a ramp
get a thrill
skate down stairs and rails
hurt yourself
wear a helmet
break bones
go to skateboarding parks
pay a fine
try new tricks
...

Playing sports

take part in a competition   score a goal   watch a game/match   train once/twice a week
hit/catch a ball   beat the other team   have a break   cheer for your team
have the right equipment   become a professional   ...

Equipment

helmet   ball   goal   kite   rope   shoulder/knee/elbow pads
skates   board   basket   (hockey/...) stick   trainers (BE)/sneakers (AE)
boat   paddle   raft   skis   sled   ...

You play/practise ...

on ...	at ...	in ...
a playing field	a club	a park
a sports field	a sports centre	a gym
the street	a fitness centre	the garden
...	...	...

F DESCRIBING PEOPLE

People's character

positive	neutral	negative
charming	curious	angry
friendly	patient	impolite
funny	quiet	mean
nice	serious	nasty
polite	shy	rude
optimistic	...	strange
...		unfriendly
		...

People's looks

beautiful   pretty   ugly   cute
good-looking   interesting
normal   scary   crazy   unusual
wild   boring   modern
natural   elegant   ...

People's clothes and accessories

dress   jacket   skirt   top
sweater   trousers   boots
trainers (BE) / sneakers (AE)
cap   hat   scarf   earring   necklace
glasses   sunglasses   tattoo   piercing   ...

People's bodies

tall   big   small   slim
skinny   thin   fat   ...

People's hair

long   short   dark   blonde
straight   braided   ...

Talking about yourself and other people

I always/usually/... wear ...
I'm proud of my ...
I enjoy wearing ...
I'm a (shy/friendly/...) person.
I prefer ...
I love ...
...

He/She is wearing ...
He/She looks a bit like ...
He/She seems to be ...
He/She might be ...
He/She looks nice/...
He/She might like ...
...

Good to know ...

He looks disgusting, like a monster, really scary. AND he is fat!

No, he's not disgusting. He's just very different and unusual. And of course, he's a big boy. I would not call him fat. He's only a bit on the large side. And he's unique!

People might hear you when you talk about them. So try not to say things that might hurt their feelings. Instead, choose a nice detail because there is always something nice to say.

WORDBANK

 FOOD

have tea   set the table   add some salt and pepper   bake a cake
cut the fruit   order takeaway food   make a salad   put something in the fridge
clean up the table/kitchen   wash the vegetables   use a fork and knife   feed the baby
eat in a cafeteria/canteen   go to a restaurant   lose/put on weight   start a diet   ...

Food can be ...
hot • cold • delicious • sweet •
traditional • disgusting • healthy •
unhealthy • high in fat/sugar •
fat-reduced • hot and spicy • fresh
• old • good • bad • tasty • ...

make	breakfast
have	lunch
cook	a meal
eat	dinner

Healthy eating
Vitamins keep your body healthy.
Carbohydrates give your body energy.
Try to eat less sugary/junk food.
People who are more active burn more calories.
Minerals in food are needed for good health.
Calcium, for example, builds strong bones.
Protein is found in milk, eggs, meat, fish and
   other food.
Try to eat many different kinds of food.
If you are overweight, you should change your
   eating habits.
...

Can I have the menu, please?
I'll have ... , please.
For dessert I'd like ..., please.
Could you bring the bill, please?

Are you ready to order?
What would you like to eat?
Would you like anything to drink?
Anything else?
How's your meal?

H JOBS

How to get a job

do work experience   write a CV   fill in an application form
apply for a job   graduate from grade ...   do your A levels   do military/civilian service
start training as a/an ...   do volunteer work   do vocational training   go to college   ...

... to have

an indoor/outdoor job.
a job where I can travel.
a job where I can earn a lot
    of money.
long holidays.
...

I would like
I wouldn't like

... to work

indoors/outdoors.
shifts.
regular hours.
full-time/part-time.
in my own country.
abroad.
in a(n) office/factory/bank/shop/
    at home/...
with my hands.
with people/children/...
in a team/on my own.
as a car mechanic/...
...

Skills you may need for work

be good with your hands   have experience in/with ...
know how to ...   be good at languages/maths/...
be reliable/punctual/flexible/creative/polite/...
work well with others   ...

Jobs can be ...
dangerous • fun • interesting •
hard • unusual • easy
• boring • exciting • special •
terrible • great • ...

WORDBANK

Jobs	What these people do
pilot	fly planes
car mechanic	repair cars
firefighter	put out fires
shop assistant	help customers, sell things
hair stylist	cut and style people's hair
electrician	repair or install electrical equipment
social worker	help people with their problems
police officer	keep people and the streets safe
check-in agent	check people's tickets at an airport
office administrator	make phone calls, prepare letters
builder	repair and build houses
receptionist	welcome visitors in a hotel or an office, answer questions
security guard	protect buildings and shops
vet's assistant	look after (ill) animals
...	...

1 ENVIRONMENT

Saving the environment

sort rubbish   turn off electrical appliances when they aren't needed
take a shower instead of a bath   use less water   use energy-saving light bulbs
use products that aren't dangerous for the environment   grow plants   recycle rubbish
repair things   reuse things   help to reduce pollution   pick up rubbish
use the bike or walk   reduce waste   save water/energy
raise money for a nature project   protect the forests
go on a sponsored walk   act green   ...

air   earth

animals

water

plants

planet

land   ocean

Let's start today to protect our environment!

Remember: Small things can make a big change!

1 Toonkoo and Ngaardi

Aboriginal Australians believe that the world was shaped[1] and everything on it was created by 'ancestor spirits'. Theses spirits arrived a very long time ago, some from the sky, some from across the water, and some from the ground. This period of time is known as the Dreamtime.

When Darama, the Great Spirit, came down to the earth, he made all the animals and the birds. He gave them all their names. He also made Toonkoo, the first man, and Ngaardi, the first woman.

One day, Toonkoo said to Ngaardi that he'd go out hunting. He went out hunting kangaroos and emus, while Ngaardi stayed home at the foot of the mountain.

While he was hunting a kangaroo, Toonkoo looked up at the sky and saw the Great Spirit watching him. Toonkoo got angry because he did not like being watched and threw his spear[2] up to the sky to hit[3] the Great Spirit. But the Great Spirit caught it, bent it and threw it back. As it came back, it turned into a boomerang. That's how we got our boomerang.

The Great Spirit was angry with Toonkoo for having thrown the spear, so he took Toonkoo away and put him in the moon[4].

In the meantime[5], Ngaardi was waiting and waiting, but Toonkoo never came home. Finally, she went up on the mountain to look for Toonkoo. When she couldn't see him anywhere, she started worrying. Then she started crying and as the tears[6] ran down her face, she made the rivers and creeks[7] come down that mountain.

She waited there all day for Toonkoo to come back with the food, but he never did.

As the moon was coming up, Ngaardi was still crying. When she saw the moon coming up over the horizon[8] and over the sea, she looked up into the full moon and there she saw her man, Toonkoo.

She laid down[9] on the mountain and said to herself that if ever he should come back, she'd leave her heart on the mountain for him to find. Today, her heart is the red flower called the Waratah.

Choose an activity

• **Find out about the flower called Waratah and tell your class about it.**

• **How does a boomerang work? Find out and prepare a two-minute talk.**

• **Australian Aborigines tell Dreamtime stories to their children. What kind of stories were you told when you were little? Tell your favourite story to your partner.**

• **Work with a partner. Imagine you are the 'ancestor spirits' and you have to create a world. What would it look like? You can write or paint or use any other material you can think of.**

---

[1]shape – *formen*; [2]spear – *Speer*; [3]hit – *hier: treffen*; [4]moon – *Mond*; [5]in the meantime – *in der Zwischenzeit*; [6]tear – *Träne*; [7]creek – *Bach*; [8]horizon – *Horizont*; [9]lay down – *sich hinlegen*

2 Fitting in

Read the story and find out who is telling it.

My mother cried a lot the first day I was brought home in a police car. My eyes were black and my lips were big and fat. Paul Murphy and I had been fighting again. I don't remember the reason for the fight. But it did not take much[1] to start the two of us fighting in those days. He would either push me or[2] I would push[3] him in the school corridor. Sometimes even a look[4] was enough. With his funny[5] accent Paul was an outsider[6] like me. He was also fatherless[7] and always angry, too. But he was white.

I was always angry then. I was angry that an Irishman[8] like Paul Murphy could fit in[9] so easily, in our school and in the community. Although I had been born in England, it seemed[10] I was

more of a foreigner[11] than he was. Then there were his blue eyes. For me they represented[12] the blue eyes that followed me every time I went into a shop. I had never stolen anything in my life but the blue English eyes always saw me as an outsider and a potential shoplifter[13]. They told me I did not fit in. They did not see that I was just as British as they were.

I often felt like hitting the blue eyes of the white shopkeepers[14]. I couldn't do that but I could fight with big Paul Murphy and I often did.

One day we were wrestling[15] when I was suddenly pulled away from Paul. A big policeman was holding me and another was holding Paul. "Why are you two boys fighting in my neighbourhood?" the big police sergeant asked. "We were only playing, sergeant," Paul lied in a cheeky[16] voice. "This isn't your neighbourhood and don't call me boy," I said just as cheekily. "Well now, do you think we should take these two hooligans with us, Constable Jones?" the Sergeant asked. "I think we should, Sergeant Branigan. I think they need to be taught a lesson[17]."

Surprisingly, we were not taken to the police station but to a boxing club. "Right, you two," Sergeant Branigan said. "If you want to fight, this is the place to do it." He gave us boxing gloves[18] and put us in the ring. "There will be three rounds of boxing with me as referee," he said. Constable Jones rang the bell[19]. Paul and I had fought lots of time, but this was different. I thought that I would easily beat him. Then, he hit me with a right to the stomach[20] and a left to the chin[21].

Paul and I went back to the boxing club the next day. We became best friends. Later, thanks to our trainer Mick Branigan, we became the best boxers in Brighton. I liked Sergeant Branigan so much that I decided to become a policeman, just like him. "No, you won't, Bobby Senoga," he said to me when I told him and my mother one evening. "You are going to do your A levels, go to university and study architecture like your father."

---

[1]it did not take much – *es brauchte nicht viel*; [2]either … or – *entweder … oder*; [3]push – *hier: anrempeln*; [4]look – *Blick*; [5]funny – *hier: seltsam*; [6]outsider – *Außenseiter*; [7]fatherless – *vaterlos*; [8]Irishman – *Ire*; [9]fit in – *sich einfügen, dazupassen*; [10]seem – *scheinen*; [11]foreigner – *Ausländer*; [12]represent sth – *etw symbolisieren*; [13]shoplifter – *Ladendieb/in*; [14]shopkeeper – *Ladenbesitzer/in*; [15]wrestle – *kämpfen*; [16]cheeky – *frech, dreist*; [17]teach sb a lesson – *jdm eine Lektion erteilen*; [18]boxing glove – *Boxhandschuh*; [19]bell – *Glocke*; [20]stomach – *Magen, Bauch*; [21]chin – *Kinn*

A few years later, Mick and my mother were sitting in the front row[22] as I was accepted into the Royal Institute of British Architects. Sitting beside[23] them was Commonwealth boxing champion Paul Murphy with his gold medal around his neck. I was on top of the world[24]. It seemed I had everything I had ever wanted. I did, except[25] the feeling of totally belonging[26]. Sure, in my office[27] and on the building site[28] I was king of the hill but it was not enough. I still wanted to fit in and have the respect that every British man should have everywhere in his own country.

You see, when I entered a strange shop where the people did not know that I was an 'important' man, I could still feel the eyes watching me.

One day I saw an advert looking for people to join the Special Constabulary[29]. I knew that these were people who helped the police in their free time but I had never thought of joining myself. I joined and completed[30] my training without telling anybody. I continued[31] working as an architect but I was happy at the weekend when I could work as a volunteer[32] policeman.

I could now help street kids the way Sergeant Mick Branigan had helped me. I knew how Paul and I might have turned out[33] if he had not taken us from the streets.

OK, so some people who didn't know me still followed me with their eyes when I was in a strange shop but I no longer cared. I knew I was helping my community, so I was no longer an outsider.

Sergeant Mick Branigan was surprised when I walked into his boxing club in my police uniform. "So Bobby has become a bobby[34]," he said grinning[35]. Then he threw me a pair of boxing gloves.

What made Bobby Senoga an outsider? Talk to a partner.

Choose an activity

- **Choose one of the people from the story and find out as much as you can about him or her. Write a short text.**

- **What happened after Sergeant Branigan had thrown Bobby a pair of boxing gloves? Discuss possible endings with a partner. Then write an ending to the story.**

- **Do you think boxing is the right sport for young people? Collect arguments for and against and present them to the class.**

---

[22]front row – *erste Reihe*; [23]beside – *neben*; [24]on top of the world – *ganz oben auf sein*; [25]except – *außer, bis auf*; [26]belong – *(dazu)gehören*; [27]office – *Büro*; [28]building site – *Baustelle*; [29]Special Constabulary – *ehrenamtlicher Polizeidienst*; [30]complete sth – *etw absolvieren*; [31]continue doing sth – *weiter(hin) etw tun*; [32]volunteer – *freiwillig, ehrenamtlich*; [33]turn out – *sich entwickeln*; [34]bobby – *Polizist*; [35]grin – *grinsen*

HOW ADVENTUROUS ARE YOU?

OK, so you think you are quite an adventurous person. The one who is always first when it comes to exciting adventures and hobbies. Are you really what you think you are?
Do our quiz – and find out!

Your best friend suggests[1] a nice weekend, doing something unusual. You have a few ideas:

A A bungee jump from a helicopter. (3)

B Skateboarding down one or two hills near your town. (2)

C Cleaning your collection of model cars. (1)

Your boyfriend/girlfriend has just had his/her tongue[2] pierced. Do you …

A … tell him/her how difficult it will be to eat sauerkraut? (2)

B … plan to get yourself a piercing immediately? (3)

C … never speak to him/her again? (1)

Friends have been away on holiday and have cooked something special. It looks – er, interesting. Do you …

A … eat it because you like trying out different dishes? (3)

B … say you'd love to try it but that you've just eaten? (2)

C … say that you have to leave immediately? (1)

---

[1]suggest – *vorschlagen*; [2]tongue – *Zunge*;
[3]car seat – *Autositz*; [4]roadside – *Straßenrand*;
[5]self-confidence – *Selbstvertrauen*;
[6]take a risk – *ein Risiko eingehen*;
[7]now and again – *von Zeit zu Zeit*;
[8]double-check – *doppelt überprüfen*

You are on a lonely road in the north of Canada. Your car broke down and you can't repair it. What do you do?

A Make as much noise as possible to keep the bears away. (2)

B Take out the car seat[3] and relax on the roadside[4]. (3)

C Put up the warning sign and wait for a car. (1)

You want to visit a friend but your train is late and you arrive much too late to get a bus or a taxi. What do you do?

A You phone home (it's 200km away) and ask for advice. (1)

B You start to walk to your friend's house. (3)

C You go to the waiting room and wait for the morning. (2)

5 – 8 points
Well, we think you should get more self-confidence[5]. Try taking some risks[6] now and again[7].

9 – 12 points
You seem to enjoy taking risks sometimes but you always double-check[8] first.

13 – 15 points
You are a real risk-taker. Have you thought about the dangers? Take time to think first.

4 Anastasia at your service[1]

In this book, Lois Lowry writes about 12-year-old Anastasia who lives in Boston with her family.

Find out why Anastasia likes eating with her family so much.

Anastasia loved suppertime[2]. Especially when they had lasagna as they did tonight. Her mother was the best lasagna-maker in the whole world. If ever there were a National Lasagna Bake-Off Contest, her mother would win, she was quite sure.

She had told her mother that once. But her mother had made a horrible[3] face. Probably her mother didn't want to win a National Lasagna Bake-Off Contest. Anastasia could understand that. Probably the prize would be something for the kitchen.

Even when they didn't have lasagna, Anastasia loved suppertime, because the whole family, all four of them, were there, and they talked a lot. Often they talked about their problems, and it was great, Anastasia thought, how problems seemed smaller if you talked about them while you ate lasagna. Or even pot roast[4], or tuna-fish[5] casserole[6].

When she was older and her spelling had improved[7] a bit, Anastasia planned to write an article for the Journal[8] of the American Psychiatric Association. In it she was going to tell all the psychiatrists[9] in America that if they served[10] dinner to their patients, preferably[11] lasagna (although pot roast or tuna-fish casserole would be okay), their patients' problems would be solved[12] much faster.

"Oh, doctor," Anastasia imagined a psychiatric patient saying, "I see red leopards sitting behind the furniture. I will kill myself if they don't go away."

"Hmmmm," the doctor would say. "Would you like some cheese on your lasagna? Tell me more about the red leopards."

"Leopards? Were we talking about leopards? Funny, I don't remember anything about red leopards. But I would like more salad. And would you give me the rolls, please?"

What is nice about eating with a family?

Choose an activity

- **Write down YOUR favourite menu for a family dinner.**

- **Find out more about Lois Lowry, the author of the book. Present your findings to the class.**

- **Can you think of a problem that can be solved at the dinner table? Work with a partner or in a group. Make up a scene and act it out.**

---

[1]at your service – *zu Diensten*; [2]suppertime – *Abendessenszeit*; [3]horrible – *schrecklich*; [4]pot roast – *Schmorbraten*; [5]tuna-fish – *Thunfisch*; [6]casserole – *Eintopf*; [7]improve – *besser werden*; [8]journal – *Zeitschrift*; [9]psychiatrist – *Psychiater/in*; [10]serve – *hier: servieren*; [11]preferably – *am besten*; [12]solve – *lösen*;

5 Teen millionaire

Read about Ashley Qualls and how she became a teen millionaire.

Ashley Qualls doesn't sound like a typical high school student. Maybe that's because the 17-year-old is the CEO[1] (Chief Executive Officer) of a million-dollar business. Ashley is the boss of *whateverlife.com*, a website she started when she was just 14 – with eight dollars borrowed from her mother. Now, just three years later, the website makes more than $1 million a year, giving Ashley and her working class[2] family a sense of security[3] they had never really known. It all began when Ashley became interested in graphic design just when online networking[4] really started.

When she saw her friends personalizing[5] their MySpace pages, she began creating and giving away MySpace background[6] designs through *whateverlife.com*. The designs are cheery[7] and colorful, with lots of hearts, Ashley's favorites. She also took lyrics from popular songs and built backgrounds around those themes. "Teenage girls love quotes[8]," Ashley says, scrolling through some of her site's 3,000 designs, more than a third of which she made herself.

Whateverlife.com began pulling in[9] more teenage girls than a Justin Timberlake concert – about a million a day. With a big audience[10], the site attracted[11] advertisers[12]. Ashley's first check was for $2,700. The next was for $5,000, the third for $10,000. Ashley's parents are divorced. She, her mother and her little sister were all living in her mother's one-bedroom apartment then.

When the first check arrived, her mother was doubtful[13], wondering if her daughter could really make money off a website. But Ashley was confident[14], telling her mother: "No, I really trust[15] this. I think it's really gonna happen." Ashley was right. The checks kept coming and the business kept growing to the point where she could afford to buy a new four-bedroom house for them to live in. Ashley also hired[16] her mother to help her with the company.

In addition to her mother, Ashley hired three friends to help with the business, teaching them design and then requiring[17] them to make at least 25 designs a week. Her mother is proud of Ashley. Before she started the business, she says, her daughter was too shy to even order a pizza by phone. Now she's making presentations to business executives[18].

Choose an activity

• What was Ashley's life like before she started *whateverlife.com*? What is her life like now? Write two diary entries: one from before she got rich and one from now.

• Have you got a clever idea how to make a lot of money? What would you need to start your own business? Present your idea to the class. How many of your classmates think your business is a good idea?

• Write an acrostic about being poor or about being rich.

---

[1]CEO – *Geschäftsführer/in*; [2]working class – *Arbeiterklasse*; [3]sense of security – *Gefühl der Sicherheit*; [4]online networking – when you use the Internet to meet new people and to let your friends know what you're doing; [5]personalize – *persönlich(er) gestalten*; [6]background – *Hintergrund*; [7]cheery – fröhlich, lustig; [8]quote – *Zitat*; [9]pull in sb – *jdn anziehen*; [10]audience – *Publikum*; [11]attract sb – *jdn anziehen*; [12]advertiser – *Werbekunde*; [13]doubtful – *zweifelnd, skeptisch*; [14]confident – *zuversichtlich*; [15]trust – *vertrauen*; [16]hire sb – *jdn einstellen*; [17]require sb to do sth – *von jdm verlangen, etw zu tun*; [18]business executive – *leitende/r Angestellte/r*

6 Tree sitting

Some people don't just go green – they also go to extremes. One of the most spectacular ways to try to save the environment is 'tree sitting'. Read Chad's story about his experience as a tree sitter.

My name is Chad Rosenberg. I'm 26 and I have been an environmentalist for as long as I can think. I was a member of my school environmental group, I helped to raise money for different projects and I tried to get everyone around me to act green.

I was born on Prince Edward Island in Canada but we moved to Humboldt County in California when I was about nine. In California there are wonderful giant redwood trees that can be up to 95m high. Some of them are over 2,500 years old.

Because these trees are so big, many lumber companies[1] cut them down to sell the wood. Near my hometown, Pacific Lumber wanted to fell[2] some of the redwoods. I think it's a crime to kill trees that have been around this area much longer than we have. That's why I joined a tree sitting group. I wanted to help saving some of the trees.

Tree sitters are people who live on platforms high up in trees so that the trees can't be cut down. Sometimes there are several tree sitters in one area. They build connections[3] between the trees so they can visit each other.

Tree sitting can be absolutely wonderful. If the weather is good, you have an amazing view. It's really quiet and peaceful up there and you have loads of time to read and think. But it can also be really hard. On my first days up there I was always afraid to fall down and when it's rainy and stormy you are cold and miserable all the time.

But it was all worth it – after half a year the lumber company said they wouldn't cut down the tree. That was one of the happiest moments of my life!

Some people say that tree sitters are idiots and that it's not a good idea to hinder lumber companies from making money. It's right that lumber companies are sometimes important for an area. They give jobs to people and wood is needed for all sorts of things. But I think our environment is at least as important as people's jobs. If we go on treating the world around us like dirt[4], it's first the trees that go and then us.

Choose an activity

- **Would YOU go to extremes to save the environment? What would or wouldn't you do? Talk to a partner about it.**

- **Imagine you are Chad, sitting in a giant redwood. Write a diary entry.**

- **Members of an environmental group want to make a leaflet to support tree sitters. Design the leaflet.**

---

[1]lumber company *(AE) – Holzfirma*; [2]fell *– fällen*; [3]connection *– Verbindung*; [4]treat sb/sth like dirt *– jdn/etw wie Dreck behandeln*

LANGUAGE IN FOCUS

Im Grammatik-Teil *Language in Focus* (**LiF**) wird die englische Sprache ganz genau unter die Lupe genommen.

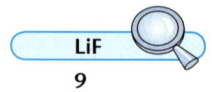

LiF
9

Immer, wenn du dieses Symbol vorn in deinem Buch siehst, kannst du hier nachsehen, welche Grammatikregeln es in der englischen Sprache gibt.

Um dir die Regeln besser einzuprägen, kannst du sie in deinen eigenen Worten und mit einigen Beispielsätzen oder Bildern notieren.

Im LiF-Teil findest du Erklärungen zu folgender Grammatik:

1	Die einfache Gegenwart	*Simple present*
2	Die Verlaufsform der Gegenwart	*Present progressive*
3	Die vollendete Gegenwart	*Present perfect*
4	Die Verlaufsform der vollendeten Gegenwart	*Present perfect progressive*
5	Die vollendete Gegenwart mit ‚since' und ‚for'	*Present perfect with since and for*
6	Die einfache Vergangenheit	*Simple past*
7	Die Verlaufsform der Vergangenheit	*Past progressive*
8	Die Vorvergangenheit	*Past perfect*
9	Die Zukunft mit ‚will'	*Will future*
10	Die Zukunft mit ‚going to'	*Going to future*
11	Bedingungssätze (Typ I)	*Conditional clauses (type I)*
12	Bedingungssätze (Typ II)	*Conditional clauses (type II)*
13	Bedingungssätze (Typ III)	*Conditional clauses (type III)*
14	Modalverben und ihre Ersatzformen	*Modal verbs and their substitute forms*
15	Das Passiv	*The passive*
16	Modalverben mit Passivformen	*Modal verbs with passive forms*
17	Indirekte Rede	*Reported speech*
18	Wortstellung und Fragebildung	*Word order and questions*
19	Die -ing-Form	*Gerund*
20	Verb + Objekt mit Infinitiv	*Verb + object + infinitive with to*
21	Substantive mit und ohne Artikel	*Nouns with and without article*
22	Adjektive als Substantive	*Adjectives as nouns*
23	Mengenangaben mit ‚much' und ‚many'	*Quantifiers: much and many*
24	Relativsätze	*Relative clauses*
25	Relativsätze ohne Pronomen	*Contact clauses*
26	Partizipien zur Verkürzung von Relativsätzen	*Participles used to shorten relative clauses*
27	Konjunktionen	*Conjunctions*

LANGUAGE IN FOCUS

1 Die einfache Gegenwart (Simple present)

- Das **simple present** benutzt du, wenn du über Gewohnheiten, Tatsachen und regelmäßig vorkommende Ereignisse sprichst.
  Signalwörter: **always, often, sometimes, never, usually, every day/week/..., on Mondays/...**

 Andy usually **rides** his BMX bike to school.

- Die Verneinung bildest du mit **don't**, bei *he, she, it* mit **doesn't**:
  I **don't** eat tomatoes.   He **doesn't** like fish.   Birds **don't** like cats.

- Ja/Nein-Fragen:

Frage	bejahende Antwort	verneinende Antwort
Do you **cook** your own meals?	Yes, I **do**.	No, I **don't**.
Is Mike good at basketball?	Yes, he **is**.	No, he **isn't**.

- Das **simple present** benutzt du auch, wenn du über einen festgelegten Zeitplan (zum Beispiel Fahrpläne von Zügen oder Bussen) sprichst, der in der Zukunft liegt.

  The plane **leaves** at 9pm.   The course **starts** next Monday.

2 Die Verlaufsform der Gegenwart (Present progressive)

- Das **present progressive** beschreibt Ereignisse und Handlungen, die gerade stattfinden.
  Signalwörter: **now, at the moment**

- Das **present progressive** bildest du so:

  Form von **be** (*am/is/are*) + Verb + **ing**

  We **are eating** at the moment.

They **are enjoying** their meal.

- Die Verneinung bildest du mit **not**:
  The sun **isn't shining**.   They **aren't skateboarding**.

- Ja/Nein-Fragen:

Frage	bejahende Antwort	verneinende Antwort
Is Jamie **cooking** dinner?	Yes, he **is**.	No, he **isn't**.

- Fragen mit Fragewort:
  What is Harry **doing** at the moment?   **Why are** you **leaving**?
  Where are you **going**?   **When is** Leyla **coming** home?

- Das **present progressive** benutzt du auch, wenn du über mit anderen vereinbarte Pläne oder Verabredungen sprichst, die in der Zukunft liegen.

  I'm meeting Brian at nine o'clock.   What **are** you **doing** on Saturday?

3 Die vollendete Gegenwart (Present perfect)

- Du benutzt das **present perfect**, um über Handlungen oder Ereignisse zu sprechen, die schon beendet sind, aber noch in die Gegenwart hineinwirken. Auch für Vorgänge, die in der Vergangenheit begonnen haben und bis in die Gegenwart andauern, verwendest du das **present perfect**.
  Signalwörter: ever, never, yet, already, just

- Das **present perfect** bildest du so: Form von **have** (*have/has*) + **Partizip** (*past participle*)

  My friend Brian **has done** kickboxing for some time (and is still doing it).
  Bob **has been** a police officer for many years (and is still working in that job).

- Regelmäßige Verben bilden das Partizip mit **-ed**.
  walk ➔ walk**ed**   play ➔ play**ed**

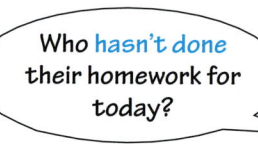

- Unregelmäßige Verben haben auch ein unregelmäßiges Partizip.

infinitive	simple past	past participle
go	went	**gone**

Who **hasn't done** their homework for today?

tip
You can find the irregular verbs on pages 253–254.

- Bei der Verneinung steht **not** hinter **have/has:**

  Ben **hasn't tried** free climbing before.
  We **haven't had** lunch yet.

- Ja/Nein-Fragen:

Frage	**bejahende Antwort**	**verneinende Antwort**
Have you ever **eaten** so much before?	Yes, I **have**.	No, I **haven't**.
Has Emily **spoken** to Leyla yet?	Yes, she **has**.	No, she **hasn't**.

- Fragen mit Fragewort:
  Where have you **been** the whole day?   **Why haven't** you **tidied** up your room yet?

4 Die Verlaufsform der vollendeten Gegenwart (Present perfect progressive)

- Du benutzt das **present perfect progressive**, um über Handlungen oder Ereignisse zu sprechen, die in der Vergangenheit begonnen haben und bis in die Gegenwart andauern. Dabei ist die Handlung oder das Ereignis selbst wichtiger als der Zeitpunkt, zu dem sie stattgefunden haben.

- Das **present perfect progressive** bildest du so:

Form von **have** (*have/has*) + been + **-ing** Form des jeweiligen Verbs

She **has been crying** for hours now.

  Jacob **has been ironing** his shirt for thirty minutes now (and is still ironing it).
  They **have been learning** English for three years (and are still learning it).

5 Die vollendete Gegenwart mit ‚since' und ‚for' (Present perfect with since and for)

> I've known my sister **since** 1993.

> I've known my sister **for** 16 years.

- **Since** und **for** werden häufig mit dem **present perfect** benutzt. Sprichst du von einem genauen Zeit<u>punkt</u>, an dem eine Handlung oder ein Ereignis begonnen hat, benutzt du **since**, z.B. **since** 1986, **since** April, **since** Monday, **since** then.

  Jason Lewis has had problems with his legs **since** his accident in Colorado.

- Wenn du hingegen einen Zeit<u>raum</u> (Monate, Jahre, Tage usw.) angibst, benutzt du das **present perfect** mit **for**, z.B. **for** six months, **for** a long time.

  Jason has made music **for** more than 25 years.

6 Die einfache Vergangenheit (Simple past)

- Für Ereignisse und Handlungen, die in der Vergangenheit liegen und abgeschlossen sind, verwendest du das **simple past**.
  Signalwörter: **yesterday, last week, two days/years/... ago**

  Mike **went** to Australia last winter.   Yesterday we **had** steak for lunch.

- Das **simple past** von regelmäßigen Verben bildest du, indem du **-ed** an den Infinitiv anhängst. Bei unregelmäßigen Verben ist das **simple past** die zweite Form in der Liste auf den Seiten 253 und 254.

- regelmäßige Verben   unregelmäßige Verben
  visit → visit**ed**   go → **went**
  look → look**ed**   leave → **left**

- Die Verneinung bildest du bei den meisten Verben mit **didn't**, bei **was/were** mit **not**:

  Ella **didn't eat anymore.**
  Jill and Judy **weren't** very happy to see us last Tuesday.

Yesterday the children **stayed** at home because the weather **was** bad.

- Ja/Nein-Fragen:

Frage	bejahende Antwort	verneinende Antwort
Did you **go** to the cinema last night?	Yes, I **did.**	No, I **didn't.**
Was it a good film?	Yes, it **was.**	No, it **wasn't.**

- Fragen mit Fragewort:
  Where did you **go** yesterday?   **Why didn't** you **ask** me to come to the party?

LANGUAGE IN FOCUS

LiF

7 **Die Verlaufsform der Vergangenheit (Past progressive)**

- Das **past progressive** drückt aus, dass eine Handlung in der Vergangenheit über einen längeren Zeitraum im Gang war. Setzt eine zweite Handlung plötzlich ein, steht diese im *simple past*.
  Signalwörter: while, when

- Das **past progressive** bildest du so:

  was/were + -ing-Form des Verbs

  When I **was walking** to school yesterday, I saw a car accident.

- Das **past progressive** benutzt du auch für gleichzeitig ablaufende Handlungen.

  The crowd **was cheering** loudly while the teams **were playing** the match.

While the woman **was taking** a picture, a man stole her bag.

- Ja/Nein-Fragen:

Frage	bejahende Antwort	verneinende Antwort
Were you **watching** the match?	Yes, I **was**.	No, I **wasn't**.

- Fragen mit Fragewort: **What were** you **doing** yesterday at four o'clock?

8 **Die Vorvergangenheit (Past perfect)**

- Wenn eine Handlung vor einer anderen Handlung in der Vergangenheit stattgefunden hat, drückst du das mit dem **past perfect** aus. Die zweite Handlung steht im *simple past*. Beide Handlungen sind abgeschlossen.

- Das **past perfect** bildest du so:

  had + Partizip *(past participle)*

  After Jamie Oliver **had started** a campaign, British schools banned junk food.

After Marylin **had hit** herself, her finger hurt for a month.

1. Handlung	2. Handlung
Because Diego **had broken** his elbow,	he was in a cast for seven weeks.
After the humans **had left** the earth,	the robots started to clean up.

9 Die Zukunft mit ‚will' (Will future)

- Wenn du über die Zukunft sprechen willst, benutzt du das **will future**. Mit dieser Zeitform kannst du auch Vermutungen ausdrücken und Vorhersagen oder Versprechen machen.
  Signalwörter: tomorrow, next week/month, in two years, probably, maybe, perhaps. Auch folgende Verben können Signalwörter sein: **think, hope, promise.**

  > On Wednesday there will be some dark clouds but there won't be any rain.

- Das **will future** bildest du so: **will + Infinitiv** des Verbs

  Michael thinks he **will** be rich one day.
  The friends **will** meet after school today.

- Verneinung: Du benutzt **will not** oder die Kurzform **won't**, um Sätze zu verneinen.

  I promise I **will not** be late.
  I hope I **won't** make any mistakes in the test.

- Ja/Nein-Fragen:

Frage	bejahende Antwort	verneinende Antwort
Will you be here tomorrow?	Yes, I **will**.	No, I **won't**.

- Fragen mit Fragewort:
  When **will** Sally be back?

10 Die Zukunft mit ‚going to' (Going to future)

- Du verwendest **going to**, wenn du sagen willst, was jemand für die Zukunft plant oder vorhat.

- Die Zukunft mit **going to** bildest du so: Form von **be** (*am/is/are*) + **going to** + Infinitiv

  I'm really tired. I'm **going to** go to bed soon.

- Bei einer Verneinung von **going to** steht **not** immer hinter (*am/is/are*).

  Aiman is very hungry. He is **going to** buy a hamburger.

  They **aren't going to** fly to San Francisco.

- Ja/Nein-Fragen:

Frage	bejahende Antwort	verneinende Antwort
Are you **going to** call your mother tonight?	Yes, I **am**.	No, I'm **not**.

- Fragen mit Fragewort:
  Where are you **going to go** on holiday?

- **Will future** oder **going to future**?

  > **will future:** Vermutungen, Versprechen, Vorhersagen, spontane Entschlüsse
  > **going to future:** Pläne, Vorhaben, feste Absichten

11 Bedingungssätze, Typ I (Conditional clauses, type I)

- Du benutzt den Bedingungssatz Typ I, um eine <u>realistische</u> Bedingung (etwas, das eintreten kann, soll oder wird) zu beschreiben. Der Hauptsatz drückt aus, was passiert, wenn die Bedingung erfüllt ist.

- Im *if*-Satz steht das **simple present**, im Hauptsatz das **will future**.

if-clause (Bedingung)	Hauptsatz (Folge)
If the weather **is** nice,	we**'ll go** on a bike ride.
If you **miss** the bus,	you **won't be** on time for school.

- Statt des **will future** kann auch **can/can't** im Hauptsatz stehen.

  If you **do** your homework now, you **can** watch TV later.

- Bedingungssätze können entweder mit dem *if*-Satz oder mit dem Hauptsatz beginnen. Wenn sie mit dem *if*-Satz beginnen, werden beide Teilsätze mit einem Komma voneinander getrennt. Steht der Hauptsatz vorne, wird kein Komma gesetzt.

  If it rains, I**'ll** stay in bed all day.
  I**'ll** stay in bed all day **if** it rains.

12 Bedingungssätze, Typ II (Conditional clauses, type II)

- Mit dem Bedingungssatz Typ II drückst du aus, was unter einer nur <u>gedachten</u> Bedingung passieren würde oder könnte. Dabei geht es um Ereignisse, die <u>unwahrscheinlich</u> oder <u>unmöglich</u> sind.

- Bei dieser Art von Bedingungssätzen steht der *if*-Satz im **simple past**. Im Hauptsatz steht **would** oder **could** vor dem Infinitiv.

  If I **had** a lot of money, I **would visit** New York.

- **Aufgepasst!** Bei *if*-Sätzen heißt es normalerweise „**I were**", aber du kannst auch „**I was**" sagen. Beide Formen sind hier richtig.

  If I **were** rich, I **could** buy a fast car.
  If I **was** a millionaire, I **would** buy lots of cars.

13 Bedingungssätze, Typ III (Conditional clauses, type III)

- Mit dem Bedingungssatz Typ III drückst du aus, was in der Vergangenheit <u>hätte</u> passieren <u>können</u>, aber nicht passiert ist.

- Bei dieser Art von Bedingungssätzen steht der *if*-Satz im **past perfect**. Im Hauptsatz steht **would** oder **could + have + Partizip** (*past participle*).

  If I **had won** the race, I **would have got** a prize.
  If she **had called** him, he **could have helped** her.

If I **hadn't missed** the last basket, we **would have won** the game.

14 Modalverben und ihre Ersatzformen (Modal verbs and their substitute forms)

- Die Modalverben geben an, ob etwas erlaubt oder notwendig ist. Die meisten Modalverben haben nur eine Form für die *present tenses*. Im *present perfect, simple past* und im *will future* musst du deshalb Ersatzformen (**substitute forms**) verwenden.

simple present	substitute	simple past	present perfect	future
can	be able to	was able to; could	have been able to	will be able to
can't	not be able to	was not able to; couldn't	haven't been able to	won't be able to
must	have to	had to	have had to	will have to
mustn't	not be allowed to	wasn't allowed to	haven't been allowed to	won't be allowed to
needn't	don't have to	didn't have to	–	won't have to

a) Fähigkeit: can/can't – be able to/not be able to

- Mit **can** und **be able to** kannst du sagen, was jemand kann. Im *simple past* kannst du auch **could** benutzen.

  Emily **wasn't able to** talk to Leyla alone.
  Sharon **could** already read when she was four.

- **Could** benutzt du auch für höfliche Bitten und Aufforderungen:

  Could someone open the window, please?

You **won't be able to** ride that bike anymore.

LANGUAGE IN FOCUS

LiF

b) Erlaubnis: can/can't – must not – be allowed to/not be allowed to

- **Can/can't, must not** und **be allowed to/not be allowed to**
  benutzt du, wenn du
  – um etwas bittest,
  – um Erlaubnis fragst oder
  – jemandem etwas erlaubst oder verbietest.

You **can** swim in the pool but you **are not allowed** to swim in the lake.
In the UK motorists **mustn't** drive on the right.

- **Aufgepasst!** M**ust not** oder die Kurzform **mustn't** klingt
  wie im Deutschen „muss nicht", heißt aber „etwas nicht dürfen"!

c) Notwendigkeit: must/have to – needn't/don't have to

- **Must** klingt wie das deutsche Wort „müssen" und heißt auch *müssen*.
  In der Regel kannst du **must** auch durch **have to/has to** ersetzen.

  Claire **must** tidy up her room.   oder   Claire **has to** tidy up her room.

- Wenn du sagen willst, was jemand nicht tun muss,
  benutzt du **don't/ doesn't have to**.

  You **don't have to** finish your meal.

- **Must** hat keine eigene Vergangenheitsform. Daher wird die
  simple past-Form von **have to** (= *had to*) benutzt.

  Before there were lights, people **had to** use candles.

- Wenn du sagen willst, dass jemand etwas nicht zu tun braucht,
  benutzt du **need not** oder die Kurzform **needn't**. **Needn't** hat die
  gleiche Bedeutung wie **don't have to**, ist aber etwas förmlicher.

  You **needn't** do your homework now.

d) Empfehlung: should/shouldn't

- Mit **should** drückst du aus, dass etwas
  deiner Ansicht nach passieren sollte:

  You **should** leave now if you want to catch the bus.

- Mit **should** kannst du auch die Meinung
  einer anderen Person erfragen.

LANGUAGE IN FOCUS

15 Das Passiv (The passive)

- Wenn mit einer Person, einem Tier oder einer Sache etwas getan wird, kannst du das durch das **Passiv** ausdrücken. Man benutzt es dann, wenn nicht wichtig oder nicht klar ist, *wer* handelt oder gehandelt hat.

  People also call elephants grey giants. → Elephants **are** also **called** grey giants.

- Das Passiv in der Gegenwart bildest du so: Form von **be** (*am/is/are*) + **past participle**

  Today letters **are written** on the computer.

  I often read those diaries on the Internet. They **are called** 'blogs'.

- Das Passiv in der Vergangenheit bildest du so: Form von **be** (*was/were*) + **past participle**

  My computer **was made** in China.   Didgeridoos **were invented** in Australia.

- Wenn du trotzdem in einem Passiv-Satz die handelnde Person oder die Ursache für etwas nennen willst, kannst du sie mit **by** an den Satz anhängen.

  The first car was invented in 1886 **by** <u>Karl Benz</u>.
  The house was destroyed **by** <u>fire</u>.
  Expedition 360 was planned **by** <u>Jason Lewis</u>.

16 Modalverben mit Passivformen (Modal verbs with passive forms)

- Du kannst Modalverben und ihre Ersatzformen wie *can*, *should*, *need*, *have to* usw. in Kombination mit dem Passiv verwenden. Damit drückst du aus, dass eine Handlung ausgeführt bzw. nicht ausgeführt werden soll, muss, kann usw.

  Animals **have to be protected** from eating plastic.

  Lots of famous people **can be seen** in Hollywood.

  Plastic bottles **shouldn't be left** on the beach.

  Zoo animals **mustn't be fed** by visitors.

17 Indirekte Rede (Reported speech)

- Wenn du berichten willst, was jemand gesagt hat, benutzt du die Form der **indirekten Rede**. Die **indirekte Rede** besteht aus einem übergeordneten Satz (*reporting clause*) und der wiedergegebenen Aussage (*reported clause*).

direct speech	reported speech	
	reporting clause	reported clause
Leyla: "I like my headscarf." →	Leyla **says (that)**	**she likes** her headscarf.

- Beide Satzteile können durch ein *that* verbunden werden, man kann es aber auch weglassen.

- Wenn du etwas berichten willst, das du gerade gehört hast und das jetzt noch stimmt oder allgemeingültig ist, benutzt du im Begleitsatz und in der wiedergegebenen Aussage die Zeitformen der Gegenwart.

- Brian: "The Great Barrier Reef **has to be protected.**" → Brian **thinks** (that) the Great Barrier Reef **has to be protected.**

- Im Allgemeinen stehen die Verben im Begleitsatz und in der wiedergegebenen Rede in der Vergangenheit. Die Zeitform der wiedergegebenen Rede rückt dann sozusagen eine Stufe weiter in die Vergangenheit als die direkte Rede. Aus dieser Tabelle kannst du ablesen, wie sich die Zeiten verändern.

direct speech		reported speech
present	→	past
past	→	past perfect
present perfect	→	past perfect
will	→	would
can	→	could
should	→	should

> Yesterday he said he loved me. Today he told me he had met someone else.

Emily: "You **look** like my grandmother!"	→	Emily told Leyla (that) she **looked** like Emily's grandmother.
Leyla: "I **saw** Nigel and Darren in the park."	→	Leyla said (that) she **had seen** Nigel and Darren in the park.
Emily: "I'll **bring** your present tomorrow."	→	Emily told Leyla (that) she **would bring** Leyla's present the next day.

- Meistens musst du Teile der indirekten Rede anpassen oder ergänzen, damit dein Gesprächspartner versteht, was du meinst. Das betrifft zum Beispiel die Pronomen und die Verbform, aber auch Angaben zu Zeit und Ort.

Emily: "**We** are taking the plane to Ireland **tomorrow.**"	→	Emily explained (that) **she and her family** were taking the plane to Ireland **the next day.**

- Wenn du eine Frage wiedergeben möchtest, die jemand anders gestellt hat, benutzt du **if** oder **whether**. Auch bei Fragen musst du darauf achten, dass die Zeitformen sich ändern:

Emily:	"Do your parents **make** you wear the hijab?"	→ Emily asked **if** Leyla's parents **made** Leyla wear the hijab.
Darren:	"Do you **live** near the park?"	→ Darren asked **whether** they **lived** near the park.

- Wenn die Frage mit einem Fragewort eingeleitet wird, übernimmst du einfach das Fragewort:

Leyla:	"**How long** will you be in Ireland?"	→ Leyla asked **how long** Emily would be in Ireland.
Emily:	"**Why** are you wearing a headscarf?"	→ Emily asked **why** Leyla was wearing a headscarf.

18 Wortstellung und Fragebildung (Word order and questions)

a) Aussagesätze

- Der Bauplan für englische Aussagesätze sieht so aus:

(Vorfeld)	Subjekt	Häufigkeits-adverb	Prädikat	Objekt	andere Ergänzungen
Last week	Ethan		was		ill.
	Amy	usually	eats	two apples	for lunch.

- Orts- und Zeitangaben stehen in der Regel am Ende eines Satzes. Dabei steht immer „Ort" vor „Zeit". Um eine Zeitangabe besonders zu betonen, kannst du sie an den Satzanfang stellen.

> **tip**
> Remember: Like nine before ten, it's 'where' before 'when'.

- Häufigkeitsadverbien (*always*, *usually*, *sometimes*, *never*) stehen meistens zwischen Subjekt und Prädikat. Aufgepasst bei *be* und *can*:
  Susan is **sometimes** late for school.
  You can **always** call me.

b) Fragen

- Ja/Nein-Fragen bildet man so:

Hilfsverb	Subjekt	Prädikat	andere Ergänzungen
Is	Brian	talking	on the phone?
Does	Phoebe	know	the answer?

- Fragen mit Fragewort folgen demselben Bauplan, aber sie beginnen mit dem Fragewort:

Fragewort	Hilfsverb	Subjekt	Prädikat	andere Ergänzungen
Why	is	the train	not going	faster?
Where	do	you	do	your homework?
How long	will	the trip	take?	

LANGUAGE IN FOCUS

LiF

19 Die -ing-Form (Gerund)

a) Die -ing-Form als Nomen

- Du verwendest die **-ing-Form**, wenn du über Tätigkeiten, Gewohnheiten und Hobbys sprichst. Im Englischen machst du dazu aus dem Verb ein Nomen, indem du ein **-ing** an das Verb hängst:

  Walking keeps you fit.   **Travelling** is a lot of fun.

b) Die -ing-Form nach bestimmten Verben

- Oft folgt die **-ing-Form** nach bestimmten Verben.
  Dazu gehören **like, love, enjoy, hate, start, stop, prefer**.

  Mareike **likes watching** TV.

  Olivia **loves going** on holiday.

  I **hate putting on** costumes.

c) Die -ing-Form nach bestimmten Ausdrücken

- Du verwendest die **-ing-Form** nach Ausdrücken wie **good at, bad at, interested in, afraid of, look forward to, fond of** und **terrible at**.

  Nicola is **good at doing** gymnastics.   He is **fond of eating** big pizzas.

20 Verb + Objekt mit Infinitiv (Verb + object + infinitive with to)

- Nach bestimmten Verben, die eine Erlaubnis, einen Wunsch oder einen Willen ausdrücken **(ask, allow, tell, want/would like)**, kannst du den **Infinitiv mit to** verwenden. **To** steht in diesen Fällen nach dem Objekt.

John	**wants**	people	**to** understand and accept each other.
Adeela	**would like**	the group	**to** keep going.
He	**asked**	me	**to** meet him at the airport.
His mother	**doesn't allow**	him	**to** come.

21 Substantive mit und ohne Artikel (Nouns with and without article)

- Wie im Deutschen gibt es auch im Englischen einen bestimmten **(the)** und einen unbestimmten **(a/an)** Artikel.

  Could I have **a** bottle of milk?   She put **the** bottles on the table in the kitchen

- Wenn du über eine Sache im Allgemeinen (das Leben, die Schule, die Politik) sprichst, lässt du im Englischen den Artikel weg.

  Life is wonderful.   **School** can be hard.

144

- Auch bestimmte Substantive werden im Englischen ohne den Artikel verwendet, z. B. Straßennamen oder Namen öffentlicher Gebäude.

  She lives on **Brook Street**.   We went to **Heathrow Airport**.

- Wenn du über den Beruf einer Person sprechen möchtest, benutzt du im Englischen immer den unbestimmten Artikel **a/an**.

  She's **an electrician**.   I work as **a painter**.   My sister is **a vet's assistant**.

22 Adjektive als Substantive (Adjectives as nouns)

- Es gibt einige Adjektive, die du in Verbindung mit dem Artikel **the** als Substantive benutzen kannst, um über eine bestimmte Gruppe von Menschen zu sprechen: z. B. **the young, the poor, the rich, the old, the blind, the unemployed**.

  The famous (= famous people) often live in Los Angeles.
  He's collecting money for **the homeless** (= homeless people).

- Einige Adjektive, die Nationalitäten bezeichnen, können auch als Substantive verwendet werden.

  The British (= British people) like football.
  I like **the French** (= French people).

23 Mengenangaben mit ‚much' und ‚many' (Quantifiers: much and many)

- Mit **how many** fragst du nach der Anzahl von Dingen.
  How many CDs have you got?   I have got **twenty** CDs.

- Mit **how much** fragst du nach unbestimmten, nicht zählbaren Mengen.
  How much time have we got?
  We've got **half an hour** before the bus leaves.

24 Relativsätze (Relative clauses)

- Um eine Person oder eine Sache genauer zu beschreiben, verwendest du Relativsätze. Ein Relativsatz beginnt meist mit einem Relativpronomen: **who, which, that**.

- **Who** steht für Personen, **which** für Tiere und Dinge und **that** für Tiere, Dinge oder Personen.

  A doctor is someone **who** works in a hospital.
  I've got a video game **which** is really good.
  I saw a band **that** played great music.

LANGUAGE IN FOCUS

LiF

25 Relativsätze ohne Pronomen (Contact clauses)

- Das Relativpronomen *(who, which, that)* kann im Englischen weggelassen werden, wenn es das Objekt des Relativsatzes ist.
  Wenn dem Relativpronomen ein <u>Verb</u> folgt, muss das Relativpronomen bleiben. Folgt ein <u>Substantiv</u>, kannst du das Relativpronomen weglassen. Im Deutschen ist dies nicht möglich.

  The people **who** <u>were</u> on the streets did not look at Oliver.
  The town **(which)** <u>Oliver</u> is going to is called London.

26 Partizipien zur Verkürzung von Relativsätzen (Participles used to shorten relative clauses)

- Im Englischen gibt es zwei Partizipien: das *present participle*, das auf *-ing* endet, und das *past participle* (= 3. Verbform), das bei regelmäßigen Verben auf *-ed* endet. Diese Partizipformen kannst du benutzen, um einen Relativsatz zu verkürzen.

  Some of the sentences **that are passed** by a teen court are letters of apology. → Some of the sentences **passed** by a teen court are letters of apology.

  Teenagers **who want to become** jurors were often offenders themselves. → Teenagers **wanting to become** jurors were often offenders themselves.

27 Konjunktionen (Conjunctions)

- Du benutzt eine **Konjunktion**, um Sätze oder Satzglieder zu verbinden. Mit Konjunktionen wie **and, but, so, or** verbindest du Hauptsätze.

Hauptsatz	Konjunktion	Hauptsatz
Christina was born in New York	**and**	she now lives in Los Angeles.
Christina Aguilera is a famous star	**but**	she likes to live a 'normal' life.

- Mit Konjunktionen wie **before, because, although, if, when** und **while** verbindest du einen Hauptsatz mit einem Nebensatz.

Hauptsatz	Konjunktion	Nebensatz
Diego had to pay a fine	**because**	he was skateboarding on the stairs of an office building.
Christina looked very young	**when**	her first album came out.

- Du kannst deinen Satz auch mit dem Nebensatz beginnen. Dann steht die Konjunktion am Anfang.

Konjunktion	Nebensatz	Hauptsatz
Although	it was late and nobody there,	Diego had to pay a fine.
While	he tried to skate down a rail,	Diego broke his foot.

GRAMMATICAL TERMS

German	LiF	English	Example
Adjektiv		adjective [ˈædʒɪktɪv]	nice, tall, big
als Substantiv	22	as noun [æz ˈnaʊn]	the British, the young
Adverb		adverb [ˈædvɜːb]	
der Art und Weise		of manner [əv ˈmænə]	angrily, quickly, badly
Häufigkeitsadverb	18	of frequency [əvˈfriːkwənsi]	sometimes, often, never
der Zeit		of time [əv ˈtaɪm]	this morning, on Saturday
Artikel	21	article [ˈɑːtɪkl]	
bestimmter		definite [ˈdefnət]	the
unbestimmter		indefinite [ɪnˈdefnət]	a, an
Aussagesatz	18	statement [ˈsteɪtmənt]	Her name is Cheryl.
Bedingungssatz, Typ I	11	conditional clause, type I [kənˌdɪʃnəl ˈklɔːz]	If it's cold outside, I'll wear a jacket.
Bedingungssatz, Typ II	12	conditional clause, type II	If it were cold outside, I would wear a jacket.
Bedingungssatz, Typ III	13	conditional clause, type III	If it had been cold outside, I would have worn a jacket.
Bestätigungsfrage		question tag [ˈkwestʃn ˌtæg]	That's Katie's wallet, isn't it?
Einzahl (Singular)		singular [ˈsɪŋjʊlə]	house, school, brother
Ersatzform	14	substitute form [ˈsʌbstɪˌtjuːt ˌfɔːm]	have to, be able to, be allowed to
Frage	18	question [ˈkwestʃn]	How old are you?
Fragewort		question word [ˈkwestʃn ˌwɜːd]	who, when, what, whose
Futur (Zukunft)		future tense [ˌfjuːtʃə ˈtens]	
einfache Gegenwart mit Futurbedeutung	1	simple present with future meaning	The movie starts at 8pm.
Futur mit *going to*	10	going to future [ˈgəʊɪŋ tʊ ˌfjuːtʃə]	She is going to buy a CD.
Futur mit *will*	9	will future [ˈwɪl ˌfjuːtʃə]	She will be a pop star.
Gegenwart		present tense [ˌpreznt ˈtens]	
einfache Gegenwart	1	simple present [ˌsɪmpl ˈpreznt]	He plays tennis on Mondays. He doesn't play soccer.
Verlaufsform der Gegenwart	2	present progressive [ˌpreznt prəʊˈgresɪv]	It is raining. It isn't snowing.
vollendete Gegenwart	3	present perfect [ˌpreznt ˈpɜːfɪkt]	We have been to Perth before.
Verlaufsform der vollendeten Gegenwart	4	present perfect progressive [ˌpreznt ˌpɜːfɪkt prəʊˈgresɪv]	I have been living here since my birth.
Genitiv		genitive [ˈdʒenətɪv]	Brian's photo, the title of the story
Imperativ (Befehlsform)		imperative [ɪmˈperətɪv]	Go and wash your hands.
indirekte Rede	17	reported speech [rɪˌpɔːtɪd ˈspiːtʃ]	I read a lot. → She says (that) she reads a lot.
Infinitiv (Grundform)		infinitive [ɪnˈfɪnɪtɪv]	be, sit, listen
***-ing*-Form (Gerundium)**	19	gerund [ˈdʒerənd]	I like going to parties.
Konjunktion	27	conjunction [kənˈdʒʌŋkʃn]	and, or, because, when, until
Kurzantwort		short answer [ˌʃɔːt ˈɑːnsə]	Yes, I do. / No, we haven't.
Kurzform		short form [ˈʃɔːt ˌfɔːm]	I'm, they've got, it's
Langform		long form [ˈlɒŋ ˌfɔːm]	I am, they have got, it is

GRAMMATICAL TERMS

German	Page	English	Example
Mehrzahl (Plural)		plural [ˈplʊərəl]	houses, schools, brothers
unregelmäßig		irregular [ɪˈregjʊlə]	child – children, tooth – teeth
Mengenangabe	23	quantifier [ˈkwɒntɪˌfaɪə]	some juice, much money
Modalverb	14	modal verb [ˌməʊdl ˈvɜːb]	can, must, should
Objekt	16	object [ˈɒbdʒekt]	We've got a <u>cat</u>. I like <u>music</u>.
Partizip Perfekt	26	past participle [ˌpɑːst ˈpɑːtɪsɪpl]	eaten, gone, started
Passiv	15	passive [ˈpæsɪv]	My watch was made in China.
Präposition		preposition [ˌprepəˈzɪʃn]	in, into, next to, on, over
Pronomen (Fürwort)		pronoun [ˈprəʊnaʊn]	
Personalpronomen		personal pronoun [ˌpɜːsnəl ˈprəʊnaʊn]	I, you, he/she/it, we, you, they
Possessivbegleiter		possessive determiner [pəˌzesɪv dɪˈtɜːmɪnə]	my, your, his/her/its, our, your, their
Possessivpronomen		possessive pronoun [pəˌzesɪv ˈprəʊnaʊn]	mine, yours, his/hers, ours, yours, theirs
Reflexivpronomen		reflexive pronoun [rɪˌfleksɪv ˈprəʊnaʊn]	myself, yourself, himself/herself/itself, ourselves, yourselves, themselves
Relativpronomen	24	relative pronoun [ˌrelətɪv ˈprəʊnaʊn]	who, which, that
Relativsatz	24	relative clause [ˌrelətɪv ˈklɔːz]	That's the man <u>who helped me</u>.
ohne Relativpronomen	25	contact clause [ˈkɒntækt ˌklɔːz]	The town <u>(that) Oliver is going to</u> is called London.
Satz	16	sentence [ˈsentəns]	
bejaht/positiv		positive [ˈpɒzətɪv]	She's from the US.
verneint/negativ		negative [ˈnegətɪv]	We haven't got a car.
Steigerung von Adjektiven		comparison [kəmˈpærɪsn]	
Grundform		positive [ˈpɒzətɪv]	tall, important
Komparativ		comparative [kəmˈpærətɪv]	taller, more important
Superlativ		superlative [sʊˈpɜːlətɪv]	(the) tallest, (the) most important
Stützwort: *one/ones*		prop word: one/ones [ˈprɒp ˌwɜːd: wʌn/wʌnz]	Which one do you like best?
Subjekt	18	subject [ˈsʌbdʒekt]	<u>We</u>'ve got a cat.
Substantiv (Hauptwort)	21	noun [naʊn]	market, Adam, brother
zählbares		countable [ˈkaʊntəbl]	bottle – bottles, tooth – teeth
unzählbares		uncountable [ʌnˈkaʊntəbl]	butter, water, sand
Verb		verb [vɜːb]	
regelmäßig		regular [ˈregjʊlə]	play, clean, like
unregelmäßig		irregular [ɪˈregjʊlə]	come, do, eat
Vergangenheit		past tense [ˌpɑːst ˈtens]	
einfache Vergangenheit	6	simple past [ˌsɪmpl ˈpɑːst]	We played games at the party.
Verlaufsform der Vergangenheit	7	past progressive [ˌpɑːst prəʊˈgresɪv]	Yesterday at 6pm Andy was cooking dinner.
Vorvergangenheit	8	past perfect [ˌpɑːst ˈpɜːfɪkt]	He didn't bring his homework because the dog <u>had eaten</u> it.
Verneinung		negation [nɪˈgeɪʃn]	No, I don't like it.
Wortstellung	18	word order [ˈwɜːdˌɔːdə]	subject – verb – object

WORDS

Alphabetische Wortlisten

In der alphabetischen Wortliste findest du den Lernwortschatz aus Camden Market 1–4 sowie alle Wörter aus diesem Buch. Wenn du also ein Wort noch nicht kennst oder dich nicht mehr an seine deutsche Bedeutung erinnerst, kannst du es im *English-German dictionary* ab **Seite 194** nachschlagen.

Wenn du für eine Aufgabe ein englisches Wort brauchst, kannst du es im *German-English dictionary* ab **Seite 229** nachschlagen.

Die Wortlisten nach *Themes*

Hier sind alle neuen Wörter in der Reihenfolge angegeben, in der sie vorne im Buch vorkommen. Wörter mit einem ° brauchst du dir nicht zu merken.

Hier siehst du, wie du die Wortlisten ab **Seite 151** benutzen kannst:

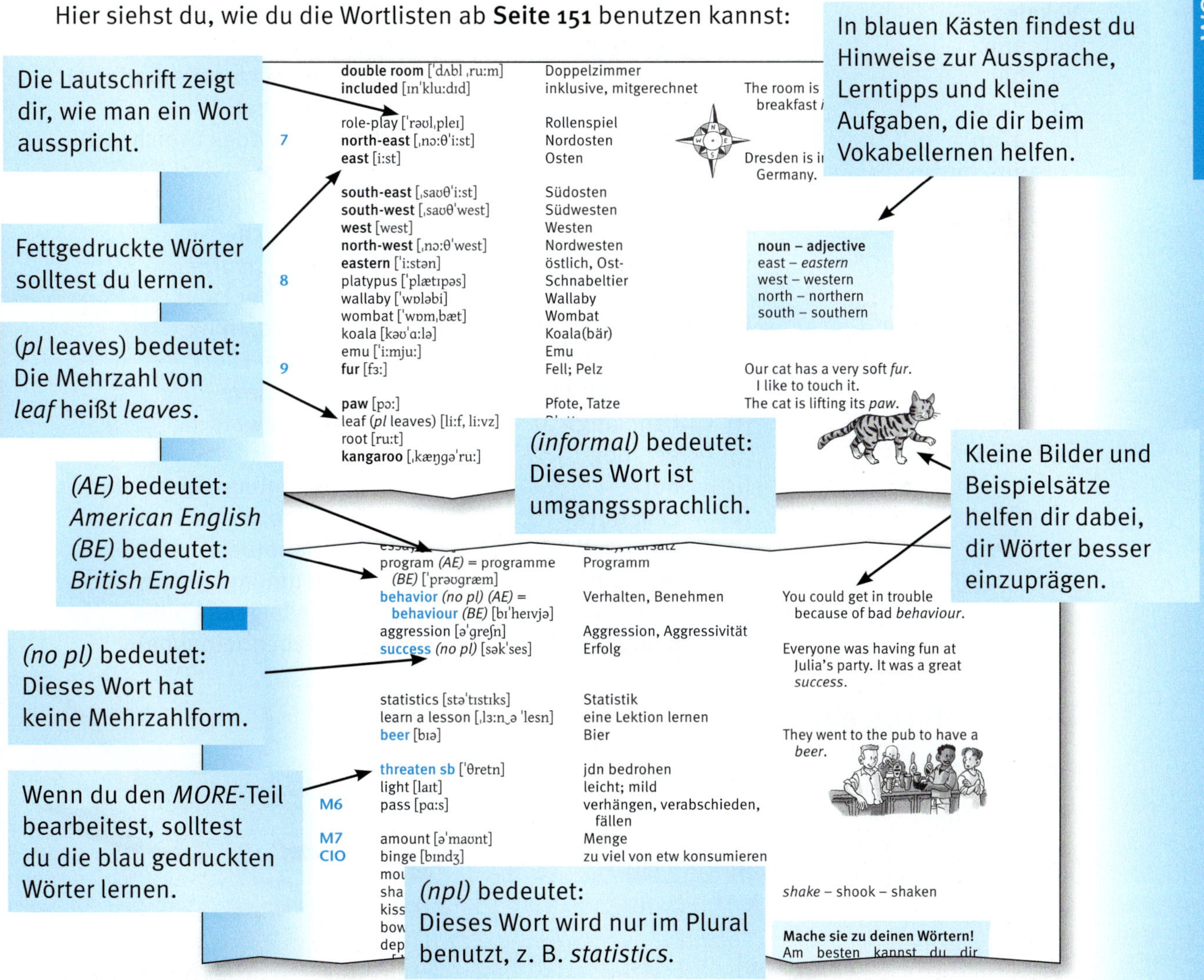

> In blauen Kästen findest du Hinweise zur Aussprache, Lerntipps und kleine Aufgaben, die dir beim Vokabellernen helfen.

> Die Lautschrift zeigt dir, wie man ein Wort ausspricht.

> Fettgedruckte Wörter solltest du lernen.

> (*pl* leaves) bedeutet: Die Mehrzahl von *leaf* heißt *leaves*.

> (AE) bedeutet: *American English*
> (BE) bedeutet: *British English*

> (no pl) bedeutet: Dieses Wort hat keine Mehrzahlform.

> Wenn du den *MORE*-Teil bearbeitest, solltest du die blau gedruckten Wörter lernen.

> (*informal*) bedeutet: Dieses Wort ist umgangssprachlich.

> Kleine Bilder und Beispielsätze helfen dir dabei, dir Wörter besser einzuprägen.

> (*npl*) bedeutet: Dieses Wort wird nur im Plural benutzt, z. B. *statistics*.

double room [ˈdʌbl ˌruːm] — Doppelzimmer
included [ɪnˈkluːdɪd] — inklusive, mitgerechnet — The room is ... breakfast ...

7 **role-play** [ˈrəʊlˌpleɪ] — Rollenspiel
north-east [ˌnɔːθˈiːst] — Nordosten
east [iːst] — Osten — Dresden is i... Germany.

south-east [ˌsaʊθˈiːst] — Südosten
south-west [ˌsaʊθˈwest] — Südwesten
west [west] — Westen
north-west [ˌnɔːθˈwest] — Nordwesten
eastern [ˈiːstən] — östlich, Ost-
8 **platypus** [ˈplætɪpəs] — Schnabeltier
wallaby [ˈwɒləbi] — Wallaby
wombat [ˈwɒmˌbæt] — Wombat
koala [kəʊˈɑːlə] — Koala(bär)
emu [ˈiːmjuː] — Emu
9 **fur** [fɜː] — Fell; Pelz — Our cat has a very soft *fur*. I like to touch it.

paw [pɔː] — Pfote, Tatze — The cat is lifting its *paw*.
leaf (*pl* leaves) [liːf, liːvz] — ...
root [ruːt] — ...
kangaroo [ˌkæŋɡəˈruː] — ...

> noun – adjective
> east – *eastern*
> west – *western*
> north – *northern*
> south – *southern*

... program (AE) = programme (BE) [ˈprəʊɡræm] — Programm
behavior (no pl) (AE) = **behaviour** (BE) [bɪˈheɪvjə] — Verhalten, Benehmen — You could get in trouble because of bad *behaviour*.
aggression [əˈɡreʃn] — Aggression, Aggressivität
success (no pl) [səkˈses] — Erfolg — Everyone was having fun at Julia's party. It was a great *success*.

statistics [stəˈtɪstɪks] — Statistik
learn a lesson [ˌlɜːn ə ˈlesn] — eine Lektion lernen
beer [bɪə] — Bier — They went to the pub to have a *beer*.

M6 **threaten sb** [ˈθretn] — jdn bedrohen
light [laɪt] — leicht; mild
pass [pɑːs] — verhängen, verabschieden, fällen
M7 **amount** [əˈmaʊnt] — Menge
CIO binge [bɪndʒ] — zu viel von etw konsumieren
mou...
sha... — *shake – shook – shaken*
kiss...
bow...
dep...

> **Mache sie zu deinen Wörtern!** Am besten kannst du dir ...

Names

Auf den **Seiten 249–251** findest du alle Namen aus den *Themes* mit Lautschrift.

Irregular verbs

Alle unregelmäßigen Verben, die in den *Themes* vorkommen, findest du auf den **Seiten 253–254**.

WORDS

English sounds

Im Englischen spricht man Wörter oft anders aus, als man sie schreibt. Das ist aber kein Problem. Denn die Aussprache der Wörter ist in jedem Wörterbuch angegeben. So kann man auch neue Wörter richtig aussprechen, ohne sie vorher gehört zu haben.
Dazu nimmt man die sogenannte Lautschrift zu Hilfe. Das ist eine Schrift, deren Symbole jeden Laut genau bezeichnen. Die Lautschrift wird in jedem Wörterbuch benutzt.

Hier findest du eine Liste mit den Symbolen dieser Lautschrift zusammen mit Beispielwörtern, in denen der entsprechende Laut vorkommt.

Vokale		Doppellaute		Konsonanten	
[ɑ:]	arm	[aɪ]	eye, buy	[p]	present, top
[ʌ]	but	[aʊ]	our	[r]	red, right
[e]	desk	[eə]	there	[s]	sister, class (scharfes s)
[ə]	a, an	[eɪ]	take, they	[t]	time, cat
[ɜ:]	girl, bird	[ɪə]	here	[z]	nose, dogs (weiches s)
[æ]	apple	[ɔɪ]	boy	[dʒ]	orange
[ɪ]	in, it	[əʊ]	go, gold	[ʃ]	sure, English
[i]	every	[ʊə]	you're	[tʃ]	child, cheese
[i:]	easy, eat			[ð]	these, mother (weicher Laut)
[ɒ]	orange, sorry	Konsonanten		[θ]	mouth, think (harter Laut)
[ɔ:]	all, call	[b]	bag, club	[v]	very, have
[ʊ]	look	[d]	duck, card	[w]	what, word
[u]	February	[f]	fish, laugh		
[u:]	food	[g]	get, dog	[']	Betonungszeichen für die folgende Silbe (Hauptbetonung)
		[h]	hot		
		[k]	can, duck	[ˌ]	Betonungszeichen für die folgende Silbe (Nebenbetonung)
		[l]	lot, small		
		[m]	more, mum		
		[n]	now, sun		
		[ŋ]	song, long		

The English alphabet

[eɪ]	[bi:]	[si:]	[di:]	[i:]	[ef]	[dʒi:]
a	b	c	d	e	f	g

[eɪtʃ]	[aɪ]	[dʒeɪ]	[keɪ]	[el]	[em]	[en]
h	i	j	k	l	m	n

[əʊ]	[pi:]	[kju:]	[ɑ:]	[es]	[ti:]	[ju:]
o	p	q	r	s	t	u

[vi:]	['dʌblju:]	[eks]	[waɪ]	[zed]		
v	w	x	y	z		

WORDS *Intro*

WORDS INTRO

The English-speaking world

1 ° English-speaking ['ɪŋglɪʃˌspiːkɪŋ] — englischsprachig

° have sth in common [hæv ˌsʌmθɪŋ ɪn 'kɒmən] — etwas gemein haben — Susan and David have *something in common* – they both like football.

° Canada ['kænədə] — Kanada
° the Pacific Ocean [ðə pəˌsɪfɪk 'əʊʃn] — der Pazifische Ozean
° the Atlantic Ocean [ðiˌətˌlæntɪk 'əʊʃn] — der Atlantische Ozean
° Europe ['jʊərəp] — Europa
° Cyprus ['saɪprəs] — Zypern
° Africa ['æfrɪkə] — Afrika — There are many countries in *Africa*.

° Egypt ['iːdʒɪpt] — Ägypten
° Cairo ['kaɪrəʊ] — Kairo
° Cameroon [ˌkæmə'ruːn] — Kamerun
° Kenya ['kenjə] — Kenia
° Rwanda [ru'ændə] — Ruanda
° Ethiopia [ˌiːθi'əʊpiə] — Äthiopien
° Republic of South Africa [rɪˌpʌblɪk əv saʊθ 'æfrɪkə] — Republik Südafrika
° Cape Town ['keɪptaʊn] — Kapstadt
° the Seychelles [ðə seɪ'ʃelz] — die Seychellen — *The Seychelles* are a group of islands in the Indian Ocean.

° Jordan ['dʒɔːdn] — Jordanien
° U.A.E. (= United Arab Emirates) [ˌjuː eɪ 'iː, juˌnaɪtɪd ˌærəb 'e mərəts] — Vereinigte Arabische Emirate
° Yemen ['jemən] — Jemen
° Asia ['eɪʃə] — Asien
° New Delhi [njuː 'deli] — Neu-Delhi
° Rangoon [ræŋ'guːn] — Rangun
° the Philippines [ðə 'fɪləpiːnz] — die Philippinen — *The Philippines* are a group of 7,107 islands in East Asia.
° the Indian Ocean [ðiˌɪndiən 'əʊʃn] — der Indische Ozean — *The Indian Ocean* lies south of India.
° Singapore [ˌsɪŋə'pɔː] — Singapur
° Micronesia [ˌmaɪkrəʊ'niːziə] — Mikronesien
° Papua New Guinea [ˌpæpuə njuː 'gɪni] — Papua-Neuguinea
° the Solomon Islands [ðə 'sɒləmən ˌaɪləndz] — die Solomonen
° Australia [ɒ'streɪliə] — Australien
° New Zealand [njuː 'ziːlənd] — Neuseeland
° mother tongue ['mʌðə ˌtʌŋ] — Muttersprache — German is the *mother tongue* of most Germans. It is the language they learn from birth.

° use [juːs] — Verwendung, Gebrauch
° semi-official [ˌsemi ə'fɪʃl] — halboffiziell

WORDS INTRO

	° capital [ˈkæpɪtl]	Hauptstadt	Berlin is the *capital* of Germany; London is the *capital* of England.
	° g'day *(Australian English; informal)* [gəˈdeɪ]	hi, hallo	
	° mate *(informal)* [meɪt]	Kumpel, Freund/in	
2	° complete [kəmˈpliːt]	vervollständigen	
	° Swahili [swɑːˈhiːli]	Swahili, Suaheli *(afrikanische Sprache)*	
	° Hindi [ˈhɪndi]	Hindi *(Amtssprache in Indien)*	How many languages do you know in English? Make a list.
	° Welsh [welʃ]	Walisisch; walisisch	
	° Japanese [ˌdʒæpəˈniːz]	Japaner/in; Japanisch; japanisch	
	° Patois [ˈpætwɑː]	Patois *(Dialekt in Jamaika)*	
	° Mandarin [ˈmændərɪn]	Mandarin *(chinesische Hochsprache)*	
3	° continent [ˈkɒntɪnənt]	Kontinent, Erdteil	A *continent* is a large area of land. The continents on earth are called Europe, Africa, North America, South America, Asia, Australia, and Antarctica.
PP	° business [ˈbɪznəs]	Handel, Gewerbe	
	° government [ˈɡʌvənmənt]	Regierung	
	° belong to sth [bɪˈlɒŋ tə ˌsʌmθɪŋ]	zu etw gehören	*belong to something* = be a member of something
	° common [ˈkɒmən]	gemeinsam	
	° nation [ˈneɪʃn]	Nation, Land	
	° head [hed]	*hier:* Oberhaupt	The *head* of a school is the headteacher.
	° colony [ˈkɒləni]	Kolonie	
	° independent [ˌɪndɪˈpendənt]	unabhängig; selbstständig	Steve likes to work alone and without any help from others. He is very *independent*.
	° better off [ˌbetəˈʳɒf]	wohlhabender, besser gestellt	
	° support [səˈpɔːt]	(unter)stützen	
	° deal with [ˈdiːl wɪð]	sich kümmern um, sich befassen mit	
	° Sweden [ˈswiːdn]	Schweden	
	° Swede [swiːd]	Schwede/Schwedin	

Nur zehn Minuten
Übe die Vokabeln immer nur fünf bis zehn Minuten, aber dafür regelmäßig! Das ist viel wirkungsvoller als eine ganze Stunde oder nur zweimal im Monat. Probiere dabei die Vokabeltipps auf den nächsten Seiten aus.

Theme 1 – Down under

I	down under *(informal)* [ˌdaʊn ˈʌndə]	Australien	
	Australia [ɒˈstreɪliə]	Australien	
	statistics *(npl)* [stəˈtɪstɪks]	Statistik	
	Aborigine [ˌæbəˈrɪdʒəni]	australische/r Ureinwohner/in, Aborigine	The *Aborigines* were the first people to live in Australia.
	culture [ˈkʌltʃə]	Kultur	
	give a presentation [ˌgɪv‿ə ˌpreznˈteɪʃn]	eine Präsentation halten	
2	**fact** [fækt]	Tatsache, Fakt	When something is true, it's a *fact*.
	coral reef [ˌkɒrəl ˈriːf]	Korallenriff	
	system [ˈsɪstəm]	System	
	individual [ˌɪndɪˈvɪdʒuəl]	einzeln	
	outer space [ˌaʊtə ˈspeɪs]	Weltall, Weltraum	
	settle [ˈsetl]	sich niederlassen	
	Asia [ˈeɪʃə]	Asien	
	holy [ˈhəʊli]	heilig	

A church is a *holy* place.

	film-maker [ˈfɪlm ˌmeɪkə]	Filmemacher/in	
	animal lover [ˈænɪml ˌlʌvə]	Tierfreund/in	
	hunter [ˈhʌntə]	Jäger/in	
	kill [kɪl]	töten	
	stingray [ˈstɪŋreɪ]	Stachelrochen	
	outback *(no pl)* [ˈaʊtˌbæk]	Hinterland (Australiens)	
	declare [dɪˈkleə]	erklären, verkünden	

verb – noun
make – *maker*
love – *lover*
hunt – *hunter*
dance – *dancer*
play – *player*

4	Greek [griːk]	Grieche/Griechin; griechisch	
	Athens [ˈæθɪnz]	Athen	
	New Zealand [ˌnjuː ˈziːlənd]	Neuseeland	
	the Philippines [ðə ˈfɪlɪpiːnz]	die Philippinen	
	Greece [griːs]	Griechenland	
	the figures *(pl)* [ðə ˈfɪgəz]	Zahlen(material)	
	fifth [fɪfθ]	Fünftel	I was only allowed to eat one *fifth* of the cake.
5	Christmas Day [ˌkrɪsməs ˈdeɪ]	erster Weihnachtsfeiertag	
	have a barbecue [ˌhæv‿ə ˈbɑːbɪˌkjuː]	grillen, eine Grillparty feiern	
	barbie *(Australian English; informal)* [ˈbɑːbi]	*Kurzform von barbecue*	
	by the way [ˌbaɪ ðə ˈweɪ]	übrigens	I talked to Paul yesterday, *by the way*.
	dingo *(pl -es)* [ˈdɪŋgəʊ, ˈdɪŋgəʊz]	Dingo, australischer Windhund	
	boarding school [ˈbɔːdɪŋ ˌskuːl]	Internat	
	all right [ɔːl ˈraɪt]	in Ordnung	
	make fun of sb [ˌmeɪk ˈfʌn‿ɒv ˌsʌmbədi]	sich über jdn lustig machen	sb = somebody
	pommy *(Australian English; informal)* [ˈpɒmi]	*abwertende Bezeichnung für einen Briten/eine Britin*	
	get on sb's nerves *(informal)* [ˌget‿ɒn sʌmbədiz ˈnɜːvz]	jdm auf die Nerven gehen	

WORDS THEME 1

153

over the radio [ˌəʊvə ðə ˈreɪdiəʊ]	über Funk	The captain spoke to the other ship *over the radio*.
schoolwork *(no pl)* [ˈskuːl ˌwɜːk]	Schularbeiten	
pyjamas *(pl)* [pəˈdʒɑːməz]	Pyjama, Schlafanzug	Danny likes his new *pyjamas*.
emergency [ɪˈmɜːdʒnsi]	Notfall	

> Get all the people out now! This is an *emergency*!

forever [fərˈevə]	ewig	We travelled for three hours. The journey took *forever*.
look forward to sth [ˌlʊk ˈfɔːwəd tuː ˌsʌmθɪŋ]	sich auf etw freuen	sth = something
distance [ˈdɪstəns]	Entfernung; Strecke	
6 halfway [ˌhɑːfˈweɪ]	auf halber Strecke, in der Mitte	
backpacker [ˈbækˌpækə]	Rucksackreisende/r	
receptionist [rɪˈsepʃnɪst]	Empfangschef/in	
book [bʊk]	buchen	

> That hotel looks nice. Let's *book* our rooms there.

per [pɜː]	pro	
private room [ˌpraɪvət ˈruːm]	*hier:* Einzelzimmer	
mixed dorm [ˌmɪkst ˈdɔːm]	*Schlafsaal, in dem Männer und Frauen übernachten*	There were lots of boys and girls in the *mixed dorm*.
AUD (= Australian Dollar) [ˌeɪ juː diː]	Australischer Dollar *(Währung in Australien)*	
single room [ˈsɪŋgl ˌruːm]	Einzelzimmer	
double room [ˈdʌbl ˌruːm]	Doppelzimmer	
included [ɪnˈkluːdɪd]	inklusive, mitgerechnet	The room is 20 AUD per night, breakfast *included*.
role-play [ˈrəʊlˌpleɪ]	Rollenspiel	
7 **north-east** [ˌnɔːθˈiːst]	Nordosten	
east [iːst]	Osten	Dresden is in the *east* of Germany.
south-east [ˌsaʊθˈiːst]	Südosten	
south-west [ˌsaʊθˈwest]	Südwesten	
west [west]	Westen	
north-west [ˌnɔːθˈwest]	Nordwesten	
eastern [ˈiːstən]	östlich, Ost-	noun – adjective
8 platypus [ˈplætɪpəs]	Schnabeltier	east – *eastern*
wallaby [ˈwɒləbi]	Wallaby	west – *western*
wombat [ˈwɒmˌbæt]	Wombat	north – *northern*
koala [kəʊˈɑːlə]	Koala(bär)	south – *southern*
emu [ˈiːmjuː]	Emu	
9 **fur** [fɜː]	Fell; Pelz	Our cat has a very soft *fur*. I like to touch it. The cat is lifting its *paw*.
paw [pɔː]	Pfote, Tatze	
leaf (*pl* leaves) [liːf, liːvz]	Blatt	
root [ruːt]	Wurzel	
kangaroo [ˌkæŋgəˈruː]	Känguru	

10	**Aboriginal** [ˌæbəˈrɪdʒnl]	... der Aboriginals	The didgeridoo is an *Aboriginal* instrument.
	aggressive [əˈgresɪv]	aggressiv; energisch	
	relaxing [rɪˈlæksɪŋ]	entspannend	
	rhythm [ˈrɪðəm]	Rhythmus, Takt	This song has a cool *rhythm*.

	instrument [ˈɪnstrʊmənt]	Instrument	
11	Dreamtime [ˈdriːmˌtaɪm]	*Traumzeit*	
	ancestor spirit [ˈænsestə ˌspɪrɪt]	*Geist eines Vorfahren/ einer Vorfahrin*	
	a long time ago [ə ˌlɒŋ ˌtaɪm ə ˈgəʊ]	vor langer Zeit	Neanderthals lived *a long time ago*.
	sky [skaɪ]	Himmel	There are lots of stars in the *sky*.

period (of time) [ˈpɪəriəd]	Zeitraum
crane [kreɪn]	Kranich
fight over sth [ˈfaɪt ˌəʊvə ˌsʌmθɪŋ]	um etw streiten
crack [kræk]	aufbrechen
kick [kɪk]	treten, schießen
explosion [ɪkˈspləʊʒn]	Explosion
yolk [jəʊk]	Eigelb, (Ei)dotter
eggshell [ˈegˌʃel]	Eierschale
warmth *(no pl)* [wɔːmθ]	Wärme
match [mætʃ]	passen zu

12	**grandmother** [ˈgrænˌmʌðə]	Großmutter	My *grandmother* makes the best tea in the world.

tribal [ˈtraɪbl]	Stammes-
religious [rəˈlɪdʒəs]	religiöse(r, s), Religions-
anyway [ˈeniˌweɪ]	sowieso, jedenfalls; *hier*: trotzdem
grandfather [ˈgrænˌfɑːðə]	Großvater
tuberculosis *(no pl)* [tjuːˌbɜːkjʊˈləʊsɪs]	Tuberkulose
support [səˈpɔːt]	unterstützen; *hier*: für den Lebensunterhalt aufkommen

train sb [ˈtreɪn ˌsʌmbədi]	jdn ausbilden

His father is *training* him, so he can take over the family business.

prison [ˈprɪzn]	Gefängnis

He is in *prison* because he stole lots of money.

home [həʊm]	*hier*: Heim
within [wɪðˈɪn]	innerhalb
strict [strɪkt]	streng
cruel [ˈkruːəl]	grausam

He beats his wife, his children and his dog. He's a very *cruel* man.

overcrowded [ˌəʊvəˈkraʊdɪd]	überfüllt
arithmetic *(no pl)* [əˈrɪθmətɪk]	Rechnen
auntie *(informal)* [ˈɑːnti]	*Kosewort für Tante*
send out sb [send ˈaʊt ˌsʌmbədi]	jdn aussenden; *hier*: jdn fortschicken
(children's) nurse [(ˈtʃɪldrənz) nɜːs]	Kindermädchen

How many names for relatives do you know in English? Make a list.

force sb (to do sth) ['fɔːs ˌsʌmbədi]	jdn zwingen (etw zu tun)	
in my opinion [ɪn 'maɪ ˌə,pɪnjən]	meiner Meinung/Ansicht nach	*In my opinion*, Manchester United is the best football team.

PP
° New Guinea [ˌnjuː ˈɡɪni]	Neuguinea	
° canoe [kəˈnuː]	Kanu, Paddelboot	
° ice age [ˈaɪs ˌeɪdʒ]	Eiszeit	
° divide [dɪˈvaɪd]	teilen; trennen	They *divided* the cake into two pieces.
° attach [əˈtætʃ]	verbinden; befestigen	The poster was *attached* to the wall.
° South-East Asia [ˌsaʊθ,iːst ˈeɪʒə]	Südostasien	
° live off sth [ˈlɪv ˌɒf ˌsʌmθɪŋ]	von etw leben	Charlie *lives off* pizza. He never eats any other food.
° pick [pɪk]	*hier:* pflücken, sammeln	
° berry [ˈberi]	Beere	I like to pick *berries* from a field near my house.
° up to [ˈʌp tuː]	bis zu	
° fight [faɪt]	Kampf, Streit	
° farm (land) [fɑːm]	(Land) bebauen	
° turn into [ˌtɜːn ˈɪntʊ]	umwandeln, verändern	
° educate [ˈedjʊkeɪt]	unterrichten, ausbilden; *hier:* erziehen	Her job was to *educate* the pupils.
° properly [ˈprɒpəli]	korrekt, richtig	If you don't do it *properly*, you can stop doing it.
° generation [ˌdʒenəˈreɪʃn]	Generation	
° native Australian [ˌneɪtɪv ɒˈstreɪliən]	australischer Ureinwohner/ australische Urein- wohnerin	
° compensate sb for sth [ˈkɒmpənseɪt ˌsʌmbədi fə ˌsʌmθɪŋ]	jdn für etw (finanziell) entschädigen	

13
timeline [ˈtaɪm,laɪn]	Zeitstrahl	
finding [ˈfaɪndɪŋ]	Entdeckung; Ergebnis	The detective had done a lot of work and had found out a lot. He told me about his *findings*.
religion [rɪˈlɪdʒn]	Religion; Glaube	
mind [maɪnd]	etw dagegen haben	 *Do you mind if I ask you a question?* *No, not at all.*

M1
World Heritage Site [ˌwɜːld ˈherɪtɪdʒ ˌsaɪt]	Weltkulturerbe, Weltkulturdenkmal	
brilliant [ˈbrɪljənt]	leuchtend, brilliant	
off [ɒf]	*hier:* vor	
reef [riːf]	Riff	A *reef* is made of rock or corals.
north-east [ˌnɔːθˈiːst]	nordöstlich, Nordost-	
include [ɪnˈkluːd]	beinhalten, einschließen	
single [ˈsɪŋɡl]	einzelne(r, s)	

structure ['strʌktʃə]	Gefüge, Struktur	
organism ['ɔːgə,nɪzm]	Organismus	
coral ['kɒrəl]	Korallen-	
polyp ['pɒlɪp]	Polyp	
tiny ['taɪni]	winzig	*tiny* = very small
join up [,dʒɔɪn‿'ʌp]	sich verbinden, miteinander verschmelzen	
colony ['kɒləni]	Kolonie	*colony* = a group of people, animals or organisms living together
shell [ʃel]	Schale	An egg has a hard *shell*.
coral ['kɒrəl]	Koralle	
make up [,meɪk‿'ʌp]	bilden	
underwater [,ʌndə'wɔːtə]	Unterwasser-	
square kilometre [,skweə kɪ'lɒmɪtə]	Quadratkilometer	
impressive [ɪm'presɪv]	beeindruckend	
constant ['kɒnstənt]	dauernd, ständig	
take on sth [,teɪk‿'ɒn ,sʌmθɪŋ]	etw annehmen	
worm [wɜːm]	Wurm	
parrotfish ['pærətfɪʃ]	Papageifisch	
clownfish ['klaʊnfɪʃ]	Clownfisch	
ideal [aɪ'dɪəl]	ideal	
wide [waɪd]	breit; breit gefächert	
range [reɪndʒ]	Reichweite; *hier:* Spektrum, Vielfalt	
turtle ['tɜːtl]	Meeresschildkröte	*Turtles* have hard shells and live in the sea.
hatch [hætʃ]	schlüpfen	
several ['sevrəl]	einige	There are *several* pieces of fruit on the table.
lay [leɪ]	legen	
whale [weɪl]	Wal	*Whales* look like big fish, but they are not fish.
frog [frɒg]	Frosch	*Frogs* are small green animals that can jump very far.
nest [nest]	nisten	
however [haʊ'evə]	aber, jedoch	She wanted to buy the book. *However*, she didn't have any money.
seem [siːm]	scheinen	The shop still *seems* to be open. It looks like it's open.
own [əʊn]	besitzen	The king *owns* this castle.
interest ['ɪntrəst]	Interesse	My main *interest* is playing sports. I do it every day.
glass-bottomed [,glɑːs 'bɒtəmd]	mit einer Unterseite aus Glas; mit einem gläsernen Boden	

Achtung Schreibweise!
Im Englischen schreibt man manche Wörter mit -re, wo im Deutschen -er steht:
kilometre – *dt. Kilometer*
theatre – *dt. Theater*
litre – *dt. Liter*

This T-shirt is *ideal*. It's exactly what I **need** for the party.

	scuba diving *(no pl)* ['skuːbə ˌdaɪvɪŋ]	Sporttauchen	*Scuba diving* is his favourite activity.
	helicopter ['helɪˌkɒptə]	Hubschrauber	
	flight [flaɪt]	Flug	
	properly ['prɒpəli]	korrekt, richtig	
	natural balance [ˌnætʃrəl 'bæləns]	ökologisches Gleichgewicht	
	disturb [dɪ'stɜːb]	stören, durcheinander- bringen	The loud music had *disturbed* him.
	overfishing *(no pl)* [ˌəʊvə'fɪʃɪŋ]	Überfischung	
	diver ['daɪvə]	Taucher/in	
	preserve [prɪ'zɜːv]	erhalten, bewahren, schützen	We need to *preserve* the forests. We can't let people cut the trees down.
	immense [ɪ'mens]	riesig, enorm	
	beauty ['bjuːti]	Schönheit	
	location [ləʊ'keɪʃn]	Lage	The *location* of Big Ben is in London.
M2	guess [ges]	Vermutung	
	relief [rɪ'liːf]	Hilfe, Unterstützung	
	organization [ˌɔːgənaɪ'zeɪʃn]	Organisation	This *organization* is a group of people who want to help animals.
	global warming *(no pl)* [ˌgləʊbl 'wɔːmɪŋ]	Erwärmung der Erdatmosphäre	
	affect sb/sth [ə'fekt ˌsʌmbədi/ ˌsʌmθɪŋ]	sich auf jdn/etw auswirken	
	ecosystem ['iːkəʊˌsɪstəm]	Ökosystem	*ecosystem* = a group of living things and the place where they live
	zooxanthella *(pl* -e) [ˌzəʊəzæn'θelə, ˌzəʊəzæn'θeli]	*Algenart*	
	temperature ['temprɪtʃə]	Temperatur	In winter, the *temperature* is really low. So it's very cold.
	stressed ['strest]	gestresst	She has so much work to do. She is really *stressed*.
	spit out [ˌspɪt 'aʊt]	ausspucken	George hated the food so he *spat* it *out*.
	helper ['helpə]	Helfer	
	process ['prəʊses]	Prozess, Vorgang	
	bleaching ['bliːtʃɪŋ]	Bleichen	
	dead [ded]	tot	
	in order to [ɪn 'ɔːdə tuː]	um zu	He got on the bus *in order to* get to town more quickly.
M3	ozone hole ['əʊzəʊn ˌhəʊl]	Ozonloch	The earth is getting hotter because there is an *ozone hole*.
	skin [skɪn]	Haut	The sun has made my *skin* go brown.
	rate [reɪt]	Rate, Quote	
	cancer ['kænsə]	Krebs *(Krankheit)*	

	slip on sth *(informal)* ['slɪp‿ɒn ˌsʌmθɪŋ]	etw anziehen
	slop on sth *(informal)* [ˌslɒp‿'ɒn ˌsʌmθɪŋ]	*hier:* etw auftragen
	slap on sth *(informal)* [ˌslæp‿'ɒn ˌsʌmθɪŋ]	*hier:* etw aufsetzen

He is *slopping on* some sunscreen.

M4	topic ['tɒpɪk]	Thema

The *topic* I want to discuss today is education.

M5	rabbit-proof fence [ˌræbɪt ˌpruːf 'fens]	*Schutzzaun in Westaustralien, der gezogen wurde, um die Ausbreitung von Kaninchen auf Ackerland zu vermeiden*
	be based on sth [bi: 'beɪst‿ɒn ˌsʌmθɪŋ]	auf etw basieren/beruhen
	summary ['sʌməri]	Zusammenfassung; Inhaltsangabe
	be set somewhere [bi: 'set sʌmweə]	irgendwo spielen/ stattfinden
	government ['gʌvənmənt]	Regierung
	settlement ['setlmənt]	Siedlung
	servant ['sɜːvnt]	Diener/in, Dienstmädchen, Bedienstete/r
	despise [dɪ'spaɪz]	verachten, hassen
	lead [li:d]	(an)führen, leiten
	flee [fli:]	fliehen
	originally [ə'rɪdʒnəli]	ursprünglich
	keep out [ˌki:p 'aʊt]	nicht hereinlassen
	tracker ['trækə]	Fährtenleser/in
	lead away [ˌli:d‿ə'weɪ]	wegführen
	capture ['kæptʃə]	(ein)fangen
	manage ['mænɪdʒ]	es schaffen
	generation [ˌdʒenə'reɪʃn]	Generation
M6	What if ...? [ˌwɒt‿'ɪf]	Was ist/wäre, wenn ...?
	fence [fens]	Zaun
	guide [gaɪd]	führen, den Weg zeigen
	authority [ɔː'θɒrəti]	Amtsgewalt; Behörde
M7	atmosphere ['ætməsˌfɪə]	Atmosphäre, Stimmung
	dreamlike ['dri:mˌlaɪk]	wie in einem Traum
	dramatic [drə'mætɪk]	dramatisch
	touching ['tʌtʃɪŋ]	(be)rührend

The *government* makes all the rules in a country.

We live in a very small *settlement* with only a few houses.

Rich people have got *servants* to do all the jobs in their houses.

They are *fleeing* the building.

He *managed* to clean the flat before his parents came home.

There are three *generations* in this family, the grandfather, the parents and the children.

The *authorities* said he had to go to school, he had no choice.

The *atmosphere* of the story in the book was very spooky.

mysterious [mɪˈstɪəriəs]	geheimnisvoll, mysteriös	He didn't know what she was thinking. She was very *mysterious*.
magical [ˈmædʒɪkl]	magisch	She can do *magical* things.
gloomy [ˈgluːmi]	trostlos, trübe, düster	
M8 e-pal [ˈiː ˌpæl]	*E-Mail-Freund/in*	I am writing an email to my *e-pal*.
portrait [ˈpɔːtrɪt]	Porträt, Darstellung	
M9 prime minister [ˌpraɪm ˈmɪnɪstə]	Premierminister/in, Ministerpräsident/in	
say sorry (to sb) [ˌseɪ ˈsɒri]	sich (bei jdm) entschuldigen	

Can you *say sorry* to your brother, please? You hurt him.

wrong [rɒŋ]	Unrecht	People should apologize for the *wrongs* they have done.
speech [spiːtʃ]	Rede	He is giving a *speech*.
° honour [ˈɒnə]	ehren, würdigen	

We want *to honour* the winners.

° indigenous [ɪnˈdɪdʒənəs]	(ein)heimisch	
° people [ˈpiːpl]	*hier:* Volk	
° continuing [kənˈtɪnjʊɪŋ]	andauernd	
° human [ˈhjuːmən]	menschlich	
° reflect on sb/sth [rɪˈflekt ˌɒn ˌsʌmbədi/ˌsʌmθɪŋ]	über jdn/etw nachdenken	
° past [pɑːst]	frühere(r, s); vergangen	
° mistreatment [ˌmɪsˈtriːtmənt]	Misshandlung, schlechte Behandlung	
° in particular [ˌɪn pəˈtɪkjʊlə]	insbesondere	
° blemished [ˈblemɪʃt]	fehlerhaft; *hier:* dunkel	He has a *blemished* past. He did things that were wrong.
° chapter [ˈtʃæptə]	Kapitel, Abschnitt	A book can have many *chapters*.
° national [ˈnæʃnəl]	national; National-	
° right sth [ˈraɪt ˌsʌmθɪŋ]	etw wiedergutmachen	
° confidence *(no pl)* [ˈkɒnfɪdns]	Vertrauen, Zuversicht	
° law [lɔː]	Gesetz	You are not allowed to smoke here. That is the *law*.
° policy [ˈpɒləsi]	Programm, Strategie; Grundsatz	

° successive [səkˈsesɪv]	aufeinander folgend	
° parliament [ˈpɑːləmənt]	Parlament	
° inflict sth on sb [ɪnˈflɪkt ˌsʌmθɪŋ ˌɒn ˌsʌmbədi]	jdm etw zufügen	
° profound [prəˈfaʊnd]	tief, heftig, groß	His leg hurt *profoundly*.
° grief [griːf]	Trauer, Leid, Schmerz	
° suffering *(no pl)* [ˈsʌfərɪŋ]	Leid	

° loss [lɒs]	Verlust	
° fellow ['feləʊ]	Mit-	Bob and his *fellow* prisoners were very angry.

° removal *(no pl)* [rɪˈmuːvl]	Entfernung, Wegnahme
° islander [ˈaɪləndə]	Inselbewohner/in
° pain [peɪn]	Schmerz, Leid
° hurt [hɜːt]	Schmerz; Kränkung
° descendant [dɪˈsendənt]	Nachkomme
° break up [breɪk ˈʌp]	zerstören; auflösen
° indignity [ɪnˈdɪgnəti]	Demütigung, Erniedrigung

It was a terrible *indignity* when the other boys laughed at him.

° degradation [ˌdegrəˈdeɪʃn]	Erniedrigung
° thus [ðʌs]	so, auf diese Weise; folglich
° respectful [rɪˈspektfl]	respektvoll
° apology [əˈpɒlədʒi]	Entschuldigung

I want to make an *apology*. I am sorry.

° receive [rɪˈsiːv]	*hier:* annehmen, gewähren
° spirit *(no pl)* [ˈspɪrɪt]	*hier:* Geiste
° healing [ˈhiːlɪŋ]	Heilung

The *healing* of a broken arm can take a long time.

° take heart [ˌteɪk ˈhɑːt]	neuen Mut schöpfen

Take heart! We'll win the next game.

° resolve [rɪˈzɒlv]	*hier:* beschließen
° take a first step [ˌteɪk ə ˌfɜːst ˈstep]	einen ersten Schritt machen/unternehmen
° acknowlegde [əkˈnɒlɪdʒ]	anerkennen; zugeben
° lay claim to sth [ˌleɪ ˈkleɪm tə ˌsʌmθɪŋ]	auf etw Anspruch erheben
° embrace [ɪmˈbreɪs]	umarmen; umfassen
° injustice [ɪnˈdʒʌstɪs]	Ungerechtigkeit
but [bʌt]	*hier:* sondern	Sarah didn't speak to Ben *but* to Mike.
over and over again [ˌəʊvə ˌən ˌəʊvə əˈgen]	immer wieder	When my brother learns a new word, he says it o*ver and over again.*

CIO

quiz sb [ˈkwɪz ˌsʌmbədi]	jdn befragen/prüfen	The teacher *quizzed* the class to see what they had learned.
nowhere [ˈnəʊweə]	nirgends, nirgendwo	
have a nap [hæv ə ˈnæp]	ein Nickerchen machen	My mum likes to *have a nap* in the afternoon.

WORDS THEME 1

| poisonous ['pɔɪznəs] | giftig | Some snakes are *poisonous*. You have to be careful. |

shake (out) ['ʃeɪk ('aʊt)]	(aus)schütteln
in case ... [ɪn 'keɪs]	für den Fall, dass ...; falls ...
° be crazy about sb/sth ['kreɪzi ə‚baʊt ‚sʌmbədi/ ‚sʌmθɪŋ]	nach jdm/etw verrückt sein

He *is crazy about* his girlfriend.

| ° time zone ['taɪm ‚zəʊn] | Zeitzone |
| ° instead (of) [ɪn'sted (‚ɒv)] | stattdessen; (an)statt |

Wortnetze ergänzen
Inzwischen weißt du ja, wie man Wortnetze *(mindmaps)* zusammenstellt. Du lernst immer mehr neue Wörter und da sind sicherlich einige dabei, die in Wortnetze passen, die du früher schon angelegt hast. Ergänze deine alten Wortnetze und sieh dir die Wörter noch einmal an. Bestimmt kannst du dich noch gut an sie erinnern, oder?

Probier's mal mit Gemütlichkeit
Nicht nur für das Vokabellernen gilt: Du solltest dich an dem Ort, an dem du arbeitest, wohl fühlen und durch nichts abgelenkt sein! Eine gewisse Ordnung erleichtert das Arbeiten. Mache regelmäßig Pausen, in denen du z. B. das Fenster öffnest, etwas trinkst und dich bewegst. So kannst du dich besser konzentrieren.

Am Computer Vokabeln lernen
Hast du einen Computer? Dann kannst du auch dort Vokabeln lernen! Lege dir deine persönliche Vokabeldatei an. Dort schreibst du alle Wörter hinein, die du lernen willst. Du kannst die Wörter auch automatisch alphabetisch sortieren lassen und dir so dein eigenes Wörterbuch erstellen.

Theme 2 – Mixed feelings

I	mixed [mɪkst]	gemischt
	difficulty ['dɪfɪklti]	Schwierigkeit, Problem
	responsibility [rɪˌspɒnsə'bɪləti]	Verantwortlichkeit, Zuständigkeit; Verantwortung
	youth [juːθ]	Jugend; Jugendliche/r; Jugend-
	tolerance ['tɒlərəns]	Toleranz
	pro [prəʊ]	Pro(-Argument)
	con [kɒn]	Kontra(-Argument)
	court [kɔːt]	Gericht
1	speech bubble ['spiːtʃ ˌbʌbl]	Sprechblase
	° make sb laugh [ˌmeɪk sʌmbədi 'lɑːf]	jdn zum Lachen bringen
	° look out for sb [ˌlʊk ˌaʊt fə sʌmbədi]	nach jdm Ausschau halten; auf jdn aufpassen
	° have sb's back [ˌhæv sʌmbədiz 'bæk]	jdn beschützen, unterstützen
	° have sb around [ˌhæv sʌmbədi ə'raʊnd]	jdn in der Nähe haben
	° shell [ʃel]	Schale; Muschel
	° feel the need to do sth [ˌfiːl ðə 'niːd tə ˌduː sʌmθɪŋ]	das Bedürfnis verspüren, etw zu tun
	° rebel yell [ˌrebəl 'jel]	(Kampf)schrei
	° 'cause (= because) (informal) [kʌz, bɪ'kɒz]	weil, da
	° keep sb's feet on the ground [ˌkiːp sʌmbədiz ˌfiːt ˌɒn ðə 'graʊnd]	dafür sorgen, dass jd realistisch/auf dem Boden bleibt
	° chorus ['kɔːrəs]	Refrain
	° pull sb aside [ˌpʊl sʌmbədi ə'saɪd]	jdn beiseite nehmen
	° ain't (AE, informal) [eɪnt]	nicht sein
	° alright [ɔːl'raɪt]	in Ordnung
2	guess [ges]	Vermutung
	intolerant [ɪn'tɒlərənt]	intolerant
	unfair [ʌn'feə]	unfair, ungerecht
	exchange [ɪks'tʃeɪndʒ]	austauschen
	headscarf ['hedˌskɑːf]	Kopftuch
	be dying to do sth [bi 'daɪɪŋ tə ˌduː sʌmθɪŋ]	darauf brennen, etw zu tun
	Muslim ['mʊzləm]	Muslim/in; muslimisch
	leave sb alone [ˌliːv sʌmbədi ə'ləʊn]	jdn in Ruhe lassen
	pay attention to sb/sth [ˌpeɪ ə'tenʃn tə sʌmbədi/ sʌmθɪŋ]	jdm/etw Aufmerksamkeit schenken
	the odd one out [ðɪ ˌɒd wʌn ˌaʊt]	das fünfte Rad am Wagen
	more or less [ˌmɔː ɔː 'les]	mehr oder weniger, ungefähr

Sing a song!
Weißt du eigentlich genau, was du singst, wenn du deinen englischen Lieblingssong vor dich hin trällerst? Übersetze ihn doch einfach mal. Anschließend kannst du singend Vokabeln üben!

Neue Wörter verstehen
Manche Adjektive verändern mit einer Vorsilbe wie zum Beispiel *in-* oder *un-* ihre Bedeutung. Diese **Vorsilben** weisen auf das Gegenteil hin:
tolerant – intolerant
correct – incorrect
fair – unfair
happy – unhappy
Fallen dir noch weitere Beispiele ein?

Alex wished the bullies would *leave him alone.*

My homework is *more or less* finished – I only have one question left to do.

rest [rest]	Rest	
in a way [ɪn ə ˈweɪ]	in gewisser Weise	
feel sorry for sb	Mitleid mit jdm haben	Jessica *felt sorry for* Dave
[ˌfiːl ˈsɒri fɔː ˈsʌmbədi]		because he looked sad.
seem [siːm]	scheinen	
imagination	Fantasie, Vorstellungskraft;	In her *imagination* Amanda was
[ɪˌmædʒɪˈneɪʃn]	Einbildung	a famous actress.
straight out [ˌstreɪt ˈaʊt]	offen, direkt	
Westerner [ˈwestənə]	*Bewohner/in der westlichen Welt*	

have a will of one's own — seinen eigenen Willen haben
[ˌhæv ə ˌwɪl əv ˈwʌnz ˈəʊn]

sex object [ˈseks ˌɒbdʒekt] — Sexualobjekt
cutie *(informal)* [ˈkjuːti] — Süße/r
phase [feɪz] — Phase
horrible [ˈhɒrəbl] — schrecklich

Roy did not like fish. He thought it smelled *horrible*.

sack [sæk] — Sack
be joking [biː ˈdʒəʊkɪŋ] — Spaß machen, scherzen

Did you say learning English is boring? You must *be joking*.

dress [dres] — sich kleiden; sich anziehen
offend sb [əˈfend ˌsʌmbədi] — jdn beleidigen; jdn kränken

If you call somebody a stupid old cow, you will *offend* them.

on the one hand — einerseits
[ɒn ðə ˈwʌn ˌhænd]

On the one hand bungee jumping is fun. *On the other hand* it can be dangerous.

on the other hand — andererseits
[ɒn ðiˈʌðə ˌhænd]
make [meɪk] — *hier:* lassen
fault [fɔːlt] — Schuld; Fehler
wonder [ˈwʌndə] — sich fragen

He *wondered* what the answer was.

all in all [ˌɔːl ɪn ˈɔːl] — alles in allem

I lost my homework, my head hurt and it rained on me. *All in all,* it was not a nice day.

pronounce [prəˈnaʊns] — aussprechen
belong to sth — zu etw gehören
[bɪˈlɒŋ tə ˌsʌmθɪŋ]

> [ɔː] <u>a</u>ll, f<u>au</u>lt, p<u>aw</u>, c<u>ou</u>rt

entry [ˈentri] — *hier:* Eintrag
3 view [vjuː] — *hier:* Ansicht, Meinung
4 certain [ˈsɜːtn] — sicher; gewisse(r, s), bestimmte(r, s)

baggy [ˈbægi] — *hier:* weit
5 **responsibility** — Verantwortlichkeit, Zuständigkeit; Verantwortung
[rɪˌspɒnsəˈbɪləti]

Being a parent is a big *responsibility*.

teenage [ˈtiːneɪdʒ] — jugendlich; *hier:* Teenager-
be responsible for sth — für etw verantwortlich sein; für etw haften
[biː rɪˈspɒnsəbl fə ˌsʌmθɪŋ]

Parents are *responsible for* looking after their children.

crime [kraɪm] — Verbrechen
commit [kəˈmɪt] — begehen *(Verbrechen)*

If you steal something, you are *committing* a crime.

restriction [rɪˈstrɪkʃn]	Einschränkung, Begrenzung	
passport [ˈpɑːspɔːt]	(Reise)pass	You need a *passport* if you want to go to another country.
get married [get ˈmærɪd]	heiraten	When two people love each other, they often *get married*.
permission *(no pl)* [pəˈmɪʃn]	Erlaubnis, Genehmigung	
vote [vəʊt]	wählen	Americans *vote* to decide who will become President of the USA.
club [klʌb]	*hier:* Disko(thek)	
fireworks *(pl)* [ˈfaɪəˌwɜːks]	Feuerwerkskörper	
California [ˌkæləˈfɔːniə]	Kalifornien	
serve [sɜːv]	dienen	
juror [ˈdʒʊərə]	Schöffe/Schöffin; Geschworene/r	
election [ɪˈlekʃn]	Wahl	If you win the *election*, you could become President!
helmet [ˈhelmɪt]	Helm	When riding a bike, it's best to wear a *helmet*.

6
PP

ruin [ˈruːɪn]	ruinieren, zerstören	
° binge [bɪndʒ]	zu viel von etw konsumieren	
° excessive [ɪkˈsesɪv]	übermäßig, exzessiv	
° known [nəʊn]	bekannt	
° study [ˈstʌdi]	Studie, (wissenschaftliche) Untersuchung	
° common [ˈkɒmən]	üblich, normal	
° clubbing [ˈklʌbɪŋ]	in die Disko gehen	
° consume [kənˈsjuːm]	konsumieren, zu sich nehmen	
° ambulance [ˈæmbjʊləns]	Rettungswagen	
° end up [ˌendˈʌp]	enden	
° poisoning [ˈpɔɪznɪŋ]	Vergiftung	

Partner quiz
Zu zweit macht das Vokabellernen viel mehr Spaß! Bilde einen Rätselsatz, in dem du ein englisches Wort umschreibst. Kann deine Partnerin/dein Partner das Wort erraten?

> You wear it when you ride your bike.

> A helmet?

7

underage [ˌʌndərˈeɪdʒ]	minderjährig	
clubbing [ˈklʌbɪŋ]	in die Disko gehen	
start [stɑːt]	*hier:* eröffnen, ins Leben rufen	After leaving school he *started* his own underage club.
in concert [ɪn ˈkɒnsət]	live	
doorman [ˈdɔːmən]	Türsteher	
in [ɪn]	herein	Tom came *in* through the garden door.
enter [ˈentə]	betreten	Please take off your shoes before you *enter*.
solution [səˈluːʃn]	Lösung	When there is a problem, you need a *solution*.
rise [raɪz]	(auf)steigen	
organise [ˈɔːgənaɪz]	organisieren	

8

discussion [dɪˈskʌʃn]	Diskussion, Erörterung	
argument [ˈɑːgjʊmənt]	Argument	Sue's *arguments* were very good.

9

virtual [ˈvɜːtʃʊəl]	virtuell	
give out [ˌgɪvˈaʊt]	bekannt geben, herausgeben	
personal [ˈpɜːsnəl]	persönlich; privat	

WORDS *Theme 2*

watch sth [wɒtʃ]	*hier:* auf etw achten	
password [ˈpɑːsˌwɜːd]	Passwort	
threatening [ˈθretnɪŋ]	drohend, Droh-; bedrohlich	
save [seɪv]	*hier:* speichern, sichern	If you write something on a computer, you should always *save* it.
print (out) [prɪnt]	(aus)drucken	After doing his homework on the computer, Paul *printed* it *out*.
click [klɪk]	(an)klicken, drücken	
join in [ˌdʒɔɪnˈɪn]	sich anschließen, mitmachen	Ben was all alone, so Becky asked him if he wanted to *join in* with their game of football.

10

brainstorm [ˈbreɪnˌstɔːm]	ein Brainstorming machen	
access code [ˈækses ˌkəʊd]	Zugangs-/Zugriffscode	
rate sb [reɪt]	jdn einschätzen	
the next day [ðə ˌnekstˈdeɪ]	am nächsten Tag	Mary saw a beautiful skirt in a shop. *The next day* she bought it.
send out sth [ˌsendˈaʊt sʌmθɪŋ]	etw verschicken	
no wonder [ˌnəʊ ˈwʌndə]	kein Wunder	It's *no wonder* you're fat when you eat so much.
turn out [ˌtɜːnˈaʊt]	sich herausstellen	
look at sb [ˈlʊk ət ˌsʌmbədi]	jdn anschauen	You should *look at* somebody when you are talking to them.
direct [dɪˈrekt]	direkt	Wendy wanted to get from London to New York and back quickly, so she took a *direct* flight.
suspend sb [səˈspend]	jdn zeitweilig ausschließen	
kick sb out *(informal)* [ˌkɪk sʌmbədiˈaʊt]	jdn hinauswerfen	
private [ˈpraɪvət]	privat; vertraulich	
the hard way [ðə ˈhɑːd ˌweɪ]	*hier:* auf die harte Tour	
express [ɪkˈspres]	ausdrücken	When I am happy, I *express* it with a smile.

11

helpline [ˈhelpˌlaɪn]	telefonischer Beratungsdienst; Notruf	

12

power [ˈpaʊə]	Macht; Einfluss	
law [lɔː]	Gesetz	
entrance fee [ˈentrəns ˌfiː]	Eintritt(sgeld)	

M1

racist [ˈreɪsɪst]	Rassist/in; rassistisch	If you bully somebody because of the colour of their skin, you are being *racist*.
attack [əˈtæk]	Angriff	I was hurt by his *attack*.
how to [haʊ tə]	wie man	
incident [ˈɪnsɪdnt]	Vorfall	
violent [ˈvaɪələnt]	brutal, gewalttätig	He is a very *violent* person.
racially motivated [ˈreɪʃli ˌməʊtɪveɪtɪd]	rassistisch motiviert	

WORDS THEME 2

	race [reɪs]	hier: Rasse	Every person on earth is part of the human *race*.
	riot ['raɪət]	Krawall, Unruhe	
	hit [hɪt]	*hier:* treffen, erschüttern	
	violence ['vaɪələns]	Gewalt, Gewalttätigkeit	I grew up in a family where there was a lot of *violence*.
	vehicle ['viːɪkl]	Fahrzeug	
	torch sth (informal) [tɔːtʃ]	etw in Brand setzen	
	mob [mɒb]	Mob, (Menschen)menge	
	set fire to sth [ˌset 'faɪə tə sʌmθɪŋ]	etw anzünden/in Brand stecken	
	petrol bomb ['petrəl ˌbɒm]	Molotowcocktail	
M2	tolerance ['tɒlərəns]	Toleranz	
	culture ['kʌltʃə]	Kultur	

Books, theatre, music and film are important parts of *culture*.
At school I was *leader* of the football team.

	leader ['liːdə]	Leiter/in, Führer/in	
	brilliant (informal) ['brɪljənt]	*hier:* toll, hervorragend	
	realise sth ['rɪəlaɪz]	sich einer Sache bewusst werden	

Fred *realised* he had forgotten his trousers.

	get to know sb [get tə 'nəʊ ˌsʌmbədi]	jdn kennenlernen	
	keep going [ˌkiːp 'gəʊɪŋ]	weitermachen, in Gang halten	
	even though [ˌiːvn 'ðəʊ]	selbst/auch wenn	
	background ['bæk.graʊnd]	Herkunft, Verhältnisse; Hintergrund	

Jim's parents had lots of money – he came from a rich *background*.
Being a parent can be *stressful*.

	stressful ['stresfl]	stressig, anstrengend	
	centre ['sentə]	Zentrum	
M3	in three months' time [ɪn ˌθriː mʌns 'taɪm]	in drei Monaten	
M5	court [kɔːt]	Gericht	
	deal with ['diːl wɪð]	sich kümmern um, sich befassen mit	
	offender [ə'fendə]	(Straf)täter/in	
	similar ['sɪmɪlə]	ähnlich	
	catch [kætʃ]	*hier:* festnehmen	

The police are going to *catch* the *offender*. Then he will be *punished*.

	punish ['pʌnɪʃ]	bestrafen	
	judge [dʒʌdʒ]	Richter/in	

The *judge* decides what happens in the court.

	jury ['dʒʊəri]	Schöffen; Geschworene	
	prosecutor ['prɒsɪkjuːtə]	Staatsanwalt/-anwältin, Ankläger/in	
	appear [ə'pɪə]	erscheinen	

After he had stolen the money, he had to *appear* in court.

	juvenile court [ˌdʒuːvənaɪl 'kɔːt]	Jugendgericht	
	criminal record [ˌkrɪmɪnl 'rekɔːd]	Vorstrafenregister	

WORDS · THEME 2

admit sth [əd'mɪt]	etw zugeben, etw eingestehen	He *admitted* that he had broken the window.
do wrong [duː 'rɒŋ]	etw falsch machen	
offence [ə'fens]	Straftat	Stealing is an *offence*.

shoplifting *(no pl)* ['ʃɒp,lɪftɪŋ]	Ladendiebstahl
criminal ['krɪmɪnl]	Kriminelle/r
serve [sɜːv]	dienen
sentence ['sentəns]	*hier:* Urteil, Strafe

His *sentence* was three years in prison.

apology [ə'pɒlədʒi]	Entschuldigung
community service *(no pl)* [kəm,juːnəti 'sɜːvɪs]	gemeinnützige Arbeit
essay ['eseɪ]	Essay, Aufsatz
program *(AE)* = programme *(BE)* ['prəʊgræm]	Programm
behavior *(no pl) (AE)* = **behaviour** *(BE)* [bɪ'heɪvjə]	Verhalten, Benehmen

You could get in trouble because of bad *behaviour*.

aggression [ə'greʃn]	Aggression, Aggressivität
success *(no pl)* [sək'ses]	Erfolg

Everyone was having fun at Julia's party. It was a great *success*.

statistics [stə'tɪstɪks]	Statistik
learn a lesson [,lɜːn‿ə 'lesn]	eine Lektion lernen
beer [bɪə]	Bier

They went to the pub to have a *beer*.

	threaten sb ['θretn]	jdn bedrohen
	light [laɪt]	leicht; mild
M6	pass [pɑːs]	verhängen, verabschieden, fällen
M7	amount [ə'maʊnt]	Menge
CIO	binge [bɪndʒ]	zu viel von etw konsumieren
	mouse-surfer ['maʊs‿,sɜːfə]	Maus-Surfer
	shake [ʃeɪk]	schütteln
	kiss [kɪs]	küssen
	bow [baʊ]	sich verbeugen
	depend on sth [dɪ'pend‿ɒn ,sʌmθɪŋ]	von etw abhängen
	uncomfortable [ʌn'kʌmftəbl]	unwohl, unbehaglich, unbequem

shake – shook – shaken

° list [lɪst]	auflisten
° widely-spoken [,waɪdli 'spəʊkən]	*hier:* weitverbreitet
° behaviour *(no pl)* [bɪ'heɪvjə]	Verhalten, Benehmen
° nationality [,næʃə'næləti]	Nationalität; Staatsangehörigkeit

Mache sie zu deinen Wörtern!
Am besten kannst du dir Wörter merken, die du selbst verwendet hast. Darum: Schreibe ein Gedicht oder eine verrückte Geschichte mit folgenden Wörtern aus dem *Theme: horrible, fault, passport, helmet, solution.*

Theme 3 – Express yourself!

I	skateboarding *(no pl)* ['skeɪtˌbɔːdɪŋ]	Skateboardfahren
	create [kri'eɪt]	erschaffen; gestalten
	expedition [ˌekspə'dɪʃn]	Expedition, (Forschungs)reise

1   **active** ['æktɪv]   aktiv

Brian is very *active*. He plays football, basketball and tennis.

Make an alphabet of sports:
A – American football
B – boxing, baseball
C – caving
D – ...

2	BMX biking *(no pl)* [ˌbiːem'eks ˌbaɪkɪŋ]	Fahren mit dem BMX-Rad
	kickboxing *(no pl)* ['kɪkˌbɒksɪŋ]	Kickboxen
	skydiving *(no pl)* ['skaɪˌdaɪvɪŋ]	Fallschirmspringen
	kite [kaɪt]	Drachen
	parkour *(no pl)* ['pɑːkʊə]	Parkour *(Sportart)*
	whitewater rafting *(no pl)* [ˌwaɪtwɔːtə 'rɑːftɪŋ]	Wildwasserfahren, (Wildwasser)rafting
	caving *(no pl)* ['keɪvɪŋ]	Höhlenexpedition; hier: Höhlenwandern

3	**kick** [kɪk]	treten, schießen, kicken
4	challenge ['tʃælɪndʒ]	herausfordern
	since [sɪns]	seit

Martin is late. Ted and Bill have been waiting for him *since* 10 o'clock.

	expedition [ˌekspə'dɪʃn]	Expedition, (Forschungs)reise
	wilderness ['wɪldənəs]	Wildnis
	skill [skɪl]	Fähigkeit; Geschick(lichkeit)
	develop [dɪ'veləp]	entwickeln
	ability [ə'bɪləti]	Fähigkeit; Talent
	care for sb/sth ['keə fə ˌsʌmbədi/ˌsʌmθɪŋ]	sich um jdn/etw kümmern
	canoeing *(no pl)* [kə'nuːɪŋ]	Kanufahren; Paddeln
	fun [fʌn]	lustig, witzig, spaßig
	experience [ɪk'spɪəriəns]	Erfahrung

Richard helps to *care for* his grandpa who is ill.

Going on holiday is *fun*! Visiting London is an interesting *experience*.

	go bush [ˌgəʊ 'bʊʃ]	*die Wildnis erleben*
	the same age [ðə ˌseɪm 'eɪdʒ]	gleichaltrig

Paula and Sue were born in the same year – they are *the same age*.

	dog sledding *(no pl)* ['dɒg ˌsledɪŋ]	Hundeschlittenfahren
	skiing *(no pl)* ['skiːɪŋ]	Skifahren, Skilaufen
	weeklong ['wiːkˌlɒŋ]	einwöchig
	ski [skiː]	Ski
	sled [sled]	Schlitten
	snow-covered ['snəʊˌkʌvəd]	schneebedeckt
	extreme [ɪk'striːm]	extrem
	manage ['mænɪdʒ]	führen, organisieren
	frozen ['frəʊzn]	gefroren

[iː] extr**e**me, sk**i**, l**ea**ve, f**ee**l, **ea**st

WORDS THEME 3

5

Get outta here! *(informal)* [ˌget‿ˈaʊtə hɪə]	Verschwinde(t)!
punk *(informal)* [pʌŋk]	*hier:* Mistkerl; Randalierer/in
property [ˈprɒpəti]	Eigentum
cop *(informal)* [kɒp]	Bulle
useless [ˈjuːsləs]	zu nichts zu gebrauchen
troublemaker [ˈtrʌblˌmeɪkə]	Unruhestifter/in
public [ˈpʌblɪk]	öffentlich

Can you sort these words in alphabetical order?
skill, develop, ability, experience, sled, ski, since, kick, active, extreme

At the train station there is a *public* toilet which anyone can use.

ramp [ræmp]	Rampe
in the country [ɪn ðə ˈkʌntri]	auf dem Land
immediately [ɪˈmiːdiətli]	sofort

Our train is leaving in 10 minutes! We have to go to the station *immediately*!

thrill [θrɪl]	Nervenkitzel, Kick
sidewalk *(AE)* [ˈsaɪdˌwɔːk]	Bürgersteig
rail [reɪl]	Geländer

In high places there is often a safety *rail*. If you hold onto it, it will stop you from falling off.

| **Canada** [ˈkænədə] | Kanada |
| **arrest sb** [əˈrest ˌsʌmbədi] | jdn verhaften |

The police are *arresting* a man because he was fighting.

skate [skeɪt]	skaten, Skateboard fahren
charge sb (with sth) [ˈtʃɑːdʒ ˌsʌmbədi]	jdn (einer Sache) beschuldigen; jdn (wegen einer Sache) anklagen
trespassing [ˈtrespəsɪŋ]	unbefugtes Betreten
vandalism [ˈvændəˌlɪzm]	Vandalismus, Sachbeschädigung
fine [faɪn]	Geldstrafe, Bußgeld

If you do something illegal, you might have to pay a *fine*.

keep doing sth [kiːp ˈduːɪŋ ˌsʌmθɪŋ]	etw weiter tun; *hier:* etw wiederholt/immer wieder tun
cast [kɑːst]	Gips(verband)
bone [bəʊn]	Knochen

If you *keep practising* your English, you will become very good at it.

The dog is trying to find his *bone*.

| **bit** [bɪt] | Stück, Stückchen |
| **screw** [skruː] | Schraube |

You might use a *screw* if you are building something.

yeah *(informal)* [jeə]	ja
so what? *(informal)* [ˌsəʊ ˈwɒt]	na und?
be worth sth [biː ˈwɜːθ ˌsʌmθɪŋ]	etw wert sein
energy [ˈenədʒi]	Energie, Kraft
professional [prəˈfeʃnəl]	professionell, Profi-
risk [rɪsk]	Risiko, Gefahr
professional [prəˈfeʃnəl]	Profi

This *is worth* a lot of money!

6

| **bother sb** [ˈbɒðə ˌsʌmbədi] | jdn stören; jdn belästigen |

When I play loud music, it *bothers* my parents.

7	basic [ˈbeɪsɪk]	grundlegend, wesentlich; Grund-	
	record [ˈrekɔːd]	Rekord	
8	**look** [lʊk]	Aussehen; Blick	They are wearing the same clothes, so they have the same *look*.
	tree hugger [ˈtriː ˌhʌgə]	Öko	
	rasta [ˈræstə]	Rasta, Rastafari	
10	forum [ˈfɔːrəm]	Forum	
	wherever [werˈevə]	wo(hin) auch immer	*Wherever* you are in the world, you can meet interesting people.
	stare at sb/sth [ˈsteəˌæt ˌsʌmbədi, ˌsʌmθɪŋ]	jdn/etw anstarren	It is unhealthy to just *stare* at the TV all day.
	be wrong [biː ˈrɒŋ]	sich irren	If you think 6 + 11 = 14, you are *wrong*.
	truth [truːθ]	Wahrheit	
	provoke [prəˈvəʊk]	provozieren	
	necklace [ˈnekləs]	(Hals)kette	That *necklace* looks expensive!
	worship [ˈwɜːʃɪp]	anbeten, verehren	
	death [deθ]	Tod	
	fear [fɪə]	fürchten, befürchten	
	accept [əkˈsept]	annehmen; *hier:* akzeptieren	
	optimistic [ˌɒptɪˈmɪstɪk]	optimistisch, zuversichtlich	
	personality [ˌpɜːsəˈnæləti]	Persönlichkeit, Charakter	I like him, he has a nice *personality*.
11	° breathe [briːð]	atmen	
	° insecure [ˌɪnsɪˈkjʊə]	unsicher	
	° pain [peɪn]	Schmerz, Leid	
	° no matter (what/who) [ˌnəʊ ˈmætə]	ganz gleich/egal (was/wer)	
	° bring down sb [ˌbrɪŋ ˈdaʊn sʌmbədi]	jdn deprimieren	
	° single [ˈsɪŋgl]	einzelne(r, s)	
	° be delirious [biː dɪˈlɪriəs]	im Delirium sein; *hier:* verrückt sein	
	° be consumed [biː kənˈsjuːmd]	versunken sein	
	° doom [duːm]	(schlimmes) Schicksal; *hier:* Untergangsstimmung	
	° emptiness *(no pl)* [ˈemptɪnəs]	Leere	
	° gone [gɒn]	weg	
	° puzzle [ˈpʌzl]	Puzzle; Rätsel	
	° undone [ʌnˈdʌn]	unvollendet; ruiniert	
	° tune [tjuːn]	Melodie	
	° shine [ʃaɪn]	scheinen *(Sonne)*	*shine* – shone – shone
	° awake [əˈweɪk]	aufwachen, erwachen	*awake* – awoke – awoken
PP	° well-known [ˌwelˈnəʊn]	berühmt, (allgemein) bekannt	
	° come up [ˌkʌmˈˈʌp]	entstehen	
	° Britain [ˈbrɪtn]	Großbritannien	
	° individual [ˌɪndɪˈvɪdʒuəl]	individuell; eigen	
	° either ... or ... [ˌaɪðə ... ˈɔː]	entweder ... oder ...	
	° shock [ʃɒk]	schockieren	

Zirkeltraining
Manchmal muss man den Kreislauf erst in Schwung bringen, damit man wieder konzentriert lernen kann. Für das Zirkeltraining schreibst du schwierige Wörter oder Formulierungen auf Zettel und verteilst diese dann in deinem Zimmer oder in der Wohnung. Dann gehst du an alle Stationen und formulierst Sätze mit den Wörtern auf den Zetteln. Kniebeugen nicht vergessen!

° society [səˈsaɪəti] — Gesellschaft
° individual [ˌɪndɪˈvɪdʒuəl] — Individuum, (selbstständige) Persönlichkeit

° exist [ɪgˈzɪst] — existieren, vorkommen
° beauty [ˈbjuːti] — Schönheit
° strength [streŋθ] — Stärke, Kraft

M1 placemat [ˈpleɪsˌmæt] — Set, Platzdeckchen
M2 route [ruːt] — Route, Strecke, Verlauf
cleaning company [ˈkliːnɪŋ ˌkʌmpəni] — Reinigungsunternehmen
human [ˈhjuːmən] — menschlich

power [ˈpaʊə] — *hier:* Kraft, Stärke

physical [ˈfɪzɪkl] — körperlich, physisch
challenge [ˈtʃælɪndʒ] — Herausforderung

raise interest [ˌreɪz ˈɪntrəst] — Interesse (er)wecken
save [seɪv] — *hier:* sparen

wooden [ˈwʊdn] — hölzern, Holz-

pedal boat [ˈpedl ˌbəʊt] — Tretboot
only [ˈəʊnli] — *hier:* erst
drunk [drʌŋk] — Betrunkene/r
hit sb [hɪt] — *hier:* jdn anfahren
finished [ˈfɪnɪʃt] — fertig, beendet

thief *(pl thieves)* [θiːf] — Dieb
signal [ˈsɪgnl] — Signal
radio [ˈreɪdiəʊ] — *hier:* Funkgerät
lifejacket [ˈlaɪfˌdʒækɪt] — Schwimmweste

water maker [ˈwɔːtə ˌmeɪkə] — *Gerät, das aus Meerwasser Trinkwasser produziert*

solar panel [ˌsəʊlə ˈpænəl] — Sonnenkollektor
Indonesia [ˌɪndəʊˈniːʒə] — Indonesien
so far [ˈsəʊ fɑː] — bisher, bis jetzt

attack [əˈtæk] — angreifen
kayak [ˈkaɪæk] — Kajak
paddle [ˈpædl] — Paddel

rebuild [ˌriːˈbɪld] — wieder aufbauen
hit [hɪt] — *hier:* treffen, erschüttern
the Himalayas [ðə ˌhɪməˈleɪəz] — der Himalaja
downhill [ˌdaʊnˈhɪl] — bergab führend
break down [ˌbreɪk ˈdaʊn] — zusammenbrechen
cyclist [ˈsaɪklɪst] — Radfahrer/in
spare part [ˌspeə ˈpɑːt] — Ersatzteil
Egypt [ˈiːdʒɪpt] — Ägypten

What are the opposites of these words?
be right – ???
useful – ???
birth – ???
passive – ???

This thing is not *human*!
He has enough *power* to lift heavy weights.

Climbing Mount Everest is very difficult – it is a *challenge*.

Tom wants to *save* enough money to buy a bike.
This bench is made of wood – it is a *wooden* bench.

I have done all my homework – it is *finished*!
A *thief* is stealing her bag!

If you are on a boat, it is safest to wear a *lifejacket*.

I am enjoying the film *so far*, but I haven't watched all of it yet.

They are using *paddles* to move their boat.

The *cyclist* is riding his bike.

	hardly ['hɑːdli]	kaum	The carpet is so heavy, he can *hardly* carry it.
	Egyptian [i'dʒɪpʃn]	Ägypter/in; ägyptisch	
	military ['mɪlɪtri]	Militär	
	spy [spaɪ]	Spion/in	
	visa ['viːzə]	Visum	
	run out [ˌrʌnˈaʊt]	ablaufen, auslaufen	
	difficulty ['dɪfɪklti]	Schwierigkeit, Problem	
	face [feɪs]	etw ausgesetzt sein, mit etw konfrontiert sein	
	definition [ˌdefə'nɪʃn]	Definition, Erklärung	In a dictionary, you can look up the *definition* of a word.

	plastic ['plæstɪk]	Plastik, Kunststoff	
	awful ['ɔːfl]	furchtbar, schrecklich	The weather outside is *awful*. You can use a telephone to *communicate* with other people.
	communicate [kə'mjuːnɪkeɪt]	sich verständigen, kommunizieren	
M4	return [rɪ'tɜːn]	Rückkehr	
M5	expert ['ekspɜːt]	Experte/Expertin	
	contact ['kɒntækt]	Kontakt	
M6	adventurous [əd'ventʃrəs]	abenteuerlich	
	draft [drɑːft]	Entwurf, Konzept	
	final ['faɪnl]	letzte(r, s); endgültig	
	copy ['kɒpi]	Abschrift; Exemplar	
M7	glamorous ['glæmərəs]	glamourös	She is a *glamorous* model. If there is more than one of something, it is not *unique*.
	unique [juː'niːk]	einzigartig	

M8	close [kləʊs]	*hier:* genau	
	translation [træns'leɪʃn]	Übersetzung	
	star [stɑː]	in einem Film/Theaterstück auftreten	He is *starring* in a play.
	album ['ælbəm]	(Musik)album	
	release [rɪ'liːs]	herausbringen, veröffentlichen	
	genie ['dʒiːni]	(Flaschen)geist	
	blonde [blɒnd]	blond	
	straight [streɪt]	glatt *(Haar)*	
	girly ['gɜːli]	mädchenhaft	
	therefore ['ðeəfɔː]	deshalb, daher	I am tired, *therefore* I will go to bed.
	strip [strɪp]	sich entkleiden	
	get rid of sth [get 'rɪd əv ˌsʌmθɪŋ]	etw loswerden	That is not an environmentally friendly way to *get rid of* your rubbish.
	braided ['breɪdɪd]	geflochten	
	dye [daɪ]	färben	
	definitely ['defnətli]	eindeutig, definitiv	I love films, so I *definitely* want to go to the cinema!
	release [rɪ'liːs]	Erleichterung	

WORDS Theme 3

WORDS THEME 3

	empowered [ɪmˈpaʊəd]	(mental) gestärkt
	award [əˈwɔːd]	Auszeichnung, Preis
	no matter [ˌnəʊ ˈmætə]	ganz gleich/egal
	elegant [ˈelɪɡənt]	elegant
	give birth to a child [gɪv ˌbɜːθˌtʊˌə ˈtʃaɪld]	ein Kind zur Welt bringen
	conjunction [kənˈdʒʌŋkʃn]	Konjunktion
M9	style [staɪl]	Stil
C10	fashion [ˈfæʃn]	Mode
	style [staɪl]	Stil
	the British (pl) [ðə ˈbrɪtɪʃ]	die Briten
	understatement [ˈʌndəˌsteɪtmənt]	Untertreibung, Understatement
	play down sth [ˌpleɪ ˈdaʊn sʌmθɪŋ]	etw herunterspielen
°	ski [skiː]	Ski fahren, Ski laufen
°	North Pole [ˌnɔːθ ˈpəʊl]	Nordpol
°	impossible [ɪmˈpɒsəbl]	unmöglich
°	lick [lɪk]	(ab)lecken
°	worldwide [ˌwɜːldˈwaɪd]	weltweit
°	appear [əˈpɪə]	erscheinen
°	the latest [ðə ˈleɪtɪst]	der/die/das letzte, der/die/das neueste
°	combination [ˌkɒmbɪˈneɪʃn]	Kombination
°	karate (no pl) [kəˈrɑːti]	Karate
°	boxing (no pl) [ˈbɒksɪŋ]	Boxen
°	originally [əˈrɪdʒnəli]	ursprünglich
°	worthless [ˈwɜːθləs]	wertlos

Konditionstraining
Schreibe einen kleinen Text mit den Wörtern, die du lernen willst. Die Liste hängst du in deinem Zimmer auf – möglichst weit weg von deinem Schreibtisch.
Gehe zu dem Blatt und merke dir einen Teil des Textes. Setze dich wieder an deinen Schreibtisch und notiere, was du behalten hast.
Das wiederholst du, bis du den gesamten Text geschrieben hast. Um zu sehen, ob du alles richtig geschrieben hast, gehst du wieder los …

Kim's game
Schreibe zehn Vokabeln auf ein Blatt Papier. Sieh dir die Wörter drei Minuten lang an. Dann drehst du das Blatt um. Versuche nun, alle Wörter auswendig auf die Rückseite zu schreiben. Wie viele hast du dir gemerkt?

Bilder fürs Gedächtnis
Manche Wörter kann man sich mithilfe von kleinen Zeichnungen leichter merken. Sieh dir z. B. das Bild zu *run* an. Fallen dir andere Wörter ein, die du zeichnen kannst?

Theme 4 – Food for thought

I	food for thought [fuːd fə ˈθɔːt]	Stoff zum Nachdenken	
	thought [θɔːt]	Nachdenken, Überlegen; Gedanke	
	junk food [ˈdʒʌŋk fuːd]	Schnellgerichte; ungesundes Essen, Fraß	
	ban sth [ˈbæn ˌsʌmθɪŋ]	etw verbieten	
	canteen [kænˈtiːn]	Kantine; Mensa	
	topic [ˈtɒpɪk]	Thema	
1	cereal [ˈsɪəriəl]	Getreide(sorte); Frühstückszerealien	Many people eat *cereal* for their breakfast.
	seaweed [ˈsiːˌwiːd]	Seegras, (See)tang	
	tofu [ˈtəʊfuː]	Tofu	
	cream cheese [ˌkriːm ˈtʃiːz]	Frischkäse	*Cream cheese* is a sweet, soft, white kind of cheese.
2	habit [ˈhæbɪt]	Gewohnheit	
3	following [ˈfɒləʊɪŋ]	folgende(r, s)	
	carbohydrate [ˌkɑːbəʊˈhaɪdreɪt]	Kohle(n)hydrat	Bread, pasta, potatoes and rice have got many *carbohydrates*.
	calorie [ˈkæləri]	Kalorie	
	protein [ˈprəʊtiːn]	Eiweiß, Protein	Chicken, fish and cheese have got much *protein*.
	sugary [ˈʃʊɡəri]	zuckerhaltig	
	fat-reduced [ˌfætrɪˈdjuːst]	fettreduziert	If you want to lose weight, you could eat *fat-reduced* food.
	vitamin [ˈvɪtəmɪn]	Vitamin	You can find many *vitamins* in fruit.
	mineral [ˈmɪnrəl]	Mineral	
4	eatwell plate [ˈiːtwel pleɪt]	*den täglichen Nahrungsbedarf anzeigendes Kreisdiagramm*	
	pie chart [ˈpaɪ tʃɑːt]	Tortendiagramm	
	section [ˈsekʃn]	Bereich, Teil	
	non-dairy [ˌnɒn ˈdeəri]	milchfrei	
	source [sɔːs]	Quelle	
	high (in) [haɪ]	reich (an)	
	fat [fæt]	Fett	It is dangerous to always eat foods with lots of *fat* in them.
	dairy food [ˈdeəri fuːd]	Milchprodukt	Milk, butter and cheese are examples of *dairy food*.
	less [les]	weniger	
	fizzy drink [ˌfɪzi ˈdrɪŋk]	süßes, kohlensäurehaltiges Getränk	
	possible [ˈpɒsəbl]	möglich	
	perfect [ˈpɜːfɪkt]	perfekt	
	diet [ˈdaɪət]	Nahrung, Ernährung; Diät	
5	canteen [kænˈtiːn]	Kantine; Mensa	Many pupils eat in the *canteen* at school.
	junk food [ˈdʒʌŋk fuːd]	Schnellgerichte; ungesundes Essen, Fraß	Many teenagers love *junk food*, like burgers, although it is unhealthy.

	ban sth [ˈbæn ˌsʌmθɪŋ]	etw verbieten	
	government [ˈgʌvənmənt]	Regierung	The *government* makes rules for the country.
	chef [ʃef]	Koch/Köchin	A *chef's* job is to cook food.
	lead [liːd]	(an)führen, leiten	*lead* – led – led
	campaign [kæmˈpeɪn]	Kampagne, Aktion	
	overweight [ˌəʊvəˈweɪt]	übergewichtig	He eats too much, so he is *overweight*.
	twice [twaɪs]	zweimal	*twice* = two times
	reaction (to) [riˈækʃn]	Reaktion (auf)	
	law [lɔː]	Gesetz	
	boss [bɒs]	Chef	When I am at work, I have to do what my *boss* tells me.

6	radio station [ˈreɪdiəʊ ˌsteɪʃn]	Radiosender	
	make sure [meɪk ˈʃɔː]	sich versichern, darauf achten	
	not see the point [nɒt ˌsiː ðə ˈpɔɪnt]	keinen Sinn in etw sehen	
	memory [ˈmemri]	Gedächtnis	
	serve [sɜːv]	*hier:* servieren	
	diet [ˈdaɪət]	Nahrung, Ernährung; Diät	It is important to eat a healthy *diet*.

	move out [ˌmuːvˈaʊt]	ausziehen
PP	° one in six [ˌwʌn ɪn ˈsɪks]	eine(r,s) von sechs
	° how to [haʊ tə]	wie man
	° series [ˈsɪəriːz]	Serie, Reihe
	° set [set]	*hier:* setzen
	° standard [ˈstændəd]	Standard; Richtlinie; Wertvorstellung
	° support *(no pl)* [səˈpɔːt]	Unterstützung
	° it takes [ɪt ˌteɪks]	man braucht
	° expect [ɪkˈspekt]	erwarten
	° massive [ˈmæsɪv]	riesig, enorm
7	include [ɪnˈkluːd]	beinhalten, einschließen, aufnehmen
	contact sb [ˈkɒntækt ˌsʌmbədi]	jdn kontaktieren, sich mit jdm in Verbindung setzen
8	aerobics *(no pl)* [eəˈrəʊbɪks]	Aerobic(kurs)
	therapy [ˈθerəpi]	Therapie, Behandlung
9	**height** [haɪt]	(Körper)größe; Höhe

False friends – nicht verwechseln!
Im Englischen gibt es viele Wörter, die deutschen Wörtern zwar sehr ähnlich sehen, aber eine ganz andere Bedeutung haben. Man nennt sie deshalb *false friends* (falsche Freunde).
Für diese Wörter kannst du dir ein Merkblatt „Vorsicht Falle" anlegen.
chef = Koch (NICHT: Chef)
capital = Hauptstadt (NICHT: Kapital)
also = auch (NICHT: also)
map = Karte (NICHT: Mappe)
become = werden (NICHT: bekommen)
kind = Art, Sorte (NICHT: Kind)
floor = Boden; Stockwerk (NICHT: Flur)

The man on the left is taller: He has a greater *height*.

	lunchtime [ˈlʌntʃˌtaɪm]	Mittagszeit; Mittagspause
	slice [slaɪs]	Scheibe
	melon [ˈmelən]	Melone
	boiled [bɔɪld]	gekocht

She needs *boiled* water to make a cup of tea.

	do exercises [duː ˈeksəsaɪzɪz]	Sport treiben
	sunbathe [ˈsʌnˌbeɪð]	sonnenbaden
	awful [ˈɔːfl]	furchtbar, schrecklich
	skinny [ˈskɪni]	dünn, mager

This fish smells *awful*!
skinny = very thin

all day [ˌɔ:l 'deɪ] — den ganzen Tag

At the weekend, I sometimes sleep *all day*.
Both sides *weigh* the same.

weigh [weɪ] — wiegen
anorexia *(no pl)* [ˌænə'reksiə] — Magersucht, Anorexie
take over [ˌteɪkˌ'əʊvə] — (die Macht) übernehmen
sick [sɪk] — krank
put on weight [ˌpʊtˌ'ɒn ˌweɪt] — zunehmen

dead [ded] — tot
within [wɪð'ɪn] — innerhalb

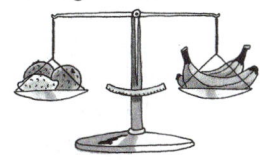

I am late – I have to be at school *within* the next ten minutes!

anorexic [ˌænə'reksɪk] — magersüchtig

She is too thin because she is *anorexic*.

live [lɪv] — *hier:* überleben
psychologist [saɪ'kɒlədʒɪst] — Psychologe/Psychologin
similar ['sɪmɪlə] — ähnlich

Two things are *similar* if they are almost the same.

high-calorie [ˌhaɪ 'kæləri] — kalorienreich
lie down [ˌlaɪ 'daʊn] — sich hinlegen
therapist ['θerəpɪst] — Therapeut/in

Talking to a *therapist* might make you feel better.

hell [hel] — Hölle
have therapy [ˌhæv 'θerəpi] — in Therapie/Behandlung sein

cured [kjʊəd] — geheilt
10 **close** [kləʊs] — *hier:* genau
illness ['ɪlnəs] — Krankheit, Erkrankung

She is in hospital because she has an *illness*.
He *reacts* in an angry way.

react [ri'ækt] — reagieren
11 **keep a diary** [ˌki:pˌə 'daɪəri] — (ein) Tagebuch führen
direct speech [dɪˌrekt 'spi:tʃ] — direkte Rede
reported speech [rɪˌpɔ:tɪd 'spi:tʃ] — indirekte Rede

the day before [ðə ˌdeɪ bɪ'fɔ:] — am vorherigen Tag
what else [wɒtˌ'els] — was noch, was sonst
missing ['mɪsɪŋ] — fehlend
expert ['ekspɜ:t] — Experte/Expertin

13 **thick** [θɪk] — dick
M2 **extra** ['ekstrə] — besonders

thick ≠ thin
I am very hungry, so tonight I will make my dinner *extra* big!

portion ['pɔ:ʃn] — Portion
dream [dri:m] — träumen

When I sleep, I *dream* that I am Tarzan, but I know my dream will never *come true*.

come true [kʌm 'tru:] — wahr werden
known [nəʊn] — bekannt
take sth to the extreme [ˌteɪk sʌmθɪŋ tə ði ˌɪk'stri:m] — etwas auf die Spitze treiben

extreme [ɪk'stri:m] — Extrem; äußerstes Ende
best-known [ˌbest'nəʊn] — bekannteste(r,s)
oz (= ounce) [aʊns] — Unze *(Maßeinheit)*
for free [fə 'fri:] — gratis, umsonst

If you don't have to pay for something, you get it *for free*.

flatline *(informal)* ['flæt,laɪn]   Todes-
fries *(AE, pl)* [fraɪz]   Pommes frites
fry [fraɪ]   frittieren, braten   For breakfast, I usually *fry* some eggs.

pure [pjʊə]   rein, pur   The water is *pure* and clean.
lard [lɑːd]   Schweinefett
jolt [dʒəʊlt]   Schock
quadruple ['kwɒdrʊpl]   vierfach
level ['levl]   Ebene, Stockwerk   The top *level* of this building is very high up.

heart attack ['hɑːt‿ə,tæk]   Herzinfarkt, Herzanfall
lb (= pound) [paʊnd]   Pfund *(Maßeinheit)*
Latin ['lætɪn]   Latein; lateinisch
M3 totally ['təʊtəli]   völlig, total
at once [ət 'wʌns]   auf einmal
no way [,nəʊ 'weɪ]   auf keinen Fall
appetite ['æpɪtaɪt]   Appetit   I eat a lot because I have a big *appetite*.

matter [mætə]   von Bedeutung sein
starve [stɑːv]   (ver)hungern   If you don't eat anything, you will *starve*.

barely ['beəli]   kaum
over-eat [,əʊvər'iːt]   zu viel essen
waste *(no pl)* [weɪst]   Verschwendung
option ['ɒpʃn]   Wahl, Möglichkeit, Option
waste [weɪst]   verschwenden
annoy [ə'nɔɪ]   ärgern, nerven   The cat and the dog *annoy* each other.

M4 interest sb ['ɪntrəst]   jdn interessieren, bei jdm Interesse wecken

M5 Europe ['jʊərəp]   Europa
think bubble ['θɪŋk ,bʌbl]   Gedankenblase
M6 novel ['nɒvl]   Roman   I am reading a really exciting *novel*.

publish ['pʌblɪʃ]   veröffentlichen
make sb aware of sth [,meɪk sʌmbədi‿ə'weə‿əv sʌmθɪŋ]   jdm etw bewusst machen
living conditions *(pl)* ['lɪvɪŋ‿kən,dɪʃnz]   Lebensbedingungen
at that time [ət 'ðæt‿,taɪm]   zu dieser Zeit
orphaned ['ɔːfnd]   elternlos   A child with no mother or father is *orphaned*.

end up [,end‿'ʌp]   enden
workhouse ['wɜːkhaʊs]   Armenhaus
go mad (with hunger) [,gəʊ 'mæd (wɪð ,hʌŋgə)]   (vor Hunger) verrückt werden
hunger ['hʌŋgə]   Hunger   *Hunger* is a huge problem in Africa, where there is not much food.

porridge ['pɒrɪdʒ]   Porridge, Haferbrei
desperate ['despɹət]   verzweifelt
master ['mɑːstə]   Hausherr

	no one [ˈnəʊ wʌn]	keiner, niemand	*No one* came to my party – I was all alone.
	dare [deə]	wagen, sich trauen	Will he *dare* to jump?

	roar [rɔː]	brüllen	
	sir [sɜː]	Herr *(Anrede)*	
M7	**repeat** [rɪˈpiːt]	wiederholen	
	caption [ˈkæpʃn]	Bildunterschrift; Titel	
	cellar [ˈselə]	Keller	There is a *cellar* under my house.

coffin

	undertaker [ˈʌndəˌteɪkə]	Leichenbestatter/in; Bestattungsinstitut	
	coffin [ˈkɒfɪn]	Sarg	
	read out [ˌriːdˈaʊt]	(laut) vorlesen	
M8	pass [pɑːs]	*hier:* vergehen, vorübergehen	
	orphan [ˈɔːfn]	Waise, Waisenkind	An *orphan* is a child with no parents.

hurry on [ˈhʌriˌɒn]	weitereilen	
snub-nosed [ˌsnʌbˈnəʊzd]	stupsnasig, mit einer Stupsnase	
rough-looking [ˈrʌfˌlʊkɪŋ]	hart und mitgenommen aussehend	
close by [ˌkləʊsˈbaɪ]	ganz in der Nähe, in unmittelbarer Nähe	

[ʌ] h**u**nger, sn**u**b-nosed, r**ou**gh-looking, c**o**me

look sb up and down [ˌlʊk sʌmbədiˌˌʌpˌənˈdaʊn]	jdn von oben bis unten mustern		
greet [griːt]	(be)grüßen		You can *greet* people by saying hello to them.
small [smɔːl]	*hier:* leise		
voice [vɔɪs]	Stimme		She has a wonderful singing *voice*.

in surprise [ɪn səˈpraɪz]	überrascht, erstaunt	
kind [kaɪnd]	nett, freundlich	
be as good as one's word [biːˌəz ˌɡʊdˌəz wʌnzˈwɜːd]	sein Wort halten	
wolf down [ˌwʊlfˈdaʊn]	verschlingen, hinunterschlingen	
rueful [ˈruːfl]	reuevoll	
suppose [səˈpəʊz]	denken, annehmen, vermuten	It's late, so I *suppose* I should go to bed.
gentleman [ˈdʒentlmən]	(vornehmer) Herr	
for nothing [fə ˈnʌθɪŋ]	umsonst	I didn't pay for this apple – the shop assistant gave it to me *for nothing*!
grateful [ˈɡreɪtfl]	dankbar	You should say thank you to show that you are *grateful*.

	artful dodger [ˌɑːtfl ˈdɒdʒə]	durchtriebenes Bürschchen
M9	leave out [ˌliːvˈaʊt]	auslassen, weglassen
	relative pronoun [ˌrelətɪv ˈprəʊnaʊn]	Relativpronomen

M10	lucky [ˈlʌki]	glücklich; Glück bringend	
	pick [pɪk]	(Aus)wahl	
	take in sb [ˌteɪk ˌɪn sʌmbədi]	jdn (bei sich) aufnehmen	
	pick pockets [ˈpɪk ˌpɒkɪts]	Taschendiebstahl begehen	*pick pockets* = steal things from people's pockets

M11	research *(no pl)* [riˈsɜːtʃ]	Forschung, Erforschung
	housing *(no pl)* [ˈhaʊzɪŋ]	Wohnungen, Unterkünfte
C10	daily [ˈdeɪli]	täglich
	rather [ˈrɑːðə]	eher
	absolutely [ˈæbsəluːtli]	absolut, völlig
	° B.C. (= before Christ) [biˌfɔː ˈkraɪst]	v. Chr.
	° North American [ˌnɔːθ əˈmerɪkən]	Nordamerikaner/in; nordamerikanisch
	° pepperoni [ˌpepəˈrəʊni]	Peperoni
	° topping [ˈtɒpɪŋ]	Garnierung, Belag
	° bee [biː]	Biene
	° produce [prəˈdjuːs]	herstellen, erzeugen, produzieren
	° to [tə]	*hier:* bis (zu)
	° honey [ˈhʌni]	Honig
	° tablespoon [ˈteɪblˌspuːn]	Esslöffel
	° orange [ˈɒrɪndʒ]	orange(farben)

Schwierige Wörter
Wenn du merkst, dass du bei der Schreibweise einiger englischer Wörter Schwierigkeiten hast, kannst du Folgendes tun: Schreibe das Wort auf ein großes Blatt und markiere die Stelle, die dir Probleme macht. Hänge das Blatt in deinem Zimmer auf. Du wirst merken, dass du das Wort bald richtig schreiben kannst!

Neue Wörter verstehen
Manche neuen Wörter enthalten Elemente, die du schon kennst.
An **Nachsilben** wie *-ship, -tion, -ness* siehst du beispielsweise, dass es sich bei dem betreffenden Wort um ein Substantiv *(noun)* handelt. Du kennst ja die deutschen Entsprechungen wie -schaft, -heit, -keit, -ung.
Hier einige Beispiele:
championship, sportsmanship, friendship, imagination, expedition, description, celebration, wilderness, illness

Theme 5 – Making a living

1

make a living [ˌmeɪk‿ə ˈlɪvɪŋ]	seinen Lebensunterhalt verdienen	
work experience *(no pl)* [ˈwɜːk‿ɪkˌspɪərɪəns]	Praktikum; Berufserfahrung	
get into debt [ˌget‿ɪntə ˈdet]	Schulden machen, sich verschulden	
application form [ˌæplɪˈkeɪʃn ˌfɔːm]	Bewerbungsformular	Make an alphabet of jobs.
abroad [əˈbrɔːd]	im Ausland	
support [səˈpɔːt]	(unter)stützen	
the homeless *(pl)* [ðə ˈhəʊmləs]	die Obdachlosen	

2

nursery teacher [ˈnɜːsəri ˌtiːtʃə]	Erzieher/in	A *nursery teacher* looks after and teaches small children.
check-in agent [ˈtʃekɪnˌeɪdʒnt]	*Mitarbeiter/in am Check-in-Schalter am Flughafen*	
builder [ˈbɪldə]	Bauarbeiter/in	A *builder* builds houses and other buildings.
scaffolder [ˈskæfəʊldə]	Gerüstbauer/in	
scaffold [ˈskæfəʊld]	Gerüst	
shift [ˈʃɪft]	Schicht	
electrician [ɪˌlekˈtrɪʃn]	Elektriker/in	
vet's assistant [ˈvets‿əˌsɪstnt]	Tierarzthelfer/in	
painter [ˈpeɪntə]	Maler/in; Anstreicher/in; Lackierer/in	When she grows up, she wants to be a *painter*.
office administrator [ˌɒfɪs‿ədˈmɪnɪˌstreɪtə]	Bürokaufmann/Bürokauffrau	
security guard [sɪˈkjʊərəti ˌgɑːd]	Sicherheitsbedienstete/r	
warehouse worker [ˈweəˌhaʊs ˌwɜːkə]	Lagerist/in	
graduate [ˈgrædʒueɪt]	die Abschlussprüfung bestehen	Last year my sister *graduated* from college.
grade [greɪd]	Klasse(nstufe)	
do military service [duː ˌmɪlɪtri ˈsɜːvɪs]	Wehrdienst leisten	After I finish school I am going to *do military service*.
afterwards [ˈɑːftəwədz]	danach, anschließend; später	
do one's A levels [duː wʌnz‿ˈeɪ ˌlevlz]	das Abitur machen	
gap year [ˈgæp jɪə]	*Zwischenjahr, in dem gereist oder gearbeitet wird*	
training [ˈtreɪnɪŋ]	Ausbildung; Schulung	I want to do special *training*, so I can become a firefighter.
do civilian service [duː səˌvɪliən ˈsɜːvɪs]	Zivildienst leisten	After I finish school I want to *do civilian service* for a year.
do volunteer work [duː ˈvɒləntɪə ˌwɜːk]	Freiwilligenarbeit leisten	
do vocational training [duː vəʊˌkeɪʃnəl ˈtreɪnɪŋ]	eine Berufsausbildung machen	I want to *do vocational training*, so I can learn how to be a car mechanic.

WORDS THEME 5

3 | score [skɔː] | punkten |
test [test]	Prüfung, Test; Klassenarbeit
panic [ˈpænɪk]	in Panik geraten
grade [greɪd]	*hier:* Note
behave [bɪˈheɪv]	sich verhalten, sich benehmen	Sometimes my brother and I *behave* very badly.
reliable [rɪˈlaɪəbl]	verlässlich, zuverlässig	Let's ask Mary to look after the children. She's very *reliable*.
stamina *(no pl)* [ˈstæmɪnə]	Durchhaltevermögen, Ausdauer
flexible [ˈfleksəbl]	flexibel, anpassungsfähig
creative [kriˈeɪtɪv]	kreativ	She is very *creative* – she likes making things and has lots of interesting ideas.
communicative [kəˈmjuːnɪkətɪv]	mitteilsam, gesprächig
punctual [ˈpʌŋktʃuəl]	pünktlich	He is never *punctual* – he is always late!
on one's own [ɒn wʌnzˈˌəʊn]	allein(e)	He does not want to play with the others – he wants to be *on his own*.
hardly ever [ˌhɑːdliˈˌevə]	kaum
conversation [ˌkɒnvəˈseɪʃn]	Gespräch, Unterhaltung

4 | **CV (= curriculum vitae)** [ˌsiːˈviː (= kəˌrɪkjʊləm ˈviːtaɪ)] | Lebenslauf |
centre [ˈsentə]	Zentrum, Center
present [ˈpreznt]	Gegenwart
primary school [ˈpraɪməri ˌskuːl]	Grundschule	Children usually go to *primary school* between the ages of 4 and 11.
excellent [ˈeksələnt]	ausgezeichnet, hervorragend	I loved the film – it was *excellent*!
teamwork [ˈtiːmˌwɜːk]	Teamarbeit
communication [kəˌmjuːnɪˈkeɪʃn]	Kommunikation	*Communication* is important – you should try and discuss things with other people.
wide [waɪd]	breit; breit gefächert
knowledge *(no pl)* [ˈnɒlɪdʒ]	Wissen, Kenntnisse
material [məˈtɪəriəl]	Material
reference [ˈrefrəns]	Empfehlungsschreiben, (Arbeits)zeugnis, Referenz
available [əˈveɪləbl]	verfügbar

5 | **work experience** *(no pl)* [ˈwɜːkɪkˌspɪəriəns] | Praktikum; Berufserfahrung | I want to do *work experience* in the summer holidays. |
local [ˈləʊkl]	hiesig, örtlich	The *local* school is just across the road.
building centre [ˈbɪldɪŋ ˌsentə]	Baumarkt
on time [ɒn ˈtaɪm]	pünktlich; rechtzeitig	He missed the bus because he did not get to the bus stop *on time*.
so far [ˈsəʊ ˌfɑː]	bisher
Yuck! *(informal)* [jʌk]	Igitt!
put [pʊt]	*hier:* eingeben

		portable ['pɔːtəbl]	tragbar
		drill [drɪl]	Bohrer, Bohrmaschine
		complete [kəm'pliːt]	vervollständigen
7		include [ɪn'kluːd]	einfügen, aufnehmen
PP	°	training on the job [ˌtreɪnɪŋ ˌɒn ðə 'dʒɒb]	Ausbildung am Arbeitsplatz
	°	train sb for sth [treɪn]	*hier:* jdn für etw ausbilden
	°	practical ['præktɪkl]	praktisch
	°	as well as [æz wel ˌæz]	und (auch), sowie
	°	theoretical [ˌθɪə'retɪkl]	theoretisch
	°	take a test [ˌteɪk ə 'test]	eine Prüfung ablegen
	°	pass [pɑːs]	*hier:* bestehen
	°	further ['fɜːðə]	zusätzlich, noch mehr
	°	qualification [ˌkwɒlɪfɪ'keɪʃn]	Qualifikation
	°	vocational [vəʊ'keɪʃnəl]	beruflich
	°	recognized ['rekəgnaɪzd]	anerkannt; zugelassen
8		portfolio [pɔːt'fəʊliəʊ]	(Akten)mappe
		edit ['edɪt]	bearbeiten, redigieren
		checklist ['tʃekˌlɪst]	Checkliste, Kontrollliste
		connect [kə'nekt]	verbinden

My computer can *connect* to the Internet.

	that's why [ðæts waɪ]	das ist der Grund, warum	

I'm feeling ill. *That's why* I didn't go to school today.

	garage ['gærɑːʒ]	*hier:* (Kfz-)Werkstatt	
	overalls *(pl)* ['əʊvərˌɔːlz]	Overall, Arbeitsanzug	
	strong [strɒŋ]	*hier:* robust, stabil	
	morning break ['mɔːnɪŋ ˌbreɪk]	Frühstückspause	
	lunch break ['lʌntʃ ˌbreɪk]	Mittagspause	
	engine ['endʒɪn]	Motor, Maschine	

The *engine* is at the front of the car.

	change [tʃeɪndʒ]	*hier:* wechseln	
	tyre ['taɪə]	Reifen	
9	definition [ˌdefə'nɪʃn]	Definition, Erklärung	
10	**millionaire** [ˌmɪljə'neə]	Millionär/in	

I need to *change* the tyre!

If I were a *millionaire*, I would buy lots of expensive things!

11		Swedish ['swiːdɪʃ]	schwedisch
		solve [sɒlv]	lösen, klären
	°	still [stɪl]	*hier:* trotzdem, dennoch
	°	penny ['peni]	Penny, Centstück
	°	wealthy ['welθi]	reich, wohlhabend
	°	not at all [nɒtˌətˌɔːl]	überhaupt nicht
	°	fool around *(informal)* [ˌfuːl ə'raʊnd]	herumblödeln, seine Zeit verschwenden
	°	have a ball *(informal)* [hævˌə 'bɔːl]	Spaß haben, sich bestens amüsieren
	°	hard [hɑːd]	hier: schwierig
	°	can't get sb/sth off one's mind [ˌkɑːnt get sʌmbədi/sʌmθɪŋ ɒf wʌnz 'maɪnd]	nicht aufhören können, an jdn/etw zu denken
	°	happen to do sth [ˌhæpən tə 'duː sʌmθɪŋ]	zufällig etw tun
	°	fortune ['fɔːtʃən]	Vermögen

Spell check
Buchstabiere ein Wort für einen Partner. Wechselt euch ab und kontrolliert anschließend gegenseitig, ob alles richtig geschrieben ist. Für jedes richtige Wort gibt es einen Punkt. Wer ist der *spelling king* oder die *spelling queen?*

Den richtigen Ton treffen
Im gesprochenen Englisch gibt es viele umgangssprachliche Wörter und Ausdrücke. Ihre Verwendung hängt sehr von der Situation und der Herkunft des Sprechers ab. Wenn du nicht weißt, ob ein Ausdruck angemessen ist, benutze ihn lieber nicht. Verwende stattdessen Wörter, die dir vertraut sind.

12	spending power *(no pl)* ['spendɪŋ ˌpaʊə]	Kaufkraft
	make up [ˌmeɪk ˈʌp]	bilden
	double circle [ˌdʌbl 'sɜːkl]	Doppelkreis
13	study ['stʌdi]	Studie, (wissenschaftliche) Untersuchung
	spending habits *(pl)* ['spendɪŋ ˌhæbɪts]	Kaufgewohnheiten
	at that time [ət 'ðæt ˌtaɪm]	zu dieser Zeit
	pocket money ['pɒkɪt ˌmʌni]	Taschengeld
	record player ['rekɔːd ˌpleɪə]	(Schall)plattenspieler
	record ['rekɔːd]	*hier:* (Schall)platte
	pay cash [peɪ 'kæʃ]	bar bezahlen
	exist [ɪgˈzɪst]	existieren, vorkommen
	take out [ˌteɪk ˈaʊt]	abheben *(Geld)*
	account [əˈkaʊnt]	Konto
	the young *(pl)* [ðə jʌŋ]	die jungen Leute
	wish [wɪʃ]	Wunsch
	grandchild *(pl* **grandchildren)** ['græn,tʃaɪld]	Enkelkind
	stuff *(informal)* [stʌf]	Zeug, Sachen
	own [əʊn]	besitzen
	loving ['lʌvɪŋ]	liebevoll, liebend
	pregnant ['pregnənt]	schwanger
	transport ['trænspɔːt]	*hier:* Fahrkarten
	and so on [ænd 'səʊ ˌɒn]	und so weiter
	afford [əˈfɔːd]	sich leisten
	save [seɪv]	*hier:* sparen
	debit card ['debɪt ˌkɑːd]	Debitkarte *(entspricht einer EC-Karte)*
	get into debt [ˌget ˌɪntə 'det]	Schulden machen, sich verschulden
	the unemployed *(pl)* [ðiˌˌʌnɪm'plɔɪd]	die Arbeitslosen
	out of work [aʊt ˌəv 'wɜːk]	arbeitslos
	try hard to do sth [ˌtraɪ 'hɑːd ˌtə du: sʌmθɪŋ]	sich sehr bemühen, etw zu tun
14	**organization** [ˌɔːgənaɪ'zeɪʃn]	Organisation
	the rich *(pl)* [ðə rɪtʃ]	die Reichen
	the wealthy *(pl)* [ðə 'welθi]	die Reichen, die Wohlhabenden
	the famous *(pl)* [ðə 'feɪməs]	die Berühmten
	the poor *(pl)* [ðə pɔː]	die Armen

| [z] | afterward**s**, A level**s**, trou**s**er**s** |
| [s] | **s**o far, **s**caffolder, habit**s** |

Every week my parents give me £5.00 *pocket money*.

He is not using his credit card, he is *paying cash*.

If I had one *wish*, it would be to fly.

Do you *own* this car?

Yes, it's mine.

He can't *afford* to buy much – he hasn't got enough money!
I *save* money by buying cheap things.

If you spend too much money, you could *get into debt*.

He does not have a job – he is *out of work*.
He is *trying hard to* lift the weights.

15	matter ['mætə]	Angelegenheit, Sache
	tip [tɪp]	Tipp
	budget ['bʌdʒɪt]	ein Budget aufstellen
	work out [ˌwɜːkˈaʊt]	*hier:* ausrechnen

He can't *work out* the answer.

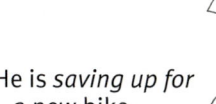

	unexpected [ˌʌnɪkˈspektɪd]	unerwartet
	amount [əˈmaʊnt]	Menge
	aim [eɪm]	zielen, zum Ziel haben
	save up for sth [ˌseɪvˈʌp fə sʌmθɪŋ]	auf/für etw sparen

He is *saving up for* a new bike.

	avoid [əˈvɔɪd]	(ver)meiden, ausweichen
	store card ['stɔː ˌkɑːd]	Kunden(kredit)karte
	be in control of sth [biˌɪn kənˈtrəʊl əv ˌsʌmθɪŋ]	etw unter Kontrolle haben
16	household spending *(no pl)* ['haʊshəʊld ˌspendɪŋ]	Haushaltsausgaben
	recreation [ˌrekriˈeɪʃn]	Freizeitbeschäftigung, Hobby
	housing *(no pl)* ['haʊzɪŋ]	Wohnungen, Unterkünfte
	miscellaneous [ˌmɪsəˈleɪniəs]	verschiedene(r, s), diverse(r, s),sonstige(r, s)
	bar chart ['bɑː ˌtʃɑːt]	Säulendiagramm, Balkendiagramm
M1	**abroad** [əˈbrɔːd]	im Ausland

I'm going *abroad* for my holidays this summer.

	provide [prəˈvaɪd]	bieten, geben, sorgen für
	opportunity [ˌɒpəˈtjuːnəti]	Möglichkeit, Chance; Gelegenheit

The weekend is a good *opportunity* to go out with your friends.

	national ['næʃnəl]	Staatsbürger/in, Staatsangehörige/r
	sort out [ˌsɔːtˈaʊt]	organisieren, sich kümmern um
	up to [ʌp tʊ]	bis zu

My baby sister can count *up to* 5.

	fast food chain [ˌfɑːst fuːd ˈtʃeɪn]	(Schnell)imbisskette
	airport ['eəˌpɔːt]	Flughafen

The plane is landing at the *airport*.

	host family ['həʊst ˌfæmli]	Gastfamilie
	have the time of one's life [hæv ðə ˌtaɪmˌəv wʌnz ˈlaɪf]	eine tolle Zeit haben
	apply (for) [əˈplaɪ]	sich bewerben (um)

I'm going to *apply for* a job.

	animal care *(no pl)* ['ænɪml ˌkeə]	Tierpflege
	South Africa [saʊθˈæfrɪkə]	Südafrika
	gain [geɪn]	erwerben, erlangen, sammeln, gewinnen

After her father had died, she *gained* lots of money. Now she is rich.

	animal carer ['ænɪml ˌkeərə]	Tierpfleger/in
	exercise ['eksəsaɪz]	trainieren; bewegen

It is healthy to *exercise* every day.

	rehabilitate [ˌriːəˈbɪlɪteɪt]	rehabilitieren

WORDS THEME 5

essential [ɪˈsenʃl]	unbedingt erforderlich, von größter Wichtigkeit	
practical [ˈpræktɪkl]	praktisch	A *practical* skill is a useful skill.
develop [dɪˈveləp]	(sich) entwickeln	If you practise your English every day, you will *develop* your language skills.
picker [ˈpɪkə]	Erntehelfer/in	
involve [ɪnˈvɒlv]	beinhalten; betreffen	
pick [pɪk]	*hier:* pflücken, sammeln	In the summer I like to *pick* fruit from the trees.
strawberry [ˈstrɔːbri]	Erdbeere	I love eating *strawberries*!
quality [ˈkwɒləti]	Qualität, Güte	
payment [ˈpeɪmənt]	Bezahlung, Entlohnung	
piecework [ˈpiːsˌwɜːk]	Akkordarbeit	
basis [ˈbeɪsɪs]	Basis, Grundlage	
flexibility [ˌfleksəˈbɪləti]	Flexibilität, Anpassungsfähigkeit	
required [rɪˈkwaɪəd]	erforderlich	
mobile home [ˌməʊbaɪl ˈhəʊm]	Wohnwagen	
wage(s) [weɪdʒ(ɪz)]	Lohn	I earn my *wage* by working.

M2	application form [ˌæplɪˈkeɪʃn fɔːm]	Bewerbungsformular	For some jobs you might need to fill in an *application form*.
	nationality [ˌnæʃəˈnæləti]	Nationalität; Staatsangehörigkeit	What is your *nationality* – which country are you from?
	position [pəˈzɪʃn]	Position, Stelle	
	previous [ˈpriːviəs]	vorherig	
	employment [ɪmˈplɔɪmənt]	Beschäftigung, Anstellung	
	qualification [ˌkwɒlɪfɪˈkeɪʃn]	Qualifikation; Abschluss	What *qualifications* have you got?
	hold [həʊld]	*hier:* besitzen	
	graduation [ˌgrædʒuˈeɪʃn]	Schulabschluss, Studienabschluss	
	improve [ɪmˈpruːv]	verbessern	If you *improve* something, you make it better.
	teammate [ˈtiːmmeɪt]	Teammitglied, Teamkollege/ Teamkollegin	
	either ... or ... [ˌaɪðə ... ˈɔː]	entweder ... oder ...	We can *either* watch a film at home *or* go to the cinema.
	resolve [rɪˈzɒlv]	lösen, klären	
	ambition [æmˈbɪʃn]	Ambition, (angestrebtes) Ziel	
	medical technician [ˌmedɪkl tekˈnɪʃn]	medizinisch-technische/r Assistent/in	
	category [ˈkætəgri]	Kategorie	
	belong [bɪˈlɒŋ]	gehören	
	applicant [ˈæplɪkənt]	Bewerber/in	
M3	impression [ɪmˈpreʃn]	Eindruck	
	job interview [ˈdʒɒbˌɪntəvjuː]	Bewerbungsgespräch, Vorstellungsgespräch	At a *job interview* you will be asked lots of questions.
	haircut [ˈheəˌkʌt]	Haarschnitt, Frisur	He is getting a *haircut*.
	eye contact *(no pl)* [ˈaɪ ˌkɒntækt]	Blickkontakt	

M4	iron [ˈaɪən]	bügeln	If you want to look good, you should *iron* your clothes.
	shirt [ʃɜːt]	Hemd	*shirt*
	for quite some time [fə ˌkwaɪt səm ˈtaɪm]	seit einer ganzen Weile	
M6	suggestion [səˈdʒestʃn]	Vorschlag; Hinweis	
M7	golden [ˈgəʊldn]	golden	
	grape [greɪp]	(Wein)traube	
	Father Christmas [ˌfɑːðə ˈkrɪsməs]	Weihnachtsmann	
	research [rɪˈsɜːtʃ]	recherchieren	
M8	acrostic [əˈkrɒstɪk]	*Gedichtform, bei der bestimmte Buchstaben aus jeder Zeile untereinander ein Wort ergeben*	enjoy work abroad skills
M9	have sth in common [hæv ˌsʌmθɪŋ ɪn ˈkɒmən]	etwas gemein haben	
	biography [baɪˈɒgrəfi]	Biografie	
M10	get on sb's nerves [ˌget ɒn sʌmbədiz ˈnɜːvz]	jdm auf die Nerven gehen	Sometimes my little brother *gets on my nerves.*
	suggest [səˈdʒest]	vorschlagen	If you are tired, I *suggest* you go to bed early.
M11	begging (no pl) [ˈbegɪŋ]	Betteln	
	beggar [ˈbegə]	Bettler/in	Have you ever given money to a *beggar*?
	off [ɒf]	weg von, raus aus	Homeless people need money to get *off* the streets.
	beg [beg]	betteln	
	founder [ˈfaʊndə]	Gründer/in	Someone who starts a company is the *founder* of the company.
	issue [ˈɪʃuː]	Thema; Frage	
	heated [ˈhiːtɪd]	hitzig, erregt; heftig	
	well-known [ˌwelˈnəʊn]	berühmt, (allgemein) bekannt	If something is *well-known*, lots of people know about it.
	idiotic [ˌɪdiˈɒtɪk]	idiotisch	That's the most stupid, *idiotic* idea I've ever heard!
	cash handout [ˈkæʃ ˌhændaʊt]	finanzielle Zuwendung, Geldzuwendung	
	murder [ˈmɜːdə]	umbringen, ermorden	
	argue [ˈɑːgju]	*hier:* argumentieren	Some people *argue* that alcohol and cigarettes should be illegal because they are dangerous drugs.
	runaway [ˈrʌnəˌweɪ]	Ausreißer/in	A *runaway* is somebody who has run away from home.
	alternative [ɔːlˈtɜːnətɪv]	Alternative	Isn't there another way of doing things – an *alternative*?
	charity organization [ˌtʃærətiˌɔːgənaɪˈzeɪʃn]	Wohltätigkeitsorganisation	
	Labour [ˈleɪbə]	*Name einer britischen Partei*	
	MP (= Member of Parliament) [ˌem ˈpiː (= ˌmembər əv ˈpɑːləmənt]	Abgeordnete/r, Parlamentsmitglied	
	solve [sɒlv]	lösen, klären	We have to *solve* this problem!

| single ['sɪŋgl] | einzelne(r, s) | |
| nowhere ['nəʊweə] | nirgends, nirgendwo | Homeless people live on the streets because they have *nowhere* to go. |

	mentally ill [ˌmentli'ɪl]	psychisch krank
	source of income [ˌsɔːs͜əv͜'ɪnkʌm]	Einkommensquelle
	spokesman/spokeswoman ['spəʊksmən, 'spəʊksˌwʊmən]	Sprecher/in
M12	record [rɪ'kɔːd]	aufnehmen, aufzeichnen
CIO	apply (for) [ə'plaɪ]	sich bewerben (um)
	unusual [ʌn'juːʒʊəl]	ungewöhnlich
	include [ɪn'kluːd]	*hier:* beifügen
	report [rɪ'pɔːt]	*hier:* Zeugnis
	former ['fɔːmə]	ehemalige(r, s), frühere(r, s)
	employer [ɪm'plɔɪə]	Arbeitgeber/in
	° average ['ævrɪdʒ]	durchschnittlich
	° worker [wɜːkə]	Arbeiter/in, Angestellte/r
	° office ['ɒfɪs]	Büro
	° architect ['ɑːkɪˌtekt]	Architekt/in
	° cotton ['kɒtn]	Baumwolle
	° linen *(no pl)* ['lɪnɪn]	Leinen
	° second-hand car [ˌsekəndˌhænd 'kɑː]	Gebrauchtwagen
	° issue ['ɪʃuː]	ausstellen, in Umlauf bringen

Find the opposites to these words in Theme 5:
(be) late – ???
(work) together – ???
spend (money) – ???

He is an *architect* – he designs buildings.

Wortbedeutungen erschließen
Bevor du zum Wörterbuch greifst, um die Bedeutung eines englischen Wortes nachzuschlagen, solltest du dir das Wort genau ansehen. Vielleicht ist es ein Wort, das aus zwei Einzelwörtern besteht. Die Bedeutung kannst du erschließen, wenn dir ein Bestandteil schon bekannt ist, z. B.:
vet's assistant
work experience
security guard
building centre

Vielseitige Verben
Im Englischen kann ein Verb ganz verschiedene Bedeutungen haben – je nachdem, mit welchen Wörtern es kombiniert wird. Zum Beispiel kann *have* wie folgt übersetzt werden:
have brown eyes – braune Augen haben
have lunch – zu Mittag essen
have a barbecue – grillen, eine Grillparty feiern
have tea – Tee trinken
have a good time – sich amüsieren
have a guess – raten, schätzen

Theme 6 – Our world, our future

I	act [ækt]	handeln, sich verhalten	
	green [griːn]	*hier:* umweltfreundlich, ökologisch	
	questionnaire [ˌkwestʃəˈneə]	Fragebogen	
	eco- [iːkəʊ]	Öko-	
	plan of action [ˌplæn ˌəv ˈækʃn]	Aktionsplan	
1	**electrical appliance** [ɪˌlektrɪkl̩ əˈplaɪəns]	Elektrogerät	
	oven [ˈʌvn]	(Back)ofen	A baker uses a special *oven* to make bread.
	microwave [ˈmaɪkrəˌweɪv]	Mikrowelle(nherd)	
	dishwasher [ˈdɪʃˌwɒʃə]	Geschirrspülmaschine	If a plate is dirty, put it in the *dishwasher*.
	washing machine [ˈwɒʃɪŋ məˌʃiːn]	Waschmaschine	
	heating [ˈhiːtɪŋ]	Heizung	It's so cold outside – I'm glad we turned the *heating* on!
2	**act** [ækt]	handeln, sich verhalten	
	green [griːn]	*hier:* umweltfreundlich, ökologisch	
	turn off [ˌtɜːn ˈɒf]	ausmachen, ausschalten	*turn off* ≠ turn on
3	**take action** [teɪk ˈækʃn]	handeln, etw unternehmen	They were not being paid enough, so they decided to *take action*.
	planet [ˈplænɪt]	Planet	
	piece of advice [ˌpiːs əv ədˈvaɪs]	Rat	
	leave [liːv]	*hier:* lassen	You should eat everything! Don't *leave* food on your plate!
	on standby [ɒn ˈstændbaɪ]	in Bereitschaft, auf Standby	
	take a shower [teɪk ə ˈʃaʊə]	duschen	
	instead (of) [ɪnˈsted (əv)]	stattdessen; (an)statt	Because she felt sick, she stayed in bed *instead of* going to school.
	take a bath [teɪk ə ˈbɑːθ]	baden	He is *taking a bath*. 
	heat [hiːt]	erhitzen	
	as [əz]	*hier:* so	
	recycle [riːˈsaɪkl]	wiederverwerten, recyclen	
	pollution [pəˈluːʃn]	(Umwelt)verschmutzung	*Pollution* in rivers and lakes can kill plants and fish.
	energy-saving [ˈenədʒi ˌseɪvɪŋ]	energiesparend	It is good for the environment to use *energy-saving* light bulbs.
	wrapped [ræpt]	eingepackt, verpackt	
	plastic [ˈplæstɪk]	Plastik, Kunststoff	Many drinks come in *plastic* bottles.
	reduce [rɪˈdjuːs]	verringern, reduzieren, verkleinern	
	reuse [riːˈjuːz]	wiederverwenden	*reuse* sth = use sth again
4	**unfortunately** [ʌnˈfɔːtʃnətli]	leider, unglücklicherweise	*Unfortunately*, she missed the bus.
	honest [ˈɒnɪst]	ehrlich	Be *honest* and tell the truth!

test [test]	prüfen, testen	
turn up [ˌtɜːn ˈʌp]	aufdrehen, höher stellen	When I am cold, I wear my *jumper*.
jumper [ˈdʒʌmpə]	Pullover	
recycled [riːˈsaɪkld]	wiederverwertet, recycelt	
ignore [ɪgˈnɔː]	ignorieren	
walk on [ˌwɔːk ˈɒn]	weiterlaufen, weitergehen	
pick up [ˌpɪk ˈʌp]	aufheben	The children had to *pick* their toys *up*.
can [kæn]	Dose	Would you like a *can* of cola?
volunteer to do sth [ˌvɒlənˈtɪə tə duː ˌsʌmθɪŋ]	sich freiwillig anbieten, etw zu tun	
finish [ˈfɪnɪʃ]	*hier:* austrinken	
keep up sth [ˌkiːp ˈʌp ˌsʌmθɪŋ]	etw fortführen, etw weiterhin tun	
be on the right track [bi ˌɒn ðə ˌraɪt ˈtræk]	auf dem richtigen Weg sein	
behaviour *(no pl)* [bɪˈheɪvjə]	Verhalten, Benehmen	Chewing gum at school is not good *behaviour*!

PP	° go green [ˌgəʊ ˈgriːn]	umweltbewusst werden
	° celebrity [səˈlebrəti]	berühmte Persönlichkeit, Star
	° found [faʊnd]	gründen
	° donate [dəʊˈneɪt]	spenden
	° sum [sʌm]	Summe, Betrag
	° environmental [ɪnˌvaɪrənˈmentl]	Umwelt-
	° conference [ˈkɒnfrəns]	Konferenz, Tagung
	° goal [gəʊl]	*hier:* Ziel
	° plant [plɑːnt]	pflanzen
	° perform [pəˈfɔːm]	*hier:* auftreten
	° billion [ˈbɪljən]	Milliarde
	° vice-president [ˌvaɪs ˈprezɪdənt]	Vizepräsident/in
	° explore [ɪkˈsplɔː]	untersuchen, erkunden
	° effect [ɪˈfekt]	(Aus)wirkung, Konsequenz, Einfluss
	° global warming *(no pl)* [ˌgləʊbl ˈwɔːmɪŋ]	Erwärmung der Erdatmosphäre
	° inconvenient [ˌɪnkənˈviːniənt]	unbequem, lästig
	° Nobel Peace Prize [nəʊˌbel ˈpiːs praɪz]	Friedensnobelpreis
5	environmental [ɪnˌvaɪrənˈmentl]	Umwelt-
	waste *(no pl)* [weɪst]	*hier:* Abfall, Müll
	least [liːst]	geringste(r, s), wenigste(r, s)
	packaging [ˈpækɪdʒɪŋ]	Verpackung(smaterial)
	donate [dəʊˈneɪt]	spenden
	item [ˈaɪtəm]	Gegenstand, Ding
	writing paper *(no pl)* [ˈraɪtɪŋ ˌpeɪpə]	Schreibpapier
6	crossword puzzle [ˈkrɒswɜːd ˌpʌzl]	Kreuzworträtsel

Verknüpfungen herstellen
Bei Wörtern, die überhaupt nicht in deinen Kopf wollen, kannst du:
- dir das Wort bildlich vorstellen,
- ein kleines Bild dazu zeichnen,
- an ein Ereignis denken, das du selbst erlebt hast,
- einen Satz, in dem das Wort vorkommt, auswendig lernen,
- dir eine Eselsbrücke (z. B. einen Reim) ausdenken.

The bin is full of *waste*.

When you buy something, it often comes in *packaging*.
Some people *donate* money to charities.

When I am writing a letter, I use *writing paper*.

	collage [ˈkɒlɑːʒ]	Collage
8	summary [ˈsʌməri]	Zusammenfassung; Inhaltsangabe
	animated film [ˌænɪmeɪtɪd ˈfɪlm]	(Zeichen)trickfilm, Animationsfilm
	be set somewhere [bi: ˈset ˌsʌmweə]	irgendwo spielen/ stattfinden
	human [ˈhjuːmən]	Mensch
	polluted [pəˈluːtɪd]	verschmutzt
	impossible [ɪmˈpɒsəbl]	unmöglich
	army [ˈɑːmi]	Armee, Heer
	robot [ˈrəʊbɒt]	Roboter
	leave behind [ˌliːv bɪˈhaɪnd]	zurücklassen
	break down [ˌbreɪk ˈdaʊn]	kaputtgehen, zusammenbrechen
	cockroach [ˈkɒkrəʊtʃ]	Küchenschabe, Kakerlake
	put away [ˌpʊt əˈweɪ]	wegräumen, aufräumen
	romantic [rəʊˈmæntɪk]	romantisch
	turn up [ˌtɜːn ˈʌp]	*hier:* erscheinen, auftauchen
	check out sth [ˌtʃek ˈaʊt ˌsʌmθɪŋ]	etw untersuchen/überprüfen
	return [rɪˈtɜːn]	zurückkehren
	arrival [əˈraɪvl]	Ankunft
	proof [pruːf]	Beweis
	fall in love (with) [ˌfɔːl ɪn ˈlʌv]	sich verlieben (in)
	lazy [ˈleɪzi]	faul, träge
	moving [ˈmuːvɪŋ]	beweglich
	autopilot [ˈɔːtəʊˌpaɪlət]	Autopilot
	programmed [ˈprəʊɡræmd]	programmiert
	keep sb from doing sth [ˈkiːp ˌsʌmbədi frəm ˌduːɪŋ ˌsʌmθɪŋ]	jdn davon abhalten, etw zu tun
	manage [ˈmænɪdʒ]	es schaffen
	fight [faɪt]	Kampf, Streit
	plant [plɑːnt]	pflanzen
	character [ˈkærɪktə]	Charakter; Figur
10	living [ˈlɪvɪŋ]	lebend
13	**pollute** [pəˈluːt]	verschmutzen
	go on doing sth [ˌɡəʊ ˈɒn ˌduːɪŋ ˌsʌmθɪŋ]	etw weiter tun
14	stand still [stænd ˈstɪl]	stillstehen
	the day after tomorrow [ðə ˌdeɪ ˌɑːftə təˈmɒrəʊ]	übermorgen
M1	global warming *(no pl)* [ˌɡləʊbl ˈwɔːmɪŋ]	Erwärmung der Erdatmosphäre
	explanation [ˌekspləˈneɪʃn]	Erklärung
	encyclopedia [ɪnˌsaɪkləˈpiːdiə]	Lexikon, Enzyklopädie
	control [kənˈtrəʊl]	regulieren, steuern

I like *animated films*, but I prefer watching real people.

You are a *human*.
Plants can't grow here because the area is so *polluted*.
I can't do it – it is *impossible*!

A *robot* is a kind of machine.

The car *broke down*, so they had to push it.

I flew to New York and then *returned* to London.

Machines like computers do what they are *programmed* to do.

Although he was tired, he *managed* to get out of bed.

He is going to *plant* the tree.

The earth is getting hotter because of *global warming*.

sunbeam ['sʌnˌbiːm]	Sonnenstrahl	*Sunbeams* come to the earth from the sun.
heat up [ˌhiːtˌˈʌp]	aufwärmen, erhitzen	
heat *(no pl)* [hiːt]	Wärme; Hitze	The cat is enjoying the *heat* from the fire.
atmosphere ['ætməsˌfɪə]	*hier:* Erdatmosphäre	
gas [gæs]	Gas	
carbon dioxide *(no pl)* [ˌkɑːbən daɪˈɒksaɪd]	Kohlen(stoff)dioxid	
greenhouse gas ['griːnˌhaʊs gæs]	Treibhausgas	
produce [prəˈdjuːs]	herstellen, erzeugen, produzieren	Fire *produces* smoke.
home [həʊm]	*hier:* Haus	
consequence ['kɒnsɪkwəns]	Folge, Konsequenz	He was late for school. As a *consequence*, his teacher was angry with him.

M2 the United Nations [ðə juːˌnaɪtɪd ˈneɪʃnz]	die Vereinten Nationen	
conference ['kɒnfrəns]	Konferenz, Tagung	
development [dɪˈveləpmənt]	Entwicklung; Wachstum	
aim [eɪm]	Ziel, Absicht	
encourage sb [ɪnˈkʌrɪdʒ ˌsʌmbədi]	jdn ermutigen, jdn unterstützen	
the media [ðə ˈmiːdiə]	die Medien	
resource [rɪˈzɔːs]	Ressource	
melt [melt]	schmelzen	
ice cap ['aɪs kæp]	Polkappe	
motivate sb to do sth ['məʊtɪveɪt ˌsʌmbədi tə duː ˌsʌmθɪŋ]	jdn motivieren/dazu bewegen, etw zu tun	

> **Can you sort these words in alphabetical order?**
> produce, heat, encyclopedia, gas, melt, control, home, explanation, consequence, conference

topic ['tɒpɪk]	Thema	Today, we will talk about the *topic* of friends and family.
tank [tæŋk]	(Flüssigkeits)behälter, (Wasser)tank	I keep my fish in a fish *tank*.
water ['wɔːtə]	gießen	If you do not *water* a plant, it will die.
usage ['juːsɪdʒ]	Verbrauch	check the *usage* of water = check how much water is being used
fountain ['faʊntɪn]	Brunnen	
refill [riːˈfɪl]	auffüllen, nachfüllen	When you have drunk all your orange juice, I will *refill* your glass.
rather than ['rɑːðə ðæn]	anstatt	
take a reading of sth [teɪkˌə ˈriːdɪŋˌəv ˌsʌmθɪŋ]	etw ablesen	
electricity [ɪˌlekˈtrɪsəti]	Elektrizität, Strom	Lights, televisions and radios all use *electricity*.

electricity

consumption [kənˈsʌmpʃn]	Verbrauch	
importance *(no pl)* [ɪmˈpɔːtns]	Bedeutung, Wichtigkeit	
create [kriˈeɪt]	erschaffen; gestalten	
tap [tæp]	Wasserhahn	Water comes out of the *taps*.

	minimization *(no pl)* [ˌmɪnɪmaɪˈzeɪʃn]	Minimierung	
	cardboard *(no pl)* [ˈkɑːdˌbɔːd]	Pappe, (Papp)karton	Many boxes are made of *cardboard*.
	printer cartridge [ˈprɪntə ˌkɑːtrɪdʒ]	Druckerpatrone	
	litter *(no pl)* [ˈlɪtə]	Müll, Abfall	She is dropping her *litter* on the floor.
	in addition to [ɪn_əˈdɪʃn tʊ]	zusätzlich zu	
	carry out sth [ˌkæriˌˈaʊt ˌsʌmθɪŋ]	etw durchführen	
	future [ˈfjuːtʃə]	zukünftig, später	
	use [juːs]	Verwendung, Gebrauch	I can't drive yet, but I bought a car for future *use*.
	painful [ˈpeɪnfl]	schmerzhaft; *hier:* schrecklich, furchtbar	

Reimwörter
Damit du dir besser merken kannst, wie bestimmte Wörter ausgesprochen werden, suche Reimwörter für sie. Dir wird auffallen, dass die Reimwörter nicht immer dieselbe Schreibweise haben.
Hier ein Beispiel:
clear – *cheer* – *here*

	clear [klɪə]	klar, eindeutig	
M3	drawing [ˈdrɔːɪŋ]	Zeichnung	
M4	**paper bank** [ˈpeɪpə bæŋk]	Altpapiercontainer	
	bottle bank [ˈbɒtl bæŋk]	Altglascontainer	
	plastic bottle bank [ˈplæstɪk ˌbɒtl bæŋk]	Plastikflaschencontainer	
	can bank [ˈkæn bæŋk]	Dosencontainer	
	compost bin [ˈkɒmpɒst bɪn]	Komposttonne	
	non-recyclable [ˌnɒn riːˈsaɪkləbl]	nicht recycelbar	
M5	exchange- [ɪksˈtʃeɪndʒ]	(Aus)tausch-	
	Hanover [ˈhænəʊvə]	Hannover	
	battery [ˈbætri]	Batterie	Some machines don't work without *batteries* inside them.
M6	**making** *(no pl)* [ˈmeɪkɪŋ]	Herstellung	
	upside down [ˌʌpsaɪdˈˈdaʊn]	verkehrt herum	
	mean to do sth [ˈmiːn tə duː ˌsʌmθɪŋ]	etw tun wollen	˙uʍop ǝpᴉsdn sᴉ ƃuᴉʇᴉɹʍ sᴉɥʇ
	damage [ˈdæmɪdʒ]	(be)schädigen	You hurt my arm and *damaged* my bike!

	fill [fɪl]	füllen	
M7	likely [ˈlaɪkli]	wahrscheinlich	
	point of view [ˌpɔɪnt_əvˈˈvjuː]	Standpunkt, Gesichtspunkt	
CIO	take seriously [teɪk ˈsɪəriəsli]	ernst nehmen	
	° yoghurt pot [ˈjɒgət pɒt]	Jogurtbecher	
	° take [teɪk]	*hier:* brauchen	
	° break down [ˌbreɪkˈdaʊn]	*hier:* sich auflösen	
	° electricity [ɪˌlekˈtrɪsəti]	Elektrizität, Strom	
	° double [dʌbl]	sich verdoppeln	
	° expression [ɪkˈspreʃn]	Ausdruck	

Vokabeln umschreiben
Wenn du dir ein Wort einfach nicht merken kannst, versuche es zu umschreiben. Überlege dir, was das Wort bedeutet, und schreibe dir einen kurzen englischen Satz dazu auf, zum Beispiel:
donate = give money to a charity
packaging = paper or plastic that you put around products

A

a [ə, eɪ] pro

do one's A levels [du: wʌnz ˈeɪ ˌlevlz] das Abitur machen V/5/2

a/an [ə, ən] ein(e)

ability [əˈbɪləti] Fähigkeit; Talent V/3/4

be able to do [bi ˌeɪbl tə ˈdu:] tun können

Aboriginal [ˌæbəˈrɪdʒnl] ... der Aboriginals V/1/10

Aborigine [ˌæbəˈrɪdʒəni] australische/r Ureinwohner/in, Aborigine V/1/I

about [əˈbaʊt] über; wegen; ungefähr

be about [ˌbi əˈbaʊt] handeln von

above [əˈbʌv] über

abroad [əˈbrɔːd] im Ausland V/5/M1

absolutely [ˈæbsəluːtli] absolut, völlig V/4/CIO

accent [ˈæksnt] Akzent

accept [əkˈsept] annehmen; akzeptieren V/3/10

access code [ˈækses ˌkəʊd] Zugangs-/Zugriffscode V/2/10

accident [ˈæksɪdnt] Unfall

by accident [baɪ ˈæksɪdnt] aus Versehen; zufällig

account [əˈkaʊnt] Konto V/5/13

° acknowlegde [əkˈnɒlɪdʒ] anerkennen; zugeben V/1/M9

across [əˈkrɒs] über

acrostic [əˈkrɒstɪk] *Gedichtform, bei der bestimmte Buchstaben aus jeder Zeile untereinander ein Wort ergeben* V/5/M8

act [ækt] handeln, sich verhalten V/6/2

act out [ækt ˈaʊt] nachspielen

action [ˈækʃn] Handlung; Aktion

active [ˈæktɪv] aktiv V/3/1

activity [ækˈtɪvəti] Aktivität

actor/actress [ˈæktə/ˈæktrəs] Schauspieler/in

actually [ˈæktʃuəli] eigentlich

add [æd] hinzufügen

in addition to [ɪn əˈdɪʃn tʊ] zusätzlich zu V/6/M2

address [əˈdres] Adresse

adjective [ˈædʒɪktɪv] Adjektiv

admit sth [ədˈmɪt] etw zugeben, etw eingestehen V/2/M5

adult [ˈædʌlt] Erwachsene/r

adventure [ədˈventʃə] Abenteuer, Erlebnis

adventurous [ədˈventʃrəs] abenteuerlich V/3/M6

advert (= advertisement) [ˈædvɜːt] Anzeige, Inserat; Werbung

advice (no pl) [ədˈvaɪs] Rat

aerobics (no pl) [eəˈrəʊbɪks] Aerobic(kurs) V/4/8

affect sb/sth [əˈfekt ˌsʌmbədi/ˌsʌmθɪŋ] sich auf jdn/etw auswirken V/1/M2

afford [əˈfɔːd] sich leisten V/5/13

be afraid (of) [ˌbi əˈfreɪd] Angst haben/sich fürchten (vor)

Africa [ˈæfrɪkə] Afrika

African American [ˌæfrɪkən əˈmerɪkən] Afroamerikaner/in; afroamerikanisch

after [ˈɑːftə] nach; nachdem

afternoon [ˌɑːftəˈnuːn] Nachmittag

in the afternoon [ˌɪn ðiː ˌɑːftəˈnuːn] am Nachmittag, nachmittags

this afternoon [ðɪs ˌɑːftəˈnuːn] heute Nachmittag

afterwards [ˈɑːftəwədz] danach, anschließend; später V/5/2

again [əˈgen] wieder, noch einmal, noch mal

over and over again [ˌəʊvə ən ˌəʊvə əˈgen] immer wieder V/1/M9

against [əˈgenst] gegen

age [eɪdʒ] Alter

aggression [əˈgreʃn] Aggression, Aggressivität V/2/M5

aggressive [əˈgresɪv] aggressiv; energisch V/1/10

(two days) ago [əˈgəʊ] vor (zwei Tagen)

agree on [əˈgriː ɒn] einer Meinung sein über; sich einigen auf

agree (with) [əˈgriː] zustimmen

aim [eɪm] zielen, zum Ziel haben V/5/15; Ziel, Absicht V/6/M2

° ain't (AE, informal) [eɪnt] nicht sein V/2/1

air [eə] Luft

airport [ˈeəˌpɔːt] Flughafen V/5/M1

alarm clock [əˈlɑːm ˌklɒk] Wecker

album [ˈælbəm] (Musik)album V/3/M8

alcohol [ˈælkəˌhɒl] Alkohol

all [ɔːl] alle(s); ganz, völlig

all day [ˌɔːl ˈdeɪ] den ganzen Tag V/4/9

all in all [ˌɔːl ɪn ˌɔːl] alles in allem V/2/2

all over [ˈɔːl ˌəʊvə] überall in/auf

all right [ˌɔːl ˈraɪt] in Ordnung V/1/5

all the time [ˌɔːl ðə ˈtaɪm] dauernd, ständig

be allowed to do sth [bi əˌlaʊd tə ˈdu: sʌmθɪŋ] etw tun dürfen

almost [ˈɔːlməʊst] fast, beinahe

alone [əˈləʊn] allein

leave sb alone [ˌliːv sʌmbədi əˈləʊn] jdn in Ruhe lassen V/2/2

along [əˈlɒŋ] entlang

aloud [əˈlaʊd] laut

alphabet [ˈælfəˌbet] Alphabet

already [ɔːlˈredi] schon

° alright [ɔːlˈraɪt] in Ordnung V/2/1

also [ˈɔːlsəʊ] auch

alternative [ɔːlˈtɜːnətɪv] Alternative V/5/M11

although [ɔːlˈðəʊ] obwohl, obgleich

always [ˈɔːlweɪz] immer

am (= ante meridiem) [ˌeɪ ˈem, ˌænti məˈrɪdiəm] morgens, vormittags *(nur hinter Uhrzeit zwischen Mitternacht und 12 Uhr mittags)*

ambition [æmˈbɪʃn] Ambition, (angestrebtes) Ziel V/5/M2

° ambulance [ˈæmbjʊləns] Rettungswagen V/2/PP

American [əˈmerɪkən] Amerikaner/in; amerikanisch

Amish [ˈɑːmɪʃ] amisch

the Amish [ðiː ˈɑːmɪʃ] die Amischen

among [əˈmʌŋ] unter

amount [əˈmaʊnt] Menge V/5/15

ancestor spirit [ˈænsestə ˌspɪrɪt] Geist eines Vorfahren/einer Vorfahrin V/1/11

and [ænd] und

and so on [ænd ˈsəʊ ˌɒn] und so weiter V/5/13

angry [ˈæŋgri] verärgert; zornig; wütend

animal [ˈænɪml] Tier

animal care *(no pl)* [ˈænɪml ˌkeə] Tierpflege V/5/M1

animal carer [ˈænɪml ˌkeərə] Tierpfleger/in V/5/M1

animal lover [ˈænɪmlˌˈlʌvə] Tierfreund/in V/1/2

animated film [ˌænɪmeɪtɪd ˈfɪlm] (Zeichen)trickfilm, Animationsfilm V/6/8

annoy [əˈnɔɪ] ärgern, nerven V/4/M3

anorexia *(no pl)* [ˌænəˈreksiə] Magersucht, Anorexie V/4/9

anorexic [ˌænəˈreksɪk] magersüchtig V/4/9

another [əˈnʌðə] noch ein(e, r, s); ein zweiter/zweites/eine zweite; ein anderer/anderes, eine andere

answer [ˈɑːnsə] (be)antworten; Antwort

any [ˈeni] irgendein(e); jede(r, s)

not anymore [nɒtˌˈeniˈmɔː] nicht mehr

anyone [ˈeniˌwʌn] jede/r, jemand

anything [ˈeniˌθɪŋ] alles; etwas

Anything else? [ˌeniθɪŋ ˈels] Darf es noch etwas sein?

anyway [ˈeniˌweɪ] sowieso, jedenfalls; trotzdem

apartment *(AE)* = flat *(BE)* [əˈpɑːtmənt] Wohnung; Apartment

apologize [əˈpɒlədʒaɪz] sich entschuldigen

apology [əˈpɒlədʒi] Entschuldigung V/2/M5

appear [əˈpɪə] erscheinen V/2/M5

appetite [ˈæpɪtaɪt] Appetit V/4/M3

apple [ˈæpl] Apfel

apple pie [ˈæpl ˌpaɪ] gedeckter Apfelkuchen

applicant [ˈæplɪkənt] Bewerber/in V/5/M2

application form [ˌæplɪˈkeɪʃn fɔːm] Bewerbungsformular V/5/M2

apply (for) [əˈplaɪ] sich bewerben (um) V/5/M1

April [ˈeɪprəl] April

° architect [ˈɑːkɪtekt] Architekt/in V/5/CIO

Are you all right? [ɑː jʊ ɔːl ˈraɪt] Ist alles in Ordnung?

area [ˈeəriə] Gebiet, Region

argue [ˈɑːgjuː] sich streiten; argumentieren V/5/M11

argument [ˈɑːgjʊmənt] Argument V/2/8

arithmetic *(no pl)* [əˈrɪθmətɪk] Rechnen V/1/12

arm [ɑːm] Arm

armchair [ˈɑːmˌtʃeə] Sessel, Lehnstuhl

army [ˈɑːmi] Armee, Heer V/6/8

around [əˈraʊnd] um; in

° have sb around [ˌhæv sʌmbədiˌəˈraʊnd] jdn in der Nähe haben V/2/1

arrest sb [əˈrest ˌsʌmbədi] jdn verhaften V/3/5

arrival [əˈraɪvl] Ankunft V/6/8

arrive [əˈraɪv] ankommen

art [ɑːt] Kunst

artful dodger [ˌɑːtfl ˈdɒdʒə] durchtriebenes Bürschchen V/4/M8

article [ˈɑːtɪkl] Artikel

artist [ˈɑːtɪst] Künstler/in

as [əz] als

as [əz] so V/6/3

as ... as ... [əz əz] (genau)so ... wie ...

as soon as [əzˈsuːnˌəz] sobald

° as well as [æz wel ˌæz] und (auch), sowie V/5/PP

be ashamed [ˌbiˌəˈʃeɪmd] sich schämen

Asia [ˈeɪʃə] Asien V/1/2

Asian [ˈeɪʒn] Asiat/in; asiatisch

° pull sb aside [ˌpʊl sʌmbədiˌəˈsaɪd] jdn beiseite nehmen V/2/1

ask [ɑːsk] fragen; bitten

ask questions [ɑːskˌˈkwestʃnz] Fragen stellen

ask sb out [ˌɑːsk sʌmbədiˈˌaʊt] sich mit jdm verabreden

be asleep [ˌbiˌəˈsliːp] schlafen

fall asleep [ˌfɔːlˌəˈsliːp] einschlafen

astronaut [ˈæstrəˌnɔːt] Astronaut/in

at [æt] auf, an, in, bei; um

at first [ət ˈfɜːst] anfangs, zuerst

at least [ət ˈliːst] mindestens, wenigstens

Athens [ˈæθɪnz] Athen V/1/4

athlete [ˈæθliːt] Athlet/in

° the Atlantic Ocean [ðiˌətˌlæntɪkˈəʊʃn] der Atlantische Ozean V/I/1

atmosphere [ˈætməsˌfɪə] Erdatmosphäre V/6/M1

atmosphere [ˈætməsˌfɪə] Atmosphäre, Stimmung V/1/M7

° attach [əˈtætʃ] verbinden; befestigen V/1/PP

attack [əˈtæk] angreifen V/3/M2; Angriff V/2/M1

pay attention to sb/sth [ˌpeɪˌəˈtenʃn tə sʌmbədi/sʌmθɪŋ] jdm/etw Aufmerksamkeit schenken V/2/2

attraction [əˈtrækʃn] Attraktion; Anziehung(skraft)

AUD (= Australian Dollar) [ˌeɪ juː ˈdiː] Australischer Dollar (Währung in Australien) V/1/6

audition [ɔːˈdɪʃn] Vorsprechen; Vorsingen; Vortanzen; Vorspielen

August [ˈɔːgəst] August

aunt [ɑːnt] Tante

auntie *(informal)* [ˈɑːnti] Kosewort für Tante V/1/12

Australia [ɒˈstreɪliə] Australien V/1/I

Australian [ɒˈstreɪliən] Australier/in; australisch

author [ˈɔːθə] Schriftsteller/in; Verfasser/in, Autor/in

authority [ɔːˈθɒrəti] Amtsgewalt; Behörde V/1/M6

autograph [ˈɔːtəˌgrɑːf] Autogramm

autopilot [ˈɔːtəʊˌpaɪlət] Autopilot V/6/8

available [əˈveɪləbl] verfügbar V/5/4

° average [ˈævrɪdʒ] durchschnittlich V/5/CIO

avoid [əˈvɔɪd] (ver)meiden, ausweichen V/5/15

° awake [əˈweɪk] aufwachen, erwachen V/3/11

award [əˈwɔːd] Auszeichnung, Preis V/3/M8

be aware of sth [biː əˈweər ɒv ˌsʌmθɪŋ] sich einer Sache bewusst sein

make sb aware of sth [ˌmeɪk sʌmbədi əˈweə əv sʌmθɪŋ] jdm etw bewusst machen V/4/M6

away [əˈweɪ] weg

awful [ˈɔːfl] furchtbar, schrecklich V/4/9

B

° B.C. (= before Christ) [biˌfɔːˈkraɪst] v. Chr. V/4/CIO

back [bæk] Rücken; Rückseite; zurück

at the back of [ət ðə ˈbæk əv] hinten in

backache [ˈbækeɪk] Rückenschmerzen

background [ˈbækˌɡraʊnd] Herkunft, Verhältnisse; Hintergrund V/2/M2

backpacker [ˈbækˌpækə] Rucksackreisende/r V/1/6

bacon [ˈbeɪkən] (Schinken)speck

bad [bæd] schlecht; schlimm

use bad language [juːz bæd ˈlæŋɡwɪdʒ] Schimpfwörter benutzen

bag [bæɡ] Tasche

baggy [ˈbæɡi] weit V/2/4

bake [beɪk] backen

baker [ˈbeɪkə] Bäcker/in

natural balance [ˌnætʃrəl ˈbæləns] ökologisches Gleichgewicht V/1/M1

ball [bɔːl] Ball

° have a ball *(informal)* [hæv ə ˈbɔːl] Spaß haben, sich bestens amüsieren V/5/11

ballpoint [ˈbɔːlˌpɔɪnt] Kugelschreiber

ban sth [ˈbæn ˌsʌmθɪŋ] etw verbieten V/4/5

banana [bəˈnɑːnə] Banane

bandage [ˈbændɪdʒ] Verband

bottle bank [ˈbɒtl bæŋk] Altglascontainer V/6/M4

can bank [ˈkæn bæŋk] Dosencontainer V/6/M4

paper bank [ˈpeɪpə bæŋk] Altpapiercontainer V/6/M4

plastic bottle bank [ˈplæstɪk ˌbɒtl bæŋk] Plastikflaschencontainer V/6/M4

bar chart [ˈbɑː ˌtʃɑːt] Säulendiagramm, Balkendiagramm V/5/16

have a barbecue [ˌhæv ə ˈbɑːbɪˌkjuː] grillen, eine Grillparty feiern V/1/5

barbie *(Australian English; informal)* [ˈbɑːbi] Kurzform von barbecue V/1/5

barely [ˈbeəli] kaum V/4/M3

bark [bɑːk] bellen

be based on sth [biː ˈbeɪst ɒn ˌsʌmθɪŋ] auf etw basieren/ beruhen V/1/M5

basic [ˈbeɪsɪk] grundlegend, wesentlich; Grund- V/3/7

basis [ˈbeɪsɪs] Basis, Grundlage V/5/M1

basket [ˈbɑːskɪt] Korb

bath [bɑːθ] (Bade)wanne; Bad(ezimmer)

take a bath [teɪk ə ˈbɑːθ] baden V/6/4

bathroom [ˈbɑːθˌruːm] Bad(ezimmer)

bathroom *(AE) here:* toilet *(BE)* [ˈbɑːθˌruːm] Toilette

battery [ˈbætri] Batterie V/6/M5

be [biː] sein

beach [biːtʃ] Strand

bean [biːn] Bohne

bear [beə] Bär

beat [biːt] schlagen; besiegen

beautiful [ˈbjuːtəfl] schön

beauty [ˈbjuːti] Schönheit V/1/M1

because [bɪˈkɒz] weil

because of [bɪˈkɒz əv] wegen

become [bɪˈkʌm] werden

bed [bed] Bett

bedroom [ˈbedruːm] Schlafzimmer

° bee [biː] Biene V/4/CIO

beer [bɪə] Bier V/2/M5

before [bɪˈfɔː] bevor; vor; zuvor, vorher

beg [beg] betteln V/5/M11

beggar [ˈbegə] Bettler/in V/5/M11

begging *(no pl)* [ˈbegɪŋ] Betteln V/5/M11

begin [bɪˈgɪn] anfangen, beginnen

beginning [bɪˈgɪnɪŋ] Anfang

behave [bɪˈheɪv] sich verhalten, sich benehmen V/5/3

behavior *(no pl) (AE)* = behaviour *(BE)* [bɪˈheɪvjə] Verhalten, Benehmen V/2/M5

behaviour *(no pl)* [bɪˈheɪvjə] Verhalten, Benehmen V/6/4

behind [bɪˈhaɪnd] hinter; dahinter

believe (in) [bɪˈliːv] glauben (an)

belong [bɪˈlɒŋ] gehören V/5/M2

below [bɪˈləʊ] unten

bench [bentʃ] Bank

bend [bend] (sich) biegen

bend over [bend ˈəʊvə] sich vorbeugen

° berry [ˈberi] Beere V/1/PP

best [best] am meisten/liebsten/ besten; beste(r, s)

best wishes [ˌbest ˈwɪʃɪz] viele/ beste Grüße

best-known [ˌbestˈnəʊn] bekannteste(r,s) V/4/M2

bet [bet] wetten

° better off [ˌbetə ˈɒf] wohlhabender, besser gestellt V/I/PP

between [bɪˈtwiːn] zwischen

bicycle [ˈbaɪsɪkl] Fahrrad

big [bɪɡ] groß

bike [baɪk] (Fahr)rad

bill [bɪl] Rechnung

° billion [ˈbɪljən] Milliarde V/6/PP

bin [bɪn] Mülleimer, Mülltonne

compost bin [ˈkɒmpɒst bɪn] Komposttonne V/6/M4

binge [bɪndʒ] zu viel von etw konsumieren V/2/CIO

biography [baɪˈɒɡrəfi] Biografie V/5/M9

biology [baɪˈɒlədʒi] Biologie
bird [bɜːd] Vogel
birth [bɜːθ] Geburt
give birth to a child [gɪv ˌbɜːθ tʊ ə ˈtʃaɪld] ein Kind zur Welt bringen V/3/M8
birthday [ˈbɜːθdeɪ] Geburtstag
biscuit [ˈbɪskɪt] Keks
bit [bɪt] Stück, Stückchen V/3/5
a bit [ə ˈbɪt] ein bisschen
bite [baɪt] beißen
black [blæk] schwarz
blackboard [ˈblækˌbɔːd] Tafel
bleaching [ˈbliːtʃɪŋ] Bleichen V/1/M2
° blemished [ˈblemɪʃt] fehlerhaft; dunkel V/1/M9
block [blɒk] blockieren, verstellen; den Weg versperren
blonde [blɒnd] blond V/3/M8
blue [bluː] blau
BMX biking *(no pl)* [ˌbiːemˈeks ˌbaɪkɪŋ] Fahren mit dem BMX-Rad V/3/2
board [bɔːd] Brett
boarding school [ˈbɔːdɪŋ ˌskuːl] Internat V/1/5
boat [bəʊt] Boot
body [ˈbɒdi] Körper
boiled [bɔɪld] gekocht V/4/9
bone [bəʊn] Knochen V/3/5
book [bʊk] Buch; buchen V/1/6
boot [buːt] Stiefel
border [ˈbɔːdə] Grenze
be bored [bi ˈbɔːd] sich langweilen
boring [ˈbɔːrɪŋ] langweilig
born [bɔːn] geboren
borrow [ˈbɒrəʊ] leihen
boss [bɒs] Chef V/4/5
both [bəʊθ] beide
bother sb [ˈbɒðə ˌsʌmbədi] jdn stören; jdn belästigen V/3/6
bottle [ˈbɒtl] Flasche
bottle bank [ˈbɒtl bæŋk] Altglascontainer V/6/M4
bottom [ˈbɒtəm] Boden; Unterseite; unteres Ende, Boden
bow [baʊ] sich verbeugen V/2/CIO
bowl [bəʊl] Schüssel

box office [ˈbɒksˌɒfɪs] Kasse *(im Kino, Theater)*
° boxing *(no pl)* [ˈbɒksɪŋ] Boxen V/3/CIO
boy [bɔɪ] Junge
boyfriend [ˈbɔɪfrend] Freund (eines Mädchens)
braided [ˈbreɪdɪd] geflochten V/3/M8
brainstorm [ˈbreɪnˌstɔːm] ein Brainstorming machen V/2/10
branch [brɑːntʃ] Zweig; Ast
brave [breɪv] mutig, unerschrocken
bread [bred] Brot
break [breɪk] (zer)brechen; verstoßen, übertreten, ignorieren; Pause
break down [ˌbreɪk ˈdaʊn] kaputtgehen, zusammenbrechen V/6/8
° break down [ˌbreɪk ˈdaʊn] sich auflösen V/6/CIO
° break up [ˌbreɪkˈʌp] zerstören; auflösen V/1/M9
breakfast [ˈbrekfəst] Frühstück
° breathe [briːð] atmen V/3/11
bridge [brɪdʒ] Brücke
bright [braɪt] hell
brilliant [ˈbrɪljənt] leuchtend, brilliant V/1/M1
brilliant *(informal)* [ˈbrɪljənt] toll, hervorragend V/2/M2
bring [brɪŋ] (mit)bringen
° bring down sb [ˌbrɪŋ ˈdaʊn sʌmbədi] jdn deprimieren V/3/11
Britain [ˈbrɪtn] Großbritannien
British [ˈbrɪtɪʃ] britische(r, s)
the British *(pl)* [ðə ˈbrɪtɪʃ] die Briten
brochure [ˈbrəʊʃə] Broschüre
broken [ˈbrəʊkən] zerbrochen, kaputt
brother [ˈbrʌðə] Bruder
brown [braʊn] braun
bruised [bruːzd] geprellt
brush [brʌʃ] (ab)bürsten; putzen
budget [ˈbʌdʒɪt] ein Budget aufstellen V/5/15
build [bɪld] bauen
builder [ˈbɪldə] Bauarbeiter/in V/5/2

building [ˈbɪldɪŋ] Gebäude, Bau
building centre [ˈbɪldɪŋ ˌsentə] Baumarkt V/5/5
bully [ˈbʊli] Tyrann, Rüpel, Rabauke; tyrannisieren, drangsalieren
bullying [ˈbʊliɪŋ] Mobbing
burn [bɜːn] (ver)brennen
bus [bʌs] Bus
bus stop [ˈbʌs ˌstɒp] Bushaltestelle
bush [bʊʃ] Busch
° business [ˈbɪznəs] Handel, Gewerbe V/I/PP
busker [ˈbʌskə] Straßenmusikant/in
busy [ˈbɪzi] beschäftigt; arbeitsreich
but [bʌt] aber
but [bʌt] sondern V/1/M9
butter [ˈbʌtə] Butter
buy [baɪ] kaufen
buyer [ˈbaɪə] Käufer/in
by [baɪ] bei, in der Nähe; mit, durch; (spätestens) bis; von
by accident [baɪ ˈæksɪdnt] aus Versehen; zufällig
by the way [baɪ ðə ˈweɪ] übrigens V/1/5
Bye! *(informal)* [baɪ] Tschüss!
Bye-bye! *(informal)* [bəˈbaɪ] Tschüss!

C

cafeteria [ˌkæfəˈtɪəriə] Cafeteria
° Cairo [ˈkaɪrəʊ] Kairo V/I/1
cake [keɪk] Kuchen
calendar [ˈkælɪndə] Kalender
California [ˌkæləˈfɔːniə] Kalifornien V/2/5
call [kɔːl] (Telefon)anruf; anrufen; nennen
call sb names [ˌkɔːl sʌmbədi ˈneɪmz] jdn beschimpfen
called [kɔːld] genannt
caller [ˈkɔːlə] Anrufer/in
calorie [ˈkæləri] Kalorie V/4/3
camera [ˈkæmrə] Kamera, Fotoapparat
cameraman/-woman [ˈkæmrəˌmæn, ˈkæmrəˌwʊmən] Kameramann/-frau

DICTIONARY *English–German*

DICTIONARY ENGLISH–GERMAN

° Cameroon [ˌkæməˈruːn] Kamerun
V/I/1

campaign [kæmˈpeɪn] Kampagne,
Aktion V/4/5

campsite [ˈkæmpˌsaɪt]
Campingplatz, Zeltplatz

can [kæn] können; Dose V/6/4

can bank [ˈkæn bæŋk]
Dosencontainer V/6/M4

° can't get sb/sth off one's mind
[ˌkɑːnt get sʌmbədi/sʌmθɪŋ ˌɒf
wʌnz ˈmaɪnd] nicht aufhören
können, an jdn/etw zu denken
V/5/11

Canada [ˈkænədə] Kanada V/3/5

cancer [ˈkænsə] Krebs *(Krankheit)*
V/1/M3

candle [ˈkændl] Kerze

° canoe [kəˈnuː] Kanu, Paddelboot
V/1/PP

canoeing *(no pl)* [kəˈnuːɪŋ]
Kanufahren; Paddeln V/3/4

canteen [kænˈtiːn] Kantine;
Mensa V/4/5

cap [kæp] Mütze, Kappe

° Cape Town [ˈkeɪptaʊn] Kapstadt
V/I/1

capital [ˈkæpɪtl] Hauptstadt

captain [ˈkæptɪn] Kapitän/-in

caption [ˈkæpʃn] Bildunterschrift;
Titel V/4/M7

capture [ˈkæptʃə] (ein)fangen
V/1/M5

car [kɑː] Auto

car boot sale [ˌkɑː ˈbuːt ˌseɪl]
*Verkauf persönlicher
Gegenstände aus dem Koffer-
raum auf einem Parkplatz*

carbohydrate [ˌkɑːbəʊˈhaɪdreɪt]
Kohle(n)hydrat V/4/3

carbon dioxide *(no pl)* [ˌkɑːbən
daɪˈɒksaɪd] Kohlen(stoff)dioxid
V/6/M1

card [kɑːd] Pappe, Karton; Karte

cardboard *(no pl)* [ˈkɑːdˌbɔːd]
Pappe, (Papp)karton V/6/M2

sb does not care [ˌsʌmbədi dʌz
nɒt ˈkeə] jdm ist es gleich/egal

care for sb/sth [ˈkeə fə ˌsʌmbədi/
ˌsʌmθɪŋ] sich um jdn/etw
kümmern V/3/4

take care of [teɪk ˈkeər ˌəv] sich
kümmern um, versorgen

career [kəˈrɪə] Beruf; Karriere

careful [ˈkeəfl] vorsichtig;
sorgfältig, gründlich

Caribbean [ˌkærɪˈbiən] karibisch

the Caribbean [ðə ˌkærɪˈbiən] die
Karibik, die Karibischen Inseln

carnival [ˈkɑːnɪvl] Volksfest;
Karneval

carpet [ˈkɑːpɪt] Teppich

carrot [ˈkærət] Möhre, Karotte,
Mohrrübe

carry [ˈkæri] tragen

carry out sth [ˌkæriˈaʊt ˌsʌmθɪŋ]
etw durchführen V/6/M2

cartoon [kɑːˈtuːn]
Zeichentrickfilm

in case ... [ɪn keɪs] für den Fall,
dass ...; falls ... V/1/CIO

cash handout [ˈkæʃ ˌhændaʊt]
finanzielle Zuwendung,
Geldzuwendung V/5/M11

cash machine [ˈkæʃ məˌʃiːn]
Geldautomat

cash *(no pl)* [kæʃ] Bargeld

cast [kɑːst] Gips(verband)
V/3/5

castle [ˈkɑːsl] Burg; Schloss

cat [kæt] Katze

catch [kætʃ] fangen; kriegen;
festnehmen V/2/M5

category [ˈkætəgri] Kategorie
V/5/M2

caterer [ˈkeɪtərə] Lieferant/-in
für Speisen und Getränke;
Partyservice

° 'cause (= because) *(informal)*
[kʌz, bɪˈkɒz] weil, da V/2/1

cause [kɔːz] Grund, Ursache;
Sache

causeway [ˈkɔːzweɪ] Damm

caving *(no pl)* [ˈkeɪvɪŋ]
Höhlenexpedition;
Höhlenwandern V/3/2

celebrate [ˈseləˌbreɪt] feiern

celebration [ˌseləˈbreɪʃn] Feier

° celebrity [səˈlebrəti] berühmte
Persönlichkeit, Star V/6/PP

cellar [ˈselə] Keller V/4/M7

cent [sent] Cent, Centmünze
(amerikanische Währung)

centre [ˈsentə] Zentrum, Center
V/5/4

century [ˈsentʃəri] Jahrhundert

cereal [ˈsɪəriəl] Getreide(sorte);
Frühstückszerealien V/4/1

certain [ˈsɜːtn] sicher; gewis-
se(r, s), bestimmte(r, s)

chain [tʃeɪn] Kette

chair [tʃeə] Stuhl

chalk *(no pl)* [tʃɔːk] Kreide

challenge [ˈtʃælɪndʒ]
Herausforderung V/3/M2

challenge [ˈtʃælɪndʒ]
herausfordern V/3/4

championship [ˈtʃæmpiənʃɪp]
Meisterschaft

chance [tʃɑːns] Möglichkeit;
Chance

change [tʃeɪndʒ] (sich)
(ver)ändern; (Ver)änderung;
Wechselgeld; wechseln V/5/8

channel [ˈtʃænl] Kanal, Programm

° chapter [ˈtʃæptə] Kapitel,
Abschnitt V/1/M9

character [ˈkærɪktə] Charakter;
Figur V/6/8

charge sb (with sth) [ˈtʃɑːdʒ
ˌsʌmbədi] jdn (einer Sache)
beschuldigen; jdn (wegen
einer Sache) anklagen
V/3/5

charity [ˈtʃærəti]
Wohltätigkeitsveranstaltung;
wohltätige Zwecke

charity organization [ˈtʃærəti
ˌɔːgənaɪˈzeɪʃn] Wohltätigkeits-
organisation V/5/M11

charming [ˈtʃɑːmɪŋ] bezaubernd,
reizend

chat-up line *(informal)* [ˈtʃætʌp
ˌlaɪn] Anmache

cheap [tʃiːp] billig, preiswert

check [tʃek] überprüfen,
kontrollieren

check out sth [ˌtʃekˈaʊt ˌsʌmθɪŋ]
etw untersuchen/überprüfen
V/6/8

check-in agent [ˈtʃekɪnˌeɪdʒnt]
Mitarbeiter/-in am Check-in-
Schalter am Flughafen V/5/2

checklist [ˈtʃekˌlɪst] Checkliste,
Kontrollliste V/5/8

cheek [tʃiːk] Wange, Backe

cheer [tʃɪə] jubeln; anfeuern

cheer up [ˌtʃɪərˈʌp] vergnügt(er)
werden; aufmuntern

198

DICTIONARY *English–German*

Cheer up! [tʃɪər ˈʌp] Lass (doch) den Kopf nicht hängen!, Kopf hoch!

cheerleading [ˈtʃɪəˌliːdɪŋ] Cheerleaden

cheese [tʃiːz] Käse

chef [ʃef] Koch/Köchin V/4/5

cherry [ˈtʃeri] Kirsche

chess [tʃes] Schach(spiel)

chest of drawers [ˌtʃest əv ˈdrɔːz] Kommode

chewing gum *(no pl)* [ˈtʃuːɪŋ ˌgʌm] Kaugummi

chicken [ˈtʃɪkɪn] Huhn

chickenpox [ˈtʃɪkɪnˌpɒks] Windpocken

chief [tʃiːf] Führer/in; Oberhaupt; Häuptling

child *(pl* **children***)* [tʃaɪld, ˈtʃɪldrən] Kind

(children's) nurse [(ˈtʃɪldrənz) nɜːs] Kindermädchen V/1/12

chimpanzee [ˌtʃɪmpænˈziː] Schimpanse

China [ˈtʃaɪnə] China

Chinese [ˌtʃaɪˈniːz] Chinese/Chinesin; chinesisch

chips *(pl)* [tʃɪps] Pommes frites

chocolate [ˈtʃɒklət] Schokolade

choice [tʃɔɪs] Wahl

choose [tʃuːz] auswählen

° **chorus** [ˈkɔːrəs] Refrain V/2/1

Christmas [ˈkrɪsməs] Weihnachten

Christmas Day [ˌkrɪsməs ˈdeɪ] erster Weihnachtsfeiertag V/1/5

church [tʃɜːtʃ] Kirche

cinema [ˈsɪnəmə] Kino

circle [ˈsɜːkl] Kreis

citizen [ˈsɪtɪzn] (Staats)bürger/in

city [ˈsɪti] (Groß)stadt

do civilian service [du səˌvɪliən ˈsɜːvɪs] Zivildienst leisten V/5/2

° **lay claim to sth** [ˌleɪ ˈkleɪm tə sʌmθɪŋ] auf etw Anspruch erheben V/1/M9

class [klɑːs] (Schul)klasse; Unterricht

(class) schedule *(AE)* = **timetable** *(BE)* [ˈklɑːs ˌskedʒəl] Stundenplan

classmate [ˈklɑːsˌmeɪt] Klassenkamerad/in, Mitschüler/in

classroom [ˈklɑːsˌruːm] Klassenzimmer

clean [kliːn] sauber; sauber machen, reinigen, putzen

clean up [kliːn ˈʌp] sauber machen, reinigen

cleaning company [ˈkliːnɪŋ ˌkʌmpəni] Reinigungsunternehmen V/3/M2

clear [klɪə] klar, eindeutig V/6/M2

clever [ˈklevə] klug, gescheit, schlau

click [klɪk] (an)klicken, drücken V/2/9

climb [klaɪm] (hinauf)steigen; (hinauf)klettern

clock [klɒk] Uhr

(eight) o'clock [əˈklɒk] (acht) Uhr

close [kləʊs] nah(e)

close [kləʊz] schließen, zumachen

close [kləʊs] genau V/4/10

close by [ˌkləʊs ˈbaɪ] ganz in der Nähe, in unmittelbarer Nähe V/4/M8

clothes *(npl)* [kləʊðz] Kleider, Bekleidung

clothing *(no pl)* [ˈkləʊðɪŋ] Kleidung

cloud [klaʊd] Wolke

cloudy [ˈklaʊdi] bewölkt, bedeckt

clownfish [ˈklaʊnfɪʃ] Clownfisch V/1/M1

club [klʌb] Klub, Verein

club [klʌb] Disko(thek) V/2/5

clubbing [ˈklʌbɪŋ] in die Disko gehen V/2/7

coach [kəʊtʃ] Trainer

coast [kəʊst] Küste

cockroach [ˈkɒkrəʊtʃ] Küchenschabe, Kakerlake V/6/8

coffee [ˈkɒfi] Kaffee

coffin [ˈkɒfɪn] Sarg V/4/M7

coin [kɔɪn] Münze, Geldstück

cold [kəʊld] kalt; Erkältung, Schnupfen; Kälte

collage [ˈkɒlɑːʒ] Collage V/6/6

collect [kəˈlekt] sammeln; abholen

college [ˈkɒlɪdʒ] Bildungseinrichtung; Universität, Hochschule

colony [ˈkɒləni] Kolonie V/1/M1

colour [ˈkʌlə] Farbe

colourful [ˈkʌləfl] farbenfroh, farbenprächtig

comb [kəʊm] Kamm

° **combination** [ˌkɒmbɪˈneɪʃn] Kombination V/3/CIO

come [kʌm] kommen

come for [ˈkʌm fə] (ab)holen, kommen wegen

come in [kʌm ˈɪn] hereinkommen

Come on! [kʌm ˈɒn] Komm(t) jetzt!, Mach(t) schon!

come out [kʌm ˈaʊt] herauskommen

come over [ˌkʌm ˈəʊvə] (her)überkommen

come to sb's mind [kʌm tə ˌsʌmbədiz ˈmaɪnd] jdm einfallen

come true [kʌm ˈtruː] wahr werden V/4/M2

° **come up** [ˌkʌm ˈʌp] entstehen V/3/PP

comedy [ˈkɒmədi] Komödie

comfortable [ˈkʌmftəbl] bequem

comment [ˈkɒment] Kommentar, Bemerkung

commercial [kəˈmɜːʃl] Werbespot; Fernseh-/Radiowerbung

commit [kəˈmɪt] begehen *(Verbrechen)* V/2/5

° **common** [ˈkɒmən] gemeinsam V/I/PP; üblich, normal V/2/PP

have sth in common [hæv ˌsʌmθɪŋ ɪn ˈkɒmən] etwas gemein haben V/5/M9

communicate [kəˈmjuːnɪkeɪt] sich verständigen, kommunizieren V/3/M2

communication [kəˌmjuːnɪˈkeɪʃn] Kommunikation V/5/4

communicative [kəˈmjuːnɪkətɪv] mitteilsam, gesprächig V/5/3

community [kəˈmjuːnəti] Gemeinde; Gemeinschaft

community service *(no pl)* [kəmˌjuːnəti ˈsɜːvɪs] gemeinnützige Arbeit V/2/M5

DICTIONARY *English–German*

DICTIONARY ENGLISH–GERMAN

company ['kʌmpni] Firma;
Gesellschaft
compare [kəm'peə] vergleichen
° **compensate sb for sth**
['kɒmpənseɪt ˌsʌmbədi fə
ˌsʌmθɪŋ] jdn für etw (finanziell)
entschädigen V/1/PP
compete (for) [kəm'pi:t]
wetteifern (um), kämpfen (um)
competition [ˌkɒmpə'tɪʃn]
Wettbewerb
complete [kəm'pli:t]
vervollständigen
compost bin ['kɒmpɒst bɪn]
Komposttonne V/6/M4
con [kɒn] Kontra(-Argument)
V/2/I
be concerned (about) [ˌbi:
kən'sɜ:nd] sich Sorgen machen
(um)
concert ['kɒnsət] Konzert
in concert [ɪn 'kɒnsət] live V/2/7
conference ['kɒnfrəns]
Konferenz, Tagung V/6/M2
° **confidence** *(no pl)* ['kɒnfɪdns]
Vertrauen, Zuversicht
V/1/M9
confused [kən'fju:zd] verwirrt,
durcheinander
congratulations *(npl)*
[kənˌgrætʃʊ'leɪʃnz]
Glückwunsch, Glückwünsche
conjunction [kən'dʒʌŋkʃn]
Konjunktion V/3/M8
connect [kə'nekt] verbinden
V/5/8
consequence ['kɒnsɪkwəns]
Folge, Konsequenz V/6/M1
constant ['kɒnstənt] dauernd,
ständig V/1/M1
° **consume** [kən'sju:m]
konsumieren, zu sich nehmen
V/2/PP
° **be consumed** [bi: kən'sju:md]
versunken sein V/3/11
consumption [kən'sʌmpʃn]
Verbrauch V/6/M2
contact ['kɒntækt] Kontakt
V/3/M5
contact sb ['kɒntækt ˌsʌmbədi]
jdn kontaktieren, sich mit jdm
in Verbindung setzen V/4/7
contest ['kɒntest] Wettbewerb

context ['kɒntekst] Kontext,
Zusammenhang
° **continent** ['kɒntɪnənt] Kontinent,
Erdteil V/I/3
° **continuing** [kən'tɪnjʊɪŋ]
andauernd V/1/M9
control [kən'trəʊl] regulieren,
steuern V/6/M1
be in control of sth [bi_ɪn
kən'trəʊl əv ˌsʌmθɪŋ] etw unter
Kontrolle haben V/5/15
conversation [ˌkɒnvə'seɪʃn]
Gespräch, Unterhaltung V/5/3
cook [kʊk] Koch/Köchin; kochen
cool [ku:l] kalt, kühl; cool
cop *(informal)* [kɒp] Bulle V/3/5
copy ['kɒpi] abschreiben;
kopieren
copy ['kɒpi] Abschrift; Exemplar
V/3/M6
coral ['kɒrəl] Koralle V/1/M1
coral ['kɒrəl] Korallen- V/1/M1
coral reef [ˌkɒrəl 'ri:f] Korallenriff
V/1/2
corn [kɔ:n] Getreide, Korn
corner ['kɔ:nə] Ecke
correct [kə'rekt] korrigieren;
richtig, korrekt
cost [kɒst] kosten
costume ['kɒstju:m] Tracht,
Kostüm
° **cotton** ['kɒtn] Baumwolle
V/5/CIO
count [kaʊnt] zählen
country ['kʌntri] Land
in the country [ɪn ðə 'kʌntri] auf
dem Land V/3/5
course [kɔ:s] Kurs
of course [əv 'kɔ:s] natürlich
court [kɔ:t] Gericht V/2/M5
cousin ['kʌzn] Cousin/e
cow [kaʊ] Kuh
coward ['kaʊəd] Feigling
crack [kræk] aufbrechen V/1/11
crane [kreɪn] Kranich V/1/11
crazy ['kreɪzi] verrückt
° **be crazy about sb/sth**
['kreɪzi_əˌbaʊt ˌsʌmbədi/
ˌsʌmθɪŋ] nach jdm/etw
verrückt sein V/1/CIO
cream [kri:m] Sahne
cream cheese [ˌkri:m 'tʃi:z]
Frischkäse V/4/1

create [kri'eɪt] erschaffen;
gestalten V/6/M2
creative [kri'eɪtɪv] kreativ V/5/3
credit card ['kredɪt ˌkɑ:d]
Kreditkarte
crime [kraɪm] Verbrechen
V/2/5
criminal ['krɪmɪnl] Kriminelle/r
V/2/M5
criminal record [ˌkrɪmɪnl 'rekɔ:d]
Vorstrafenregister V/2/M5
crisps *(npl)* [krɪsps] Chips
crocodile ['krɒkədaɪl] Krokodil
cross [krɒs] durchqueren;
überqueren
crossword puzzle ['krɒsw3:d
ˌpʌzl] Kreuzworträtsel V/6/6
crowd [kraʊd] (Menschen)menge,
Zuschauermenge
crown [kraʊn] Krone
cruel ['kru:əl] grausam V/1/12
cry [kraɪ] Weinen; Schrei; Ruf;
weinen; schreien
cucumber ['kju:ˌkʌmbə]
(Salat)gurke
culture ['kʌltʃə] Kultur
V/2/M2
cup [kʌp] Tasse
cupboard ['kʌbəd] Schrank
cured [kjʊəd] geheilt V/4/9
curious ['kjʊəriəs] neugierig
curry ['kʌri] Curry(gericht)
curtain ['k3:tn] Vorhang
cushion ['kʊʃn] Kissen
custom ['kʌstəm] Brauch, Sitte
customer ['kʌstəmə] Kunde/
Kundin
cut [kʌt] schneiden; mähen
cut down [kʌt 'daʊn] umhauen,
fällen
cute [kju:t] süß, niedlich
cutie *(informal)* ['kju:ti] Süße/r
V/2/2
CV (= curriculum vitae)
[ˌsi: 'vi: (= kəˌrɪkjʊləm 'vi:taɪ)]
Lebenslauf V/5/4
cycle ['saɪkl] Rad fahren
cycling ['saɪklɪŋ] Radfahren,
Radeln
cyclist ['saɪklɪst] Radfahrer/in
V/3/M2
° **Cyprus** ['saɪprəs] Zypern
V/I/1

D

dad *(informal)* [dæd] Papa, Vati
daily ['deɪli] täglich
  V/4/CIO
dairy food ['deəri fuːd]
  Milchprodukt V/4/4
damage ['dæmɪdʒ] (be)schädigen
  V/6/M6
dance [dɑːns] Tanz; tanzen
dancer ['dɑːnsə] Tänzer/in
dancing ['dɑːnsɪŋ] Tanzen
danger ['deɪndʒə] (Lebens)gefahr
dangerous ['deɪndʒərəs]
  gefährlich
dare [deə] wagen, sich trauen
  V/4/M6
dark [dɑːk] dunkel
date [deɪt] Datum; Termin;
  Verabredung; Rendezvous
date of birth ['deɪt ˌəv ˌbɜːθ]
  Geburtsdatum
date sb *(informal)* ['deɪt
  ˌsʌmbədi] mit jdm gehen; sich
  mit jdm verabreden
daughter ['dɔːtə] Tochter
day [deɪ] Tag
the day after tomorrow
  [ðə ˌdeɪ ˌɑːftə təˈmɒrəʊ]
  übermorgen V/6/14
the day before [ðə ˌdeɪ bɪˈfɔː] am
  vorherigen Tag V/4/11
dead [ded] tot V/4/9
deal with ['diːl wɪð] sich
  kümmern um, sich befassen
  mit V/2/M5
dear [dɪə] liebe(r) *(Anrede)*
death [deθ] Tod V/3/10
debit card ['debɪt ˌkɑːd]
  Debitkarte *(entspricht einer
  EC-Karte)* V/5/13
get into debt [ˌget ˌɪntə 'det]
  Schulden machen, sich
  verschulden V/5/13
December [dɪˈsembə] Dezember
decide [dɪˈsaɪd] sich entscheiden;
  beschließen
declare [dɪˈkleə] erklären,
  verkünden V/1/2
decorate ['dekəreɪt] schmücken
deep [diːp] tief
defend [dɪˈfend] verteidigen
definitely ['defnətli] eindeutig,
  definitiv V/3/M8

definition [ˌdefəˈnɪʃn] Definition,
  Erklärung V/3/M2
° **degradation** [ˌdegrəˈdeɪʃn]
  Erniedrigung V/1/M9
delicious [dɪˈlɪʃəs] köstlich, lecker
° **be delirious** [bi: dɪˈlɪriəs] im
  Delirium sein; verrückt sein
  V/3/11
depart [dɪˈpɑːt] abfahren
department store [dɪˈpɑːtmənt
  ˌstɔː] Kaufhaus
depend on sth [dɪˈpend ˌɒn ˌsʌmθɪŋ]
  von etw abhängen V/2/CIO
deputy head ['depjʊti ˌhed]
  Konrektor
° **descendant** [dɪˈsendənt]
  Nachkomme V/1/M9
describe [dɪˈskraɪb] beschreiben
description [dɪˈskrɪpʃn]
  Beschreibung
desert ['dezət] Wüste
design [dɪˈzaɪn] entwerfen
desk [desk] Schreibtisch
desperate ['desprət] verzweifelt
  V/4/M6
despise [dɪˈspaɪz] verachten,
  hassen V/1/M5
dessert [dɪˈzɜːt] Nachtisch,
  Dessert
destroy [dɪˈstrɔɪ] zerstören
detail ['diːteɪl] Detail, Einzelheit
detective [dɪˈtektɪv]
  (Privat)detektiv/in
develop [dɪˈveləp] (sich) entwickeln V/3/4
development [dɪˈveləpmənt] Ent-
  wicklung; Wachstum V/6/M2
dialogue ['daɪəlɒg] Gespräch,
  Dialog
diary ['daɪəri] Tagebuch
keep a diary [ˌkiːp ə 'daɪəri] (ein)
  Tagebuch führen V/4/11
dictionary ['dɪkʃənri] Wörterbuch
die [daɪ] sterben
diet ['daɪət] Nahrung, Ernährung;
  Diät V/4/6
difference ['dɪfrəns] Unterschied
different ['dɪfrənt] anders,
  andere(r, s); verschieden
difficult ['dɪfɪklt] schwierig,
  schwer
difficulty ['dɪfɪklti] Schwierigkeit,
  Problem V/3/M2

dingo *(pl -es)* ['dɪŋgəʊ, 'dɪŋgəʊz]
  Dingo, australischer Windhund
  V/1/5
dining room ['daɪnɪŋ ˌruːm]
  Esszimmer
dinner ['dɪnə] Abendessen;
  Mittagessen
dinosaur ['daɪnəˌsɔː] Dinosaurier
direct [dɪˈrekt] direkt V/2/10
direct speech [dɪˌrekt 'spiːtʃ]
  direkte Rede V/4/11
give directions [ˌgɪv dɪˈrekʃnz]
  den Weg beschreiben
dirty ['dɜːti] dreckig, schmutzig
disabled [dɪsˈeɪbld] behindert
disagree [ˌdɪsəˈgriː] nicht übereinstimmen; nicht einverstanden sein
disappear [ˌdɪsəˈpɪə] verschwinden
disappointed [ˌdɪsəˈpɔɪntɪd]
  enttäuscht
discover [dɪˈskʌvə] herausfinden,
  entdecken
discuss [dɪˈskʌs] besprechen
discuss [dɪˈskʌs] diskutieren
  V/2/M7
discussion [dɪˈskʌʃn] Diskussion,
  Erörterung V/2/8
disease [dɪˈziːz] Krankheit
disgusting [dɪsˈgʌstɪŋ] widerlich
dish *(pl -es)* [dɪʃ] Schale;
  Gericht
dishwasher ['dɪʃˌwɒʃə] Geschirrspülmaschine V/6/1
dislikes *(pl)* [dɪsˈlaɪks]
  Abneigungen
distance ['dɪstəns] Entfernung;
  Strecke V/1/5
disturb [dɪˈstɜːb] stören,
  durcheinanderbringen V/1/M1
diver ['daɪvə] Taucher/in V/1/M1
° **divide** [dɪˈvaɪd] teilen; trennen
  V/1/PP
divorced [dɪˈvɔːst] geschieden
do [duː] machen, tun
do civilian service [duː səˈvɪliən
  'sɜːvɪs] Zivildienst leisten V/5/2
do military service [duː ˌmɪlɪtri
  'sɜːvɪs] Wehrdienst leisten
  V/5/2
do one's A levels [duː wʌnzˌ 'eɪ
  ˌlevlz] das Abitur machen
  V/5/2

do vocational training [duː
vəʊˌkeɪʃnəl ˈtreɪnɪŋ] eine
Berufsausbildung machen
V/5/2

do volunteer work [duː ˈvɒləntɪə
ˌwɜːk] Freiwilligenarbeit leisten
V/5/2

do wrong [duː ˈrɒŋ] etw falsch
machen V/2/M5

doctor [ˈdɒktə] Arzt/Ärztin

documentary [ˌdɒkjʊˈmentri]
Dokumentation,
Dokumentarfilm

dog [dɒg] Hund

dog sledding *(no pl)* [ˈdɒg ˌsledɪŋ]
Hundeschlittenfahren V/3/4

doll [dɒl] Puppe

dolphin [ˈdɒlfɪn] Delphin

donate [dəʊˈneɪt] spenden V/6/5

° **doom** [duːm]
(schlimmes) Schicksal;
Untergangsstimmung V/3/11

door [dɔː] Tür

doorbell [ˈdɔːbel] Türklingel,
Türglocke

doorman [ˈdɔːmən] Türsteher
V/2/7

dos and don'ts [ˌduːz ˌənd
ˈdəʊnts] was man tun und was
man nicht tun sollte

° **double** [dʌbl] sich verdoppeln
V/6/CIO

double circle [ˌdʌbl ˈsɜːkl]
Doppelkreis V/5/12

double room [ˈdʌbl ˌruːm]
Doppelzimmer V/1/6

down [daʊn] hinunter, hinab

down under *(informal)*
[ˌdaʊn ˈʌndə] Australien V/1/I

downhill [ˌdaʊnˈhɪl] bergab
führend V/3/M2

draft [drɑːft] Entwurf, Konzept
V/3/M6

dragon [ˈdrægən] Drache

drama *(no pl)* [ˈdrɑːmə]
Schauspielerei; Theater

dramatic [drəˈmætɪk] dramatisch
V/1/M7

draw [drɔː] zeichnen

drawing [ˈdrɔːɪŋ] Zeichnung
V/6/M3

dream [driːm] Traum; träumen
V/4/M2

dreamlike [ˈdriːmˌlaɪk] wie in
einem Traum V/1/M7

Dreamtime [ˈdriːmˌtaɪm]
Traumzeit V/1/11

dress [dres] Kleid; sich kleiden;
sich anziehen V/2/2

dress up [ˌdresˈʌp] sich
herausputzen; sich verkleiden

drill [drɪl] Bohrer, Bohrmaschine
V/5/5

drink [drɪŋk] trinken; Getränk;
Drink

drive [draɪv] fahren

driver [ˈdraɪvə] Fahrer/in

drop [drɒp] fallen lassen

drug [drʌg] Medikament; Droge

drunk [drʌŋk] Betrunkene/r
V/3/M2

dry [draɪ] trocken

duck [dʌk] Ente

dumpling [ˈdʌmplɪŋ] Knödel,
Kloß

during [ˈdjʊərɪŋ] während

dye [daɪ] färben V/3/M8

be dying to do sth [biː ˈdaɪɪŋ tə
ˌduː ˈsʌmθɪŋ] darauf brennen,
etw zu tun V/2/2

E

e-pal [ˈiː ˌpæl] E-Mail-Freund/in
V/1/M8

each [iːtʃ] jede(r, s)

each other [iːtʃ ˈʌðə] einander

ear [ɪə] Ohr

early [ˈɜːli] früh

earn [ɜːn] verdienen

earring [ˈɪərɪŋ] Ohrring

earth [ɜːθ] die Erde

earthquake [ˈɜːθˌkweɪk] Erdbeben

east [iːst] Osten V/1/7; östlich,
Ost-

Easter [ˈiːstə] Ostern, Osterfest

eastern [ˈiːstən] östlich, Ost-
V/1/7

easy [ˈiːzi] einfach; leicht

eat [iːt] essen

eating habits *(npl)* [ˌiːtɪŋ ˈhæbɪts]
Essgewohnheiten

eatwell plate [ˈiːtwel pleɪt] *den
täglichen Nahrungsbedarf
anzeigendes Kreisdiagramm*
V/4/4

eco- [iːkəʊ] Öko- V/6/I

ecosystem [ˈiːkəʊˌsɪstəm]
Ökosystem V/1/M2

edit [ˈedɪt] bearbeiten, redigieren
V/5/8

° **educate** [ˈedjʊkeɪt] unterrichten,
ausbilden; erziehen V/1/PP

education [ˌedjʊˈkeɪʃn]
(Aus)bildung

° **effect** [ɪˈfekt] (Aus)wirkung,
Konsequenz, Einfluss V/6/PP

egg [eg] Ei

eggshell [ˈegˌʃel] Eierschale
V/1/11

Egypt [ˈiːdʒɪpt] Ägypten V/3/M2

Egyptian [iˈdʒɪpʃn] Ägypter/in;
ägyptisch V/3/M2

either ... or ... [ˌaɪðə ... ˈɔː]
entweder ... oder ... V/5/M2

elbow [ˈelbəʊ] Ellbogen

election [ɪˈlekʃn] Wahl V/2/5

elective *(AE)* [ɪˈlektɪv] Wahlfach,
Wahlkurs

electrical appliance
[ɪˌlektrɪklˌəˈplaɪəns]
Elektrogerät V/6/1

electrician [ɪˌlekˈtrɪʃn] Elektri-
ker/in V/5/2

electricity [ɪˌlekˈtrɪsəti]
Elektrizität, Strom V/6/M2

elegant [ˈelɪgənt] elegant V/3/M8

what else [wɒtˈels] was noch,
was sonst V/4/11

Anything else? [ˌeniθɪŋ ˈels] Darf
es noch etwas sein?

embarrassed [ɪmˈbærəst]
verlegen, peinlich berührt

embarrassing [ɪmˈbærəsɪŋ]
peinlich

° **embrace** [ɪmˈbreɪs] umarmen;
umfassen V/1/M9

emergency [ɪˈmɜːdʒnsi] Notfall
V/1/5

employer [ɪmˈplɔɪə] Arbeitge-
ber/in V/5/CIO

employment [ɪmˈplɔɪmənt]
Beschäftigung, Anstellung
V/5/M2

empowered [ɪmˈpaʊəd] (mental)
gestärkt V/3/M8

° **emptiness** *(no pl)* [ˈemptinəs]
Leere V/3/11

empty [ˈempti] leer

emu [ˈiːmjuː] Emu V/1/8

encourage sb [ɪnˈkʌrɪdʒ ˌsʌmbədi] jdn ermutigen, jdn unterstützen V/6/M2

encyclopedia [ɪnˌsaɪkləˈpiːdiə] Lexikon, Enzyklopädie V/6/M1

end [end] (be)enden; Ende

in the end [ˌɪn ðiˈend] letzten Endes; schließlich

end up [ˌendˈʌp] enden V/4/M6

ending [ˈendɪŋ] Ende, Schluss

energy [ˈenədʒi] Energie, Kraft V/3/5

energy-saving [ˈenədʒi ˌseɪvɪŋ] energiesparend V/6/3

engine [ˈendʒɪn] Motor, Maschine V/5/8

England [ˈɪŋglənd] England

English [ˈɪŋglɪʃ] englisch

in English [ˌɪnˈɪŋglɪʃ] auf Englisch

° English-speaking [ˈɪŋglɪʃˌspiːkɪŋ] englischsprachig V/I/1

enjoy [ɪnˈdʒɔɪ] genießen

Enjoy your meal! [ɪnˌdʒɔɪ jəˈmiːl] Guten Appetit!

enough [ɪˈnʌf] genügend, ausreichend, genug

enter [ˈentə] betreten V/2/7

entrance fee [ˈentrəns ˌfiː] Eintritt(sgeld) V/2/12

entry [ˈentri] Eintrag V/2/2

entry form [ˈentri ˌfɔːm] Anmeldeformular

envelope [ˈenvələʊp] Briefumschlag, Kuvert

environment [ɪnˈvaɪrənmənt] Umgebung; Umwelt

environmental [ɪnˌvaɪrənˈmentl] Umwelt- V/6/5

episode [ˈepɪsəʊd] Episode, Folge

equal [ˈiːkwəl] gleich; gleichberechtigt

equipment [ɪˈkwɪpmənt] Ausrüstung, Ausstattung

escalator [ˈeskəˌleɪtə] Rolltreppe

escape [ɪˈskeɪp] (ent)fliehen; entkommen

especially [ɪˈspeʃli] besonders

essay [ˈeseɪ] Essay, Aufsatz V/2/M5

essential [ɪˈsenʃl] unbedingt erforderlich, von größter Wichtigkeit V/5/M1

° Ethiopia [ˌiːθiˈəʊpiə] Äthiopien V/I/1

Europe [ˈjʊərəp] Europa V/4/M5

European [ˌjʊərəˈpiːən] Europäer/in; europäisch

even [ˈiːvn] selbst; sogar

even though [ˌiːvn ˈðəʊ] selbst/ auch wenn V/2/M2

evening [ˈiːvnɪŋ] Abend

in the evening [ˌɪn ðiˈiːvnɪŋ] am Abend, abends

ever [ˈevə] jemals

every [ˈevri] jede(r, s)

everybody [ˈevriˌbɒdi] jede(r); alle

everyday [ˈevrideɪ] alltäglich

everyone [ˈevriwʌn] jede(r); alle

everything [ˈevriˌθɪŋ] alles

everywhere [ˈevriˌweə] überall

exactly [ɪgˈzæktli] genau

example [ɪgˈzɑːmpl] Beispiel

for example [ˌfɔːr ɪgˈzɑːmpl] zum Beispiel

excellent [ˈeksələnt] ausgezeichnet, hervorragend V/5/4

° excessive [ɪkˈsesɪv] übermäßig, exzessiv V/2/PP

exchange [ɪksˈtʃeɪndʒ] austauschen V/2/2

exchange- [ɪksˈtʃeɪndʒ] (Aus)tausch- V/6/M5

excited [ɪkˈsaɪtɪd] aufgeregt

exciting [ɪkˈsaɪtɪŋ] aufregend; spannend

excuse [ɪkˈskjuːs] Entschuldigung, Grund

Excuse me! [ɪkˈskjuːz ˌmi] Entschuldigen Sie bitte!, Entschuldigung!

exercise [ˈeksəsaɪz] Übung

exercise [ˈeksəsaɪz] trainieren; bewegen V/5/M1

exercise book [ˈeksəsaɪz ˌbʊk] Heft

do exercises [duːˈeksəsaɪzɪz] Sport treiben V/4/9

exhausted [ɪgˈzɔːstɪd] erschöpft

exhibition [ˌeksɪˈbɪʃn] Ausstellung

exist [ɪgˈzɪst] existieren, vorkommen V/5/13

exit [ˈeksɪt] Ausgang

expect [ɪkˈspekt] erwarten

expedition [ˌekspəˈdɪʃn] Expedition, (Forschungs)reise V/3/4

expensive [ɪkˈspensɪv] teuer

experience [ɪkˈspɪəriəns] Erfahrung V/3/4

expert [ˈekspɜːt] Experte/Expertin V/4/11

explain [ɪkˈspleɪn] erklären

explanation [ˌekspləˈneɪʃn] Erklärung V/6/M1

° explore [ɪkˈsplɔː] untersuchen, erkunden V/6/PP

explorer [ɪkˈsplɔːrə] Forscher/in, Entdecker/in

explosion [ɪkˈspləʊʒn] Explosion V/1/11

express [ɪkˈspres] ausdrücken V/2/10

° expression [ɪkˈspreʃn] Ausdruck V/6/CIO

extra [ˈekstrə] zusätzlich; besonders V/4/M2

extreme [ɪkˈstriːm] extrem V/3/4

extreme [ɪkˈstriːm] Extrem; äußerstes Ende V/4/M2

take sth to the extreme [ˌteɪk sʌmθɪŋ tə ðiˌɪkˈstriːm] etw auf die Spitze treiben V/4/M2

eye [aɪ] Auge

eye contact (no pl) [ˈaɪ ˌkɒntækt] Blickkontakt V/5/M3

F

face [feɪs] Gesicht

face [feɪs] etw ausgesetzt sein, mit etw konfrontiert sein V/3/M2

fact [fækt] Tatsache, Fakt V/1/2

fact file [ˈfækt ˌfaɪl] Steckbrief

factory [ˈfæktri] Fabrik; Werk

faint [feɪnt] ohnmächtig werden

fall [fɔːl] fallen; stürzen

fall (AE) = autumn (BE) [fɔːl] Herbst

fall asleep [ˌfɔːl əˈsliːp] einschlafen

fall in love (with) [ˌfɔːl ɪn ˈlʌv] sich verlieben (in) V/6/8

fall off [ˈfɔːl ɒf] herunterfallen

false [fɔːls] falsch

family [ˈfæmli] Familie

famous [ˈfeɪməs] berühmt

the famous (pl) [ðə ˈfeɪməs] die Berühmten V/5/14

fancy dress [ˌfænsi ˈdres]
Verkleidung, Kostüm
fancy *(informal)* [ˈfænsi] wollen,
mögen
fantastic *(informal)* [fænˈtæstɪk]
fantastisch
fantasy [ˈfæntəsi] Fantasie
far [fɑː] von weit her; weit
so far [ˈsəʊ ˌfɑː] bisher V/5/5
farm [fɑːm] Bauernhof
farm (land) [fɑːm] (Land)
bebauen
farmer [ˈfɑːmə] Bauer/Bäuerin,
Farmer/in
fashion [ˈfæʃn] Mode V/3/CIO
fast [fɑːst] schnell
fast food chain [ˌfɑːst fuːd ˈtʃeɪn]
(Schnell)imbisskette V/5/M1
fat [fæt] dick, fett; Fett V/4/4
fat-reduced [ˌfætrɪˈdjuːst]
fettreduziert V/4/3
father [ˈfɑːðə] Vater
Father Christmas [ˌfɑːðə ˈkrɪsməs]
Weihnachtsmann V/5/M7
fault [fɔːlt] Schuld; Fehler V/2/2
favourite [ˈfeɪvrət] Liebling;
Favorit/in; Lieblings-
fear [fɪə] fürchten, befürchten
V/3/10
feather [ˈfeðə] Feder
February [ˈfebruəri] Februar
feed [fiːd] zu essen geben,
füttern
feeding time [ˈfiːdɪŋ ˌtaɪm]
Fütterungszeit
feel [fiːl] (sich) fühlen
feel sorry for sb [ˌfiːl ˈsɒri fə
sʌmbədi] Mitleid mit jdm
haben V/2/2
° **feel the need to do sth** [ˌfiːl
ðə ˈniːd tə ˌduː sʌmθɪŋ] das
Bedürfnis verspüren, etwas zu
tun V/2/1
feeling [ˈfiːlɪŋ] Gefühl
° **keep sb's feet on the ground**
[ˌkiːp sʌmbədiz ˌfiːt ɒn ðə
ˈɡraʊnd] dafür sorgen, dass
jd realistisch/auf dem Boden
bleibt V/2/1
° **fellow** [ˈfeləʊ] Mit- V/1/M9
female [ˈfiːmeɪl] weiblich
fence [fens] Zaun V/1/M6
ferry [ˈferi] Fähre

few [fjuː] einige; wenige
a few [ə ˈfjuː] einige
field [fiːld] Wiese, Weide, Feld
fifth [fɪfθ] Fünftel V/1/4
fight [faɪt] Kampf, Streit V/6/8;
kämpfen, streiten
fight over sth [ˈfaɪt ˌəʊvə ˌsʌmθɪŋ]
um etw streiten V/1/11
figure out [ˌfɪɡərˈaʊt]
herausfinden; ausrechnen;
verstehen
the figures *(pl)* [ðə ˈfɪɡəz]
Zahlen(material) V/1/4
fill [fɪl] füllen V/6/M6
fill in [fɪlˈɪn] ausfüllen; einsetzen
fill out [fɪlˈaʊt] ausfüllen
film [fɪlm] Film
film studio [ˈfɪlm ˌstjuːdiəʊ]
Filmstudio
film-maker [ˈfɪlmˌmeɪkə]
Filmemacher/in V/1/2
final [ˈfaɪnl] letzte(r, s); endgültig
V/3/M6
finally [ˈfaɪnli] schließlich,
endlich
find [faɪnd] finden
find out [faɪndˈaʊt] herausfinden
finding [ˈfaɪndɪŋ] Entdeckung;
Ergebnis V/1/13
fine [faɪn] in Ordnung, gut;
Geldstrafe, Bußgeld V/3/5
finger [ˈfɪŋɡə] Finger
finish [ˈfɪnɪʃ] Ziel; beenden,
aufhören; austrinken V/6/4
finished [ˈfɪnɪʃt] fertig, beendet
V/3/M2
fire [ˈfaɪə] Feuer
be on fire [ˌbiː ɒn ˈfaɪə] brennen,
in Flammen stehen
set fire to sth [ˌset ˈfaɪə tə sʌmθɪŋ]
etw anzünden/in Brand
stecken V/2/M1
firefighter [ˈfaɪəˌfaɪtə]
Feuerwehrmann/-frau
firework [ˈfaɪəˌwɜːk] Feuerwerk
fireworks *(pl)* [ˈfaɪəˌwɜːks]
Feuerwerkskörper V/2/5
first [fɜːst] erste(r, s); zuerst; als
Erstes
at first [ət ˈfɜːst] anfangs, zuerst
first language [ˌfɜːst ˈlæŋɡwɪdʒ]
Muttersprache
first name [ˈfɜːst ˌneɪm] Vorname

° **take a first step** [ˌteɪk ə ˌfɜːst ˈstep]
einen ersten Schritt machen/
unternehmen V/1/M9
fish [fɪʃ] fischen, angeln
fish *(pl fish)* [fɪʃ] Fisch
fit [fɪt] sich eignen; passen
fitting room [ˈfɪtɪŋ ˌruːm]
Umkleide, Anprobe
fizzy drink [ˌfɪzi ˈdrɪŋk] süßes,
kohlensäurehaltiges Getränk
V/4/4
flag [flæɡ] Fahne; Flagge
flame [fleɪm] Flamme
flat [flæt] Wohnung
flatline *(informal)* [ˈflætˌlaɪn]
Todes- V/4/M2
flee [fliː] fliehen V/1/M5
flexibility [ˌfleksəˈbɪləti]
Flexibilität,
Anpassungsfähigkeit
V/5/M1
flexible [ˈfleksəbl] flexibel,
anpassungsfähig V/5/3
flight [flaɪt] Flug V/1/M1
floor [flɔː] Boden; Stockwerk
flour [ˈflaʊə] Mehl
flower [ˈflaʊə] Blume
fly [flaɪ] fliegen
fog [fɒɡ] Nebel
foggy [ˈfɒɡi] neblig
fold [fəʊld] (zusammen)falten
folder [ˈfəʊldə] Mappe,
Schnellhefter
follow [ˈfɒləʊ] folgen
following [ˈfɒləʊɪŋ] folgende(r, s)
V/4/3
be fond of sth/doing sth [bi:
ˈfɒnd əv ˌsʌmθɪŋ, ˌduːɪŋ ˌsʌmθɪŋ]
etw gerne mögen/machen
food for thought [fuːd fə ˈθɔːt]
Stoff zum Nachdenken V/4/I
food *(no pl)* [fuːd] Essen
° **fool around** *(informal)*
[ˌfuːl əˈraʊnd] herumblödeln,
seine Zeit verschwenden
V/5/11
foot *(pl feet)* [fʊt, fiːt] Fuß
foot *(pl foot or feet)* [fʊt, fiːt] Fuß
(= 0,3048 Meter)
football [ˈfʊtˌbɔːl] Fußball
for [fɔː] für; nach; seit
for example [ˌfɔːr ɪɡˈzɑːmpl] zum
Beispiel

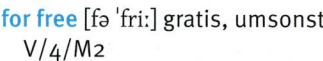
for free [fə 'friː] gratis, umsonst V/4/M2

for quite some time [fə ˌkwaɪt səm 'taɪm] seit einer ganzen Weile V/5/M4

force sb (to do sth) ['fɔːs ˌsʌmbədi] jdn zwingen (etw zu tun) V/1/12

foreign ['fɒrɪn] ausländisch, fremd

foreign country [ˌfɒrɪn 'kʌntri] Ausland

foreigner ['fɒrɪnə] Ausländer/in

forest ['fɒrɪst] Wald

forever [fər'evə] ewig V/1/5

forget [fə'get] vergessen

fork [fɔːk] Gabel

form [fɔːm] bilden, formen; Form; Formular

former ['fɔːmə] ehemalige(r, s), frühere(r, s) V/5/CIO

° **fortune** ['fɔːtʃən] Vermögen V/5/11

fortune-teller ['fɔːtʃən ˌtelə] Wahrsager/in

forum ['fɔːrəm] Forum V/3/10

forward ['fɔːwəd] nach vorn(e)

look forward to sth [ˌlʊk 'fɔːwəd tə sʌmθɪŋ] sich auf etw freuen V/1/5

found [faʊnd] gründen

founder ['faʊndə] Gründer/in V/5/M11

fountain ['faʊntɪn] Brunnen V/6/M2

France [frɑːnts] Frankreich

free [friː] frei; gratis, umsonst

for free [friː] gratis, umsonst V/4/M2

free time [ˌfriː 'taɪm] Freizeit

freedom *(no pl)* ['friːdəm] Freiheit, Unabhängigkeit

freeze [friːz] gefrieren, einfrieren, zufrieren

French [frentʃ] Franzose/ Französin; französisch

French fries *(AE, npl)* = chips *(BE, pl)* [ˌfrentʃ 'fraɪz] Pommes frites

fresh [freʃ] frisch, neu

Friday ['fraɪdeɪ] Freitag

fridge *(informal)* [frɪdʒ] Kühlschrank

fried chicken [ˌfraɪd 'tʃɪkɪn] Brathähnchen

fried egg [ˌfraɪd 'eg] Spiegelei

friend [frend] Freund/in

friendly ['frendli] freundlich

friendly match [ˌfrendli 'mætʃ] Freundschaftsspiel

make friends (with sb) [meɪk 'frendz] sich (mit jdm) anfreunden, einen Freund gewinnen

friendship ['frendʃɪp] Freundschaft

fries *(AE, pl)* [fraɪz] Pommes frites V/4/M2

be frightened [bi 'fraɪtnd] sich fürchten

frightening ['fraɪtnɪŋ] Furcht erregend, beängstigend

frog [frɒg] Frosch V/1/M1

from [frəm] von, aus

in front [ɪn 'frʌnt] vorn(e)

in front of [ɪn 'frʌnt ˌəv] vor

at the front of [ət ðə 'frʌnt ˌəv] vorne in

frown [fraʊn] die Stirn runzeln

frozen ['frəʊzn] gefroren V/3/4

fruit [fruːt] Frucht; Obst

fry [fraɪ] frittieren, braten V/4/M2

full [fʊl] voll

full-time ['fʊlˌtaɪm] Ganztags-, Vollzeit-

fun [fʌn] Spaß; lustig, witzig, spaßig V/3/4

be fun [bi 'fʌn] Spaß machen

make fun of sb [meɪk 'fʌn ˌəv ˌsʌmbədi] sich über jdn lustig machen V/1/5

funny ['fʌni] lustig, witzig, komisch

fur [fɜː] Fell; Pelz V/1/9

furniture *(no pl)* ['fɜːnɪtʃə] Möbel

° **further** ['fɜːðə] zusätzlich, noch mehr V/5/PP

future ['fjuːtʃə] Zukunft

future ['fjuːtʃə] zukünftig, später V/6/M2

G

° **g'day** *(Australian English; informal)* [gə'deɪ] hi, hallo V/I/1

gadget ['gædʒɪt] Gerät

gain [geɪn] erwerben, erlangen, sammeln, gewinnen V/5/M1

gallery ['gæləri] Galerie, Ausstellung

game [geɪm] Spiel

gap year ['gæp jɪə] *Zwischenjahr, in dem gereist oder gearbeitet wird* V/5/2

garage ['gærɑːʒ] Garage; (Kfz-) Werkstatt V/5/8

garden ['gɑːdn] Garten

gardener ['gɑːdnə] Gärtner/in

garlic ['gɑːlɪk] Knoblauch

gas [gæs] Gas V/6/M1

generation [ˌdʒenə'reɪʃn] Generation V/1/M5

genie ['dʒiːni] (Flaschen)geist V/3/M8

gentleman ['dʒentlmən] (vornehmer) Herr V/4/M8

geography [dʒiːˈɒgrəfi] Erdkunde, Geographie

German ['dʒɜːmən] Deutsche/r; deutsch

Germany ['dʒɜːməni] Deutschland

get [get] erhalten, bekommen; gelangen; werden; holen; kapieren, verstehen

get along (with sb) [getˌə'lɒŋ] sich (mit jdm) verstehen

get back [get 'bæk] zurückbekommen; zurückkommen

get into debt [ˌget ˌɪntə 'det] Schulden machen, sich verschulden V/5/13

get lost [get 'lɒst] sich verirren; sich verlaufen

get married [get 'mærɪd] heiraten V/2/5

get on [getˌ'ɒn] einsteigen (in); aufsteigen (auf)

get on sb's nerves *(informal)* [ˌgetˌɒn sʌmbədiz 'nɜːvz] jdm auf die Nerven gehen V/1/5

Get outta here! *(informal)* [ˌgetˌ'aʊtə hɪə] Verschwinde(t)! V/3/5

get rid of sth [get 'rɪd ˌəv ˌsʌmθɪŋ] etw loswerden V/3/M8

get sb sth ['get sʌmbədi ˌsʌmθɪŋ] jdm etw bringen

DICTIONARY   *English – German*

get to know sb [ˌget tə ˈnəʊ ˌsʌmbədi] jdn kennenlernen V/2/M2

get (to) [get] (an)kommen

get together [get təˈgeðə] sich treffen

get up [ˌgetˈʌp] aufstehen

get used to sth [get ˈjuːsd tə ˌsʌmθɪŋ] sich an etw gewöhnen

get well [get ˈwel] gesund werden

get well card [get ˈwel ˌkɑːd] Genesungskarte

Get well soon! [ˌget wel ˈsuːn] Gute Besserung!

ghost [gəʊst] Geist, Gespenst

giant [ˈdʒaɪənt] Riese; riesig

girl [gɜːl] Mädchen

girly [ˈgɜːli] mädchenhaft V/3/M8

give [gɪv] geben

give a presentation [ˌgɪv ə ˌpreznˈteɪʃn] eine Präsentation halten V/1/I

give a talk [ˌgɪv ə ˈtɔːk] einen Vortrag halten V/I/4

give directions [ˌgɪv dɪˈrekʃnz] den Weg beschreiben

give out [ˌgɪvˈaʊt] bekannt geben, herausgeben V/2/9

give sb a hard stare [ˌgɪv sʌmbədi ə hɑːd ˈsteə] jdm einen bösen Blick zuwerfen

glacier [ˈglæsiə] Gletscher

glad [glæd] glücklich, froh

glamorous [ˈglæmərəs] glamourös V/3/M7

glass [glɑːs] Glas

glass-bottomed [ˌglɑːs ˈbɒtəmd] mit einer Unterseite aus Glas; mit einem gläsernen Boden V/1/M1

glasses *(npl)* [ˈglɑːsɪz] Brille

global warming *(no pl)* [ˌgləʊbl ˈwɔːmɪŋ] Erwärmung der Erdatmosphäre V/6/M1

globe [gləʊb] die Erde; Globus

gloomy [ˈgluːmi] trostlos, trübe, düster V/1/M7

go [gəʊ] gehen; werden

go bush [ˌgəʊ ˈbʊʃ] die Wildnis erleben V/3/4

go for a walk [ˌgəʊ fər ə ˈwɔːk] spazieren gehen

° **go green** [ˌgəʊ ˈgriːn] umweltbewusst werden V/6/PP

go in [gəʊ ˈɪn] hineingehen

go mad (with hunger) [ˌgəʊ ˈmæd (wɪð ˌhʌŋgə)] (vor Hunger) verrückt werden V/4/M6

go on [gəʊ ˈɒn] weitergehen; weitermachen; passieren

go on doing sth [ˌgəʊˈɒn ˌduːɪŋ ˌsʌmθɪŋ] etw weiter tun V/6/13

go out [gəʊˈaʊt] (hinaus)gehen; ausgehen

go with [ˈgəʊ wɪð] gehören zu

goal [gəʊl] Tor

° **goal** [gəʊl] Ziel V/6/PP

score a goal [ˌskɔːr ə ˈgəʊl] ein Tor schießen

goalkeeper [ˈgəʊlˌkiːpə] Tormann/Torfrau

god [gɒd] Gott

golden [ˈgəʊldn] golden V/5/M7

goldfish [ˈgəʊldˌfɪʃ] Goldfisch

° **gone** [gɒn] weg V/3/11

good [gʊd] gut

be as good as one's word [biː əz ˌgʊd əz wʌnz ˈwɜːd] sein Wort halten V/4/M8

be good at sth [biː ˈgʊd ˌæt ˌsʌmθɪŋ] gut in etw sein

good luck [gʊd ˈlʌk] Glück

Good luck! [gʊd ˈlʌk] Viel Glück!

have a good time [ˌhæv ə gʊd ˈtaɪm] sich amüsieren

good-looking [ˌgʊdˈlʊkɪŋ] gut aussehend

Goodbye! [ˌgʊdˈbaɪ] Auf Wiedersehen!

government [ˈgʌvənmənt] Regierung V/4/5

grade [greɪd] Klasse(nstufe) V/5/2; Note V/5/3

graduate [ˈgrædʒueɪt] die Abschlussprüfung bestehen V/5/2

graduation [ˌgrædʒuˈeɪʃn] Schulabschluss, Studienabschluss V/5/M2

graffer *(informal)* [ˈgræfə] Graffitikünstler

grammar [ˈgræmə] Grammatik

grandchild *(pl* **grandchildren)** [ˈgrænˌtʃaɪld] Enkelkind V/5/13

grandfather [ˈgrænˌfɑːðə] Großvater V/1/12

grandma [ˈgrænˌmɑː] Oma, Omi

grandmother [ˈgrænˌmʌðə] Großmutter V/1/12

grandpa [ˈgrænˌpɑː] Opa, Opi

grandparents *(pl)* [ˈgrænˌpeərənts] Großeltern

grape [greɪp] (Wein)traube V/5/M7

graphic artist [ˌgræfɪkˈɑːtɪst] Grafiker/in

grass [grɑːs] Gras

grateful [ˈgreɪtfl] dankbar V/4/M8

graveyard [ˈgreɪvˌjɑːd] Friedhof

great [greɪt] groß, riesig; großartig, wunderbar

Great Britain [ˌgreɪt ˈbrɪtn] Großbritannien

Greece [griːs] Griechenland V/1/4

Greek [griːk] Grieche/Griechin; griechisch V/1/4

green [griːn] grün; umweltfreundlich, ökologisch V/6/2

° **go green** [ˌgəʊ ˈgriːn] umweltbewusst werden V/6/PP

greenhouse gas [ˈgriːnˌhaʊs gæs] Treibhausgas V/6/M1

greet [griːt] (be)grüßen V/4/M8

grey [greɪ] grau

grid [grɪd] Gitter; Tabelle

° **grief** [griːf] Trauer, Leid, Schmerz V/1/M9

grill [grɪl] grillen

ground [graʊnd] (Erd)boden, Erde; Gelände

group [gruːp] Gruppe

grow [grəʊ] wachsen

grow up [ˌgrəʊˈʌp] erwachsen werden

guard [gɑːd] bewachen

guess [ges] (er)raten; vermuten

guess [ges] Vermutung V/2/2

have a guess [ˌhæv ə ˈges] raten, schätzen

Guess what! [ges ˈwɒt] Stell dir vor!

guest [gest] Gast

guide [gaɪd] führen, den Weg zeigen V/1/M6

guilty ['gɪlti] schuldig
guitar [gɪ'tɑ:] Gitarre
guy *(informal)* [gaɪ] Kerl, Typ
gym (= gymnasium) [dʒɪm, dʒɪm'neɪziəm] Turnhalle
gymnastics *(npl)* [dʒɪm'næstɪks] Turnen

H

habit ['hæbɪt] Gewohnheit V/4/2
hair *(no pl)* [heə] Haar(e)
hair stylist ['heə ˌstaɪlɪst] Friseur/Friseuse
haircut ['heəˌkʌt] Haarschnitt, Frisur V/5/M3
half [hɑ:f] halb
half past (eight) ['hɑ:f ˌpɑ:st] halb (neun)
half *(pl halves)* [hɑ:f, hɑ:vz] Hälfte
halfway [ˌhɑ:f'weɪ] auf halber Strecke, in der Mitte V/1/6
hall [hɔ:l] Korridor; Halle
ham [hæm] Schinken
hand [hænd] Hand
on the one hand [ɒn ðə 'wʌn ˌhænd] einerseits V/2/2
on the other hand [ɒn ði'ʌðə ˌhænd] andererseits V/2/2
hang [hæŋ] hängen
hang out *(informal)* [hæŋ 'aʊt] Zeit verbringen, abhängen
hang up [ˌhæŋ'ʌp] auflegen, einhängen
hang up sth ['hæŋ ʌp ˌsʌmθɪŋ] etw aufhängen
Hanover ['hænəʊvə] Hannover V/6/M5
happen ['hæpən] geschehen, passieren
° happen to do sth [ˌhæpən tə 'du: sʌmθɪŋ] zufällig etw tun V/5/11
happy ['hæpi] glücklich; zufrieden; fröhlich
Happy birthday! [ˌhæpi 'bɜ:θdeɪ] Alles Gute zum Geburtstag!
hard [hɑ:d] hart; angestrengt
° hard [hɑ:d] schwierig V/5/11
try hard to do sth [ˌtraɪ 'hɑ:d tə du: sʌmθɪŋ] sich sehr bemühen, etw zu tun V/5/13
the hard way [ðə 'hɑ:d ˌweɪ] auf die harte Tour V/2/10

hardly ['hɑ:dli] kaum V/3/M2
hardly ever [ˌhɑ:dli 'evə] kaum V/5/3
harvest ['hɑ:vɪst] Ernte; Ertrag
hat [hæt] Hut
hatch [hætʃ] schlüpfen V/1/M1
hate [heɪt] hassen, nicht ausstehen können
hate *(no pl)* [heɪt] Hass
have [hæv] haben; essen
have a guess [ˌhəv ə 'ges] raten, schätzen
° have a ball (informal) [hæv ə 'bɔ:l] Spaß haben, sich bestens amüsieren V/5/11
have a barbecue [ˌhæv ə 'bɑ:bɪˌkju:] grillen, eine Grillparty feiern V/1/5
have a meal [ˌhæv ə 'mi:l] eine Mahlzeit zu sich nehmen
have a will of one's own [ˌhæv ə ˌwɪl əv wʌnz 'əʊn] seinen eigenen Willen haben V/2/2
have got [hæv 'gɒt] haben
° have sb around [ˌhæv sʌmbədi ə'raʊnd] jdn in der Nähe haben V/2/1
° have sb's back [ˌhæv sʌmbədiz 'bæk] jdn beschützen, unterstützen V/2/1
have sth ['hæv ˌsʌmθɪŋ] etw zu sich nehmen, etw bestellen
have sth in common [hæv ˌsʌmθɪŋ ɪn 'kɒmən] etwas gemein haben V/5/M9
have tea [hæv 'ti:] Tee trinken
have the time of one's life [hæv ðə ˌtaɪm əv wʌnz 'laɪf] eine tolle Zeit haben V/5/M1
have to ['hæv tə] müssen
Hawaiian [hə'waɪən] Hawaiianer/in; hawai(an)isch
he [hi] er
head [hed] Kopf
° head [hed] Oberhaupt V/I/PP
headline ['hedˌlaɪn] Schlagzeile
headscarf ['hedˌskɑ:f] Kopftuch V/2/2
headteacher [ˌhed'ti:tʃə] Schulleiter/in, Rektor/in
° healing ['hi:lɪŋ] Heilung V/1/M9
health [helθ] Gesundheit
healthy ['helθi] gesund

hear [hɪə] hören
heart ['hɑ:t] Herz
take heart [ˌteɪk 'hɑ:t] neuen Mut schöpfen V/1/M9
heart attack ['hɑ:t əˌtæk] Herzinfarkt, Herzanfall V/4/M2
heat [hi:t] erhitzen V/6/3
heat *(no pl)* [hi:t] Wärme; Hitze V/6/M1
heat up [ˌhi:t 'ʌp] aufwärmen, erhitzen V/6/M1
heated ['hi:tɪd] hitzig, erregt; heftig V/5/M11
heating ['hi:tɪŋ] Heizung V/6/1
heavy ['hevi] schwer
height [haɪt] (Körper)größe; Höhe V/4/9
helicopter ['helɪˌkɒptə] Hubschrauber V/1/M1
hell [hel] Hölle V/4/9
hello [hə'ləʊ] hallo
say hello to [ˌseɪ hə'ləʊ tə] (be)grüßen
helmet ['helmɪt] Helm V/2/5
help [help] helfen; Hilfe
help out [help ˌaʊt] (aus)helfen, unterstützen
helper ['helpə] Helfer V/1/M2
helpless ['helpləs] hilflos
helpline ['helpˌlaɪn] telefonischer Beratungsdienst; Notruf V/2/11
hen [hen] Henne, Huhn
her [hɜ:] sie; ihr(e, n)
here [hɪə] hier
Here you are. [ˌhɪə ju: 'ɑ:] Hier, bitte!, Bitte schön!
hero *(pl -es)* ['hɪərəʊ, 'hɪərəʊz] Held
hers [hɜ:z] ihre(r, s)
herself [hə'self] sich (selbst); selbst
hide [haɪd] (sich) verstecken
high [haɪ] hoch
high (in) [haɪ] reich (an) V/4/4
high school ['haɪ ˌsku:l] *weiterführende Schule in den USA (Klasse 9-12)*
high-calorie [ˌhaɪ 'kæləri] kalorienreich V/4/9
highway ['haɪˌweɪ] Bundesstraße, Highway
hike [haɪk] wandern

hiking [ˈhaɪkɪŋ] Wandern

hill [hɪl] Hügel

him [hɪm] ihm, ihn

the Himalayas [ðə ˌhɪməˈleɪəz] der Himalaja V/3/M2

° **Hindi** [ˈhɪndi] Hindi *(Amtssprache in Indien)* V/I/2

hippopotamus [ˌhɪpəˈpɒtəməs] Nilpferd

his [hɪz] sein(e, r)

Hispanic [hɪˈspænɪk] Hispano-Amerikaner/in; hispanisch

history [ˈhɪstri] Geschichte

hit [hɪt] schlagen (auf)

hit [hɪt] treffen, erschüttern V/2/M1

hit sb [hɪt] jdn anfahren V/3/M2

hold [həʊld] (fest)halten

hold [həʊld] besitzen V/5/M2

holiday [ˈhɒlɪdeɪ] Urlaub, Ferien

be on holiday [ˌbi ɒn ˈhɒlɪdeɪ] Urlaub haben, im Urlaub sein

holy [ˈhəʊli] heilig V/1/2

home [həʊm] zu Hause; nach Hause; Zuhause; Heim V/1/12

home [həʊm] Haus V/6/M1

at home [ət ˈhəʊm] zu Hause

homecoming *(AE)* [ˈhəʊmˌkʌmɪŋ] *Amerikanisches Schulfest mit Ehemaligentreffen*

homeless [ˈhəʊmləs] heimatlos, obdachlos

the homeless *(pl)* [ðə ˈhəʊmləs] die Obdachlosen V/5/I

be homesick [bi ˈhəʊmˌsɪk] Heimweh haben

homework *(no pl)* [ˈhəʊmˌwɜːk] Hausaufgaben

honest [ˈɒnɪst] ehrlich V/6/4

honey [ˈhʌni] Honig

° **honour** [ˈɒnə] ehren, würdigen V/1/M9

hope [həʊp] hoffen; Hoffnung

horrible [ˈhɒrəbl] schrecklich V/2/2

horse [hɔːs] Pferd

hospital [ˈhɒspɪtl] Krankenhaus

host family [ˈhəʊst ˌfæmli] Gastfamilie V/5/M1

hot [hɒt] heiß; scharf

hotel [həʊˈtel] Hotel

hour [ˈaʊə] Stunde

house [haʊs] Haus

household spending *(no pl)* [ˈhaʊshəʊld ˌspendɪŋ] Haushaltsausgaben V/5/16

housing *(no pl)* [ˈhaʊzɪŋ] Wohnungen, Unterkünfte V/5/16

how [haʊ] wie

How about ...? [haʊ əˈbaʊt] Was ist mit ...?, Wie wäre es mit ...?

How are things? [ˌhaʊ ɑː ˈθɪŋz] Wie geht's?

How are you doing? [ˌhaʊ ə jə ˈduːɪŋ] Wie geht es dir/Ihnen/euch?

How are you? [haʊ ˈɑː juː] Wie geht es dir/Ihnen/euch?

How much is/are ... ? [ˌhaʊ mʌtʃ ˈɪz/ɑː] Was kostet/kosten ...?

how to [haʊ tə] wie man V/I/4

however [haʊˈevə] aber, jedoch V/1/M1

huge [hjuːdʒ] riesig, riesengroß

human [ˈhjuːmən] Mensch V/6/8

human [ˈhjuːmən] menschlich V/3/M2

hundred [ˈhʌndrəd] Hundert

hunger [ˈhʌŋgə] Hunger V/4/M6

hungry [ˈhʌŋgri] hungrig

hunt [hʌnt] jagen

hunter [ˈhʌntə] Jäger/in V/1/2

hurry [ˈhʌri] sich beeilen; hetzen

hurry on [ˈhʌri ɒn] weitereilen V/4/M8

hurt [hɜːt] verletzt, verwundet; wehtun, schmerzen; schaden

° **hurt** [hɜːt] Schmerz; Kränkung V/1/M9

hyena [haɪˈiːnə] Hyäne

I

I [aɪ] ich

I'll have ... [aɪl ˈhæv] Ich hätte gern ...; Ich nehme ...

ice [aɪs] Eis

° **ice age** [ˈaɪs ˌeɪdʒ] Eiszeit V/1/PP

ice cap [ˈaɪs kæp] Polkappe V/6/M2

ice cream [ˈaɪs ˌkriːm] Eiskrem

idea [aɪˈdɪə] Idee

ideal [aɪˈdɪəl] ideal V/1/M1

identification (= ID) *(no pl)* [aɪˌdentɪfɪˈkeɪʃn] Identifizierung; Ausweis

idiotic [ˌɪdiˈɒtɪk] idiotisch V/5/M11

if [ɪf] wenn, falls

ignore [ɪgˈnɔː] ignorieren

ill [ɪl] krank

illegal [ɪˈliːgl] rechtswidrig, illegal

illness [ˈɪlnəs] Krankheit, Erkrankung V/4/10

imagination [ɪˌmædʒɪˈneɪʃn] Fantasie, Vorstellungskraft; Einbildung V/2/2

imagine [ɪˈmædʒɪn] sich vorstellen

immediately [ɪˈmiːdiətli] sofort V/3/5

immense [ɪˈmens] riesig, enorm V/1/M1

immigrant [ˈɪmɪgrənt] Einwanderer/in

immigrate [ˈɪmɪˌgreɪt] einwandern

immigration [ˌɪmɪˈgreɪʃn] Einwanderung, Immigration

impolite [ˌɪmpəˈlaɪt] unhöflich

importance *(no pl)* [ɪmˈpɔːtns] Bedeutung, Wichtigkeit V/6/M2

important [ɪmˈpɔːtnt] wichtig

impossible [ɪmˈpɒsəbl] unmöglich V/6/8

impression [ɪmˈpreʃn] Eindruck V/5/M3

impressive [ɪmˈpresɪv] beeindruckend V/1/M1

improve [ɪmˈpruːv] verbessern V/5/M2

in [ɪn] in; herein V/2/7

° **one in six** [ˌwʌn ɪn ˈsɪks] eine(r,s) von sechs V/4/PP

in the end [ɪn ði ˈend] letzten Endes; schließlich

in three months' time [ɪn ˌθriː mʌns ˈtaɪm] in drei Monaten V/2/M3

incident [ˈɪnsɪdnt] Vorfall V/2/M1

include [ɪnˈkluːd] beinhalten, einschließen, aufnehmen V/4/7; einfügen V/5/7; beifügen V/5/CIO

included [ɪnˈkluːdɪd] inklusive, mitgerechnet V/1/6

° **inconvenient** [ˌɪnkənˈviːniənt] unbequem, lästig V/6/PP

incredible [ɪnˈkredəbl]
unglaublich

° **independent** [ˌɪndɪˈpendənt]
unabhängig; selbstständig
V/I/PP

India [ˈɪndiə] Indien

Indian [ˈɪndiən] Inder/in;
Indianer/in; indisch; indianisch

° **the Indian Ocean** [ðiˌɪndiənˈəʊʃn]
der Indische Ozean V/I/1

° **indigenous** [ɪnˈdɪdʒənəs]
(ein)heimisch V/1/M9

° **indignity** [ɪnˈdɪgnəti]
Demütigung, Erniedrigung
V/1/M9

individual [ˌɪndɪˈvɪdʒuəl]
Einzelperson

individual [ˌɪndɪˈvɪdʒuəl] einzeln
V/1/2

° **individual** [ˌɪndɪˈvɪdʒuəl]
individuell; eigen; Individuum,
(selbstständige) Persönlichkeit
V/3/PP

Indonesia [ˌɪndəʊˈniːʒə]
Indonesien V/3/M2

indoor(s) [ɪnˈdɔː] drinnen; zu
Hause; Innen-

° **inflict sth on sb** [ɪnˈflɪkt
ˌsʌmθɪŋ ˌɒn ˌsʌmbədi] jdm etw
zufügen V/1/M9

information *(no pl)* [ˌɪnfəˈmeɪʃn]
Information

ingredient [ɪnˈgriːdiənt]
Bestandteil, Zutat

injured [ˈɪndʒəd] verletzt

° **injustice** [ɪnˈdʒʌstɪs]
Ungerechtigkeit V/1/M9

° **insecure** [ˌɪnsɪˈkjʊə] unsicher
V/3/11

inside [ˈɪnˌsaɪd] (in …) hinein;
innen; im Inneren

instead (of) [ɪnˈsted (ˌəv)]
stattdessen; (an)statt V/6/3

instruction [ɪnˈstrʌkʃn]
Anweisung, Anleitung

instructor [ɪnˈstrʌktə] Lehrer/in;
Betreuer/in

instrument [ˈɪnstrʊmənt]
Instrument V/1/10

insult [ˈɪnsʌlt] Beleidigung

intelligent [ɪnˈtelɪdʒnt] intelligent

interest [ˈɪntrəst] Interesse
V/1/M1

interest sb [ˈɪntrəst] jdn
interessieren, bei jdm
Interesse wecken V/4/M4

interested (in) [ˈɪntrəstɪd]
interessiert (an)

be interested in [biˈɪntrəstɪdˌɪn]
sich interessieren für

interesting [ˈɪntrəstɪŋ] interessant

intern *(AE)* = **trainee** *(BE)* [ˈɪntɜːn]
Praktikant/in

on the Internet [ˌɒn ðiˈɪntənet]
im Internet

interview [ˈɪntəˌvjuː] befragen

into [ˈɪntʊ] in

intolerant [ɪnˈtɒlərənt] intolerant

introduce [ˌɪntrəˈdjuːs] vorstellen

invent [ɪnˈvent] erfinden

invention [ɪnˈvenʃn] Erfindung

invitation [ˌɪnvɪˈteɪʃn] Einladung

invite [ɪnˈvaɪt] einladen

involve [ɪnˈvɒlv] beinhalten;
betreffen V/5/M1

Ireland [ˈaɪələnd] Irland

Irish [ˈaɪərɪʃ] irisch

iron [ˈaɪən] bügeln V/5/M4

island [ˈaɪlənd] Insel

° **islander** [ˈaɪləndə] Insel-
bewohner/in V/1/M9

issue [ˈɪʃuː] Thema; Frage
V/5/M11; ausstellen, in
Umlauf bringen V/5/CIO

it [ɪt] es

Italian [ɪˈtæljən] Italiener/in;
italienisch

Italy [ˈɪtəli] Italien

item [ˈaɪtəm] Gegenstand, Ding
V/6/5

itself [ɪtˈself] sich (selbst); selbst

J

jacket [ˈdʒækɪt] Jacke

January [ˈdʒænjuəri] Januar

° **Japanese** [ˌdʒæpəˈniːz] Japa-
ner/in; Japanisch; japanisch
V/I/2

jealous [ˈdʒeləs] eifersüchtig

jelly [ˈdʒeli] Gelee; Marmelade

Jewish [ˈdʒuːɪʃ] jüdisch

job [dʒɒb] Arbeit, Stelle,
Tätigkeit, Aufgabe

job interview [ˈdʒɒbˌɪntəvjuː]
Bewerbungsgespräch,
Vorstellungsgespräch V/5/M3

join [dʒɔɪn] mitmachen bei;
beitreten; (sich) anschließen

join in [ˌdʒɔɪnˈɪn] sich
anschließen, mitmachen
V/2/9

join up [ˌdʒɔɪnˈʌp] sich
verbinden, miteinander
verschmelzen V/1/M1

joke [dʒəʊk] Witz

be joking [biˈdʒəʊkɪŋ] Spaß
machen, scherzen V/2/2

jolt [dʒəʊlt] Schock V/4/M2

° **Jordan** [ˈdʒɔːdn] Jordanien V/I/1

journey [ˈdʒɜːni] Reise

judge [dʒʌdʒ] Richter/in V/2/M5

juggler [ˈdʒʌglə] Jongleur/in

juice [dʒuːs] Saft

July [dʒʊˈlaɪ] Juli

jump [dʒʌmp] springen

jump up [dʒʌmpˈʌp]
aufspringen, hochspringen

jumper [ˈdʒʌmpə] Pullover
V/6/4

June [dʒuːn] Juni

junk food [ˈdʒʌŋk fuːd]
Schnellgerichte; ungesundes
Essen, Fraß V/4/5

juror [ˈdʒʊərə] Schöffe/Schöffin;
Geschworene/r V/2/5

jury [ˈdʒʊəri] Schöffen;
Geschworene V/2/M5

just [dʒʌst] gleich; genau; nur;
einfach; gerade

just a minute [ˌdʒʌstəˈmɪnɪt]
einen Augenblick/Moment
bitte

juvenile court [ˌdʒuːvənaɪlˈkɔːt]
Jugendgericht V/2/M5

K

kangaroo [ˌkæŋgəˈruː] Känguru
V/1/9

° **karate** *(no pl)* [kəˈrɑːti] Karate
V/3/CIO

kayak [ˈkaɪæk] Kajak V/3/M2

keep [kiːp] (be)halten

keep a diary [ˌkiːpəˈdaɪəri] (ein)
Tagebuch führen V/4/11

keep doing sth [kiːpˈduːɪŋ
ˌsʌmθɪŋ] etw weiter tun; etw
wiederholt/immer wieder tun
V/3/5

keep fit [ˌkiːpˈfɪt] sich fit halten

DICTIONARY ENGLISH–GERMAN

keep going [ˌkiːp ˈɡəʊɪŋ]
weitermachen, in Gang halten
V/2/M2

keep out [ˌkiːpˌˈaʊt] nicht
hereinlassen V/1/M5

keep sb from doing sth [ˈkiːp
ˌsʌmbədi frəm ˌduːɪŋ ˌsʌmθɪŋ]
jdn davon abhalten, etw zu tun
V/6/8

° keep sb's feet on the ground
[ˌkiːp sʌmbədiz ˌfiːtˌɒn ðə
ˈɡraʊnd] dafür sorgen, dass
jd realistisch/auf dem Boden
bleibt V/2/1

keep up sth [ˌkiːpˌˈʌp ˌsʌmθɪŋ]
etw fortführen, etw weiterhin
tun V/6/4

° **Kenya** [ˈkenjə] Kenia V/I/1

key [kiː] Schlüssel

keyword [ˈkiːˌwɜːd] Schlüsselwort

kick [kɪk] treten, schießen,
kicken V/3/3

kick sb out *(informal)* [ˌkɪk
sʌmbədiˌˈaʊt] jdn hinauswerfen
V/2/10

kickboxing *(no pl)* [ˈkɪkˌbɒksɪŋ]
Kickboxen V/3/2

kill [kɪl] töten V/1/2

kilo [ˈkiːləʊ] Kilo

kind [kaɪnd] Art, Sorte; nett,
freundlich V/4/M8

kindergarten *(AE)* = nursery
school *(BE)* *(no pl)*
[ˈkɪndəˌɡɑːtn] Kindergarten;
Vorschule

king [kɪŋ] König

kiss [kɪs] Kuss; küssen

kitchen [ˈkɪtʃən] Küche

kite [kaɪt] Drachen V/3/2

kitten [ˈkɪtn] Kätzchen, junge
Katze

knee [niː] Knie

knife *(pl knives)* [naɪf, naɪvz]
Messer

know [nəʊ] wissen; kennen

know about [ˈnəʊ əˌbaʊt]
Bescheid wissen über

get to know sb [getˌtə ˈnəʊ
ˌsʌmbədi] jdn kennenlernen
V/2/M2

knowledge *(no pl)* [ˈnɒlɪdʒ]
Wissen, Kenntnisse
V/5/4

known [nəʊn] bekannt V/4/M2

koala [kəʊˈɑːlə] Koala(bär) V/1/8

L

Labour [ˈleɪbə] *Name einer
britischen Partei* V/5/M11

lacrosse *(no pl)* [ləˈkrɒs]
Lacrosse *(Ballsportart)*

lady [ˈleɪdi] Frau; Dame

lake [laɪk] See

lamb [læm] Lamm

lamp [læmp] Lampe

land [lænd] (Fest)land; landen

landscape [ˈlændˌskeɪp]
Landschaft

language [ˈlæŋɡwɪdʒ] Sprache

use bad language [juːz bæd
ˈlæŋɡwɪdʒ] Schimpfwörter
benutzen

lard [lɑːd] Schweinefett
V/4/M2

large [lɑːdʒ] groß

last [lɑːst] letzte(r, s)

last but not least [ˌlɑːst bət nɒt
ˈliːst] nicht zuletzt

late [leɪt] (zu) spät

later [ˈleɪtə] später

° the latest [ðə ˈleɪtɪst] der/die/das
letzte, der/die/das neueste
V/3/CIO

Latin [ˈlætɪn] Latein; lateinisch
V/4/M2

Latino *(AE)* [læˈtiːnəʊ] Latino;
latino

laugh [lɑːf] lachen

° make sb laugh [ˌmeɪk sʌmbədi
ˈlɑːf] jdn zum Lachen bringen
V/2/1

laugh at sb [ˈlɑːfˌət ˌsʌmbədi] jdn
auslachen

laugh at sth [ˈlɑːfˌət ˌsʌmθɪŋ]
über etw lachen

law [lɔː] Gesetz V/4/5

lawnmower [ˈlɔːnˌməʊə]
Rasenmäher

lawyer [ˈlɔːjə] Rechtsanwalt/
-anwältin

lay [leɪ] legen V/1/M1

lazy [ˈleɪzi] faul, träge V/6/8

lb (= pound) [paʊnd] Pfund
(Maßeinheit) V/4/M2

lead [liːd] (an)führen, leiten
V/4/5

lead away [ˌliːdˌəˈweɪ] wegführen
V/1/M5

leader [ˈliːdə] Leiter/in, Führer/in
V/2/M2

leaf *(pl leaves)* [liːf, liːvz] Blatt
V/1/9

leaflet [ˈliːflət] Prospekt

learn [lɜːn] lernen

learn a lesson [ˌlɜːnˌə ˈlesn] eine
Lektion lernen V/2/M5

least [liːst] geringste(r, s),
wenigste(r, s) V/6/5

at least [ət ˈliːst] mindestens,
wenigstens

leave [liːv] verlassen; da lassen;
abfahren; hinterlassen;
lassen; weggehen;
zurücklassen

leave behind [ˌliːv bɪˈhaɪnd]
zurücklassen V/6/8

leave out [ˌliːvˌˈaʊt] auslassen,
weglassen V/4/M9

left [left] (nach) links; übrig

on the left [ˌɒn ðə ˈleft] links

leg [leg] Bein

legend [ˈledʒənd] Legende, Sage

lemon [ˈlemən] Zitrone

less [les] weniger V/4/4

lesson [ˈlesn] Stunde

learn a lesson [ˌlɜːnˌə ˈlesn] eine
Lektion lernen V/2/M5

let [let] lassen

let off [ˌletˌˈɒf] laufen lassen;
abfeuern

let sb down [ˌlet sʌmbədi ˈdaʊn]
jdn enttäuschen, jdn im Stich
lassen

let's (= let us) [lets, ˈletˌəs] lass(t)
uns

Let's go! [lets ˈɡəʊ] Los! Los
geht's!

letter [ˈletə] Brief; Buchstabe

lettuce [ˈletɪs] Blattsalat;
Kopfsalat

level [ˈlevl] Ebene, Stockwerk
V/4/M2

library [ˈlaɪbrəri] Bibliothek,
Bücherei

licence [ˈlaɪsns] Genehmigung,
Erlaubnis

° lick [lɪk] (ab)lecken V/3/CIO

lie [laɪ] lügen; liegen; sich
hinlegen

lie down [ˌlaɪ ˈdaʊn] sich hinlegen V/4/9
life (*pl* **lives**) [laɪf, laɪvz] Leben
lifeguard [ˈlaɪfˌgɑːd] Rettungsschwimmer/in; Bademeister/in
lifejacket [ˈlaɪfˌdʒækɪt] Schwimmweste V/3/M2
lift [lɪft] (hoch)heben; Aufzug, Lift
light [laɪt] Licht
light [laɪt] leicht; mild V/2/M5
light bulb [ˈlaɪt ˌbʌlb] Glühbirne
like [laɪk] mögen; wie
like this [laɪk ˈðɪs] so; solche(r, s)
I'd like (to) [ˌaɪd ˈlaɪk] ich würde gern
What's ... like? [wɒts ˈlaɪk] Wie ist ...?
likely [ˈlaɪkli] wahrscheinlich V/6/M7
likes (*pl*) [laɪks] Vorlieben
line [laɪn] Linie; Zeile
° **linen** (*no pl*) [ˈlɪnɪn] Leinen V/5/CIO
lines (*pl*) [laɪnz] Text
link [lɪŋk] verbinden
lion [ˈlaɪən] Löwe
list [lɪst] Liste
° **list** [lɪst] auflisten V/2/CIO
listen (to) [ˈlɪsn] zuhören
litter (*no pl*) [ˈlɪtə] Müll, Abfall V/6/M2
little [ˈlɪtl] klein
a little [ə ˈlɪtl] ein bisschen
live [lɪv] leben, wohnen
live [lɪv] überleben V/4/9
° **live off sth** [ˈlɪv ˌɒf ˌsʌmθɪŋ] von etw leben V/1/PP
living [ˈlɪvɪŋ] lebend V/6/10
make a living [ˌmeɪk ə ˈlɪvɪŋ] seinen Lebensunterhalt verdienen V/5/I
living conditions (*pl*) [ˈlɪvɪŋ kənˌdɪʃnz] Lebensbedingungen V/4/M6
living room [ˈlɪvɪŋ ˌruːm] Wohnzimmer
local [ˈləʊkl] hiesig, örtlich V/5/5
location [ləʊˈkeɪʃn] Lage V/1/M1
locker [ˈlɒkə] Schließfach, Spind

lonely [ˈləʊnli] einsam
long [lɒŋ] lang
a long time ago [ə ˌlɒŋ ˌtaɪm ˌəˈgəʊ] vor langer Zeit V/1/11
look [lʊk] Aussehen; Blick V/3/8; sehen, schauen; aussehen
look after [lʊk ˈɑːftə] sich kümmern um
look around [ˌlʊk əˈraʊnd] sich umsehen/umschauen (in)
look at [ˈlʊk ˌət] betrachten, sehen
look at sb [ˈlʊk ˌət ˌsʌmbədi] jdn anschauen V/2/10
look for [ˈlʊk ˌfə] suchen nach
look forward to sth [ˌlʊk ˈfɔːwəd ˌtə ˌsʌmθɪŋ] sich auf etw freuen V/1/5
° **look out for sb** [ˌlʊk ˈaʊt fə ˌsʌmbədi] nach jdm Ausschau halten; auf jdn aufpassen V/2/1
look sb up and down [ˌlʊk ˌsʌmbədiˌˌʌp ən ˈdaʊn] jdn von oben bis unten mustern V/4/M8
look up [lʊk ˈʌp] nachschlagen
look up to [lʊk ˈʌp tə] aufblicken zu
lose [luːz] verlieren
° **loss** [lɒs] Verlust V/1/M9
a lot (of) [ə ˈlɒt] sehr; viele
lots of [ˈlɒts ˌəv] viel, jede Menge
loud [laʊd] laut
love [lʌv] Liebe; lieben; sehr gern mögen; herzliche Grüße, alles Liebe
be in love (with sb) [ˌbi ˌɪn ˈlʌv] (in jdn) verliebt sein
fall in love (with) [ˌfɔːl ˌɪn ˈlʌv] sich verlieben (in)
lovely [ˈlʌvli] schön, hübsch
loving [ˈlʌvɪŋ] liebevoll, liebend V/5/13
low [ləʊ] niedrig
lucky [ˈlʌki] glücklich; Glück bringend V/4/M10
be lucky [bi ˈlʌki] Glück haben
lunch [lʌntʃ] Mittagessen
lunch break [ˈlʌntʃ ˌbreɪk] Mittagspause V/5/8

lunchtime [ˈlʌntʃˌtaɪm] Mittagszeit; Mittagspause V/4/9
lyrics [ˈlɪrɪks] (Lied)text

M

machine [məˈʃiːn] Maschine
mad [mæd] böse, wütend, sauer
go mad (with hunger) [ˌgəʊ ˈmæd (wɪð ˌhʌŋgə)] (vor Hunger) verrückt werden V/4/M6
magazine [ˌmægəˈziːn] Zeitschrift, Magazin
magic [ˈmædʒɪk] Magie, Zauber
magic trick [ˌmædʒɪk ˈtrɪk] Zaubertrick
magical [ˈmædʒɪkl] magisch V/1/M7
magician [məˈdʒɪʃn] Zauberer/Zauberin
mail [meɪl] (Briefe/E-Mails) schreiben
main [meɪn] Haupt-
main dish [meɪn ˈdɪʃ] Hauptspeise
mainly [ˈmeɪnli] hauptsächlich, in erster Linie
make [meɪk] machen
make [meɪk] lassen V/2/2
make a living [ˌmeɪk ə ˈlɪvɪŋ] seinen Lebensunterhalt verdienen V/5/I
make friends (with sb) [meɪk ˈfrendz] sich (mit jdm) anfreunden, einen Freund gewinnen
make fun of sb [meɪk ˈfʌn ˌəv ˌsʌmbədi] sich über jdn lustig machen V/1/5
make it up with sb [ˌmeɪk ˌɪt ˌʌp wɪð ˈsʌmbədi] sich (wieder) mit jdm vertragen
make money [meɪk ˈmʌni] Geld verdienen
make notes (on) [ˌmeɪk ˈnəʊts] (sich) Notizen machen (zu, über)
make sb aware of sth [ˌmeɪk ˌsʌmbədi əˈweə ˌəv ˌsʌmθɪŋ] jdm etw bewusst machen V/4/M6
make sb do sth [ˌmeɪk ˌsʌmbədi ˈduː ˌsʌmθɪŋ] jdn dazu bringen/veranlassen etw zu tun

° make sb laugh [ˌmeɪk sʌmbədi ˈlɑːf] jdn zum Lachen bringen V/2/1

make sure [ˌmeɪk ˈʃɔː] sich versichern, darauf achten

make up [ˌmeɪkˌˈʌp] bilden V/5/12

make up sth [meɪkˌˈʌp sʌmθɪŋ] etw erfinden, (sich) ausdenken

make-up artist [ˌmeɪkʌpˌˈɑːtɪst] Maskenbildner/in, Visagist/in

making *(no pl)* [ˈmeɪkɪŋ] Herstellung V/6/M6

male [meɪl] männlich

mall [mɔːl] Einkaufspassage, Einkaufszentrum

man *(pl men)* [mæn, men] Mann

manage [ˈmænɪdʒ] es schaffen V/6/8

manage [ˈmænɪdʒ] führen, organisieren V/3/4

manager [ˈmænɪdʒə] Geschäftsführer/in

° Mandarin [ˈmændərɪn] Mandarin *(chinesische Hochsprache)* V/I/2

many [ˈmeni] viele

map [mæp] (Land)karte

marathon [ˈmærəθn] Marathon(lauf)

March [mɑːtʃ] März

mark [mɑːk] Note

market [ˈmɑːkɪt] Markt

get married [get ˈmærid] heiraten V/2/5

marry [ˈmæri] heiraten

martial arts *(npl)* [ˌmɑːʃˌˈɑːts] Kampfsport

mashed potatoes [ˌmæʃt pəˈteɪtəʊz] Kartoffelbrei

° massive [ˈmæsɪv] riesig, enorm V/4/PP

master [ˈmɑːstə] Hausherr V/4/M6

match [mætʃ] Streichholz, Zündholz

match [mætʃ] passen zu V/1/11

match (with) [mætʃ] zuordnen

° mate *(informal)* [meɪt] Kumpel, Freund/in V/I/1

material [məˈtɪəriəl] Material V/5/4

maths [mæθs] Mathe

matter [ˈmætə] Angelegenheit, Sache V/5/15; von Bedeutung sein V/4/M3

° no matter (what/who) [ˌnəʊ ˈmætə] ganz gleich/egal (was/wer) V/3/11

May [meɪ] Mai

maybe [ˈmeɪbi] vielleicht, möglicherweise

mayonnaise [ˌmeɪəˈneɪz] Majonäse

me [miː] mir, mich

meal [miːl] Mahlzeit, Essen

have a meal [ˌhæv ə ˈmiːl] eine Mahlzeit zu sich nehmen

mean [miːn] bedeuten; meinen; gemein, fies

mean to do sth [ˈmiːn tə duː ˌsʌmθɪŋ] etw tun wollen V/6/M6

meaning [ˈmiːnɪŋ] Bedeutung

meat *(no pl)* [miːt] Fleisch

mechanic [mɪˈkænɪk] Mechaniker/in

the media [ðə ˈmiːdiə] die Medien V/6/M2

medical technician [ˌmedɪkl tekˈnɪʃn] medizinisch-technische/r Assistent/in V/5/M2

medicine *(no pl)* [ˈmedsn] Medizin, Medikament(e)

meet [miːt] (sich) treffen

melon [ˈmelən] Melone V/4/9

melt [melt] schmelzen V/6/M2

member [ˈmembə] Mitglied

memory [ˈmemri] Gedächtnis V/4/6

mentally ill [ˌmentliˈɪl] psychisch krank V/5/M11

menu [ˈmenjuː] Speisekarte; Menü

mess [mes] Unordnung, Durcheinander

message [ˈmesɪdʒ] Nachricht

metal [ˈmetl] Metall

metre [ˈmiːtə] Meter

Mexican [ˈmeksɪkən] Mexikaner/in, mexikanisch

Mexico [ˈmeksɪˌkəʊ] Mexiko

° Micronesia [ˌmaɪkrəʊˈniːziə] Mikronesien V/I/1

microwave [ˈmaɪkrəˌweɪv] Mikrowelle(nherd) V/6/1

the Middle East [ðə ˌmɪdlˈˈiːst] der Nahe Osten

in the middle of [ˌɪn ðə ˈmɪdlˌəv] mitten in; in der Mitte

midnight [ˈmɪdˌnaɪt] Mitternacht

might [maɪt] könnte; vielleicht tun

mile [maɪl] Meile

military [ˈmɪlɪtri] Militär V/3/M2

do military service [duː ˌmɪlɪtri ˈsɜːvɪs] Wehrdienst leisten V/5/2

milk [mɪlk] Milch

million [ˈmɪljən] Million

millionaire [ˌmɪljəˈneə] Millionär/in V/5/10

mind [maɪnd] etw dagegen haben V/1/13

° can't get sb/sth off one's mind [ˌkɑːnt get sʌmbədi/sʌmθɪŋˌɒf wʌnz ˈmaɪnd] nicht aufhören können, an jdn/etw zu denken V/5/11

come to sb's mind [kʌm tə ˌsʌmbədiz ˈmaɪnd] jdm einfallen

mindmap [ˈmaɪndmæp] Wortnetz

mine [maɪn] meine(r, s); mir

mineral [ˈmɪnrəl] Mineral V/4/3

minimization *(no pl)* [ˌmɪnɪmaɪˈzeɪʃn] Minimierung V/6/M2

minute [ˈmɪnɪt] Minute

mirror [ˈmɪrə] Spiegel

miscellaneous [ˌmɪsəˈleɪniəs] verschiedene(r, s), diverse(r, s), sonstige(r, s) V/5/16

Miss [mɪs] Fräulein (Anrede)

miss [mɪs] versäumen, verpassen; vermissen

missing [ˈmɪsɪŋ] fehlend V/4/11

mistake [mɪˈsteɪk] Fehler, Irrtum, Versehen

° mistreatment [ˌmɪsˈtriːtmənt] Misshandlung, schlechte Behandlung V/1/M9

mixed [mɪkst] gemischt V/2/I

mixed dorm [ˌmɪkstˌˈdɔːm] *Schlafsaal, in dem Männer und Frauen übernachten* V/1/6

mob [mɒb] Mob, (Menschen)menge V/2/M1

mobile home [ˌməʊbaɪl ˈhəʊm] Wohnwagen V/5/M1

mobile phone [ˌməʊbaɪl ˈfəʊn] Mobiltelefon, Handy
modern [ˈmɒdən] modern
moment [ˈməʊmənt] Moment, Augenblick
at the moment [ˌæt ðə ˈməʊmənt] im Augenblick, momentan
Monday [ˈmʌndeɪ] Montag
money [ˈmʌni] Geld
make money [meɪk ˈmʌni] Geld verdienen
raise money [reɪz ˈmʌni] Geld aufbringen/auftreiben
monkey [ˈmʌŋki] Affe
month [mʌnθ] Monat
more [mɔː] mehr
more or less [ˌmɔːˌɔː ˈles] mehr oder weniger, ungefähr V/2/2
morning [ˈmɔːnɪŋ] Morgen
in the morning [ˌɪn ðə ˈmɔːnɪŋ] morgens, am Morgen, vormittags
this morning [ðɪs ˈmɔːnɪŋ] heute Morgen
morning break [ˈmɔːnɪŋ ˌbreɪk] Frühstückspause V/5/8
(the) most [məʊst] am/die meisten
mother [ˈmʌðə] Mutter
° **mother tongue** [ˈmʌðə ˌtʌŋ] Muttersprache V/I/1
motivate sb to do sth [ˈməʊtɪveɪt ˌsʌmbədi tə duː ˌsʌmθɪŋ] jdn motivieren/dazu bewegen, etw zu tun V/6/M2
mountain [ˈmaʊntɪn] Berg
mouse-surfer [ˈmaʊsˌsɜːfə] Maus-Surfer V/2/CIO
mouth [maʊθ] Mund
move [muːv] sich bewegen; umziehen
move out [ˌmuːvˈaʊt] ausziehen V/4/6
movie (AE) = film (BE) [ˈmuːvi] (Kino-, Spiel)film
moving [ˈmuːvɪŋ] beweglich V/6/8
MP (= Member of Parliament) [ˌem ˈpiː (= ˌmembərˌəv ˈpɑːləmənt] Abgeordnete/r, Parlamentsmitglied V/5/M11
Mr [ˈmɪstə] Herr (Anrede)

Mrs [ˈmɪsɪz] Frau (Anrede)
much [mʌtʃ] viel; sehr
mum (informal) [mʌm] Mama, Mutti
murder [ˈmɜːdə] umbringen, ermorden V/5/M11
museum [mjuːˈziːəm] Museum
mushroom [ˈmʌʃruːm] Pilz
music [ˈmjuːzɪk] Musik
Muslim [ˈmʊzləm] Muslim/in; muslimisch V/2/2
must [mʌst] müssen
must not [ˌmʌst ˈnɒt] nicht dürfen
my [maɪ] mein(e)
my name is [maɪ ˈneɪmˌɪz] ich heiße
myself [maɪˈself] mich, mir; selbst
mysterious [mɪˈstɪəriəs] geheimnisvoll, mysteriös V/1/M7

N

name [neɪm] (be)nennen; Name
my name is [maɪ ˈneɪmˌɪz] ich heiße
What's your name? [ˌwɒts jə ˈneɪm] Wie heißt du?, Wie heißen Sie?
call sb names [ˌkɔːl sʌmbədi ˈneɪmz] jdn beschimpfen
have a nap [ˌhævˌə ˈnæp] ein Nickerchen machen V/1/CIO
narrator [nəˈreɪtə] Erzähler/in
nasty [ˈnɑːsti] scheußlich, grässlich, widerlich
° **nation** [ˈneɪʃn] Nation, Land V/I/PP
national [ˈnæʃnəl] national; National-
national [ˈnæʃnəl] Staatsbürger/in, Staatsangehörige/r V/5/M1
national park [ˌnæʃnəl ˈpɑːk] Nationalpark
nationality [ˌnæʃəˈnæləti] Nationalität; Staatsangehörigkeit V/5/M2
Native American [ˌneɪtɪvˌəˈmerɪkən] amerikanischer Ureinwohner/ amerikanische Ureinwohnerin; indianisch

° **native Australian** [ˌneɪtɪvˌɒˈstreɪliən] australischer Ureinwohner/ australische Ureinwohnerin V/1/PP
natural [ˈnætʃrəl] natürlich, naturbelassen
natural balance [ˌnætʃrəl ˈbæləns] ökologisches Gleichgewicht V/1/M1
natural history museum [nætʃrəl ˌhɪstri mjuːˈziːəm] Naturkundemuseum
nature [ˈneɪtʃə] Natur
near [nɪə] nahe
nearly [ˈnɪəli] fast, beinahe
neck [nek] Hals; Nacken
necklace [ˈnekləs] (Hals)kette V/3/10
need [niːd] brauchen
need to [ˈniːd tə] müssen
° **feel the need to do sth** [ˌfiːl ðə ˈniːdˌtə ˌduː sʌmθɪŋ] das Bedürfnis verspüren, etw zu tun V/2/1
neighbour [ˈneɪbə] Nachbar/in
neighbourhood [ˈneɪbəhʊd] Viertel; Nachbarschaft
nephew [ˈnefjuː] Neffe
get on sb's nerves [ˌgetˌɒn sʌmbədiz ˈnɜːvz] jdm auf die Nerven gehen V/5/M10
nervous [ˈnɜːvəs] nervös
nest [nest] nisten V/1/M1
never [ˈnevə] nie(mals)
new [njuː] neu
° **New Delhi** [njuː ˈdeli] Neu-Delhi V/I/1
° **New Guinea** [njuː ˈgɪni] Neuguinea V/1/PP
New Year (no pl) [ˌnjuː ˈjɪə] Neujahr
New Zealand [njuː ˈziːlənd] Neuseeland V/1/4
the news [ðə njuːz] Nachrichtensendung
news (no pl) [njuːz] Neuigkeit; Nachrichten
newsagent [ˈnjuːzˌeɪdʒnt] Zeitschriftengeschäft; Zeitungshändler/in
newspaper [ˈnjuːzˌpeɪpə] Zeitung

next [nekst] dann, gleich darauf; nächste(r, s)

the next day [ðə ˌnekst ˈdeɪ] am nächsten Tag V/2/10

next to [ˈnekst tə] neben

nice [naɪs] schön, angenehm; nett, freundlich

Nice to meet you. [ˌnaɪs tə ˈmiːt jə] Es freut mich, Sie/dich kennen zu lernen.

night [naɪt] Nacht; Abend

no [nəʊ] kein(e); nein

no matter [ˌnəʊ ˈmætə] ganz gleich/egal V/3/M8

no one [ˈnəʊ wʌn] keiner, niemand V/4/M6

° Nobel Peace Prize [nəʊˌbel ˈpiːs praɪz] Friedensnobelpreis V/6/PP

nobody [ˈnəʊbɒdi] niemand

nod [nɒd] nicken

noise [nɔɪz] Lärm, Krach; Geräusch

noisy [ˈnɔɪzi] laut

non-dairy [ˌnɒn ˈdeəri] milchfrei V/4/4

non-recyclable [ˌnɒn riːˈsaɪkləbl] nicht recyclebar V/6/M4

noodle [ˈnuːdl] Nudel

normal [ˈnɔːml] normal, üblich

normally [ˈnɔːmli] normalerweise

north [nɔːθ] Norden

North America [ˌnɔːθ əˈmerɪkə] Nordamerika

° North American [ˌnɔːθ əˈmerɪkən] Nordamerikaner/in; nordamerikanisch V/4/CIO

° North Pole [ˌnɔːθ ˈpəʊl] Nordpol V/3/CIO

north-east [ˌnɔːθ ˈiːst] Nordosten V/1/7

north-east [ˌnɔːθ ˈiːst] nordöstlich, Nordost- V/1/M1

north-west [ˌnɔːθ ˈwest] Nordwesten V/1/7

Northern Ireland [ˌnɔːðn ˈaɪələnd] Nordirland

nose [nəʊz] Nase

not [nɒt] nicht

° not at all [nɒt ət ˈɔːl] überhaupt nicht V/5/11

note [nəʊt] Notiz

note down [nəʊt ˈdaʊn] (sich) notieren

take/make notes (on) [ˌteɪk/ ˌmeɪk ˈnəʊts] (sich) Notizen machen (zu, über)

nothing [ˈnʌθɪŋ] nichts

for nothing [fə ˈnʌθɪŋ] umsonst V/4/M8

notice [ˈnəʊtɪs] bemerken

noun [naʊn] Hauptwort, Substantiv

novel [ˈnɒvl] Roman V/4/M6

November [nəʊˈvembə] November

now [naʊ] jetzt

nowhere [ˈnəʊweə] nirgends, nirgendwo V/5/M11

number [ˈnʌmbə] Zahl; Ziffer, Nummer

nurse [nɜːs] (Kranken)schwester, (Kranken)pfleger

nursery teacher [ˈnɜːsəri ˌtiːtʃə] Erzieher/in V/5/2

O

(eight) o'clock [əˈklɒk] (acht) Uhr

object [ˈɒbdʒekt] Objekt, Gegenstand, Sache

ocean [ˈəʊʃn] Meer; Ozean

October [ɒkˈtəʊbə] Oktober

the odd one out [ði ˌɒd wʌn ˈaʊt] das fünfte Rad am Wagen V/2/2

off [ɒf] weg von, raus aus V/5/M11

off [ɒf] vor V/1/M1

be off [bi ˈɒf] weggehen

offence [əˈfens] Straftat V/2/M5

offend sb [əˈfend ˌsʌmbədi] jdn beleidigen; jdn kränken V/2/2

offender [əˈfendə] (Straf)täter/in V/2/M5

offer [ˈɒfə] (an)bieten; Angebot

° office [ˈɒfɪs] Büro V/5/CIO

office administrator [ˌɒfɪs ədˈmɪnɪˌstreɪtə] Bürokaufmann/Bürokauffrau V/5/2

official [əˈfɪʃl] offiziell, amtlich

often [ˈɒfn] oft, häufig

Oh dear! [əʊ ˈdɪə] Du meine Güte!

oil [ɔɪl] Öl

old [əʊld] alt

olive [ˈɒlɪv] Olive

on [ɒn] auf; am, an; über; bei; im

on one's own [ˌɒn wʌnz ˈəʊn] allein(e) V/5/3

on the one hand [ɒn ðə ˈwʌn ˌhænd] einerseits V/2/2

on the other hand [ɒn ði ˈʌðə ˌhænd] andererseits V/2/2

once [wʌns] einmal

at once [ət ˈwʌns] auf einmal V/4/M3

one day [ˌwʌn ˈdeɪ] eines Tages

onion [ˈʌnjən] Zwiebel

only [ˈəʊnli] nur

only [ˈəʊnli] erst V/3/M2

open [ˈəʊpən] (sich) öffnen; offen, geöffnet; eröffnet werden

opinion [əˈpɪnjən] Meinung, Ansicht

in my opinion [ɪn ˈmaɪ əˌpɪnjən] meiner Meinung/Ansicht nach V/1/12

opponent [əˈpəʊnənt] Gegner/in; Gegenspieler/in

opportunity [ˌɒpəˈtjuːnəti] Möglichkeit, Chance; Gelegenheit V/5/M1

opposite [ˈɒpəzɪt] Gegenteil; gegenüber

optimistic [ˌɒptɪˈmɪstɪk] optimistisch, zuversichtlich V/3/10

option [ˈɒpʃn] Wahl, Möglichkeit, Option V/4/M3

or [ɔː] oder

° orange [ˈɒrɪndʒ] orange(farben) V/4/CIO

orange juice [ˈɒrɪndʒ ˌdʒuːs] Orangensaft

order [ˈɔːdə] bestellen; Ordnung, Reihenfolge

in order to [ɪn ˈɔːdə tʊ] um zu V/1/M2

organise [ˈɔːgənaɪz] organisieren V/2/7

organism [ˈɔːgəˌnɪzm] Organismus V/1/M1

organization [ˌɔːgənaɪˈzeɪʃn] Organisation V/5/14

originally [əˈrɪdʒnəli] ursprünglich V/1/M5

orphan [ˈɔːfn] Waise, Waisenkind V/4/M8

orphaned [ˈɔːfnd] elternlos V/4/M6

other [ˈʌðər] andere(r, s)
our [aʊə] unser(e)
ours [aʊəz] unsere(r, s)
ourselves [aʊəˈselvz] uns; selbst
out of [aʊt ˈɒv] aus
outback *(no pl)* [ˈaʊtˌbæk] Hinterland (Australiens) V/1/2
outdoor(s) [ˌaʊtˈdɔː] draußen; im Freien; Outdoor-
outer space [ˌaʊtə ˈspeɪs] Weltall, Weltraum V/1/2
outside [ˌaʊtˈsaɪd] außen, außerhalb; im Freien, draußen
oven [ˈʌvn] (Back)ofen V/6/1
over [ˈəʊvə] hinüber; vorbei; über
over and over again [ˌəʊvə ˌən ˌəʊvə əˈgen] immer wieder V/1/M9
over the radio [ˌəʊvə ðə ˈreɪdiəʊ] über Funk V/1/5
over-eat [ˌəʊvərˈiːt] zu viel essen V/4/M3
overalls *(pl)* [ˈəʊvərˌɔːlz] Overall, Arbeitsanzug V/5/8
overcrowded [ˌəʊvəˈkraʊdɪd] überfüllt V/1/12
overfishing *(no pl)* [ˌəʊvəˈfɪʃɪŋ] Überfischung V/1/M1
overweight [ˌəʊvəˈweɪt] übergewichtig V/4/5
own [əʊn] besitzen V/5/13; eigene(r, s)
on one's own [ɒn wʌnzˈ ˌəʊn] allein(e) V/5/3
oz (= ounce) [aʊns] Unze (Maßeinheit) V/4/M2
ozone hole [ˈəʊzəʊn ˌhəʊl] Ozonloch V/1/M3

P

p (= penny, pence) [piː, ˈpeni, pens] Penny, Centstück V/5/11
° **the Pacific Ocean** [ðə pəˌsɪfɪkˈ ˌəʊʃn] der Pazifische Ozean V/I/1
pack [pæk] packen
packaging [ˈpækɪdʒɪŋ] Verpackung(smaterial) V/6/5
packet [ˈpækɪt] Packung, Schachtel
pad [pæd] -schützer
paddle [ˈpædl] Paddel V/3/M2
page [peɪdʒ] Seite

° **pain** [peɪn] Schmerz, Leid V/1/M9
painful [ˈpeɪnfl] schmerzhaft; schrecklich, furchtbar V/6/M2
paint [peɪnt] malen; anstreichen
painter [ˈpeɪntə] Maler/in; Anstreicher/in; Lackierer/in V/5/2
painting [ˈpeɪntɪŋ] Bild, Gemälde
pair [peə] Paar
panic [ˈpænɪk] in Panik geraten
paper [ˈpeɪpə] Papier
paper bank [ˈpeɪpə bæŋk] Altpapiercontainer V/6/M4
° **Papua New Guinea** [ˌpæpuə njuːˈgɪni] Papua-Neuguinea V/I/1
parade [pəˈreɪd] Parade, Umzug
paragraph [ˈpærəˌgrɑːf] Absatz, Abschnitt
paramedic [ˌpærəˈmedɪk] Rettungssanitäter/in
parents [ˈpeərənts] Eltern
park [pɑːk] Park, Parkanlagen
park ranger [ˈpɑːk ˌreɪndʒə] Parkaufseher/in, Ranger/in
parkour *(no pl)* [ˈpɑːkʊə] Parkour *(Sportart)* V/3/2
° **parliament** [ˈpɑːləmənt] Parlament V/1/M9
parrotfish [ˈpærətfɪʃ] Papageifisch V/1/M1
part [pɑːt] Teil; Rolle
part-time [ˌpɑːtˈtaɪm] Teilzeit-
° **in particular** [ɪn pəˈtɪkjʊlə] insbesondere V/1/M9
partner [ˈpɑːtnə] Partner
pass [pɑːs] verhängen, verabschieden, fällen V/2/M6; vergehen, vorübergehen V/4/M8; bestehen V/5/PP
passport [ˈpɑːspɔːt] (Reise)pass V/2/5
password [ˈpɑːsˌwɜːd] Passwort V/2/9
past [pɑːst] Vergangenheit; vorbei/vorüber an
° **past** [pɑːst] frühere(r, s); vergangen V/1/M9
pasta [ˈpæstə] Nudeln, Teigwaren
path [pɑːθ] Weg, Pfad
patient [ˈpeɪʃnt] geduldig; Patient/in

° **Patois** [ˈpætwɑː] Patois *(Dialekt in Jamaika)* V/I/2
paw [pɔː] Pfote, Tatze V/1/9
pay [peɪ] bezahlen
pay attention to sb/sth [ˌpeɪ əˈtenʃn tə sʌmbədi/sʌmθɪŋ] jdm/etw Aufmerksamkeit schenken V/2/2
pay cash [peɪ ˈkæʃ] bar bezahlen V/5/13
payment [ˈpeɪmənt] Bezahlung, Entlohnung V/5/M1
PE (= physical education) [ˌpiː ˈiː, ˌfɪzɪkl ˌedjuˈkeɪʃn] Sport(unterricht)
pea [piː] Erbse
peace [piːs] Friede
peanut [ˈpiːˌnʌt] Erdnuss
pear [peə] Birne
pedal boat [ˈpedl ˌbəʊt] Tretboot V/3/M2
pen [pen] Feder, Stift
pencil [ˈpensl] Bleistift
pencil case [ˈpensl ˌkeɪs] Federmäppchen
penguin [ˈpeŋgwɪn] Pinguin
° **penny** [ˈpeni] Penny, Centstück V/5/11
° **people** [ˈpiːpl] Volk V/1/M9
people *(pl)* [ˈpiːpl] Leute, Menschen
pepper [ˈpepə] Pfeffer; Paprika
° **pepperoni** [ˌpepəˈrəʊni] Peperoni V/4/CIO
per [pɜː] pro V/1/6
per cent [pəˈsent] Prozent
perfect [ˈpɜːfɪkt] perfekt V/4/4
perform [pəˈfɔːm] vorführen; aufführen
° **perform** [pəˈfɔːm] auftreten V/6/PP
perhaps [pəˈhæps] vielleicht
period (of time) [ˈpɪəriəd] Zeitraum V/1/11
permission *(no pl)* [pəˈmɪʃn] Erlaubnis, Genehmigung V/2/5
person [ˈpɜːsn] Person, Mensch
personal [ˈpɜːsnəl] persönlich; privat V/2/9
personality [ˌpɜːsəˈnæləti] Persönlichkeit, Charakter V/3/10

pet [pet] Haustier
petrol bomb ['petrəl ˌbɒm] Molotowcocktail V/2/M1
phase [feɪz] Phase V/2/2
the Philippines [ðə 'fɪləpiːnz] die Philippinen V/1/4
phone [fəʊn] anrufen; Telefon
photo ['fəʊtəʊ] Foto
take photos [ˌteɪk 'fəʊtəʊz] Bilder machen, fotografieren
phrase [freɪz] Satz; Ausdruck, (Rede)wendung
physical ['fɪzɪkl] körperlich, physisch V/3/M2
pick [pɪk] pflücken, sammeln V/5/M1
pick [pɪk] (Aus)wahl V/4/M10
pick on sb ['pɪk ɒn ˌsʌmbədi] auf jdm herumhacken
pick pockets ['pɪk ˌpɒkɪts] Taschendiebstahl begehen V/4/M10
pick up [ˌpɪk ʹʌp] abholen; aufheben V/6/4
picker ['pɪkə] Erntehelfer/in V/5/M1
picnic ['pɪknɪk] Picknick
picture ['pɪktʃə] Bild, Foto
pie [paɪ] Pastete; Kuchen
pie chart ['paɪ tʃɑːt] Tortendiagramm V/4/4
pie-eating contest [ˌpaɪ iːtɪŋ 'kɒntest] Kuchenwettessen
piece [piːs] Stück
piece of advice [ˌpiːs əv əd'vaɪs] Rat V/6/3
piece of paper [ˌpiːs əv 'peɪpə] Blatt Papier, Zettel
piecework ['piːsˌwɜːk] Akkordarbeit V/5/M1
pig [pɪg] Schwein
The Pilgrims *(pl)* [ðə 'pɪlgrɪms] die Pilger(väter)
pilot ['paɪlət] Pilot/in
pink [pɪŋk] rosa, pink
pizza ['piːtsə] Pizza
place [pleɪs] Ort; Platz
placemat ['pleɪsˌmæt] Set, Platzdeckchen V/3/M1
plan [plæn] Plan; planen
plan of action [ˌplæn əvˈ'ækʃn] Aktionsplan V/6/l
plane [pleɪn] Flugzeug

planet ['plænɪt] Planet V/6/3
plant [plɑːnt] Pflanze; pflanzen V/6/8
plastic ['plæstɪk] Plastik, Kunststoff V/6/3
plastic bottle bank ['plæstɪk ˌbɒtl bæŋk] Plastikflaschencontainer V/6/M4
plate [pleɪt] Teller
platform ['plætˌfɔːm] Plattform; Bahnsteig
platypus ['plætɪpəs] Schnabeltier V/1/8
play [pleɪ] Spiel; (Theater)stück; spielen
play down sth [ˌpleɪ 'daʊn sʌmθɪŋ] etw herunterspielen V/3/CIO
player ['pleɪə] Spieler/in
playful ['pleɪfl] spielerisch, scherzhaft; verspielt
playground ['pleɪˌgraʊnd] Spielplatz
playing field ['pleɪɪŋ ˌfiːld] Sportplatz; Spielfeld
please [pliːz] bitte
Pleased to meet you. [ˌpliːzd tə 'miːt jʊ] Freut mich, dich/euch/ Sie kennen zu lernen.
plenty ['plenti] mehr als genug
pm (= post meridiem) [ˌpiː 'em, ˌpəʊst məˌrɪdiəm] nachmittags, abends *(nur hinter Uhrzeit zwischen 12 Uhr mittags und Mitternacht)*
pocket ['pɒkɪt] Tasche
pocket money ['pɒkɪt ˌmʌni] Taschengeld V/5/13
poem ['pəʊɪm] Gedicht
point [pɔɪnt] Punkt
not see the point [nɒt ˌsiː ðə 'pɔɪnt] keinen Sinn in etw sehen V/4/6
point of view [ˌpɔɪnt əvˈ'vjuː] Standpunkt, Gesichtspunkt V/6/M7
° poisoning ['pɔɪznɪŋ] Vergiftung V/2/PP
poisonous ['pɔɪznəs] giftig V/1/CIO
police *(npl)* [pə'liːs] Polizei
police officer [pə'liːs ˌɒfɪsə] Polizeibeamter/-beamtin

policeman/-woman [pə'liːsmən, pə'liːsˌwʊmən] Polizist/in
° policy ['pɒləsi] Programm, Strategie; Grundsatz V/1/M9
polite [pə'laɪt] höflich
pollute [pə'luːt] verschmutzen V/6/13
polluted [pə'luːtɪd] verschmutzt V/6/8
pollution [pə'luːʃn] (Umwelt)verschmutzung V/6/3
polyp ['pɒlɪp] Polyp V/1/M1
pommy *(Australian English; informal)* ['pɒmi] *abwertende Bezeichnung für einen Briten/ eine Britin* V/1/5
pony ['pəʊni] Pony
poor [pɔː] arm
the poor *(pl)* [ðə pɔː] die Armen V/5/14
popsicle ['pɒpsɪkl] Eis am Stiel
popular ['pɒpjʊlə] beliebt
population [ˌpɒpjʊ'leɪʃn] Bevölkerung
porridge ['pɒrɪdʒ] Porridge, Haferbrei V/4/M6
portable ['pɔːtəbl] tragbar V/5/5
portfolio [pɔːt'fəʊliəʊ] (Akten)mappe V/1/9
portion ['pɔːʃn] Portion V/4/M2
portrait ['pɔːtrɪt] Porträt, Darstellung V/1/M8
position [pə'zɪʃn] Position, Stelle V/5/M2
possible ['pɒsəbl] möglich V/4/4
post office ['pəʊst ˌɒfɪs] Postamt
post sth ['pəʊst ˌsʌmθɪŋ] etw ins Internet stellen
postcard ['pəʊstˌkɑːd] Postkarte
potato *(pl -es)* [pə'teɪtəʊ, pə'teɪtəʊz] Kartoffel
pound (£) [paʊnd] Pfund
power ['paʊə] Kraft, Stärke V/3/M2
power ['paʊə] Macht; Einfluss V/2/12
powerful ['paʊəfl] mächtig
practical ['præktɪkl] praktisch V/5/M1
practice ['præktɪs] Übung; Training
practise ['præktɪs] üben; praktizieren, ausüben

prefer [prɪˈfɜː] vorziehen, bevorzugen

pregnant [ˈpregnənt] schwanger V/5/13

prejudice [ˈpredʒʊdɪs] Vorurteil

prepare [prɪˈpeə] vorbereiten

present [ˈpreznt] Geschenk

present [ˈpreznt] Gegenwart V/5/4

present (to) [prɪˈzent] bieten; präsentieren

presentation [ˌpreznˈteɪʃn] Präsentation

give a presentation [ˌgɪv ə ˌpreznˈteɪʃn] eine Präsentation halten V/1/I

preserve [prɪˈzɜːv] erhalten, bewahren, schützen V/1/M1

president [ˈprezɪdənt] Präsident/in; Vorsitzende/r

press [pres] drücken

pretty [ˈprɪti] hübsch; ziemlich

previous [ˈpriːviəs] vorherig V/5/M2

price [praɪs] Preis

pride [praɪd] Stolz

primary school [ˈpraɪməri ˌskuːl] Grundschule V/5/4

prime minister [ˌpraɪm ˈmɪnɪstə] Premierminister/in, Ministerpräsident/in V/1/M9

prince [prɪns] Prinz

print (out) [prɪnt] (aus)drucken V/2/9

printer cartridge [ˈprɪntə ˌkɑːtrɪdʒ] Druckerpatrone V/6/M2

prison [ˈprɪzn] Gefängnis V/1/12

prisoner [ˈprɪznə] Gefangene/r

private [ˈpraɪvət] privat; vertraulich V/2/10

private room [ˌpraɪvət ˈruːm] Einzelzimmer V/1/6

prize [praɪz] Preis, Gewinn

pro [prəʊ] Pro(-Argument) V/2/I

probably [ˈprɒbəbli] wahrscheinlich

problem [ˈprɒbləm] Problem

process [ˈprəʊses] Prozess, Vorgang V/1/M2

produce [prəˈdjuːs] herstellen, erzeugen, produzieren V/6/M1

producer [prəˈdjuːsə] Produzent/in; Hersteller

product [ˈprɒdʌkt] Produkt, Erzeugnis

professional [prəˈfeʃnəl] professionell, Profi-; Profi V/3/5

° **profound** [prəˈfaʊnd] tief, heftig, groß V/1/M9

program *(AE)* = programme *(BE)* [ˈprəʊɡræm] Programm V/2/M5

programme [ˈprəʊɡræm] Programm; Sendung

programmed [ˈprəʊɡræmd] programmiert V/6/8

project [ˈprɒdʒekt] Projekt

promise [ˈprɒmɪs] versprechen

pronounce [prəˈnaʊns] aussprechen V/2/2

proof [pruːf] Beweis V/6/8

properly [ˈprɒpəli] korrekt, richtig V/1/M1

property [ˈprɒpəti] Eigentum V/3/5

prosecutor [ˈprɒsɪkjuːtə] Staatsanwalt/-anwältin, Ankläger/in V/2/M5

protect [prəˈtekt] schützen

protein [ˈprəʊtiːn] Eiweiß, Protein V/4/3

proud [praʊd] stolz

provide [prəˈvaɪd] bieten, geben, sorgen für V/5/M1

provoke [prəˈvəʊk] provozieren V/3/10

psychologist [saɪˈkɒlədʒɪst] Psychologe/Psychologin V/4/9

pub [pʌb] Kneipe

public [ˈpʌblɪk] öffentlich V/3/5

publish [ˈpʌblɪʃ] veröffentlichen V/4/M6

pull [pʊl] ziehen

° **pull sb aside** [ˌpʊl sʌmbədi ə'saɪd] jdn beiseite nehmen V/2/1

punctual [ˈpʌŋktʃuəl] pünktlich V/5/3

punish [ˈpʌnɪʃ] bestrafen V/2/M5

punk *(informal)* [pʌŋk] Mistkerl; Randalierer/in V/3/5

pupil [ˈpjuːpl] Schüler/in

puppy [ˈpʌpi] junger Hund, Welpe

pure [pjʊə] rein, pur V/4/M2

push [pʊʃ] schieben; drücken; stoßen

put [pʊt] setzen, legen, stellen

put [pʊt] eingeben V/5/5

put away [ˌpʊt əˈweɪ] wegräumen, aufräumen V/6/8

put on [pʊt ˈɒn] anziehen; sich eincremen mit

put on weight [ˌpʊt ˈɒn ˌweɪt] zunehmen V/4/9

put out sth [pʊt ˈaʊt ˌsʌmθɪŋ] etw löschen; etw ausmachen

put up [pʊt ˈʌp] aufhängen

° **puzzle** [ˈpʌzl] Puzzle; Rätsel V/3/11

pyjamas *(pl)* [pəˈdʒɑːməz] Pyjama, Schlafanzug V/1/5

Q

quadruple [ˈkwɒdrʊpl] vierfach V/4/M2

qualification [ˌkwɒlɪfɪˈkeɪʃn] Qualifikation; Abschluss V/5/M2

° qualification [ˌkwɒlɪfɪˈkeɪʃn] Qualifikation V/5/PP

quality [ˈkwɒləti] Qualität, Güte V/5/M1

quarter (past/to) [ˈkwɔːtə] Viertel (nach/vor)

queen [kwiːn] Königin

question [ˈkwestʃn] Frage

questionnaire [ˌkwestʃəˈneə] Fragebogen V/6/I

ask questions [ɑːsk ˈkwestʃnz] Fragen stellen

queue [kjuː] Schlange, Reihe

quick [kwɪk] schnell

quiet [ˈkwaɪət] leise, ruhig

quite [kwaɪt] ziemlich

quiz sb [ˈkwɪz ˌsʌmbədi] jdn befragen/prüfen V/1/CIO

R

rabbit [ˈræbɪt] Kaninchen

rabbit-proof fence [ˌræbɪt ˌpruːf ˈfens] *Schutzzaun in Westaustralien, der gezogen wurde, um die Ausbreitung von Kaninchen auf Ackerland zu vermeiden* V/1/M5

race [reɪs] Rennen

race [reɪs] Rasse V/2/M1

racially motivated [ˈreɪʃli ˌməʊtɪveɪtɪd] rassistisch motiviert V/2/M1

racist [ˈreɪsɪst] Rassist/in; rassistisch V/2/M1

radio [ˈreɪdiəʊ] Radio

radio [ˈreɪdiəʊ] Funkgerät V/3/M2

radio station [ˈreɪdiəʊ ˌsteɪʃn] Radiosender V/4/6

raft [rɑːft] Floß

rail [reɪl] Geländer V/3/5

railroad (AE) = railway (BE) [ˈreɪlˌrəʊd] Schienen; (Eisen)bahn

rain [reɪn] Regen; regnen

rainforest [ˈreɪnˌfɒrɪst] Regenwald

rainy [ˈreɪni] regnerisch

raise interest [ˌreɪzˈɪntrəst] Interesse (er)wecken V/3/M2

raise money [reɪzˈmʌni] Geld aufbringen/auftreiben

ramp [ræmp] Rampe V/3/5

range [reɪndʒ] Reichweite; Spektrum, Vielfalt V/1/M1

° Rangoon [ræŋˈguːn] Rangun V/I/1

rank [ræŋk] einstufen; anordnen

rasta [ˈræstə] Rasta, Rastafari V/3/8

rat [ræt] Ratte

rate [reɪt] Rate, Quote V/1/M3

rate sb [reɪt] jdn einschätzen V/2/10

rather [ˈrɑːðə] eher V/4/CIO

rather than [ˈrɑːðə ðæn] anstatt V/6/M2

raven [ˈreɪvn] Rabe

reach [riːtʃ] greifen; erreichen

react [riˈækt] reagieren V/4/10

reaction (to) [riˈækʃn] Reaktion (auf) V/4/5

read [riːd] lesen

read along [ˌriːd əˈlɒŋ] mitlesen

read out [ˌriːdˈaʊt] (laut) vorlesen V/4/M7

take a reading of sth [teɪk ə ˈriːdɪŋ əv ˌsʌmθɪŋ] etw ablesen V/6/M2

ready [ˈredi] fertig

(Are you) ready to order? [ˌredi təˈɔːdə] Möchten Sie schon bestellen?

real [rɪəl] wirklich; echt

realise sth [ˈrɪəlaɪz] sich einer Sache bewusst werden V/2/M2

really [ˈrɪəli] wirklich

reason [ˈriːzn] Grund

° rebel yell [ˌrebəlˈjel] (Kampf)schrei V/2/1

rebuild [ˌriːˈbɪld] wieder aufbauen V/3/M2

receipt [rɪˈsiːt] Beleg; Kassenbon

° receive [rɪˈsiːv] annehmen, gewähren V/1/M9

receptionist [rɪˈsepʃnɪst] Empfangschef/in V/1/6

recipe [ˈresəpi] Rezept

° recognized [ˈrekəgnaɪzd] anerkannt; zugelassen V/5/PP

record [ˈrekɔːd] Rekord V/3/7; (Schall)platte V/5/13

record [rɪˈkɔːd] aufnehmen, aufzeichnen V/5/M12

record player [ˈrekɔːd ˌpleɪə] (Schall)plattenspieler V/5/13

recreation [ˌrekriˈeɪʃn] Freizeitbeschäftigung, Hobby V/5/16

recycle [riːˈsaɪkl] wiederverwerten, recyclen V/6/3

recycled [riːˈsaɪkld] wiederverwertet, recycelt V/6/4

red [red] rot

reduce [rɪˈdjuːs] verringern, reduzieren, verkleinern V/6/3

reef [riːf] Riff V/1/M1

referee [ˌrefəˈriː] Schiedsrichter/in

reference [ˈrefrəns] Empfehlungsschreiben, (Arbeits)zeugnis, Referenz V/5/4

refill [riːˈfɪl] auffüllen, nachfüllen V/6/M2

° reflect on sb/sth [rɪˈflekt ɒn ˌsʌmbədi/ˌsʌmθɪŋ] über jdn/ etw nachdenken V/1/M9

regular [ˈregjʊlə] regelmäßig; üblich, normal

rehabilitate [ˌriːəˈbɪlɪteɪt] rehabilitieren V/5/M1

relative [ˈrelətɪv] Verwandte/r, Angehörige/r

relative pronoun [ˌrelətɪv ˈprəʊnaʊn] Relativpronomen V/4/M9

relaxing [rɪˈlæksɪŋ] entspannend V/1/10

release [rɪˈliːs] herausbringen, veröffentlichen V/3/M8

release [rɪˈliːs] Erleichterung V/3/M8

reliable [rɪˈlaɪəbl] verlässlich, zuverlässig V/5/3

relief [rɪˈliːf] Hilfe, Unterstützung V/1/M2

religion [rɪˈlɪdʒn] Religion; Glaube

religious [rəˈlɪdʒəs] religiöse(r, s), Religions-

rely on [rɪˈlaɪ ɒn] sich verlassen auf

remember [rɪˈmembə] sich erinnern (an)

° removal (no pl) [rɪˈmuːvl] Entfernung, Wegnahme V/1/M9

remove [rɪˈmuːv] entfernen

rent [rent] Miete

repair [rɪˈpeə] reparieren

repeat [rɪˈpiːt] Wiederholung; wiederholen V/4/M6

replace [rɪˈpleɪs] ersetzen

report [rɪˈpɔːt] Bericht; berichten; (sich) melden

report [rɪˈpɔːt] Zeugnis V/5/CIO

reported speech [rɪˌpɔːtɪd ˈspiːtʃ] indirekte Rede V/4/11

reporter [rɪˈpɔːtə] Reporter/in

° Republic of South Africa [rɪˌpʌblɪk əv saʊθ ˈæfrɪkə] Republik Südafrika V/I/1

request [rɪˈkwest] Bitte, Anfrage; Wunsch; bitten (um); (sich) wünschen

required [rɪˈkwaɪəd] erforderlich V/5/M1

rescue [ˈreskjuː] retten

research [rɪˈsɜːtʃ] recherchieren V/5/M7

research (no pl) [rɪˈsɜːtʃ] Forschung, Erforschung V/4/M11

reservation [ˌrezəˈveɪʃn] Reservierung; Reservat (= ein den Indianern vorbehaltenes Gebiet) resolve [rɪˈzɒlv] lösen, klären V/5/M2; beschließen V/1/M9

resource [rɪˈzɔːs] Ressource V/6/M2

respect [rɪˈspekt] Respekt, Achtung; respektieren, anerkennen

° respectful [rɪˈspektfl] respektvoll V/1/M9

responsibility [rɪˌspɒnsəˈbɪləti] Verantwortlichkeit, Zuständigkeit; Verantwortung V/2/5

be responsible for sth [biː rɪˈspɒnsəbl fə ˌsʌmθɪŋ] für etw verantwortlich sein; für etw haften V/2/5

rest [rest] Rest V/2/2

restaurant [ˈrestrɒnt] Restaurant

restriction [rɪˈstrɪkʃn] Einschränkung, Begrenzung V/2/5

result [rɪˈzʌlt] Folge; Ergebnis

return [rɪˈtɜːn] zurückkehren V/6/8

return [rɪˈtɜːn] Rückkehr V/3/M4

return (ticket) [rɪˈtɜːn] Hin- und Rückfahrkarte

reuse [riːˈjuːz] wiederverwenden V/6/3

rhythm [ˈrɪðəm] Rhythmus, Takt V/1/10

rice [raɪs] Reis

rich [rɪtʃ] reich

the rich (pl) [ðə rɪtʃ] die Reichen V/5/14

get rid of sth [get ˈrɪd əv ˌsʌmθɪŋ] etw loswerden V/3/M8

ride [raɪd] fahren; reiten

rider [ˈraɪdə] Reiter/in

riding [ˈraɪdɪŋ] Reiten

right [raɪt] (nach) rechts; Recht; richtig

be right [bi raɪt] Recht haben

on the right [ˌɒn ðə ˈraɪt] rechts, auf der rechten Seite

° right sth [ˈraɪt ˌsʌmθɪŋ] etw wiedergutmachen V/1/M9

be on the right track [bi ɒn ðə ˌraɪt ˈtræk] auf dem richtigen Weg sein V/6/4

ring [rɪŋ] klingeln, läuten

riot [ˈraɪət] Krawall, Unruhe V/2/M1

rise [raɪz] (auf)steigen V/2/7

risk [rɪsk] Risiko, Gefahr V/3/5

river [ˈrɪvə] Fluss

road [rəʊd] Straße

roar [rɔː] brüllen V/4/M6

robot [ˈrəʊbɒt] Roboter V/6/8

rock [rɒk] Stein, Fels(en)

role [rəʊl] Rolle

role-play [ˈrəʊlˌpleɪ] Rollenspiel V/1/6

roll [rəʊl] Brötchen

romance [rəʊˈmæns] Romanze; Liebesfilm

romantic [rəʊˈmæntɪk] romantisch V/6/8

room [ruːm] Zimmer

root [ruːt] Wurzel V/1/9

rope [rəʊp] Seil

rough-looking [ˈrʌf ˌlʊkɪŋ] hart und mitgenommen aussehend V/4/M8

route [ruːt] Route, Strecke, Verlauf V/3/M2

rubber (BE) [ˈrʌbə] Gummi; Radiergummi

rubbish [ˈrʌbɪʃ] Müll

rude [ruːd] unhöflich

rueful [ˈruːfl] reuevoll V/4/M8

ruin [ˈruːɪn] ruinieren, zerstören V/2/6

rule [ruːl] Regel

ruler [ˈruːlə] Lineal

run [rʌn] laufen, rennen

run after [ˌrʌn ˈɑːftə] hinterherlaufen

run away [rʌn əˈweɪ] weglaufen

run into [rʌn ˈɪntʊ] in jdn/etw hineinrennen; jdm über den Weg laufen

run out [ˌrʌn ˈaʊt] ablaufen, auslaufen V/3/M2

runaway [ˈrʌnəˌweɪ] Ausreißer/in V/5/M11

° Rwanda [ruˈændə] Ruanda V/I/1

S

sack [sæk] Sack V/2/2

sad [sæd] traurig

safe [seɪf] sicher

safety [ˈseɪfti] Sicherheit

sail [seɪl] segeln

salad [ˈsæləd] Salat

be on sale [biː ˌɒn ˈseɪl] reduziert sein; im Angebot sein

salesperson [ˈseɪlzˌpɜːsn] Verkäufer/in

salt [sɔːlt] Salz

the same [ðə ˈseɪm] der-/die-/dasselbe

same here [seɪm ˈhɪə] ich/wir auch

Saturday [ˈsætədeɪ] Samstag

sauce [sɔːs] Soße

sausage [ˈsɒsɪdʒ] Wurst, Würstchen

save [seɪv] retten; sparen V/5/13; speichern, sichern V/2/9

save up for sth [ˌseɪv ˈʌp fə sʌmθɪŋ] auf/für etw sparen V/5/15

say [seɪ] sagen

say hello to [ˌseɪ həˈləʊ tə] (be)grüßen

say sorry (to sb) [ˌseɪ ˈsɒri] sich (bei jdm) entschuldigen V/1/M9

saying [ˈseɪɪŋ] Sprichwort

scaffold [ˈskæfəʊld] Gerüst V/5/2

scaffolder [ˈskæfəʊldə] Gerüstbauer/in V/5/2

scare [skeə] Angst machen, erschrecken

scared [skeəd] verängstigt

be scared [bi ˈskeəd] Angst haben

scarf (pl -s or scarves) [skɑːf, skɑːvz] Schal

scary [ˈskeəri] Furcht erregend; unheimlich

scene [siːn] Szene

school [skuːl] Schule

schoolbag [ˈskuːlbæg] Schultasche

schoolwork (no pl) [ˈskuːl ˌwɜːk] Schularbeiten V/1/5

science [ˈsaɪəns] Naturwissenschaft

scientist [ˈsaɪəntɪst] Wissenschaftler/in

(pair of) scissors [ˈsɪzəz] Schere

scooter [ˈskuːtə] (Tret)roller

score [skɔː] Punktestand

score [skɔː] einen Punkt machen, punkten

score [skɔː] punkten V/5/3

DICTIONARY *English–German*

score a goal [ˌskɔːr ə ˈgəʊl] ein Tor schießen
Scotland [ˈskɒtlənd] Schottland
Scottish [ˈskɒtɪʃ] schottisch
scratch [skrætʃ] (zer)kratzen
scream [skriːm] schreien; kreischen
screw [skruː] Schraube V/3/5
scuba diving *(no pl)* [ˈskuːbə ˌdaɪvɪŋ] Sporttauchen V/1/M1
sea [siː] Meer
search [sɜːtʃ] (durch)suchen
search engine [ˌsɜːtʃ ˈendʒɪn] Suchmaschine
seasick [ˈsiːˌsɪk] seekrank
seaweed [ˈsiːˌwiːd] Seegras, (See)tang V/4/1
second [ˈsekənd] Sekunde
° **second-hand car** [ˌsekəndˌhænd ˈkɑː] Gebrauchtwagen V/5/CIO
secondary school [ˈsekəndri ˌskuːl] höhere/weiterführende Schule
secret [ˈsiːkrət] geheim; Geheimnis
secretary [ˈsekrətri] Sekretär/in
section [ˈsekʃn] Bereich, Teil V/4/4
security camera [sɪˈkjʊərəti ˌkæmrə] Überwachungskamera
security guard [sɪˈkjʊərəti ˌgɑːd] Sicherheitsbedienstete/r V/5/2
security *(no pl)* [sɪˈkjʊərəti] Sicherheit; Sicherheitsdienst
see [siː] sehen; einsehen, verstehen
See you! *(informal)* [ˈsiː jʊ] Bis bald!
seem [siːm] scheinen V/5/13
sell [sel] verkaufen
seller [ˈselə] Verkäufer/in
° **semi-official** [ˌsemi əˈfɪʃl] halboffiziell V/I/1
semifinal [ˌsemiˈfaɪnl] Halbfinale
send [send] (zu)schicken
send out sb [ˌsend ˈaʊt sʌmbədi] jdn aussenden; jdn fortschicken V/1/12
send out sth [ˌsend ˈaʊt sʌmθɪŋ] etw verschicken V/2/10
sentence [ˈsentəns] Satz; Urteil, Strafe V/2/M5

September [sepˈtembə] September
° **series** [ˈsɪəriːz] Serie, Reihe V/4/PP
serious [ˈsɪəriəs] ernst
servant [ˈsɜːvnt] Diener/in, Dienstmädchen, Bedienstete/r V/1/M5
serve [sɜːv] servieren V/4/6
serve [sɜːv] dienen V/2/M5
° **set** [set] setzen V/4/PP
set fire to sth [ˌset ˈfaɪə tə sʌmθɪŋ] etw anzünden/in Brand stecken V/2/M1
be set somewhere [bi ˈset ˌsʌmweə] irgendwo spielen/stattfinden V/6/8
set the table [ˌset ðə ˈteɪbl] den Tisch decken
settle [ˈsetl] sich niederlassen
settlement [ˈsetlmənt] Siedlung V/1/M5
settler [ˈsetlə] Siedler/in
several [ˈsevrəl] einige V/1/M1
sex object [ˈseks ˌɒbdʒekt] Sexualobjekt V/2/2
° **the Seychelles** [ðə seɪˈʃelz] die Seychellen V/I/1
shake (out) [ˈʃeɪk (ˈaʊt)] (aus)schütteln V/1/CIO
share [ʃeə] teilen
shark *(pl -s or -)* [ʃɑːk, ʃɑːks] Hai(fisch)
sharp [ʃɑːp] scharf
she [ʃiː] sie
shed [ʃed] Schuppen
sheep *(pl sheep)* [ʃiːp] Schaf
shelf *(pl shelves)* [ʃelf, ʃelvz] Regal
shell [ʃel] Schale V/1/M1
° **shell** [ʃel] Schale; Muschel V/2/1
shift [ˈʃɪft] Schicht V/5/2
shift work *(no pl)* [ˈʃɪft ˌwɜːk] Schichtarbeit, Schichtdienst
° **shine** [ʃaɪn] scheinen *(Sonne)* V/3/11
ship [ʃɪp] Schiff
shirt [ʃɜːt] Hemd V/5/M4
° **shock** [ʃɒk] schockieren V/3/PP
shocked [ʃɒkt] schockiert, entsetzt
shoe [ʃuː] Schuh
shop [ʃɒp] Geschäft, Laden

shop assistant [ˈʃɒp əˌsɪstnt] Verkäufer/in
shoplifting *(no pl)* [ˈʃɒpˌlɪftɪŋ] Ladendiebstahl V/2/M5
short [ʃɔːt] kurz
should [ʃʊd] sollte/müsste
shoulder [ˈʃəʊldə] Schulter
shout [ʃaʊt] schreien, rufen
show [ʃəʊ] zeigen
take a shower [teɪk ə ˈʃaʊə] duschen V/6/3
shy [ʃaɪ] schüchtern
sick [sɪk] krank V/4/9
side [saɪd] Seite
side order [ˈsaɪd ˌɔːdə] Beilage
sidewalk *(AE)* [ˈsaɪdˌwɔːk] Bürgersteig V/3/5
sigh [saɪ] seufzen
sight [saɪt] Sehleistung; Sehenswürdigkeit
sign [saɪn] unterschreiben; signieren; Zeichen; (Straßen-/Verkehrs)schild
signal [ˈsɪgnl] Signal V/3/M2
signature [ˈsɪgnətʃə] Unterschrift
silly [ˈsɪli] albern, dumm
similar [ˈsɪmɪlə] ähnlich V/4/9
simple [ˈsɪmpl] einfach
since [sɪns] da, weil; seit V/3/4
sing [sɪŋ] singen
° **Singapore** [ˌsɪŋəˈpɔː] Singapur V/I/1
singer [ˈsɪŋə] Sänger/in
single [ˈsɪŋgl] einzelne(r, s) V/5/M11
single room [ˈsɪŋgl ˌruːm] Einzelzimmer V/1/6
single (ticket) [ˈsɪŋgl] Einzelfahrkarte
sink [sɪŋk] untergehen, sinken
sir [sɜː] Herr *(Anrede)* V/4/M6
sister [ˈsɪstə] Schwester
sit [sɪt] sitzen
sit down [sɪt ˈdaʊn] sich (hin)setzen
situation [ˌsɪtʃuˈeɪʃn] Situation, Lage
size [saɪz] Größe
skate [skeɪt] Schlittschuh; Skate-Veranstaltung; skaten, Skateboard fahren V/3/5
skateboarding *(no pl)* [ˈskeɪtˌbɔːdɪŋ] Skateboardfahren V/3/I

D

skeleton ['skelɪtn] Skelett
ski [skiː] Ski V/3/4
° ski [skiː] Ski fahren, Ski laufen V/3/CIO
skiing (no pl) ['skiːɪŋ] Skifahren, Skilaufen V/3/4
skill [skɪl] Fähigkeit; Geschick(lichkeit) V/3/4
skin [skɪn] Haut V/1/M3
skinny ['skɪni] dünn, mager V/4/9
skirt [skɜːt] Rock
sky [skaɪ] Himmel V/1/11
skydiving (no pl) ['skaɪˌdaɪvɪŋ] Fallschirmspringen V/3/2
skyline ['skaɪˌlaɪn] Skyline, Horizont
skyscraper ['skaɪˌskreɪpə] Wolkenkratzer
slap on sth (informal) [ˌslæpˈɒn sʌmθɪŋ] etw aufsetzen V/1/M3
slave [sleɪv] Sklave/Sklavin
sled [sled] Schlitten V/3/4
sleep [sliːp] schlafen
slice [slaɪs] Scheibe V/4/9
slim [slɪm] schlank, schmal, dünn
slip on sth (informal) ['slɪpˌɒn ˌsʌmθɪŋ] etw anziehen V/1/M3
slop on sth (informal) [ˌslɒpˈɒn sʌmθɪŋ] etw auftragen V/1/M3
slow [sləʊ] langsam
small [smɔːl] klein
small [smɔːl] leise V/4/M8
smell [smel] Geruch; Duft; Gestank; riechen
smile [smaɪl] lächeln
smoke [sməʊk] Rauch; rauchen
snack bar ['snæk ˌbɑː] Imbissstube
snake [sneɪk] Schlange
snow [snəʊ] Schnee
snow-covered ['snəʊˌkʌvəd] schneebedeckt V/3/4
snub-nosed [ˌsnʌb ˈnəʊzd] stupsnasig, mit einer Stupsnase V/4/M8
so [səʊ] also, so
so far ['səʊ fɑː] bisher, bis jetzt V/3/M2
so what? (informal) [ˌsəʊ ˈwɒt] na und? V/3/5

soap (opera) ['səʊpˌɒprə] Seifenoper
soccer (AE) = football (BE) (no pl) ['sɒkə] Fußball
social worker ['səʊʃl ˈwɜːkə] Sozialarbeiter/in
° society [səˈsaɪəti] Gesellschaft V/3/PP
sock [sɒk] Socke
sofa ['səʊfə] Sofa, Couch
soft [sɒft] weich
solar panel [ˌsəʊlə ˈpænəl] Sonnenkollektor V/3/M2
° the Solomon Islands [ðə ˈsɒləmənˌaɪləndz] die Solomonen V/I/1
solution [səˈluːʃn] Lösung V/2/7
solve [sɒlv] lösen, klären V/5/M11
some [sʌm] einige; etwas
somebody ['sʌmbədi] jemand
someone ['sʌmwʌn] jemand
something ['sʌmθɪŋ] etwas
sometimes ['sʌmtaɪmz] manchmal
somewhere ['sʌmweə] irgendwo
son [sʌn] Sohn
song [sɒŋ] Lied
soon [suːn] bald
sore [sɔː] schlimm, weh; wund
feel sorry for sb [ˌfiːl ˈsɒri fə sʌmbədi] Mitleid mit jdm haben V/2/2
say sorry (to sb) [ˌseɪ ˈsɒri] sich (bei jdm) entschuldigen V/1/M9
Sorry. ['sɒri] Verzeihung!, Entschuldigung!; Wie bitte?
I'm sorry. [aɪm ˈsɒri] Das tut mir leid.
sort [sɔːt] sortieren
sort out [ˌsɔːtˈaʊt] organisieren, sich kümmern um V/5/M1
sound [saʊnd] Geräusch, Klang; Ton; klingen, sich anhören
soup [suːp] Suppe
source [sɔːs] Quelle V/4/4
source of income [ˌsɔːs_əvˈɪnkʌm] Einkommensquelle V/5/M11
south [saʊθ] Süden
South Africa [saʊθ ˈæfrɪkə] Südafrika V/5/M1

South America [ˌsaʊθ_əˈmerɪkə] Südamerika
south-east [ˌsaʊθˈiːst] Südosten V/1/7
° South-East Asia [ˌsaʊθˌiːstˈeɪʒə] Südostasien V/1/PP
south-west [ˌsaʊθˈwest] Südwesten V/1/7
space [speɪs] Raum, Weltraum
spaceship ['speɪsˌʃɪp] Raumschiff
Spain [speɪn] Spanien
Spanish ['spænɪʃ] Spanier/in; spanisch; Spanisch
spare part [ˌspeə ˈpɑːt] Ersatzteil V/3/M2
speak [spiːk] sprechen
speak up [spiːkˈʌp] lauter sprechen
special ['speʃl] besondere(r, s)
speech [spiːtʃ] Rede V/1/M9
speech bubble ['spiːtʃ ˌbʌbl] Sprechblase V/2/1
spell [spel] buchstabieren
spelling ['spelɪŋ] Rechtschreibung
spend [spend] ausgeben (Geld); verbringen (Zeit)
spending habits (pl) ['spendɪŋ ˌhæbɪts] Kaufgewohnheiten V/5/13
spending power (no pl) ['spendɪŋ ˌpaʊə] Kaufkraft V/5/12
spicy ['spaɪsi] würzig; scharf
spider ['spaɪdə] Spinne
° spirit (no pl) ['spɪrɪt] Geiste V/1/M9
spit out [ˌspɪtˈaʊt] ausspucken V/1/M2
split up [splɪtˈʌp] sich teilen; sich trennen
spokesman/spokeswoman ['spəʊksmən, 'spəʊksˌwʊmən] Sprecher/in V/5/M11
sponsor ['spɒnsə] sponsern, als Sponsor finanzieren
sponsored walk [ˌspɒnsəd ˈwɔːk] Wohltätigkeitslauf
spooky (informal) ['spuːki] schaurig; unheimlich
spoon [spuːn] Löffel
sport [spɔːt] Sport; Sportart
sports field ['spɔːts ˌfiːld] Spielfeld, Sportplatz

sports programme ['spɔːts ˌprəʊɡræm] Sportsendung
sportsmanship (no pl) ['spɔːtsmənʃɪp] Fairness
sportsperson ['spɔːtsˌpɜːsn] Sportler/in
spot [spɒt] entdecken
spray [spreɪ] (be)sprühen
spring [sprɪŋ] Frühling
spy [spaɪ] Spion/in V/3/M2
square [skweə] Quadrat; Platz
square kilometre [ˌskweə kɪˈlɒmɪtə] Quadratkilometer V/1/M1
stable ['steɪbl] Stall, Box
stadium (pl -s or -ia) ['steɪdiəm, 'steɪdiəmz, 'steɪdiə] Stadion
stage [steɪdʒ] Bühne
stairs (npl) [steəz] Treppe
stall [stɔːl] (Verkaufs)stand
stamina (no pl) ['stæmɪnə] Durchhaltevermögen, Ausdauer V/5/3
stamp [stæmp] Stempel; Briefmarke
stand [stænd] stehen; ertragen, aushalten
stand still [stænd 'stɪl] stillstehen V/6/14
stand up [ˌstænd ˈʌp] aufstehen
° **standard** ['stændəd] Standard; Richtlinie; Wertvorstellung V/4/PP
on standby [ɒn 'stændbaɪ] in Bereitschaft, auf Standby V/6/3
star [stɑː] Stern
star [stɑː] in einem Film/ Theaterstück auftreten V/3/M8
stare at sb/sth ['steə ət ˌsʌmbədi, ˌsʌmθɪŋ] jdn/etw anstarren V/3/10
start [stɑːt] Anfang, Beginn; anfangen; eröffnen, ins Leben rufen V/2/7
starter ['stɑːtə] Vorspeise
starve [stɑːv] (ver)hungern V/4/M3
state [steɪt] (Bundes)staat
statement ['steɪtmənt] Aussage; Äußerung
station ['steɪʃn] Bahnhof; Station
statistics (npl) [stəˈtɪstɪks] Statistik V/1/I

the Statue of Liberty [ðə 'stætʃuː‿əv ˌlɪbəti] die Freiheitsstatue
stay [steɪ] bleiben; untergebracht sein, wohnen
steal [stiːl] stehlen
step [step] Stufe; treten
take a first step [ˌteɪk‿ə ˌfɜːst 'step] einen ersten Schritt machen/unternehmen V/1/M9
stereo ['steriəʊ] (Stereo)anlage
stick [stɪk] kleben; Stock
still [stɪl] (immer) noch, noch immer
° **still** [stɪl] trotzdem, dennoch V/5/11
stingray ['stɪŋreɪ] Stachelrochen V/1/2
stomach ache ['stʌmək‿eɪk] Magenschmerzen, Bauchschmerzen
stone [stəʊn] Stein
stop [stɒp] aufhören, beenden; anhalten
Stop it! ['stɒp‿ɪt] Hör(t) auf (damit)!
store card ['stɔː‿ˌkɑːd] Kunden(kredit)karte V/5/15
storm [stɔːm] Sturm
story ['stɔːri] Geschichte, Erzählung
straight [streɪt] gerade(aus)
straight [streɪt] glatt (Haar) V/3/M8
straight out [ˌstreɪt‿ˈaʊt] offen, direkt V/2/2
strange [streɪndʒ] sonderbar; ungewöhnlich; fremd
stranger ['streɪndʒə] Fremde/r
strawberry ['strɔːbri] Erdbeere V/5/M1
street [striːt] Straße
° **strength** [streŋθ] Stärke, Kraft V/3/PP
stressed ['strest] gestresst V/1/M2
stressful ['stresfl] stressig, anstrengend V/2/M2
stretch [stretʃ] (sich) dehnen
strict [strɪkt] streng V/1/12
strip [strɪp] sich entkleiden V/3/M8

stroke [strəʊk] streicheln
strong [strɒŋ] stark; robust, stabil V/5/8
structure ['strʌktʃə] Gefüge, Struktur V/1/M1
student ['stjuːdnt] Student/in, Studierende/r; Schüler/in
study ['stʌdi] studieren; lernen
study ['stʌdi] Studie, (wissenschaftliche) Untersuchung V/5/13
stuff (informal) [stʌf] Zeug, Sachen V/5/13
stunt performer ['stʌnt pəˌfɔːmə] Stuntman, Stuntgirl
stupid ['stjuːpɪd] dumm, blöd
style [staɪl] Stil V/3/CIO
subject ['sʌbdʒɪkt] Thema; (Schul)fach
subway (AE) = underground (BE) ['sʌbˌweɪ] U-Bahn
success (no pl) [səkˈses] Erfolg V/2/M5
successful [səkˈsesfl] erfolgreich
° **successive** [səkˈsesɪv] aufeinander folgend V/1/M9
such as ['sʌtʃ‿əz] wie (zum Beispiel)
suddenly ['sʌdnli] plötzlich, auf einmal
° **suffering** (no pl) ['sʌfərɪŋ] Leid V/1/M9
sugar ['ʃʊɡə] Zucker
sugary ['ʃʊɡəri] zuckerhaltig V/4/3
suggest [səˈdʒest] vorschlagen V/5/M10
suggestion [səˈdʒestʃn] Vorschlag; Hinweis V/5/M6
suit [suːt] passen, recht sein; stehen
° **sum** [sʌm] Summe, Betrag V/6/PP
summary ['sʌməri] Zusammen- fassung; Inhaltsangabe V/6/8
summer ['sʌmə] Sommer
summer camp ['sʌmə ˌkæmp] Ferienlager
sun [sʌn] Sonne
sunbathe ['sʌnˌbeɪð] sonnenbaden V/4/9
sunbeam ['sʌnˌbiːm] Sonnenstrahl V/6/M1

D

Sunday ['sʌndeɪ] Sonntag

sunny ['sʌni] sonnig

sunscreen ['sʌn،skriːn] Sonnencreme

supermarket ['suːpə،maːkɪt] Supermarkt

support [sə'pɔːt] (unter)stützen

support [sə'pɔːt] unterstützen; für den Lebensunterhalt aufkommen V/1/12

° support *(no pl)* [sə'pɔːt] Unterstützung V/4/PP

suppose [sə'pəʊz] denken, annehmen, vermuten V/4/M8

sure [ʃɔː] sicher

make sure [،meɪk 'ʃɔː] sich versichern, darauf achten

surname ['sɜː،neɪm] Familienname, Nachname

surprise [sə'praɪz] Überraschung

in surprise [ɪn sə'praɪz] überrascht, erstaunt V/4/M8

surprised [sə'praɪzd] überrascht

surprising [sə'praɪzɪŋ] überraschend

survey ['sɜːveɪ] Untersuchung, Umfrage

survival [sə'vaɪvl] Überleben

survive [sə'vaɪv] überleben

suspend sb [sə'spend] jdn zeitweilig ausschließen V/2/10

° Swahili [swɑː'hiːli] Swahili, Suaheli *(afrikanische Sprache)* V/I/2

swap [swɒp] tauschen

sweater ['swetə] Pullover, Sweater

° Swede [swiːd] Schwede/ Schwedin V/I/PP

° Sweden ['swiːdn] Schweden V/I/PP

Swedish ['swiːdɪʃ] schwedisch V/5/11

sweet [swiːt] süß; Süßigkeit(en)

swim [swɪm] schwimmen

swimming ['swɪmɪŋ] Schwimmen

symbol ['sɪmbl] Symbol, Zeichen

system ['sɪstəm] System V/1/2

T

table ['teɪbl] Tisch

set the table [،set ðə 'teɪbl] den Tisch decken

° tablespoon ['teɪbl،spuːn] Esslöffel V/4/CIO

tackle sb ['tækl ،sʌmbədi] jdn angreifen

take [teɪk] (mit)nehmen; dauern

° take [teɪk] brauchen V/6/CIO

take a bath [teɪk ،ə 'bɑːθ] baden V/6/3

take a reading of sth [teɪk ،ə 'riːdɪŋ ،əv ،sʌmθɪŋ] etw ablesen V/6/M2

take a shower [teɪk ،ə 'ʃaʊə] duschen V/6/3

° take a test [،teɪk ə 'test] eine Prüfung ablegen V/5/PP

take action [teɪk ،'ækʃn] handeln, etw unternehmen V/6/3

take care of [teɪk ،'keər ،əv] sich kümmern um, versorgen

° take heart [،teɪk 'hɑːt] neuen Mut schöpfen V/1/M9

take in sb [،teɪk ،'ɪn sʌmbədi] jdn (bei sich) aufnehmen V/4/M10

take notes (on) [،teɪk 'nəʊts] (sich) Notizen machen (zu, über)

take off [teɪk ،'ɒf] abnehmen; ausziehen

take on sth [،teɪk ،'ɒn sʌmθɪŋ] etw annehmen V/1/M1

take out [،teɪk ،'aʊt] herausnehmen

take out [،teɪk ،'aʊt] abheben *(Geld)* V/5/13

take over [،teɪk ،'əʊvə] (die Macht) übernehmen V/4/9

take part (in) [،teɪk 'pɑːt] teilnehmen (an)

take photos [،teɪk 'fəʊtəʊz] Bilder machen, fotografieren

take place [teɪk 'pleɪs] stattfinden

take seriously [teɪk 'sɪəriəsli] ernst nehmen V/6/CIO

take sth to the extreme [،teɪk sʌmθɪŋ tə ðɪ ،ɪk'striːm] etw auf die Spitze treiben V/4/M2

take turns [،teɪk 'tɜːnz] sich abwechseln

takeaway ['teɪkə،weɪ] Essen zum Mitnehmen

° it takes [ɪt ،teɪks] man braucht V/4/PP

talk [tɔːk] Gespräch, Unterhaltung; Referat

give a talk [،gɪv ،ə 'tɔːk] einen Vortrag halten V/1/M4

talk (to) [tɔːk] sprechen/reden (mit)

tall [tɔːl] hoch; groß

tank [tæŋk] (Flüssigkeits)behälter, (Wasser)tank V/6/M2

tap [tæp] Wasserhahn V/6/M2

task [tɑːsk] Aufgabe

taste [teɪst] schmecken

tasty ['teɪsti] schmackhaft, lecker

tea [tiː] Tee

have tea [hæv 'tiː] Tee trinken

teach [tiːtʃ] unterrichten, beibringen

teacher ['tiːtʃə] Lehrer/in

teammate [tiːmmeɪt] Teammitglied, Teamkollege/ Teamkollegin V/5/M2

teamwork ['tiːm،wɜːk] Teamarbeit V/5/4

teenage ['tiːneɪdʒ] jugendlich; Teenager-

telephone ['telɪ،fəʊn] anrufen; Telefon

television ['telɪ،vɪʒən] Fernseher; Fernsehen

tell [tel] erzählen; sagen

temperature ['temprɪtʃə] Temperatur V/1/M2

terrible ['terəbl] schrecklich, furchtbar

test [test] Prüfung, Test; Klassenarbeit V/5/3

test [test] prüfen, testen V/1/13

° take a test [،teɪk ə 'test] eine Prüfung ablegen V/5/PP

text message ['tekst ،mesɪdʒ] SMS (Short Message Service)

Thai [taɪ] Thai, Thailänder/in; thailändisch

than [ðæn] als

thank [θæŋk] danken

Thank goodness! [،θæŋk 'gʊdnəs] Gott sei Dank!

thank you ['θæŋk juː] danke

thanks [θæŋks] danke

Thanks a lot! [،θæŋks ،ə 'lɒt] Vielen Dank!

Thanksgiving [ˈθæŋks.gɪvɪŋ] Thanksgiving *(amerikanisches Erntedankfest)*

that [ðæt] das; der/die/das

That'll be ... *(informal)* [ðætl ˈbiː] Das macht dann ... ; Das beläuft sich auf ...

that's why [ðæts waɪ] das ist der Grund, warum V/5/8

the [ðə] der/die/das

the same age [ðə ˌseɪmˈeɪdʒ] gleichaltrig V/3/4

theatre [ˈθɪətə] Theater

their [ðeə] ihr(e)

theirs [ðeəz] ihr(e, es)

them [ðem] sie, ihnen

theme [θiːm] Thema; Lektion, Kapitel V/1/I

theme park [ˈθiːm ˌpɑːk] Themenpark; Freizeitpark

themselves [ðəmˈselvz] sich (selbst); selbst

then [ðen] damals; dann

° **theoretical** [ˌθɪəˈretɪkl] theoretisch V/5/PP

therapist [ˈθerəpɪst] Therapeut/in V/4/9

therapy [ˈθerəpi] Therapie, Behandlung V/4/8

have therapy [ˌhæv ˈθerəpi] in Therapie/Behandlung sein V/4/9

there [ðeə] dort(hin)

there are [ðeərˈɑː] es gibt, da sind

there is [ðeərˈɪz] es gibt

therefore [ˈðeəfɔː] deshalb, daher V/3/M8

these *(pl of this)* [ðiːz] diese

they [ðeɪ] sie

thick [θɪk] dick V/4/13

thief *(pl* **thieves)** [θiːf] Dieb V/3/M2

thin [θɪn] dünn

thing [θɪŋ] Ding, Gegenstand

think [θɪŋk] denken, glauben, meinen; nachdenken

think about (sb/sth) [ˈθɪŋk ə.baʊt] an (jdn/etw) denken; sich (etw) überlegen

think bubble [ˈθɪŋk ˌbʌbl] Gedankenblase V/4/M5

think of [ˈθɪŋk əv] denken an; sich ausdenken

third [θɜːd] Drittel

this [ðɪs] diese(r, s)

this afternoon [ðɪs ˌɑːftəˈnuːn] heute Nachmittag

this morning [ðɪs ˈmɔːnɪŋ] heute Morgen

those *(pl of* that) [ðəʊz] diese; jene

thought [θɔːt] Nachdenken, Überlegen; Gedanke V/4/I

thousand [ˈθaʊzənd] Tausend

thousands *(pl)* [ˈθaʊzndz] Tausende

threaten sb [ˈθretn] jdn bedrohen V/2/M5

threatening [ˈθretnɪŋ] drohend, Droh-; bedrohlich V/2/9

thrill [θrɪl] Nervenkitzel, Kick V/3/5

through [θruː] durch

throw [θrəʊ] werfen

Thursday [ˈθɜːzdeɪ] Donnerstag

° **thus** [ðʌs] so, auf diese Weise; folglich V/1/M9

ticket [ˈtɪkɪt] Karte

ticket counter [ˈtɪkɪt ˌkaʊntə] Fahrkartenschalter

tidy [ˈtaɪdi] ordentlich

tidy up [ˌtaɪdiˈʌp] aufräumen

tiger [ˈtaɪgə] Tiger

till [tɪl] bis

time [taɪm] (Uhr)zeit; Mal

(just) in time [ɪn ˈtaɪm] (gerade noch) rechtzeitig

at that time [ət ˈðæt ˌtaɪm] zu dieser Zeit V/5/13

have a good time [ˌhæv ə gʊd ˈtaɪm] sich amüsieren

in three months' time [ɪn ˌθriː mʌns ˈtaɪm] in drei Monaten V/2/M3

on time [ɒn ˈtaɪm] pünktlich; rechtzeitig V/5/5

a long time ago [ə ˌlɒŋ ˌtaɪm əˈgəʊ] vor langer Zeit V/1/11

What time (is it)? [wɒt ˈtaɪm (ˌɪz ɪt)] Wie spät/Wie viel Uhr (ist es)?

have the time of one's life [hæv ðə ˌtaɪm əv wʌnz ˈlaɪf] eine tolle Zeit haben V/5/M1

time out [ˌtaɪm ˈaʊt] Auszeit

° **time zone** [ˈtaɪm ˌzəʊn] Zeitzone V/1/CIO

What's the time? [ˌwɒts ðə ˈtaɪm] Wie viel Uhr ist es?

timeline [ˈtaɪm.laɪn] Zeitstrahl V/1/13

timetable [ˈtaɪm.teɪbl] Stundenplan; Fahrplan

tin [tɪn] Büchse, Dose

tiny [ˈtaɪni] winzig V/1/M1

tip [tɪp] Tipp V/I/PP

tired [ˈtaɪəd] müde

title [ˈtaɪtl] Titel

to [tə] in, nach, zu, an; vor

° **to** [tə] bis (zu) V/4/CIO

today [təˈdeɪ] heute

toe [təʊ] Zeh(e)

tofu [ˈtəʊfuː] Tofu V/4/1

together [təˈgeðə] zusammen, gemeinsam

toilet [ˈtɔɪlət] Toilette, Klo

tolerance [ˈtɒlərəns] Toleranz V/2/M2

tomato *(pl* **-es)** [təˈmɑːtəʊ, təˈmɑːtəʊz] Tomate

tomorrow [təˈmɒrəʊ] morgen

tonight [təˈnaɪt] heute Abend

too [tuː] zu; auch

too bad [ˌtuː ˈbæd] zu schade

tool [tuːl] Werkzeug

tooth *(pl* **teeth)** [tuːθ, tiːθ] Zahn

top [tɒp] oberes Ende, Spitze

on top [ɒn ˈtɒp] oben

topic [ˈtɒpɪk] Thema V/6/M2

° **topping** [ˈtɒpɪŋ] Garnierung, Belag V/4/CIO

torch sth *(informal)* [tɔːtʃ] etw in Brand setzen V/2/M1

total [ˈtəʊtl] Gesamt-; völlig

totally [ˈtəʊtəli] völlig, total V/4/M3

totem pole [ˈtəʊtəm ˌpəʊl] Totempfahl

touch [tʌtʃ] berühren

touching [ˈtʌtʃɪŋ] (be)rührend V/1/M7

tour guide [ˈtʊə gaɪd] Reiseführer/in, Reiseleiter/in

toward(s) [təˈwɔːd(z)] in Richtung

tower [ˈtaʊə] Turm

town [taʊn] Stadt

toy [tɔɪ] Spielzeug

be on the right track [bi ˌɒn ðə ˌraɪt ˈtræk] auf dem richtigen Weg sein V/6/4

tracker [ˈtrækə] Fährtenleser/in V/1/M5

tradition [trəˈdɪʃn] Tradition, Brauch

traditional [trəˈdɪʃnəl] traditionell

traffic [ˈtræfɪk] Verkehr

trail [treɪl] Weg, Pfad

train [treɪn] trainieren; Zug

train ride [ˈtreɪn ˌraɪd] Zugfahrt

train sb [ˈtreɪn ˌsʌmbədi] jdn ausbilden V/1/12

° train sb for sth [treɪn] jdn für etw ausbilden V/5/PP

trainer *(BE)* [ˈtreɪnə] Turnschuh

training [ˈtreɪnɪŋ] Ausbildung; Schulung V/5/2

° training on the job [ˌtreɪnɪŋ ˌɒn ðə ˈdʒɒb] Ausbildung am Arbeitsplatz V/5/PP

translate [trænsˈleɪt] übersetzen

translation [trænsˈleɪʃn] Übersetzung V/3/M8

transport [ˈtrænspɔːt] Transport, Beförderung

transport [ˈtrænspɔːt] Fahrkarten V/5/13

travel [ˈtrævl] reisen

travel guide [ˈtrævl gaɪd] Reiseführer

tree [triː] Baum

tree hugger [ˈtriː ˌhʌgə] Öko V/3/8

trespassing [ˈtrespəsɪŋ] unbefugtes Betreten V/3/5

tribal [ˈtraɪbl] Stammes- V/1/12

tribe [traɪb] Stamm

trip [trɪp] Ausflug; Reise, Fahrt

trolley [ˈtrɒli] Einkaufswagen

trouble [ˈtrʌbl] Schwierigkeiten, Ärger

troublemaker [ˈtrʌblˌmeɪkə] Unruhestifter/in V/3/5

trousers *(npl)* [ˈtraʊzəz] Hose

true [truː] wahr

come true [kʌm ˈtruː] wahr werden V/4/M2

truth [truːθ] Wahrheit V/3/10

try [traɪ] versuchen; probieren

try hard to do sth [ˌtraɪ ˈhɑːd tə duː sʌmθɪŋ] sich sehr bemühen, etw zu tun V/5/13

try on [traɪ ˈɒn] anprobieren

the tube [ðə ˈtjuːb] die (Londoner) U-Bahn

tuberculosis *(no pl)* [tjuːˌbɜːkjʊˈləʊsɪs] Tuberkulose V/1/12

Tuesday [ˈtjuːzdeɪ] Dienstag

tug-of-war [ˌtʌg əv ˈwɔː] Tauziehen

° tune [tjuːn] Melodie V/3/11

turkey [ˈtɜːki] Truthahn/-henne, Pute/r

turn [tɜːn] sich drehen; abbiegen; umblättern

° turn into [ˌtɜːn ˈɪntʊ] umwandeln, verändern V/1/PP

turn off [ˌtɜːn ˈɒf] ausmachen, ausschalten V/6/2

turn on [ˌtɜːn ˈɒn] einschalten

turn out [ˌtɜːn ˈaʊt] sich herausstellen V/2/10

turn over [tɜːn ˈəʊvə] (sich) umdrehen

turn round [tɜːn ˈraʊnd] (sich) umdrehen

turn up [ˌtɜːn ˈʌp] aufdrehen, höher stellen V/6/4

turn up [ˌtɜːn ˈʌp] erscheinen, auftauchen V/6/8

take turns [ˌteɪk ˈtɜːnz] sich abwechseln

turtle [ˈtɜːtl] Meeresschildkröte V/1/M1

watch TV [ˌwɒtʃ tiːˈviː] fernsehen

TV (= television) [ˌtiːˈviː, ˈtelɪˌvɪʒn] Fernseher; Fernsehen

TV guide [tiːˌviː ˈgaɪd] Fernsehzeitschrift

TV studio [tiː ˈviː ˌstjuːdiəʊ] Fernsehstudio

twice [twaɪs] zweimal V/4/5

type [taɪp] Art; Typ; Maschine schreiben, tippen

typical [ˈtɪpɪkl] typisch

tyre [ˈtaɪə] Reifen V/5/8

U

° U.A.E. (= United Arab Emirates) [juːˌeɪ ˈiː, juːˌnaɪtɪd ˌærəb ˈemərəts] Vereinigte Arabische Emirate V/I/1

ugly [ˈʌgli] hässlich

UK (= United Kingdom) [juː ˈkeɪ, juːˌnaɪtɪd ˈkɪŋdəm] Vereinigtes Königreich

uncle [ˈʌŋkl] Onkel

uncomfortable [ʌnˈkʌmftəbl] unwohl, unbehaglich, unbequem V/2/CIO

under [ˈʌndə] unter

underage [ˌʌndərˈeɪdʒ] minderjährig V/2/7

underground [ˈʌndəˌgraʊnd] U-Bahn

underline [ˌʌndəˈlaɪn] unterstreichen

understand [ˌʌndəˈstænd] verstehen

understatement [ˈʌndəˌsteɪtmənt] Untertreibung, Understatement V/3/CIO

undertaker [ˈʌndəˌteɪkə] Leichenbestatter/in; Bestattungsinstitut V/4/M7

underwater [ˌʌndəˈwɔːtə] Unterwasser- V/1/M1

° undone [ʌnˈdʌn] unvollendet; ruiniert V/3/11

the unemployed *(pl)* [ðiˌʌnɪmˈplɔɪd] die Arbeitslosen V/5/13

unexpected [ˌʌnɪkˈspektɪd] unerwartet V/5/15

unfair [ʌnˈfeə] unfair, ungerecht V/2/2

unfortunately [ʌnˈfɔːtʃnətli] leider, unglücklicherweise V/6/4

unfriendly [ʌnˈfrendli] unfreundlich

unhappy [ʌnˈhæpi] unglücklich

unhealthy [ʌnˈhelθi] kränklich, ungesund

uniform [ˈjuːnɪˌfɔːm] Uniform

unique [juːˈniːk] einzigartig V/3/M7

the United Nations [ðə juːˌnaɪtɪd ˈneɪʃnz] die Vereinten Nationen V/6/M2

the United States [ðə juːˌnaɪtɪd ˈsteɪts] die Vereinigten Staaten

university [juːnɪˈvɜːsəti] Universität

unpaid [ʌnˈpeɪd] unbezahlt
until [ənˈtɪl] bis
unusual [ʌnˈjuːʒʊəl] ungewöhnlich
up to [ʌp tʊ] bis zu V/5/M1
upset [ʌpˈset] aufgeregt, aufgebracht
upside down [ˌʌpsaɪdˈdaʊn] verkehrt herum V/6/M6
upstairs [ʌpˈsteəz] (nach) oben
us [ʌs] uns
the US (= United States) [ðə ˌjuːˈes, juːˌnaɪtɪd ˈsteɪts] die USA
USA [ˌjuː es ˈeɪ] USA (= Vereinigte Staaten von Amerika)
usage [ˈjuːsɪdʒ] Verbrauch V/6/M2
use [juːz] benutzen
use [juːs] Verwendung, Gebrauch V/6/M2
use bad language [juːz bæd ˈlæŋgwɪdʒ] Schimpfwörter benutzen
used to … (+ infinitive) [ˈjuːsd tə] früher …
get used to sth [get ˈjuːsd tə ˌsʌmθɪŋ] sich an etw gewöhnen
useful [ˈjuːsfl] nützlich, brauchbar
useless [ˈjuːsləs] zu nichts zu gebrauchen V/3/5
usually [ˈjuːʒʊəli] gewöhnlich, normalerweise

V

vacation (AE) = holiday (BE) [vəˈkeɪʃn] Ferien, Urlaub
valley [ˈvæli] Tal
vandalism [ˈvændəˌlɪzm] Vandalismus, Sachbeschädigung
vegetable [ˈvedʒtəbl] Gemüse
vegetarian [ˌvedʒəˈteəriən] Vegetarier/in
vehicle [ˈviːɪkl] Fahrzeug V/2/M1
vending machine [ˈvendɪŋ məˌʃiːn] Automat
very [ˈveri] sehr
vet [vet] Tierarzt/-ärztin
vet's assistant [ˈvets əˌsɪstnt] Tierarzthelfer/in V/5/2
° vice-president [ˌvaɪs ˈprezɪdənt] Vizepräsident/in V/6/PP

view [vjuː] Sicht; (Aus)blick, Aussicht
view [vjuː] Ansicht, Meinung V/2/3
point of view [ˌpɔɪnt əvˈvjuː] Standpunkt, Gesichtspunkt V/6/M7
village [ˈvɪlɪdʒ] Dorf
vinegar [ˈvɪnɪgə] Essig
violence [ˈvaɪələns] Gewalt, Gewalttätigkeit V/2/M1
violent [ˈvaɪələnt] brutal, gewalttätig V/2/M1
virtual [ˈvɜːtʃʊəl] virtuell V/2/9
visa [ˈviːzə] Visum V/3/M2
visit [ˈvɪzɪt] Besuch; besuchen
visitor [ˈvɪzɪtə] Besucher/in
vitamin [ˈvɪtəmɪn] Vitamin V/4/3
° vocational [vəʊˈkeɪʃnəl] beruflich V/5/PP
do vocational training [duː vəʊˌkeɪʃnəl ˈtreɪnɪŋ] eine Berufsausbildung machen V/5/2
voice [vɔɪs] Stimme V/4/M8
volcano (pl -oes or -os) [vɒlˈkeɪnəʊ, vɒlˈkeɪnəʊz] Vulkan
volunteer to do sth [ˌvɒlənˈtɪə tə duː ˌsʌmθɪŋ] sich freiwillig anbieten, etw zu tun V/6/4
do volunteer work [duː ˈvɒləntɪə ˌwɜːk] Freiwilligenarbeit leisten V/5/2
vote [vəʊt] wählen V/2/5

W

wage(s) [weɪdʒ(ɪz)] Lohn V/5/M1
Wait a second! [ˌweɪt ə ˈsekənd] Moment mal!
wait (for) [weɪt] warten (auf)
waiter/waitress [ˈweɪtə/ˈweɪtrəs] Bedienung, Kellner/in
waiting room [ˈweɪtɪŋ ˌruːm] Wartezimmer
wake up [weɪkˈʌp] aufwecken; aufwachen
walk [wɔːk] (zu Fuß) gehen; Gehen; Spaziergang
go for a walk [ˌgəʊ fər ə ˈwɔːk] spazieren gehen
walk on [ˌwɔːkˈɒn] weiterlaufen, weitergehen V/6/4

walk up [wɔːkˈʌp] hinaufgehen
wall [wɔːl] Wand
wallaby [ˈwɒləbi] Wallaby V/1/8
wallet [ˈwɒlɪt] Brieftasche
want [wɒnt] wünschen; wollen
war [wɔː] Krieg
wardrobe [ˈwɔːdrəʊb] Kleiderschrank
warehouse worker [ˈweəˌhaʊs ˌwɜːkə] Lagerist/in V/5/2
warm [wɔːm] warm
warm up [wɔːmˈʌp] sich aufwärmen
warm-up exercise [ˈwɔːmˌʌp eksəsaɪz] Aufwärmübung
warmth (no pl) [wɔːmθ] Wärme V/1/11
wash [wɒʃ] (sich) waschen
wash up [wɒʃˈʌp] abspülen, abwaschen
washing machine [ˈwɒʃɪŋ məˌʃiːn] Waschmaschine V/6/1
waste [weɪst] verschwenden; Verschwendung V/4/M3
waste (no pl) [weɪst] Abfall, Müll V/6/5
waste of time [ˌweɪst əv ˈtaɪm] Zeitverschwendung
watch [wɒtʃ] beobachten; zusehen, zuschauen; anschauen; Uhr
watch TV [ˌwɒtʃ tiːˈviː] fernsehen
watch sth [wɒtʃ] auf etw achten V/2/9
water [ˈwɔːtə] Wasser
water [ˈwɔːtə] gießen V/6/M2
water maker [ˈwɔːtə ˌmeɪkə] Gerät, das aus Meerwasser Trinkwasser produziert V/3/M2
waterfall [ˈwɔːtəˌfɔːl] Wasserfall
wave [weɪv] winken; schwenken; Welle
wax [wæks] Wachs
way [weɪ] Weg; Art, Weise
by the way [baɪ ðə ˈweɪ] übrigens V/1/5
in a way [ɪn ə ˈweɪ] in gewisser Weise V/2/2
no way [ˌnəʊ ˈweɪ] auf keinen Fall V/4/M3

way of life [ˌweɪ ˌəv ˈlaɪf] Lebensweise

we [wiː] wir

° wealthy [ˈwelθi] reich, wohlhabend V/5/11

the wealthy (pl) [ðə ˈwelθi] die Reichen, die Wohlhabenden V/5/14

wear [weə] tragen

weather [ˈweðə] Wetter

Wednesday [ˈwenzdeɪ] Mittwoch

week [wiːk] Woche

weekend [ˌwiːkˈend] Wochenende

weeklong [ˈwiːkˌlɒŋ] einwöchig V/3/4

weekly [ˈwiːkli] wöchentlich

weigh [weɪ] wiegen V/4/9

weight [weɪt] Gewicht

put on weight [ˌpʊt ˈɒn ˌweɪt] zunehmen V/4/9

You're welcome. [jɔː ˈwelkəm] Gern geschehen.

well [wel] nun (ja), tja

Well done! [ˌwel ˈdʌn] Gut gemacht!

well-known [ˌwelˈnəʊn] berühmt, (allgemein) bekannt V/5/M11

Welsh [welʃ] walisisch

° Welsh [welʃ] Walisisch; walisisch V/I/2

west [west] Westen V/1/7; westlich, West-

the West Indies (npl) [ðə ˌwestˌˈɪndiz] die Westindischen Inseln

Westerner [ˈwestənə] Bewohner/in der westlichen Welt V/2/2

wet [wet] nass

whale [weɪl] Wal V/1/M1

what [wɒt] was; welche(r, s)

What about ...? (informal) [ˌwɒtˌəˈbaʊt] Was ist mit ...?, Wie wäre es mit ...?

what else [wɒtˌˈels] was noch, was sonst V/4/11

What if ...? [wɒtˌɪf] Was ist/wäre, wenn ...? V/1/M6

What time (is it)? [wɒtˌˈtaɪm (ˌɪz ɪt)] Wie spät/Wie viel Uhr (ist es)?

What's ... like? [wɒts ˈlaɪk] Wie ist ...?

What's on? [wɒtsˌˈɒn] Was gibt's?; Was läuft?

What's the time? [ˌwɒts ðə ˈtaɪm] Wie viel Uhr ist es?

What's your name? [ˌwɒts jə ˈneɪm] Wie heißt du?, Wie heißen Sie?

wheel [wiːl] Rad

wheelchair [ˈwiːlˌtʃeə] Rollstuhl

when [wen] als; wann; wenn

where [weə] wo(hin)

Where are you from? [ˌweərˌɑː jə ˈfrɒm] Wo kommst du her?

wherever [werˈevə] wo(hin) auch immer V/3/10

whether [ˈweðə] ob

which [wɪtʃ] welche(r, s); der/die/das

while [waɪl] während

whisper [ˈwɪspə] flüstern

whistle [ˈwɪsl] pfeifen

white [waɪt] weiß

whitewater rafting (no pl) [ˌwaɪtwɔːtə ˈrɑːftɪŋ] Wildwasserfahren, (Wildwasser)rafting V/3/2

who [huː] wer; wen; wem; der/die/das

whole [həʊl] ganz

whose [huːz] wessen

why [waɪ] warum

wide [waɪd] breit; breit gefächert V/5/4

° widely-spoken [ˌwaɪdli ˈspəʊkən] weitverbreitet V/2/CIO

wife (pl wives) [waɪf, waɪvz] Ehefrau

wild [waɪld] wild

wildebeest (pl - or -s) [ˈvɪldəˌbiːst] Gnu

wilderness [ˈwɪldənəs] Wildnis V/3/4

wildfire [ˈwaɪldˌfaɪə] Lauffeuer, nicht zu kontrollierender (Großflächen)brand

wildlife [ˈwaɪldˌlaɪf] Tier- und Pflanzenwelt

will [wɪl] werden

have a will of one's own [ˌhæv ə ˌwɪl ˌəv ˌwʌnz ˈəʊn] seinen eigenen Willen haben V/2/2

win [wɪn] gewinnen

wind [wɪnd] Wind

window [ˈwɪndəʊ] Fenster

windy [ˈwɪndi] windig

wing [wɪŋ] Flügel

winner [ˈwɪnə] Gewinner/in, Sieger/in

winter [ˈwɪntə] Winter

wish [wɪʃ] (sich) wünschen; Wunsch V/5/13

best wishes [ˌbest ˈwɪʃɪz] viele/beste Grüße

with [wɪð] mit

within [wɪðˈɪn] innerhalb V/4/9

without [wɪðˈaʊt] ohne

wolf down [ˌwʊlf ˈdaʊn] verschlingen, hinunterschlingen V/4/M8

woman (pl women) [ˈwʊmən, ˈwɪmɪn] Frau

wombat [ˈwɒmˌbæt] Wombat V/1/8

wonder [ˈwʌndə] sich fragen V/2/2

no wonder [ˌnəʊ ˈwʌndə] kein Wunder V/2/10

wonderful [ˈwʌndəfl] wunderbar, wundervoll

wood [wʊd] Holz

wooden [ˈwʊdn] hölzern, Holz- V/3/M2

word [wɜːd] Wort

be as good as one's word [biː ˌəz ˌgʊd ˌəz wʌnz ˈwɜːd] sein Wort halten V/4/M8

wordbank [ˈwɜːdbæŋk] Wortfeld V/1/4

work [wɜːk] Arbeit; arbeiten; funktionieren

out of work [aʊt ˌəv ˈwɜːk] arbeitslos V/5/13

work experience (no pl) [ˈwɜːk ɪkˌspɪəriəns] Praktikum; Berufserfahrung V/5/5

work out [ˌwɜːk ˈaʊt] funktionieren, klappen; ausrechnen V/5/15

workbook [ˈwɜːkˌbʊk] Arbeitsbuch

° worker [ˈwɜːkə] Arbeiter/in, Angestellte/r V/5/CIO

workhouse [ˈwɜːkhaʊs] Armenhaus V/4/M6

working hours ['wɜːkɪŋ ˌaʊəz] Arbeitszeit
world [wɜːld] Welt, Erde
World Heritage Site [ˌwɜːld 'herɪtɪdʒ ˌsaɪt] Weltkulturerbe, Weltkulturdenkmal V/1/M1
world record [wɜːld 'rekɔːd] Weltrekord
° **worldwide** [ˌwɜːld'waɪd] weltweit V/3/CIO
worm [wɜːm] Wurm V/1/M1
worried ['wʌrid] beunruhigt, besorgt
worry ['wʌri] sich Sorgen machen; Sorge
worship ['wɜːʃɪp] anbeten, verehren V/3/10
be worth sth [bi: 'wɜːθ ˌsʌmθɪŋ] etw wert sein V/3/5
° **worthless** ['wɜːθləs] wertlos V/3/CIO
would [wʊd] würde(st/n/t)
wrap [ræp] einpacken, (ein)wickeln
wrapped [ræpt] eingepackt, verpackt V/6/3
write [raɪt] schreiben

write down [raɪt 'daʊn] aufschreiben
writing paper *(no pl)* ['raɪtɪŋ ˌpeɪpə] Schreibpapier V/6/5
wrong [rɒŋ] falsch
wrong [rɒŋ] Unrecht V/1/M9
be wrong [bi 'rɒŋ] nicht stimmen; sich irren V/3/10

Y

yeah *(informal)* [jeə] ja V/3/5
year [jɪə] Jahr
yearbook ['jɪəˌbʊk] Jahresausgabe; Jahrbuch
yellow ['jeləʊ] gelb
° Yemen ['jemən] Jemen V/I/1
yes [jes] ja
yesterday ['jestədeɪ] gestern
yet [jet] bis jetzt; schon
not yet [nɒt 'jet] noch nicht
° **yoghurt pot** ['jɒgət pɒt] Jogurtbecher V/6/CIO
yolk [jəʊk] Eigelb, (Ei)dotter V/1/11
you [juː] du, dich, dir, Sie, Ihnen; ihr, euch

You're welcome. [ˌjɔː 'welkəm] Gern geschehen.
young [jʌŋ] jung
the young *(pl)* [ðə jʌŋ] die jungen Leute V/5/13
your [jɔː] dein(e); euer/eure; Ihr(e)
yours [jɔːz] deine(r, s); eure(r, s); Ihre(r, s)
yourself *(pl* **yourselves)** [jə'self, jə'selvz] dich, dir; selbst/ihr, euch; selbst
youth [juːθ] Jugend; Jugendliche/r; Jugend- V/2/I
youth centre ['juːθ ˌsentə] Jugendzentrum
youth hostel ['juːθ ˌhɒstl] Jugendherberge
Yuck! *(informal)* [jʌk] Igitt! V/5/5

Z

zoo [zuː] Zoo
zooxanthella *(pl -e)* [ˌzəʊəzæn'θelə, ˌzəʊəzæn'θeli] *Algenart* V/1/M2

A

abbiegen turn
(ab)holen come for
Abend evening, night
Abendessen dinner
abends in the evening, pm
(= post meridiem) *(nur hinter Uhrzeit)*
Abenteuer adventure
aber but, however
abfahren depart, leave
Abfall waste, litter *(no pl)*
abfeuern let off
abhängen hang out *(informal)*
abholen collect, pick up
das Abitur machen do one's A levels
abnehmen take off
Abneigungen dislikes *(pl)*
... der Aboriginals Aboriginal
Aborigine Aborigine
Absatz paragraph
Abschluss qualification
die Abschlussprüfung bestehen graduate
Abschnitt paragraph
abschreiben copy
abspülen wash up
abwaschen wash up
sich abwechseln take turns
darauf achten make sure
Achtung respect
Adjektiv adjective
Adresse address
Affe monkey
Afrika Africa
Afroamerikaner/in African American
afroamerikanisch African American
aggressiv aggressive
ähnlich similar
Aktion action, campaign
aktiv active
Aktivität activity
Akzent accent
akzeptieren accept
albern silly
Alkohol alcohol
alle everybody, everyone
allein alone
allein(e) on one's own
alles everything

Alles Gute zum Geburtstag! Happy birthday!
alles in allem all in all
alle(s) all
alles anything
alltäglich everyday
Alphabet alphabet
als as, than *(Vergleich),* when
also so
alt old
Alter age
Alternative alternative
Altglascontainer bottle bank
Altpapiercontainer paper bank
am on
am Abend in the evening
am besten best
am liebsten best
am meisten best
am Nachmittag in the afternoon
am nächsten Tag the next day
am/die meisten (the) most
Amerikaner/in American
amerikanisch American
amisch Amish
die Amischen the Amish
amtlich official
Amtsgewalt authority
sich amüsieren have a good time
an to, on, at
(an)bieten offer
andere(r, s) other; different
ein anderer/anderes, eine andere another
andererseits on the other hand
anders different
(sich) ändern change
(Ver)änderung change
anerkennen respect
Anfang beginning, start
anfangen start, begin
anfangs at first
anfeuern cheer
Anfrage request
sich (mit jdm) anfreunden make friends (with sb)
(an)führen lead
Angebot offer
im Angebot sein be on sale
Angehörige/r relative
angeln fish
angenehm nice

angestrengt hard
angreifen attack, tackle
Angriff attack
Angst haben be scared, be afraid
Angst machen scare
anhalten stop
sich anhören sound
Animationsfilm animated film
(an)klicken click
ankommen arrive, get (to)
Ankunft arrival
Anleitung instruction
Anmache chat-up line *(informal)*
Anmeldeformular entry form
annehmen accept; suppose
anordnen rank
Anorexie anorexia *(no pl)*
anpassungsfähig flexible
Anpassungsfähigkeit flexibility
anprobieren try on
anrufen phone, telephone, call
Anrufer/in caller
anschauen watch, look at
sich anschließen join (in)
anschließend afterwards
Ansicht opinion
jdn/etw anstarren stare at sb/sth
(an)statt instead (of)
anstreichen paint
Anstreicher/in painter
anstrengend stressful
Antwort answer
(be)antworten answer
Anweisung instruction
Anzeige advert (= advertisement)
anziehen put on
sich anziehen dress
Anziehung(skraft) attraction
Apfel apple
gedeckter Apfelkuchen apple pie
Appetit appetite
April April
Arbeit work, job
arbeiten work
Arbeitsbuch workbook
arbeitslos out of work
arbeitsreich busy
Arbeitszeit working hours
Ärger trouble

DICTIONARY GERMAN–ENGLISH

ärgern annoy
Argument argument
argumentieren argue
Arm arm
arm poor
Armee army
Art kind, type; way
Artikel article
Arzt/Ärztin doctor
Asiat/in Asian
asiatisch Asian
Asien Asia
Ast branch
Astronaut/in astronaut
Athlet/in athlete
Attraktion attraction
auch also, too
auf on, at
auf einmal at once; suddenly
Auf Wiedersehen! Goodbye!
aufbewahren keep
aufblicken zu look up to
aufdrehen turn up
aufführen perform
auffüllen refill
Aufgabe task
aufgebracht upset
aufgeregt excited, upset
etw aufhängen hang up sth, put
 up sth
aufheben pick up
aufhören stop, finish
auflegen *(Telefon)* hang up
aufmuntern cheer up
aufräumen tidy up
aufregend exciting
aufschreiben write down
aufspringen jump up
aufstehen get up, stand up
aufsteigen (auf) get on
aufwachen wake up
sich aufwärmen warm up
Aufwärmübung warm-up
 exercise
aufwecken wake up
Aufzug lift
Auge eye
Augenblick moment
im Augenblick at the moment
August August
aus out of, from
aus Versehen by accident
(Aus)bildung education

(Aus)blick view
sich ausdenken think of, make
 up
(aus)drucken print (out)
(aus)helfen help out
ausbilden train
Ausbildung training
Ausdruck phrase
ausdrücken express
Ausflug trip
ausfüllen fill out, fill in
Ausgang exit
ausgeben *(Geld)* spend
ausgehen go out
ausgezeichnet excellent
aushalten stand
jdn auslachen laugh at sb
Ausland foreign country
im Ausland abroad
Ausländer/in foreigner
ausländisch foreign
ausmachen turn off, put out
ausrechnen work out, figure out
ausreichend enough
Ausreißer/in runaway
Ausrüstung equipment
Aussage statement
ausschalten turn off
aussehen look
Aussehen look
außen outside
außerhalb outside
Aussicht view
ausspucken spit out
Ausstattung equipment
Ausstellung exhibition
Australien Australia
Australier/in Australian
australisch Australian
australische/r Ureinwohner/in
 Aborigine
austrinken finish
ausüben practise
auswählen choose
Ausweis identification (= ID)
 (no pl)
Auszeichnung award
Auszeit time out
ausziehen take off
Auto car
Autogramm autograph
Automat vending machine
Autor/in author

B

Backe cheek
(Back)ofen oven
backen bake
Bäcker/in baker
Bademeister/in lifeguard
baden take a bath
(Bade)wanne bath
Bad(ezimmer) bathroom, bath
Bahnhof station
Bahnsteig platform
bald soon
Ball ball
Banane banana
Bank bench
Bär bear
bar bezahlen pay cash
Bargeld cash *(no pl)*
Batterie battery
Bau building
Bauarbeiter/in builder
Bauchschmerzen stomach ache
bauen build
Bauer/Bäuerin farmer
Bauernhof farm
Baum tree
beängstigend frightening
(Land) bebauen farm (land)
bedeuten mean
Bedeutung meaning;
 importance *(no pl)*
Bedienstete/r servant
Bedienung waiter/waitress
jdn bedrohen threaten sb
sich beeilen hurry
beeindruckend impressive
beenden finish, stop
Beförderung transport
befragen interview
befürchten fear
begehen *(Verbrechen)* commit
Beginn start
beginnen begin
Behandlung therapy
behindert disabled
Behörde authority
bei by, at
beibringen teach
beide both
Beilage side order
Bein leg
beinahe almost, nearly
Beispiel example

beißen bite
beitreten join
(allgemein) bekannt known, well-known
Bekleidung clothes *(npl)*
bekommen get
belästigen bother
Beleg receipt
beleidigen offend
Beleidigung insult
beliebt popular
bellen bark
bemerken notice
Bemerkung comment
sich sehr bemühen, etw zu tun try hard to do sth
Benehmen behaviour *(BE)*, behavior *(AE)*
sich benehmen behave
(be)nennen name
benutzen use
beobachten watch
bequem comfortable
Berg mountain
Bericht report
berichten report
Beruf career
eine Berufsausbildung machen do vocational training
Berufserfahrung work experience *(no pl)*
berühmt famous, well-known
berühren touch
(be)schädigen damage
beschäftigt busy
Bescheid wissen über know about
jdn beschimpfen call sb names
beschließen decide
beschreiben describe
Beschreibung description
besiegen beat
besitzen own
besondere(r, s) special
besonders especially, extra
besorgt worried
besprechen discuss
(be)sprühen spray
Bestandteil ingredient
Bestattungsinstitut undertaker
(etw) bestellen order; have sth
beste(r, s) best
bestimmte(r, s) certain

bestrafen punish
Besuch visit
besuchen visit
Besucher/in visitor
betrachten look at
betreten enter
Betreuer/in instructor
Bett bed
betteln beg
Bettler/in beggar
beunruhigt worried
Bevölkerung population
bevor before
bevorzugen prefer
bewachen guard
sich bewegen move; exercise
sich bewerben (um) apply (for)
Bewerbungsformular application form
Bewerbungsgespräch job interview
bewölkt cloudy
sich einer Sache bewusst sein be aware of sth
sich einer Sache bewusst werden realise sth
bezahlen pay
bezaubernd charming
Bibliothek library
(sich) biegen bend
Bier beer
bieten present (to)
Bild picture, painting
Bilder machen take photos
billig cheap
Biologie biology
Birne pear
(spätestens) bis till, until, by
Bis bald! See you! *(informal)*
bis jetzt yet
bis zu up to
bisher so far
bitte please
Bitte request
bitten (um) request, ask
Bitteschön! Here you are.
Blatt Papier piece of paper
Blattsalat lettuce
blau blue
bleiben stay
Bleistift pencil
Blick look

blockieren block
blöd stupid
blond blonde
Blume flower
Boden floor, bottom
Bohne bean
Boot boat
böse mad
jdm einen bösen Blick zuwerfen give sb a hard stare
braten fry
Brathähnchen fried chicken
Brauch custom, tradition
brauchbar useful
brauchen need
braun brown
(zer)brechen break
brennen be on fire
Brett board
Brief letter
Briefmarke stamp
Brieftasche wallet
Briefumschlag envelope
Brille glasses *(npl)*
(mit)bringen bring
jdm etw bringen get sb sth
jdn dazu bringen etw zu tun make sb do sth
die Briten the British *(pl)*
britische(r, s) British
Brötchen roll
Broschüre brochure
Brot bread
Brücke bridge
Bruder brother
brüllen roar
Brunnen fountain
brutal violent
Buch book
buchen book
Büchse tin
Buchstabe letter
buchstabieren spell
Bücherei library
bügeln iron
Bühne stage
(Bundes)staat state
Bundesstraße highway
Burg castle
(Staats)bürger/in citizen
(ab)bürsten brush
Bus bus
Busch bush

DICTIONARY *German–English*

DICTIONARY GERMAN–ENGLISH

Bushaltestelle bus stop
Bußgeld fine
Butter butter

C

Cafeteria cafeteria
Campingplatz campsite
Cent(münze) cent
Center centre
Centstück p (= penny, pence)
Chance chance, opportunity
Charakter personality
Chef boss
China China
Chinese/Chinesin Chinese
chinesisch Chinese
Chips crisps *(npl)*
Couch sofa
Cousin/e cousin
Curry(gericht) curry

D

da since
da lassen leave
daher therefore
dahinter behind
damals then
Dame lady
Damm causeway
danach afterwards
dankbar grateful
danke thank you, thanks
danken thank
dann then, next
Darf es noch etwas sein?
   Anything else?
das the, that, which
**Das macht dann ... ; Das beläuft
   sich auf ...** That'll be ...
   (informal)
dasselbe the same
Datum date
dauern take
dauernd all the time;
   constant
Definition definition
definitiv definitely
(sich) dehnen stretch
dein(e) your
deine(r, s) yours
Delphin dolphin
denken think, suppose
denken an think of

an (jdn/etw) denken think about
   (sb/sth)
der the, that, which
derselbe the same
deshalb therefore
Dessert dessert
Detail detail
(Privat)detektiv/in detective
deutsch German
Deutsche/r German
Deutschland Germany
Dezember December
Diät diet
Dialog dialogue
dich yourself *(pl* yourselves), you
dick thick, fat
die the, that, which
Dieb thief *(pl* thieves)
dienen serve
Diener/in servant
Dienstag Tuesday
Dienstmädchen servant
diese these *(pl of* this), those
   (pl of that)
diese(r, s) this
dieselbe the same
Ding thing
Dingo dingo *(pl* -es)
Dinosaurier dinosaur
dir yourself *(pl* yourselves), you
direkt direct
Diskussion discussion
**Dokumentation,
   Dokumentarfilm** documentary
Donnerstag Thursday
Doppelzimmer double room
Dorf village
dort(hin) there
Dose can, tin
Dosencontainer can bank
Drache dragon
drangsalieren bully
draußen outdoor(s), outside
dreckig dirty
sich drehen turn
drinnen indoor(s)
Drittel third
Droge drug
drücken press, click, push
Druckerpatrone printer cartridge
Du meine Güte! Oh dear!
du you
Duft smell

dumm silly, stupid
dunkel dark
dünn thin, slim, skinny
durch through
Durcheinander mess
durcheinander confused
durcheinanderbringen disturb
durchqueren cross
(durch)suchen search
etw tun dürfen be allowed to
   do sth
duschen take a shower

E

Ebene level
echt real
Ecke corner
jdm ist es egal sb does not care
Ehefrau wife *(pl* wives)
ehrlich honest
Ei egg
eifersüchtig jealous
eigene(r, s) own
eigentlich actually
sich eignen fit
ein(e) a/an
ein bisschen a bit, a little
einander each other
Einbildung imagination
sich eincremen mit put on
eindeutig definitely, clear
einen Augenblick/Moment bitte
   just a minute
einer Meinung sein über
   agree on
einerseits on the one hand
eines Tages one day
einfach easy, simple; just
jdm einfallen come to sb's mind
eingestehen admit
einhängen hang up
einhundert one hundred
einige (a) few, several, some
sich einigen auf agree on
Einkaufspassage mall
Einkaufswagen trolley
Einkaufszentrum mall
einladen invite
Einladung invitation
einmal once
einpacken wrap
einsam lonely
einschalten turn on

einschlafen fall asleep
einsehen see
einsetzen fill in
einsteigen (in) get on
einstufen rank
Einwanderer/in immigrant
einwandern immigrate
Einwanderung immigration
(ein)wickeln wrap
Einzelfahrkarte single (ticket)
Einzelheit detail
einzelne(r, s) single
Einzelperson individual
Einzelzimmer single room,
  private room
einzigartig unique
Eis ice
Eis am Stiel popsicle
(Eisen)bahn railway *(BE)*,
  railroad *(AE)*
Eiskrem ice cream
Eiweiß protein
Elefant elephant
elegant elegant
Elektriker/in electrician
Elektrizität electricity
Elektrogerät electrical appliance
Ellbogen elbow
Eltern parents
elternlos orphaned
Empfangschef/in receptionist
Ende end, ending
(be)enden end
endlich finally
Energie energy
energiesparend energy-saving
energisch aggressive
England England
englisch English
auf Englisch in English
Enkelkind grandchild
  (pl grandchildren)
entdecken spot, discover
Entdecker/in explorer
Ente duck
entfernen remove
(ent)fliehen escape
entkommen escape
entlang along
sich entscheiden decide
sich entschuldigen apologize
Entschuldigen Sie bitte!
  Excuse me!

Entschuldigung! Excuse me!,
  Sorry!
Entschuldigung apology, excuse
entsetzt shocked
entspannend relaxing
jdn enttäuschen let sb down
enttäuscht disappointed
entweder ... oder ... either ... or ...
entwerfen design
(sich) entwickeln develop
Episode episode
er he
(er)raten guess
Erbse pea
Erdatmosphäre atmosphere
Erdbeben earthquake
Erdbeere strawberry
(Erd)boden ground
Erde earth, world, globe; ground
Erdkunde geography
Erdnuss peanut
Erfahrung experience
erfinden invent, make up
Erfindung invention
Erfolg success *(no pl)*
erfolgreich successful
Ergebnis result
erhalten get
erhitzen heat
sich erinnern (an) remember
Erkältung cold
erklären explain
Erklärung definition
erlangen gain
Erlaubnis licence
Erlebnis adventure
ermorden murder
Ernährung diet
ernst serious
Ernte harvest
eröffnen start
eröffnet werden open
Erörterung discussion
erreichen reach
erschaffen create
erscheinen appear
erschöpft exhausted
erschrecken scare
ersetzen replace
erst only
erste(r, s) first
als Erstes (at) first
Ertrag harvest

ertragen stand
erwachsen werden grow up
Erwachsene/r adult
Erwärmung der Erdatmosphäre
  global warming *(no pl)*
erwarten expect
erwerben gain
erzählen tell
Erzähler/in narrator
Erzählung story
erzeugen produce
Erzeugnis product
Erzieher/in nursery teacher
es it
Es freut mich, Sie/dich kennen
  zu lernen. Nice to meet you.
es gibt there is, there are
essen eat, have
Essen food *(no pl)*, meal
Essen zum Mitnehmen takeaway
zu essen geben feed
Essgewohnheiten eating habits
  (npl)
Essig vinegar
Esszimmer dining room
etwas anything, something,
  some
euch yourself *(pl* yourselves),
  you
euer/eure your
eure(r, s) yours
Europa Europe
Europäer/in European
europäisch European
ewig forever
existieren exist
Expedition expedition
extrem extreme

F

Fabrik factory
(Schul)fach subject
Fähigkeit skill, ability
Fahne flag
Fähre ferry
fällen cut down
fahren drive, ride
Fahrer/in driver
Fahrkartenschalter ticket
  counter
Fahrplan timetable
Fahrrad bicycle, bike
Fahrt trip

Fairness sportsmanship *(no pl)*
Fakt fact
fallen fall
fallen lassen drop
falls if
falsch false, wrong
(zusammen)falten fold
Familie family
Familienname surname
fangen catch
Fantasie fantasy, imagination
fantastisch fantastic *(informal)*
Farbe colour
färben dye
farbenfroh colourful
farbenprächtig colourful
fast almost, nearly
faul lazy
Favorit/in favourite
Februar February
Feder feather
Federmäppchen pencil case
Fehler mistake, fault
Feier celebration
feiern celebrate
Feigling coward
Feld field
Fell fur
Fels(en) rock
Fenster window
Ferien holiday *(BE)*, vacation *(AE)*
Ferienlager summer camp
fernsehen watch TV
Fernsehen; Fernseher TV
  (= television)
Fernsehstudio TV studio
Fernsehzeitschrift TV guide
fertig ready, finished
(fest)halten hold
(Fest)land land
festnehmen catch
Fett fat
fett fat
fettreduziert fat-reduced
Feuer fire
Feuerwehrmann/-frau firefighter
Feuerwerk firework
fies mean
Film film
in einem Film/Theaterstück
  auftreten star
Filmstudio film studio
finden find

Finger finger
Firma company
Fisch fish *(pl* fish)
fischen fish
sich fit halten keep fit
Flagge flag
Flamme flame
Flasche bottle
Fleisch meat *(no pl)*
flexibel flexible
Flexibilität flexibility
fliegen fly
Floß raft
Flügel wing
Flughafen airport
Flugzeug plane
Fluss river
(Flüssigkeits)behälter tank
flüstern whisper
Folge episode; consequence,
  result
folgen follow
Form form
formen form
Formular form
Forscher/in explorer
(Forschungs)reise expedition
Foto photo, picture
Fotoapparat camera
fotografieren take photos
Frage question
fragen ask
sich fragen wonder
Fragen stellen ask questions
Frankreich France
Franzose/Französin; französisch
  French
Fraß junk food
Frau woman *(pl* women), lady
Frau (Anrede) Mrs
Fräulein (Anrede) Miss
frei free
im Freien outdoors, outside
Freiheit freedom *(no pl)*
die Freiheitsstatue the Statue of
  Liberty
Freitag Friday
Freizeit free time
Freizeitpark theme park
fremd strange, foreign
Fremde/r stranger
Freund (eines Mädchens)
  boyfriend

Freund/in friend
freundlich friendly, kind, nice
Freundschaft friendship
Freundschaftsspiel friendly
  match
sich auf etw freuen look forward
  to sth
Freut mich, dich/euch/Sie
  kennen zu lernen. Pleased to
  meet you., Nice to meet you.
Friede peace
Friedhof graveyard
frisch fresh
Frischkäse cream cheese
Friseur/Friseuse hair stylist
Frisur haircut
frittieren fry
froh glad
fröhlich happy
Frosch frog
Frucht fruit
früh early
früher ... used to ... *(+ infinitive)*
Frühling spring
Frühstück breakfast
Frühstückszerealien cereal
(sich) fühlen feel
Führer/in leader, chief
füllen fill
Fünftel fifth
für for
funktionieren work (out)
Furcht erregend frightening,
  scary
furchtbar awful, terrible
fürchten fear
sich fürchten be frightened, be
  afraid
Fuß foot *(pl* feet)
Fuß (= 0,3048 Meter) foot
  (pl foot *or* feet)
Fußball football *(BE)*, soccer *(AE)*
füttern feed
Fütterungszeit feeding time

G

Gabel fork
Galerie gallery
ganz whole; all
Ganztags- full-time
Garage garage
Garten garden
Gärtner/in gardener

D

Gas gas
Gast guest
Gebäude building
geben give
Gebiet area
geboren born
Gebrauch use
Geburt birth
Geburtsdatum date of birth
Geburtstag birthday
Gedicht poem
geduldig patient
gefährlich dangerous
Gefahr risk
Gefangene/r prisoner
Gefängnis prison
gefrieren freeze
Gefühl feeling
gegen against
Gegenstand thing, object
Gegenteil opposite
gegenüber opposite
Gegner/in opponent
geheim secret
Geheimnis secret
(zu Fuß) gehen walk
gehen go
mit jdm gehen date sb
  (informal)
Gehen walk
gehören zu go with
Geist ghost
gekocht boiled
Gelände ground
Geländer rail
gelangen get
gelb yellow
Geld money
Geld aufbringen/auftreiben
  raise money
Geld verdienen make money
Geldautomat cash machine
Geldstrafe fine
Geldstück coin
Gelee jelly
Gelegenheit opportunity
Gemälde painting
gemein mean
Gemeinde community
gemeinsam together
Gemeinschaft community
Gemüse vegetable
genannt called

genau exactly, just
(genau)so ... wie ... as ... as ...
Genehmigung licence
Generation generation
Genesungskarte get well card
genießen enjoy
genügend enough
genug enough
geöffnet open
Geographie geography
geprellt bruised
gerade just
gerade(aus) straight
Gerät gadget
Geräusch sound, noise
Gericht *(Nahrung)* dish *(pl* -es)
Gericht court
Gern geschehen. You're
  welcome.
Geruch smell
Gesamt- total
Geschäft shop
Geschäftsführer/in manager
geschehen happen
gescheit clever
Geschenk present
Geschichte history, story
Geschick(lichkeit) skill
geschieden divorced
Geschirrspülmaschine
  dishwasher
Gesellschaft company
Gesetz law
Gesicht face
Gespenst ghost
Gespräch dialogue, talk
gesprächig communicative
gestalten create
Gestank smell
gestern yesterday
gestresst stressed
gesund healthy
gesund werden get well
Gesundheit health
Getränk drink
Getreide, Korn corn
Getreide(sorte) cereal
Gewalt violence
gewalttätig violent
Gewalttätigkeit violence
Gewicht weight
Gewinn prize
gewinnen win, gain

Gewinner/in winner
gewisse(r, s) certain
sich an etw gewöhnen get used
  to sth
gewöhnlich usually
gießen water
Gitarre guitar
Gitter grid
glamourös glamorous
Glas glass
glatt *(Haar)* straight
Glaube religion
glauben (an) believe (in)
gleich just; equal
gleichaltrig the same age
gleichberechtigt equal
Gletscher glacier
Globus globe
Glück good luck
Glück haben be lucky
glücklich happy, glad
Glückwunsch congratulations
  (npl)
Glühbirne light bulb
Gnu wildebeest *(pl - or* -s)
Goldfisch goldfish
Gott god
Gott sei Dank! Thank goodness!
grässlich nasty
Graffitikünstler graffer *(informal)*
Grafiker/in graphic artist
Grammatik grammar
Gras grass
gratis (for) free
grau grey
grausam cruel
greifen reach
Grenze border
Griechenland Greece
grillen grill, have a barbecue
eine Grillparty feiern have a
  barbecue
groß big, large, tall, great
großartig great
(Groß)stadt city
Großbritannien Britain, Great
  Britain
Größe size
Großeltern grandparents *(pl)*
Großmutter grandmother
Großvater grandfather
grün green
beste Grüße best wishes

herzliche Grüße love
Grund reason, cause
das ist der Grund, warum that's why
gründen found
Gründer/in founder
gründlich careful
Grundschule primary school
Gruppe group
(be)grüßen greet, say hello to
Gummi rubber *(Material)*, rubber *(BE) (Radiergummi)*
(Salat)gurke cucumber
Güte quality
gut good, fine
gut aussehend good-looking
Gut gemacht! Well done!
gut in etw sein be good at sth
Gute Besserung! Get well soon!
Guten Appetit! Enjoy your meal!

H

Haar(e) hair *(no pl)*
Haarschnitt haircut
haben have got, have
für etw haften be responsible for sth
Hai(fisch) shark *(pl -s or -)*
halb half
halb (neun) half past (eight)
Halbfinale semifinal
Hälfte half *(pl halves)*
Halle hall
hallo hello
Hals neck
(Hals)kette necklace
(be)halten keep
Hand hand
handeln take action, act
handeln von be about
Handlung action
Handy mobile phone
hängen hang
hart hard
Hass hate *(no pl)*
hassen hate
hässlich ugly
Haupt- main
häufig often
Häuptling chief
hauptsächlich mainly
Hauptspeise main dish
Hauptstadt capital

Hauptwort noun
Haus house
Hausaufgaben homework *(no pl)*
nach Hause home
zu Hause (at) home
Haustier pet
Haut skin
hawai(an)isch Hawaiian
Hawaiianer/in Hawaiian
Heer army
Heft exercise book
heilig holy
Heim home
heimatlos homeless
Heimweh haben be homesick
heiraten get married, marry
heiß hot
ich heiße my name is
Wie heißt du?/ Wie heißen Sie? What's your name?
Heizung heating
Held hero *(pl -es)*
helfen help
hell bright
Helm helmet
Hemd shirt
Henne hen
herausbringen release
herausfinden find out, discover, figure out
Herausforderung challenge
herauskommen come out
herausnehmen take out
sich herausputzen dress up
Herbst autumn *(BE)*, fall *(AE)*
herein in
hereinkommen come in
Herkunft background
Herr *(Anrede)* Mr
(vornehmer) Herr gentleman
herstellen produce
Hersteller producer
(her)überkommen come over
auf jdm herumhacken pick on sb
herunterfallen fall off
hervorragend excellent
Herz heart
Herzanfall heart attack
Herzinfarkt heart attack
hetzen hurry
heute today
heute Abend tonight
heute Morgen this morning

heute Nachmittag this afternoon
hier here
Hier, bitte! Here you are.
hiesig local
Highway highway
Hilfe help
hilflos helpless
Himmel sky
hinab down
Hin- und Rückfahrkarte return (ticket)
hinaufgehen walk up
(hinauf)klettern climb
(hinauf)steigen climb
(hinaus)gehen go out
hineingehen go in
in jdn/etw hineinrennen run into
sich hinlegen lie (down)
sich (hin)setzen sit down
hinten in at the back of
hinter behind
Hintergrund background
hinterherlaufen run after
Hinterland (Australiens) outback *(no pl)*
hinterlassen leave
hinüber over
hinunter down
hinzufügen add
hispanisch Hispanic
Hispano-Amerikaner/in Hispanic
Hitze heat *(no pl)*
hoch high, tall
(hoch)heben lift
Hochschule college
hochspringen jump up
Höhe height
höher stellen turn up
hoffen hope
Hoffnung hope
höflich polite
höhere/weiterführende Schule secondary school
holen get
Hölle hell
Holz wood
Holz- wooden
hölzern wooden
Honig honey
hören hear
Horizont skyline

Hör(t) auf (damit)! Stop it!
Hose trousers *(npl)*
Hotel hotel
hübsch pretty, lovely
Hügel hill
Huhn chicken, hen
Hund dog
Hundert hundred
Hunger hunger
hungrig hungry
Hut hat
Hyäne hyena

I

ich I
Ich hätte gern ... I'll have ...
Ich nehme ... I'll have ...
ich würde gern I'd like (to)
ich/wir auch same here
ideal ideal
Idee idea
Identifizierung identification
  (= ID) *(no pl)*
idiotisch idiotic
ignorieren ignore, break
ihm him
ihn him
ihnen them
Ihnen you
ihr you
Ihr(e) your
ihr(e) their
ihr(e, es) theirs
ihr(e, n) her
ihre(r, s) hers
Ihre(r, s) yours
Imbissstube snack bar
immer always
(immer) noch still
Immigration immigration
in in, at, to, around, into
(in ...) hinein inside
in Ordnung fine
in Richtung toward(s)
Inder/in Indian
Indianer/in Native American,
  Indian
indianisch Native American,
  Indian
Indien India
indisch Indian
Information information *(no pl)*
illegal illegal

inklusive included
innen inside, indoor(s)
im Inneren inside
innerhalb within
Insel island
Inserat advert (= advertisement)
Instrument instrument
intelligent intelligent
interessant interesting
Interesse interest
sich interessieren für be
  interested in
interessiert (an) interested (in)
Internat boarding school
im Internet on the Internet
etw ins Internet stellen
  post sth
intolerant intolerant
irgendein(e) any
irgendwo somewhere
irisch Irish
Irland Ireland
sich irren be wrong
Irrtum mistake
Italien Italy
Italiener/in Italian
italienisch Italian

J

ja yes
Jacke jacket
jagen hunt
Jahr year
Jahrbuch yearbook
Jahresausgabe yearbook
Jahrhundert century
Januar January
jedenfalls anyway
jede/r anyone, everyone,
  everybody
jede(r, s) each, every, any
jedoch however
jemals ever
jemand somebody, someone,
  anyone
jene those *(pl of* that*)*
jetzt now
Jongleur/in juggler
jubeln cheer
jüdisch Jewish
Jugendherberge youth hostel
jugendlich teenage
Jugendzentrum youth centre

Juli July
jung young
Junge boy
junger Hund puppy
Juni June

K

Kaffee coffee
Kalender calendar
Kalorie calorie
kalt cool
Kälte cold
Kamera camera
Kameramann/-frau
  cameraman/-woman
Kamm comb
Kampagne campaign
Kampf fight
kämpfen (um) fight (for),
  compete (for)
Kampfsport martial arts *(npl)*
Kanada Canada
Kanal channel
Känguru kangaroo
Kaninchen rabbit
Kantine canteen
kapieren get
Kapitän/in captain
Kappe cap
kaputt broken
kaputtgehen break down
die Karibik the Caribbean
karibisch Caribbean
die Karibischen Inseln the
  Caribbean
Karneval carnival
Karotte carrot
Karriere career
Karte ticket, card
Kartoffel potato *(pl* -es*)*
Kartoffelbrei mashed potatoes
Karton card
Käse cheese
Kasse *(im Kino, Theater)* box
  office
Kassenbon receipt
Kätzchen kitten
Katze cat
kaufen buy
Käufer/in buyer
Kaufhaus department store
Kaugummi chewing gum *(no pl)*
kaum hardly

kein(e) no
keiner no one
Keks biscuit
Keller cellar
Kellner/in waiter/waitress
kennen know
jdn kennenlernen get to know sb
Kerl guy *(informal)*
Kerze candle
Kette chain
kicken kick
Kilo kilo
Kind child *(pl* children*)*
Kindergarten nursery school *(BE)*, kindergarten *(AE)*
Kino cinema
(Kino-, Spiel)film film *(BE)*, movie *(AE)*
Kirche church
Kirsche cherry
Kissen cushion
klären solve
Klang sound
klappen work out
klar clear
(Schul)klasse class
Klassenarbeit test
Klassenkamerad/in classmate
Klasse(nstufe) grade
Klassenzimmer classroom
kleben stick
Kleid dress
sich kleiden dress
Kleider clothes *(npl)*
Kleiderschrank wardrobe
Kleidung clothing *(no pl)*
klein little, small
klingeln ring
klingen sound
Klo toilet
Kloß dumpling
Klub club
klug clever
Kneipe pub
Knie knee
Knoblauch garlic
Knochen bone
Knödel dumpling
Koch/Köchin chef, cook
kochen cook
Kohle(n)hydrat carbohydrate
Kolonie colony
komisch funny

kommen come
kommen wegen come for
Kommentar comment
Kommode chest of drawers
Komm(t) jetzt! Come on!
Kommunikation communication
kommunizieren communicate
Komödie comedy
Komposttonne compost bin
König king
Königin queen
können can
könnte might
Konrektor deputy head
Konsequenz consequence
Kontakt contact
Kontext context
Konto account
kontrollieren check
Konzert concert
Kopf head
Kopf hoch! Cheer up!
Kopfsalat lettuce
kopieren copy
Koralle coral
Korallenriff coral reef
Korb basket
Körper body
(Körper)größe height
körperlich physical
korrekt correct
Korridor hall
korrigieren correct
kosten cost
köstlich delicious
Kostüm fancy dress, costume
Krach noise
Kraft power, energy
krank ill, sick
(Kranken)schwester/ (Kranken)pfleger nurse
Krankenhaus hospital
Krankheit disease, illness
kränken offend
kränklich unhealthy
(zer)kratzen scratch
kreativ creative
Krebs *(Krankheit)* cancer
Kreditkarte credit card
Kreide chalk *(no pl)*
Kreis circle
kreischen scream
Krieg war

kriegen catch
Kriminelle/r criminal
Krokodil crocodile
Krone crown
Küche kitchen
Kuchen cake, pie
Kugelschreiber ballpoint
Kuh cow
kühl cool
Kühlschrank fridge *(informal)*
sich kümmern um look after, take care of, care for
Kultur culture
Kunde/Kundin customer
Kunst art
Künstler/in artist
Kunststoff plastic
Kurs course
kurz short
Kuss kiss
küssen kiss
Küste coast

L

Laden shop
lächeln smile
lachen laugh
über etw lachen laugh at sth
Lackierer/in painter
Lage location; situation
Lamm lamb
Lampe lamp
Land country
landen land
(Land)karte map
Landschaft landscape
lang long
langsam slow
sich langweilen be bored
langweilig boring
Lärm noise
Lass (doch) den Kopf nicht hängen! Cheer up!
lassen let, leave
lass(t) uns let's (= let us)
latino Latino *(AE)*
Latino Latino *(AE)*
laufen lassen let off
laufen run
Lauffeuer wildfire
laut loud, noisy, aloud
läuten ring
lauter sprechen speak up

Leben life (*pl* lives)
leben live
Lebensbedingungen living conditions (*pl*)
(Lebens)gefahr danger
Lebenslauf CV (= curriculum vitae)
Lebensweise way of life
lecker tasty, delicious
leer empty
legen put
Legende legend
Lehnstuhl armchair
Lehrer/in teacher, instructor
Leichenbestatter/in undertaker
leicht easy
Das tut mir leid. I'm sorry.
leider unfortunately
leihen borrow
leise quiet
sich leisten afford
leiten lead
Leiter/in leader
lernen learn, study
lesen read
letzten Endes in the end
letzte(r, s) last
Leute people (*pl*)
Licht light
Liebe love
alles Liebe love
lieben love
liebe(r) (*Anrede*) dear
Liebesfilm romance
Liebling favourite
Lieblings- favourite
Lied song
(Lied)text lyrics
Lieferant/in für Speisen und Getränke caterer
Lift lift
liegen lie
Lineal ruler
Linie line
links on the left
Liste list
Löffel spoon
löschen put out
Lohn wage(s)
Los! Los geht's! Let's go!
etw loswerden get rid of sth
lösen solve
Lösung solution

Löwe lion
Luft air
lügen lie
lustig funny, fun

M

machen make, do
Mach(t) schon! Come on!
etw gerne machen be fond of doing sth
mächtig powerful
Mädchen girl
mähen cut
Magazin magazine
Magenschmerzen stomach ache
mager skinny
Magersucht anorexia (*no pl*)
magersüchtig anorexic
Magie magic
Mahlzeit meal
eine Mahlzeit zu sich nehmen have a meal
Mai May
Majonäse mayonnaise
Mal time
malen paint
Maler/in painter
Mama mum (*informal*)
manchmal sometimes
Mann man (*pl* men)
männlich male
Mappe folder
Marathon(lauf) marathon
Markt market
Marmelade jelly
März March
Maschine machine, engine
Maschine schreiben type
Maskenbildner/in make-up artist
Material material
Mathe maths
Mechaniker/in mechanic
Medikament drug, medicine (*no pl*)
Medizin medicine (*no pl*)
Meer sea, ocean
Meeresschildkröte turtle
Mehl flour
mehr more
mehr als genug plenty
mehr oder weniger more or less
Meile mile
mein(e) my

meinen mean, think
meiner Meinung nach in my opinion
meine(r, s) mine
Meinung opinion
Meisterschaft championship
(sich) melden report
Melone melon
Menge amount
jede Menge lots of
Mensa canteen
Mensch human, person
Menschen people (*pl*)
(Menschen)menge crowd
menschlich human
Menü menu
Messer knife (*pl* knives)
Metall metal
Meter metre
Mexikaner/in Mexican
mexikanisch Mexican
Mexiko Mexico
mich myself, me
Miete rent
Mikrowelle(nherd) microwave
Milch milk
Milchprodukt dairy food
Million million
Millionär/in millionaire
mindestens at least
Mineral mineral
Minute minute
mir me, myself
mit with, by
mitgerechnet included
Mitglied member
Mitleid mit jdm haben feel sorry for sb
mitlesen read along
mitmachen bei join
Mitschüler/in classmate
Mittagessen lunch, dinner
Mittagszeit lunchtime
in der Mitte in the middle of
mitteilsam communicative
mitten in in the middle of
Mitternacht midnight
Mittwoch Wednesday
Mobbing bullying
Möbel furniture (*no pl*)
Mobiltelefon mobile phone
Möchten Sie schon bestellen? (Are you) ready to order?

modern modern
mögen like, fancy *(informal)*
sehr gern mögen love
etw gerne mögen be fond of sth
möglich possible
möglicherweise maybe
Möglichkeit opportunity, chance
Möhre carrot
momentan at the moment
Moment mal! Wait a second!
Moment moment
Monat month
Montag Monday
Morgen morning
morgen tomorrow
am Morgen in the morning
morgens in the morning, am
　　(= ante meridiem) *(nur hinter
　　Uhrzeit)*
Motor engine
müde tired
Müll rubbish, litter, waste
　　(no pl)
Mülleimer bin
Mülltonne bin
Mund mouth
Münze coin
Museum museum
Musik music
(Musik)album album
müssen have to, must, need to
müsste should
mutig brave
Mutter mother
Muttersprache first language
Mutti mum *(informal)*
Mütze cap

N

nach after; for, to
nach vorn(e) forward
(nach) links left
(nach) oben upstairs
(nach) rechts right
Nachbar/in neighbour
Nachbarschaft neighbourhood
nachdem after
nachdenken think
nachfüllen refill
Nachmittag afternoon
nachmittags in the afternoon,
　　pm (= post meridiem) *(nur
　　hinter Uhrzeit)*

Nachname surname
Nachricht message
Nachrichten news *(no pl)*
Nachrichtensendung the news
nachschlagen look up
nachspielen act out
nächste(r, s) next
Nacht night
Nachtisch dessert
Nacken neck
nah(e) near, close
der Nahe Osten the Middle East
in der Nähe by
Nahrung diet
Name name
Nase nose
nass wet
National- national
national national
Nationalität nationality
Nationalpark national park
Natur nature
naturbelassen natural
Naturkundemuseum natural
　　history museum
natürlich of course; natural
Naturwissenschaft science
Nebel fog
neben next to
neblig foggy
Neffe nephew
(mit)nehmen take
etw zu sich nehmen have sth
nein no
nennen call
nerven annoy
jdm auf die Nerven gehen get on
　　sb's nerves
nervös nervous
nett kind, nice
neu new, fresh
neugierig curious
Neuigkeit news *(no pl)*
Neujahr New Year *(no pl)*
Neuseeland New Zealand
nicht not
nicht dürfen must not
nicht einverstanden sein
　　disagree
nicht mehr not anymore
nicht stimmen be wrong
nicht übereinstimmen disagree
nicht zuletzt last but not least

nichts nothing
zu nichts zu gebrauchen useless
nicken nod
sich niederlassen settle
niedlich cute
niedrig low
nie(mals) never
niemand nobody, no one
Nilpferd hippopotamus
nirgends nowhere
nirgendwo nowhere
noch ein(e, r, s) another
noch (ein)mal again
noch nicht not yet
(immer) noch, noch immer still
Nordamerika North America
Norden north
Nordirland Northern Ireland
Nordost- north-east
Nordosten north-east
nordöstlich north-east
Nordwesten north-west
normal normal, regular
normalerweise normally, usually
Note mark, grade
Notfall emergency
(sich) notieren note down
Notiz note
(sich) Notizen machen (zu, über)
　　take/make notes (on)
November November
Nudel noodle
Nudeln pasta
Nummer number
nun (ja) well
nur only, just
nützlich useful

O

ob whether
obdachlos homeless
oben on top
oberes Ende top
Oberhaupt chief
obgleich although
Objekt object
Obst fruit
obwohl although
oder or
offen open
öffentlich public
(sich) öffnen open
offiziell official

oft often
ohne without
ohnmächtig werden faint
Ohr ear
Ohrring earring
ökologisch green
Oktober October
Öl oil
Olive olive
Oma grandma
Omi grandma
Onkel uncle
Opa grandpa
Opi grandpa
optimistisch optimistic
Orangensaft orange juice
ordentlich tidy
Ordnung order
Ist alles in Ordnung? Are you all
  right?
Organisation organization
organisieren organise
Ort place
örtlich local
Ost- east, eastern
Osten east
Ostern Easter
östlich east, eastern
Ozean ocean
Ozonloch ozone hole

P

Paar pair
packen pack
Packung packet
Paddel paddle
in Panik geraten panic
Papa dad *(informal)*
Papier paper
Pappe card, cardboard *(no pl)*
(Papp)karton card, cardboard
  (no pl)
Paprika pepper
Parade parade
Park(anlagen) park
Parkaufseher/in park ranger
Partner partner
Partyservice caterer
passen suit, fit
passieren happen, go on
Passwort password
Pastete pie
Patient/in patient

Pause break
peinlich embarrassing
peinlich berührt embarrassed
Pelz fur
Person person
persönlich personal
Persönlichkeit personality
Pfad path, trail
Pfeffer pepper
pfeifen whistle
Pferd horse
Pflanze plant
pflanzen plant
pflücken pick
Pfote paw
Pfund pound (£)
die Philippinen the Philippines
physisch physical
Picknick picnic
die Pilger(väter) the Pilgrims *(pl)*
Pilot/in pilot
Pilz mushroom
Pinguin penguin
pink pink
Pizza pizza
Plan plan
planen plan
Planet planet
Plastik plastic
Plastikflaschencontainer plastic
  bottle bank
Plattform platform
Platz place, square
plötzlich suddenly
Polizei police *(npl)*
Polizeibeamter/-beamtin police
  officer
Polizist/in policeman/-woman
Pommes frites chips *(BE, pl)*,
  French fries *(AE, npl)*
Pony pony
Portion portion
Postamt post office
Postkarte postcard
Praktikant/in trainee *(BE)*,
  intern *(AE)*
Praktikum work experience
  (no pl)
praktisch practical
praktizieren practise
präsentieren present (to)
Präsentation presentation
Präsident/in president

Preis price; prize, award
preiswert cheap
Prinz prince
privat private, personal
pro per, a
probieren try
Problem problem, difficulty
Produkt product
Produzent/in producer
produzieren produce
professionell professional
Profi professional
Programm programme; channel
programmiert programmed
Projekt project
Prospekt leaflet
Protein protein
provozieren provoke
Prozent per cent
Prüfung test
Psychologe/Psychologin
  psychologist
Pullover jumper, sweater
Punkt point
einen Punkt machen score
punkten score
Punktestand score
pünktlich punctual, on time
Puppe doll
pur pure
Pute/r turkey
putzen clean (up), brush
Pyjama pyjamas *(pl)*

Q

Quadrat square
Qualifikation qualification
Qualität quality

R

Rabauke bully
Rabe raven
Rad wheel
Radeln cycling
Rad fahren cycle
Radfahren cycling
Radfahrer/in cyclist
Radiergummi rubber *(BE)*
Radio radio
Rampe ramp
Rasenmäher lawnmower
Rasse race
Rassist/in racist

rassistisch racist
Rat advice *(no pl)*
raten have a guess
Ratte rat
Rauch smoke
rauchen smoke
Raum space
Raumschiff spaceship
raus aus off
reagieren react
Reaktion (auf) reaction (to)
Rechnung bill
Recht right
Recht haben be right
recht sein suit
rechts right, on the right
Rechtsanwalt/-anwältin lawyer
Rechtschreibung spelling
rechtswidrig illegal
rechtzeitig on time
(gerade noch) rechtzeitig (just)
   in time
recyclen recycle
reden (mit) talk (to)
(Rede)wendung phrase
reduzieren reduce
reduziert sein be on sale
Referat talk
Regal shelf *(pl shelves)*
Regel rule
regelmäßig regular
Regen rain
Regenwald rainforest
Regierung government
Region area
regnen rain
regnerisch rainy
reich rich
Reihe queue
Reihenfolge order
rein pure
reinigen clean (up)
Reis rice
Reise journey, trip
Reiseführer travel guide
Reiseführer/in tour guide
Reiseleiter/in tour guide
reisen travel
(Reise)pass passport
reiten ride
Reiten riding
Reiter/in rider
reizend charming

Rektor/in headteacher
Religion religion
Religions- religious
religiöse(r, s) religious
Rendezvous date
Rennen race
rennen run
reparieren repair
Reporter/in reporter
Reservierung reservation
Reservat *(= ein den Indianern
   vorbehaltenes Gebiet)*
   reservation
Respekt respect
respektieren respect
Rest rest
Restaurant restaurant
retten save, rescue
Rettungssanitäter/in
   paramedic
Rettungsschwimmer/in
   lifeguard
Rezept recipe
Rhythmus rhythm
Richter/in judge
richtig right, correct
riechen smell
Riese giant
riesengroß huge
riesig huge, giant
Riff reef
Risiko risk
Roboter robot
robust strong
Rock skirt
Rolle role, part
(Tret)roller scooter
Rollstuhl wheelchair
Rolltreppe escalator
Roman novel
romantisch romantic
Romanze romance
rosa pink
rot red
Rücken back
Rückenschmerzen backache
Rückseite back
Rüpel bully
Ruf cry
rufen shout
jdn in Ruhe lassen leave sb
   alone
ruhig quiet

S

Sachbeschädigung vandalism
Sache object, thing
Saft juice
Sage legend
sagen say, tell
Sahne cream
Salat salad
Salz salt
sammeln collect, pick; gain
Samstag Saturday
Sänger/in singer
Sarg coffin
Satz sentence, phrase
sauber clean
sauber machen clean (up)
sauer mad
Schach(spiel) chess
Schachtel packet
zu schade too bad
schaden hurt
Schaf sheep *(pl sheep)*
es schaffen manage
Schal scarf *(pl -s or scarves)*
Schale shell; dish *(pl -es)*
sich schämen be ashamed
scharf sharp; hot, spicy
schätzen have a guess
schauen look
schaurig spooky *(informal)*
Schauspieler/in actor/actress
Schauspielerei drama *(no pl)*
Scheibe slice
scheinen seem
Schere (pair of) scissors
scherzen be joking
scherzhaft playful
scheußlich nasty
Schicht shift
Schichtarbeit shift work *(no pl)*
Schichtdienst shift work *(no pl)*
(zu)schicken send
schieben push
Schiedsrichter/in referee
Schienen railway *(BE)*,
   railroad *(AE)*
schießen kick
Schiff ship
(Straßen-/Verkehrs)schild sign
Schimpanse chimpanzee
Schimpfwörter benutzen use
   bad language
Schinken ham

(Schinken)speck bacon
Schlafanzug pyjamas *(pl)*
schlafen sleep, be asleep
Schlafsaal *(in dem Männer und Frauen übernachten)* mixed dorm
Schlafzimmer bedroom
schlagen (auf) hit, beat
Schlagzeile headline
Schlange snake; queue
schlank slim
schlau clever
schlecht bad
schließen close
Schließfach locker
schließlich finally, in the end
schlimm bad; sore
Schlitten sled
Schlittschuh skate
Schloss castle
Schluss ending
Schlüssel key
Schlüsselwort keyword
schmackhaft tasty
schmal slim
schmecken taste
schmerzen hurt
schmücken decorate
schmutzig dirty
Schnee snow
schneiden cut
schnell fast, quick
Schnellgerichte junk food
Schnellhefter folder
Schnupfen cold
schockiert shocked
Schokolade chocolate
schon already, yet
schön beautiful, nice, lovely
schottisch Scottish
Schottland Scotland
Schrank cupboard
Schraube screw
schrecklich horrible, awful, terrible
Schrei cry
schreiben write
(Briefe/E-Mails) schreiben mail
Schreibpapier writing paper *(no pl)*
Schreibtisch desk
schreien cry, shout, scream
Schriftsteller/in author

schüchtern shy
Schuh shoe
Schulabschluss graduation
Schularbeiten schoolwork *(no pl)*
Schuld fault
Schulden machen get into debt
schuldig guilty
Schule school
Schüler/in pupil, student
Schulleiter/in headteacher
Schultasche schoolbag
Schulter shoulder
Schulung training
Schuppen shed
Schüssel bowl
schützen protect
-schützer pad
schwanger pregnant
schwarz black
Schwein pig
schwenken wave
schwer heavy; difficult
Schwester sister
schwierig difficult
Schwierigkeit difficulty
Schwierigkeiten trouble
Schwimmen swimming
schwimmen swim
Schwimmweste lifejacket
See lake
seekrank seasick
segeln sail
sehen see, look (at)
Sehenswürdigkeit sight
Sehleistung sight
sehr very, much, a lot (of)
Seifenoper soap (opera)
Seil rope
sein be
sein(e, r) his
seit since, for
Seite page, side
Sekretär/in secretary
Sekunde second
selbst myself, yourself, herself, himself, itself, ourselves, yourselves, themselves; even
Sendung programme
September September
servieren serve
Sessel armchair
setzen put

seufzen sigh
sicher safe; sure, certain
Sicherheit safety, security *(no pl)*
Sicherheitsdienst security *(no pl)*
sichern save
Sicht view
sie she, they, them, her
Sie you
Siedler/in settler
Siedlung settlement
Sieger/in winner
Signal signal
signieren sign
singen sing
sinken sink
Sitte custom
Situation situation
sitzen sit
Skateboard fahren skate
Skate-Veranstaltung skate
skaten skate
Skelett skeleton
Ski ski
Sklave/Sklavin slave
SMS *(Handy)* text message
so so, like this
sobald as soon as
Socke sock
Sofa sofa
sofort immediately
sogar even
Sohn son
solche(r, s) like this
sollte should
Sommer summer
sonderbar strange
Sonne sun
Sonnencreme sunscreen
Sonnenstrahl sunbeam
sonnig sunny
Sonntag Sunday
Sorge worry
sich Sorgen machen (um) worry, be concerned (about)
sorgfältig careful
Sorte kind
sortieren sort
Soße sauce
sowieso anyway
Sozialarbeiter/in social worker
Spanien Spain
Spanier/in Spanish

spanisch Spanish
spannend exciting
sparen save
Spaß fun
spaßig fun, funny
Spaß machen be fun; be joking
(zu) spät late
später later, afterwards
Spaziergang walk
spazieren gehen go for a walk
speichern save
Speisekarte menu
spenden donate
Spiegel mirror
Spiegelei fried egg
Spiel game, play
spielen play
Spieler/in player
spielerisch playful
Spielfeld playing field, sports field
Spielplatz playground
Spielzeug toy
Spind locker
Spinne spider
Spion/in spy
Spitze top
sponsern sponsor
als Sponsor finanzieren sponsor
Sport(art) sport
Sportler/in sportsperson
Sportplatz sports field, playing field
Sportsendung sports programme
Sport(unterricht) PE (= physical education)
Sprache language
sprechen (mit) speak, talk (to)
Sprichwort saying
springen jump
Staatsangehörigkeit nationality
stabil strong
Stadion stadium (*pl* -s or -ia)
Stadt town
Stall stable
Stamm (*Volk*) tribe
ständig all the time
Stärke power
stark strong
Station station
stattdessen instead (of)
stattfinden take place

Steckbrief fact file
stehen stand; suit
stehlen steal
Stein stone, rock
Stell dir vor! Guess what!
Stelle job
stellen put
Stempel stamp
sterben die
(Stereo)anlage stereo
Stern star
jdn im Stich lassen let sb down
Stiefel boot
Stift pen
Stimme voice
die Stirn runzeln frown
Stock stick
Stockwerk floor, level
Stolz pride
stolz proud
stören disturb, bother
stoßen push
Strafe sentence
(Straf)täter/in offender
Straftat offence
Strand beach
Straße road, street
Straßenmusikant/in busker
streicheln stroke
Streichholz match
Streit fight
sich streiten argue, fight
streng strict
stressig stressful
Strom electricity
Stück piece, bit
Stückchen bit
Student/in student
Studienabschluss graduation
studieren study
Studierende/r student
stürzen fall
Stufe step
Stuhl chair
Stunde hour, lesson
Stundenplan timetable (*BE*), (class) schedule (*AE*)
Stuntgirl/Stuntman stunt performer
Sturm storm
Substantiv noun
suchen nach look for
Suchmaschine search engine

Südamerika South America
Süden south
Südosten south-east
Südwesten south-west
Supermarkt supermarket
Suppe soup
süß sweet; cute
süßes, kohlensäurehaltiges Getränk fizzy drink
Süßigkeit(en) sweet
Symbol symbol
Szene scene

T

Tabelle grid
Tafel blackboard
Tag day
den ganzen Tag all day
Tagebuch diary
eines Tages one day
Takt rhythm
Tal valley
Talent ability
Tante aunt
Tanz dance
Tanzen dancing
tanzen dance
Tänzer/in dancer
Tasche bag, pocket
Taschendiebstahl begehen pick pockets
Taschengeld pocket money
Tasse cup
Tätigkeit job
Tatsache fact
Tatze paw
tauschen swap
Tausend thousand
Tausende thousands (*pl*)
Tauziehen tug-of-war
Teamarbeit teamwork
Teamkollege/Teamkollegin teammate
Teammitglied teammate
Tee tea
Tee trinken have tea
Teenager- teenage
Teigwaren pasta
Teil part
teilen share
sich teilen split up
teilnehmen (an) take part (in)
Teilzeit- part-time

Telefon (tele)phone
(Telefon)anruf call
Teller plate
Temperatur temperature
Teppich carpet
Termin date
Test test
teuer expensive
Thai Thai
Thailänder/in Thai
thailändisch Thai
Theater theatre; drama *(no pl)*
(Theater)stück play
Thema topic, subject
Themenpark theme park
Therapeut/in therapist
Therapie therapy
tief deep
Tier animal
Tier- und Pflanzenwelt wildlife
Tierarzt/-ärztin vet
Tiger tiger
tippen type
Tisch table
den Tisch decken set the table
Titel title
tja well
Tochter daughter
Tod death
Toilette toilet *(BE)*, bathroom
  (AE)
Toleranz tolerance
Tomate tomato *(pl -es)*
Ton sound
Tor goal
ein Tor schießen score a goal
Tormann/Torfrau goalkeeper
tot dead
total totally
Totempfahl totem pole
töten kill
Tracht costume
Tradition tradition
traditionell traditional
träge lazy
tragen carry; wear
Trainer coach
trainieren train, exercise
Training practice
Transport transport
sich trauen dare
Traum dream
träumen dream

traurig sad
(sich) treffen meet, get together
sich trennen split up
Treppe stairs *(npl)*
treten step; kick
trinken drink
trocken dry
trotzdem anyway
Truthahn/-henne turkey
Tschüss! Bye! *(informal)*, Bye-
  bye! *(informal)*
tun do
tun können be able to do
Tür door
Türglocke doorbell
Türklingel doorbell
Turm tower
Turnen gymnastics *(npl)*
Turnhalle gym (= gymnasium)
Turnschuh trainer *(BE)*
Typ guy *(informal)*; type
typisch typical
Tyrann bully
tyrannisieren bully

U

U-Bahn underground *(BE)*,
  subway *(AE)*
die (Londoner) U-Bahn the tube
üben practise
über about, above, across, over
über Funk over the radio
überall everywhere
überall in/auf all over
übergewichtig overweight
Überleben survival
überleben survive
überlegen think about
überprüfen check
überqueren cross
überraschend surprising
überrascht surprised
Überraschung surprise
übersetzen translate
übertreten *(Vorschrift)* break
Überwachungskamera security
  camera
üblich normal, regular
übrig left
übrigens by the way
Übung exercise, practice
Uhr clock, watch
um around, at

um zu in order to
umblättern turn
umbringen murder
(sich) umdrehen turn over, turn
  round
Umfrage survey
Umgebung environment
umhauen cut down
Umkleide fitting room
sich umschauen (in) look around
sich umsehen (in) look around
umsonst for nothing; (for) free
Umwelt environment
umweltfreundlich green
(Umwelt)verschmutzung
  pollution
umziehen move
Umzug parade
Unabhängigkeit freedom *(no pl)*
unbezahlt unpaid
und and
unfair unfair
Unfall accident
unfreundlich unfriendly
ungefähr about, more or less
ungerecht unfair
ungesund unhealthy
ungesundes Essen junk food
ungewöhnlich unusual, strange
unglaublich incredible
unglücklich unhappy
unglücklicherweise
  unfortunately
unheimlich scary, spooky
  (informal)
unhöflich impolite, rude
Uniform uniform
Universität university, college
unmöglich impossible
Unordnung mess
uns us, ourselves
unser(e) our
unsere(r, s) ours
unten below
unter under, among
unteres Ende bottom
untergebracht sein stay
untergehen sink
Unterhaltung talk
etw unternehmen take action
Unterricht class
unterrichten teach
Unterschied difference

unterschreiben sign
Unterschrift signature
Unterseite bottom
unterstreichen underline
unterstützen help out, support
Untersuchung survey
amerikanischer Ureinwohner/ amerikanische Ureinwohnerin Native American
Urlaub holiday *(BE)*, vacation *(AE)*
Urlaub haben be on holiday
im Urlaub sein be on holiday
Ursache cause
Urteil sentence
USA (= Vereinigte Staaten von Amerika) USA
die USA the US (= United States)

V

Vandalismus vandalism
Vati dad *(informal)*
Vater father
Vegetarier/in vegetarian
(Ver)änderung change
(ver)brennen burn
(ver)hungern starve
sich mit jdm verabreden ask sb out, date sb *(informal)*
Verabredung date
(sich) verändern change
verängstigt scared
für etw verantwortlich sein be responsible for sth
Verantwortlichkeit responsibility
Verantwortung responsibility
verärgert angry
Verband bandage
verbessern improve
etw verbieten ban sth
verbinden connect, link
Verbrauch usage
Verbrechen crime
verbringen *(Zeit)* spend
verdienen earn
Verein club
die Vereinigten Staaten the United States
Vereinigtes Königreich UK (= United Kingdom)
Verfasser/in author
Vergangenheit past
vergessen forget

vergleichen compare
vergnügt(er) werden cheer up
verhaften arrest
sich verhalten behave, act
Verhalten behaviour *(BE)*, behavior *(AE)*
Verhältnisse background
sich verirren get lost
verkaufen sell
Verkäufer/in salesperson, seller, shop assistant
(Verkaufs)stand stall
Verkehr traffic
verkehrt herum upside down
sich verkleiden dress up
Verkleidung fancy dress
verkleinern reduce
verlassen leave
sich verlassen auf rely on
verlässlich reliable
sich verlaufen get lost
verlegen embarrassed
verletzt injured, hurt
sich verlieben (in) fall in love (with)
(in jdn) verliebt sein be in love (with sb)
verlieren lose
vermissen miss
vermuten guess, suppose
veröffentlichen publish, release
Verpackung(smaterial) packaging
verpassen miss
verringern reduce
verrückt crazy
versäumen miss
verschieden different
verschmutzen pollute
verschmutzt polluted
sich verschulden get into debt
verschwenden waste
Verschwendung waste *(no pl)*
verschwinden disappear
Versehen mistake
sich versichern make sure
versorgen take care of
den Weg versperren block
verspielt playful
versprechen promise
sich verständigen communicate
(sich) verstecken hide

verstehen understand, see, get, figure out
sich (mit jdm) verstehen get along (with sb)
verstoßen break
versuchen try
verteidigen defend
sich (wieder) mit jdm vertragen make it up with sb
vertraulich private
vervollständigen complete
Verwandte/r relative
Verwendung use
verwirrt confused
verwundet hurt
Verzeihung! Sorry.
verzweifelt desperate
viel lots of, much
Viel Glück! Good luck!
viele many, a lot (of)
viele Grüße best wishes
Vielen Dank! Thanks a lot!
vielleicht perhaps, maybe
vielleicht tun might
Viertel (nach/vor) quarter (past/to)
Viertel neighbourhood
Visagist/in make-up artist
Vitamin vitamin
Vogel bird
Volksfest carnival
voll full
völlig totally
Vollzeit- full-time
von from, by
von weit her far
vor before, in front of, to
vorbei over
vor langer Zeit a long time ago
vor (zwei Tagen) (two days) ago
vorbei/vorüber an past
vorbereiten prepare
sich vorbeugen bend over
vorführen perform
Vorhang curtain
vorher before
vorkommen exist
Vorlieben likes *(pl)*
vormittags in the morning, am (= ante meridiem) *(nur hinter Uhrzeit)*
vorn(e) in front
Vorname first name

vorne in at the front of
vorschlagen suggest
Vorschule nursery school *(BE, no pl)*, kindergarten *(AE)*
vorsichtig careful
Vorsingen audition
Vorsitzende/r president
Vorspeise starter
Vorspielen audition
Vorsprechen audition
vorstellen introduce
sich vorstellen imagine
Vorstellungsgespräch job interview
Vorstellungskraft imagination
Vortanzen audition
Vorurteil prejudice
vorziehen prefer
Vulkan volcano *(pl -oes or -os)*

W

Wachs wax
wachsen grow
wagen dare
Wahl choice, election
wählen vote
Wahlfach elective *(AE)*
Wahlkurs elective *(AE)*
wahr true
wahr werden come true
während during, while
Wahrheit truth
Wahrsager/in fortune-teller
wahrscheinlich probably
Waise orphan
Waisenkind orphan
Wal whale
Wald forest
walisisch Welsh
Wand wall
Wandern hiking
wandern hike
Wange cheek
wann when
warm warm
Wärme heat *(no pl)*
warten (auf) wait (for)
Wartezimmer waiting room
warum why
was what
Was gibt's? What's on?

Was ist mit ...? How about ...?, What about ...? *(informal)*
Was kostet/kosten ...? How much is/are ...?
Was läuft? What's on?
(sich) waschen wash
Waschmaschine washing machine
Wasser water
Wasserfall waterfall
Wasserhahn tap
(Wasser)tank tank
Wecker alarm clock
Wechselgeld change
wechseln change
Weg way, path, trail
den Weg beschreiben give directions
jdm über den Weg laufen run into
weg away
weg von off
wegen because of; about
weggehen leave, be off
weglaufen run away
weh sore
Wehrdienst leisten do military service
wehtun hurt
weiblich female
weich soft
Weide field
Weihnachten Christmas
weil because, since
Weinen cry
weinen cry
Weise way
weit far
weitergehen go on
weitermachen go on
etw weiter tun keep doing sth
weiß white
welche(r, s) what, which
Welle wave
Welpe puppy
Welt world
Weltraum space
Weltrekord world record
wenige few
weniger less
wenigstens at least
wenn if, when
wer who

Werbespot commercial
Werbung advert (= advertisement)
werden become, go, will, get
werfen throw
(Kfz-)Werkstatt garage
Werkzeug tool
etw wert sein be worth sth
wessen whose
West- west
Westen west
die Westindischen Inseln the West Indies *(npl)*
westlich west
Wettbewerb competition, contest
wetteifern (um) compete (for)
wetten bet
Wetter weather
wichtig important
Wichtigkeit importance *(no pl)*
widerlich disgusting, nasty
wie how, like
Wie geht es dir/Ihnen/euch? How are you doing?, How are you?
Wie geht's? How are things?
Wie heißt du?/ Wie heißen Sie? What's your name?
Wie ist ...? What's ... like?
Wie spät/Wie viel Uhr (ist es)? What time (is it)?
Wie viel Uhr ist es? What's the time?
Wie wäre es mit ...? How about ...?, What about ...? *(informal)*
wie (zum Beispiel) such as
wieder again
wieder aufbauen rebuild
wiederholen repeat
etw wiederholt tun keep doing sth
Wiederholung repeat
wiederverwenden reuse
wiederverwerten recycle
wiegen weigh
Wiese field
wild wild
Wind wind
(australischer) Windhund dingo
windig windy
Windpocken chickenpox

winken wave
Winter winter
winzig tiny
wir we
wirklich really, real
wissen know
Wissenschaftler/in scientist
Witz joke
witzig fun, funny
Wo kommst du her? Where are
  you from?
wo(hin) where
wo(hin) auch immer wherever
Woche week
Wochenende weekend
wöchentlich weekly
wohltätige Zwecke charity
Wohltätigkeitslauf sponsored
  walk
Wohltätigkeitsveranstaltung
  charity
wohnen live
Wohnung flat *(BE)*,
  apartment *(AE)*
Wohnzimmer living room
Wolke cloud
Wolkenkratzer skyscraper
wollen want, fancy *(informal)*
Wort word
Wörterbuch dictionary
Wortnetz mindmap
wund sore
kein Wunder no wonder
wunderbar wonderful, great
wundervoll wonderful
Wunsch wish, request
(sich) wünschen wish, want,
  request
würde(st/n/t) would
Wurm worm
Wurst sausage
würzig spicy

Wüste desert
wütend angry, mad

Z

Zahl number
zählen count
Zahn tooth (*pl* teeth)
Zauber magic
Zauberer/Zauberin magician
Zaubertrick magic trick
Zeh(e) toe
Zeichen sign, symbol
(Zeichen)trickfilm animated
  film, cartoon
zeichnen draw
zeigen show
Zeile line
(Uhr)zeit time
Zeit verbringen hang out
  (informal)
Zeitschrift magazine
Zeitschriftengeschäft newsagent
Zeitung newspaper
Zeitungshändler/in newsagent
Zeitverschwendung waste of
  time
Zeltplatz campsite
Zentrum centre
zerbrochen broken
zerstören destroy
Zettel piece of paper
ziehen pull
Ziel finish
ziemlich pretty, quite
Ziffer number
Zimmer room
Zitrone lemon
Zivildienst leisten do civilian
  service
Zoo zoo
zornig angry
zu too; to

Zucker sugar
zuerst first, at first
zufällig by accident
zufrieren freeze
Zug train
etw zugeben admit sth
Zugfahrt train ride
Zuhause home
zuhören listen (to)
Zukunft future
zum Beispiel for example
zumachen close
Zündholz match
zunehmen put on weight
zuordnen match (with)
zurück back
zurückbekommen get back
zurückkehren return
zurückkommen get back
zurücklassen leave
zusammen together
zusammenbrechen break down
Zusammenhang context
zusätzlich extra
zuschauen watch
Zuschauermenge crowd
zusehen watch
Zuständigkeit responsibility
zustimmen agree (with)
Zutat ingredient
zuverlässig reliable
zuversichtlich optimistic
zuvor before
Zweig branch
zweimal twice
ein(e) zweite(r, s) another
Zwiebel onion
jdn zwingen (etw zu tun) force
  sb (to do sth)
zwischen between

NAMES

Girls/Women

Adeela [əˈdiːlə]
An [æn]
Camilla [kəˈmɪlə]
Claire [kleə]
Daisy [ˈdeɪzi]
Dolly [ˈdɒli]
Doris [ˈdɒrɪs]
Elizabeth [iˈlɪzəbəθ]
Ella [ˈelə]
Emily [ˈeməli]
Esther [ˈestə]
Eve [iːv]
Gail [geɪl]
Gita [ˈgiːtə]
Glenda [ˈglendə]
Grace [greɪs]
Gracie [ˈgreɪsi]
Hannah [ˈhænə]
Hyun-Chung [ˌhaɪən ˈtʃʌŋ]
Isabel [ˈɪzəbel]
Jeannie [ˈdʒiːni]
Jennifer [ˈdʒenɪfə]
Katie [ˈkeɪti]
Laura [ˈlɔːrə]
Leyla [ˈleɪlə]
Lilly [ˈlɪli]
Lisa [ˈliːsə]
Maryam [ˈmeəriəm]
Maxi [ˈmæksi]
May [meɪ]
Melanie [ˈmeləni]
Molly [ˈmɒli]
Muna [ˈmuːnə]
Nadia [ˈneɪdiə]
Natasha [nəˈtæʃə]
Nicola [ˈnɪkələ]
Nugi [ˈnuːgi]
Olivia [əˈlɪviə]
Paula [ˈpɔːlə]
Phoebe [ˈfiːbi]
Pippa [ˈpɪpə]
Rachel [ˈreɪtʃl]
Rebecca [riˈbekə]
Rhiannon [riˈænən]
Susan [ˈsuːzn]
Victoria [vɪkˈtɔːriə]
Violet [ˈvaɪələt]
Xie [ʒi]

Boys/Men

Aiman [ˈeɪmən]
Ben [ben]
Bob [bɒb]
Bruce [bruːs]
Darren [ˈdærən]
David [ˈdeɪvɪd]
Diego [diˈeɪgəʊ]
Ed [ed]
Fagin [ˈfeɪgɪn]
George [dʒɔːdʒ]
Harry [ˈhæri]
Henry [ˈhenri]
Isaac [ˈaɪzək]
Jack [dʒæk]
Jacob [ˈdʒeɪkəb]
Jamie [ˈdʒeɪmi]
Jason [ˈdʒeɪsən]
Jerome [dʒəˈrəʊm]
John [dʒɒn]
Josh [dʒɒʃ]
Kenneth [ˈkenəθ]
Kevin [ˈkevɪn]
Laurie [ˈlɒri]
Luca [ˈluːkə]
Martin [ˈmaːtɪn]
Max [mæks]
Nick [nɪk]
Nigel [ˈnaɪdʒəl]
Oliver [ˈɒlɪvə]
Pete [piːt]
Sam [sæm]
Sanjeev [ˈsændʒiːv]
Steve [stiːv]
Tomasz [ˈtɒmaʃ]
Wayne [weɪn]
Zuberi [zuˈberi]

Families

Bird [bɜːd]
Brownlow [ˈbraʊnləʊ]
Burkin [ˈbɜːkɪn]
Clements [ˈklemənts]
Crum [krʌm]
Dawkins [ˈdɔːkɪnz]
Garimara [gæriˈmaːrə]
Hempleman-Adams
  [ˌheplmən ˈædəmz]
Jackson [ˈdʒæksən]
Kilcoyne [ˈkɪlkɔɪn]
Kumar [ˈkuːmə]
Lewis [ˈluːɪs]
Lurie [ˈlʊəri]

McLeod [məkˈlaʊd]
Neville [ˈnevəl]
Pilkington [ˈpɪlkɪŋtən]
Qiuping [ˌtʃiuˈpɪŋ]
Turnbell [ˈtɜːnbl]
Veysey [ˈviːzi]

Other Names

ABBA [ˈæbə]
Agile Wallaby [ædʒaɪəl ˈwɒləbi]
Al Gore [ˌæl ˈgɔː]
Allanhill Farm [ˌælənhɪl ˈfaːm]
American Express
  [əˌmerɪkən ɪkˈspres]
Artful Dodger [ˌaːtfl ˈdɒdʒə]
Auto [ˈɔːtəʊ]
Axiom [ˈæksiəm]
Bales College [ˌbeɪlz ˈkɒlɪdʒ]
Beckiboo [ˈbekiˌbuː]
Brent Street [ˈbrent striːt]
Cameron Diaz [ˌkæmrən ˈdiːæs]
Casino Royale [kəˌsiːnəʊ rɔɪˈaːl]
Charles Dickens [ˌtʃaːlz ˈdɪkɪnz]
Christina Aguilera [krɪˈstiːnə
  ˌægɪˈleərə]
the Church of England [ðə
  ˌtʃɜːtʃ əv ˈɪŋglənd]
the Commonwealth [ðə
  ˈkɒmənwelθ]
Cootamundra Home
  [ˌkuːtəˈmʌndrə həʊm]
Crickhowell High School
  [krɪkˌhaʊəl ˈhaɪ skuːl]
David Beckham [ˌdeɪvɪd ˈbekəm]
Disney [ˈdɪzni]
Earth Day [ˈɜːθ deɪ]
Environmental Youth Conference
  [ɪnˌvaɪrənmentl ˈjuːθ ˌkɒnfrəns]
Erin Brokovich [ˌerɪn ˈbrɒkəvɪtʃ]
the European Union [ðə
  ˌjʊərəˌpiːən ˈjuːnjən]
Evening Standard [ˌiːvnɪŋ
  ˈstændəd]
Father Christmas [ˌfaːðə ˈkrɪsməs]
Feversham College [ˌfevəʃəm
  ˈkɒlɪdʒ]
Fizz Pop [ˈfɪz pɒp]
Gatwick Airport [ˌgætwɪkˈeəpɔːt]
Gold Dust Backpackers Hostel
  [ˌgəʊldˌdʌst ˌbækpækəz ˈhɒstəl]
The Guardian [ðə ˈgaːdiən]
Heathrow Airport
  [ˌhiːθrəʊˈeəpɔːt]

Hendon School [ˌhendən ˈsku:l]
Hollywood [ˈhɒliˌwʊd]
James Bond [ˌdʒeɪmz ˈbɒnd]
James Cook [ˌdʒeɪmz ˈkʊk]
Jamie Oliver [ˌdʒeɪmiˌˈɒlɪvə]
Jordin Sparks [ˌdʒɒdɪn ˈspa:ks]
Kempsey [ˈkempsi]
Kevin Rudd [ˈkevɪn rʌd]
Kylie Minogue [ˌkaɪli mɪˈnəʊg]
Labour [ˈleɪbə]
Leonardo DiCaprio [ˌli:əʊˌna:dəʊ
   diˈkæpriəʊ]
Little Richard [ˌlɪtl ˈrɪtʃəd]
Mickey Mouse [ˌmɪki ˈmaʊs]
Million Trees LA [ˌmɪljən
   ˌtri:zˌelˈeɪ]
Moksha [ˈmɒkʃə]
Moore River Native Settlement
   [ˌmʊə ˌrɪvə ˌneɪtɪv ˈsetlmənt]
Oliver Twist [ˌɒlɪvə ˈtwɪst]
Outward Bound [ˌaʊtwəd ˈbaʊnd]
Perth Zoo [ˌpɜ:θ ˈzu:]
Pixar [ˈpɪksa:]
PowerPoint [ˈpaʊəpɔɪnt]
Quadruple Bypass Burger
   [ˌkwɒdrʊpl ˈbaɪpa:s ˌbɜ:gə]
Reef Relief [ˈri:f rɪˌli:f]
Shuttleworth Road [ˈʃʌtlwɜ:θ ˌrəʊd]
Slip-Slop-Slap [ˌslɪp slɒp ˈslæp]
Spade&Shovel [ˌspeɪdˌən ˈʃʌvl]
St Mary Primary School [sənt
   ˌmeəri ˈpraɪməri ˌsku:l]
Steve Irwin [sti:v ˈɜ:wɪn]
The Big Issue [ðə ˌbɪg ˈɪʃu:]
The Big Texan Steak Ranch [ðə
   ˌbɪg ˌteksn ˈsteɪk ra:ntʃ]
The Heart Attack Grill [ðə ˌha:t
   əˌtæk ˈgrɪl]
Vanessa Hudgens [vəˌnesə
   ˈhʌdʒɪnz]
Victoria Park [vɪkˌtɔːriə ˈpa:k]
Wall-E [ˈwɒli]
Waterfall Hospital [wɔ:təˌfɔ:l
   ˈhɒspɪtəl]
Yothu Yindi [jəʊtu: ˈjɪndi:]

Geographical Names

Abuja [əˈbu:dʒə]
Accra [əˈkra:]
Addis Abeba [ˌædɪsˌˈæbəbə]
Africa [ˈæfrɪkə]
Alice Springs [ˌælɪs ˈsprɪŋz]
Amarillo [ˌæməˈrɪləʊ]

Amsterdam [ˈæmstədæm]
Anchorage [ˈæŋkərɪdʒ]
Antigua and Barbuda
   [ænˌti:gəˌænd ba:ˈbju:də]
Arizona [ˌærɪˈzəʊnə]
Asia [ˈeɪʃə]
Athens [ˈæθɪnz]
the Atlantic Ocean
   [ðiˌətˌlæntɪkˌˈəʊʃn]
Australia [ɒˈstreɪliə]
Ayers Rock [ˌeəz ˈrɒk]
the Bahamas [ðə bəˈha:məz]
Banda Aceh [ˌbændəˌˈætʃeɪ]
Bandya [ˈbændja:]
Bangkok [ˌbæŋˈkɒk]
Bangladesh [ˌbæŋgləˈdeʃ]
Barbados [ba:ˈbeɪdɒs]
Belize [biˈli:z]
Bermuda Islands
   [bəˈmju:dəˌaɪləndz]
Blue Mountains [blu: ˈmaʊntɪnz]
Botswana [bɒtˈswa:nə]
Bradford [ˈbrædfəd]
Brisbane [ˈbrɪzbən]
Brunei [ˈbru:naɪ]
Caims [keɪmz]
Cairns [keənz]
Cairo [ˈkaɪrəʊ]
California [ˌkæləˈfɔ:niə]
Cameroon [ˌkæməˈru:n]
Canada [ˈkænədə]
Canberra [ˈkænbərˌə]
Cape Town [ˈkeɪptaʊn]
Chennai [ˈtʃenaɪ]
Chicago [ʃɪˈka:gəʊ]
China [ˈtʃaɪnə]
Colorado [ˌkɒləˈra:dəʊ]
Cyprus [ˈsaɪprəs]
Dodoma [ˈdəʊdəmə]
Dominica [ˌdɒmɪˈni:kə]
Dorset [ˈdɔ:sɪt]
Dublin [ˈdʌblɪn]
Durban [ˈdɜ:bən]
Egypt [ˈi:dʒɪpt]
Eritrea [ˌerɪˈtreɪə]
Ethiopia [ˌi:θɪˈəʊpiə]
Europe [ˈjʊərəp]
Falkland Islands
   [ˈfɔ:lkləndˌaɪləndz]
Fiji [ˈfi:dʒi:]
Freetown [ˈfri:taʊn]
Gaborone [ˌgæbəˈrəʊni]
Gambia [ˈgæmbiə]

Georgetown [ˈdʒɔ:dʒtaʊn]
Ghana [ˈga:nə]
Great Barrier Reef [ˌgreɪt
   ˈbæriə ri:f]
Greece [gri:s]
Greenwich [ˈgrenɪtʃ]
Grenada [grɪˈneɪdə]
Guyana [gaɪˈænə]
Hanover [ˈhænəʊvə]
Harare [həˈra:ri]
Hawaiian Islands
   [həˈwaɪənˌaɪləndz]
Hendon [ˈhendən]
the Himalayas [ðə ˌhɪməˈleɪəz]
Hongkong [ˌhɒŋˈkɒŋ]
Hull [hʌl]
the Indian Ocean
   [ðiˌɪndiənˌˈəʊʃn]
Indonesia [ˌɪndəʊˈni:ʒə]
Islamabad [ɪsˈla:məbæd]
Israel [ˈɪzreɪl]
Jamaica [dʒəˈmeɪkə]
Jordan [ˈdʒɔ:dn]
Kalgoorlie [kælˈgʊəli]
Kampala [kæmˈpa:lə]
Kenya [ˈkenjə]
Key West [ˌki: ˈwest]
Khartoum [ˌka:ˈtu:m]
Kigali [kɪˈga:li]
Kingston [ˈkɪŋstən]
Kiribati [ˌkɪrɪˈba:ti]
Kuala Lumpur [ˌkwa:lə
   ˈlʊmpʊə]
Kuwait [kuˈweɪt]
Lake Nasser [ˌleɪk ˈnæsə]
Las Vegas [læs ˈveɪgəs]
Leeds [li:dz]
Lesotho [ləˈsu:tu:]
Liberia [laɪˈbɪəriə]
Lilongwe [lɪˈlɒŋweɪ]
London [ˈlʌndən]
Los Angeles [lɒsˌˈændʒəli:z]
Lusaka [luˈsa:kə]
Malawi [məˈla:wi]
Malaysia [məˈleɪzi]
Malta [ˈmɔ:ltə]
Manchester [ˈmæntʃɪstə]
Manila [məˈnɪlə]
the Marshall-Islands [ðə
   ˈma:ʃlˌaɪləndz]
Mauritius [məˈrɪʃəs]
Melbourne [ˈmelbən]
Miami [maɪˈæmi]

Micronesia [ˌmaɪkrəʊˈniːziə]
Mogadishu [ˌmɒɡəˈdɪʃuː]
Monaco [ˈmɒnəkəʊ]
Monrovia [mənˈrəʊviə]
Montreal [ˌmɒntriˈɔːl]
Mumbai [ˌmʊmˈbaɪ]
Muscat [ˈmʌskæt]
Myanmar [ˈmiːənmɑː]
Nairobi [naɪˈrəʊbi]
Namibia [nəˈmɪbiə]
Nauru [nəˈruː]
Nepal [nɪˈpɔːl]
New Delhi [njuː ˈdeli]
New Guinea [njuː ˈɡɪni]
New York [njuː ˈjɔːk]
New Zealand [njuː ˈziːlənd]
Nigeria [naɪˈdʒɪəriə]
North Pole [ˌnɔːθ ˈpəʊl]
Oman [əʊˈmɑːn]
Ottawa [ˈɒtəwə]
the Pacific Ocean [ðə pəˌsɪfɪk ˈəʊʃn]
Pakistan [ˌpaːkɪˈstɑːn]
Palau [pəˈlaʊ]
Papua New Guinea [ˌpæpuə njuː ˈɡɪni]
Perth [pɜːθ]
the Philippines [ðə ˈfɪləpiːnz]
Port Moresby [pɔːt ˈmɔːzbi]
Pretoria [priˈtɔːriə]
Puerto Rico [ˌpwɜːtəʊ ˈriːkəʊ]

Queensland [ˈkwiːnzlənd]
Rangoon [ræŋˈɡuːn]
Republic of South Africa [riˌpʌblɪk əv saʊθ ˈæfrɪkə]
Rockdale [ˈrɒkdeɪəl]
Rwanda [ruˈændə]
Samoa [səˈməʊ]
San Francisco [ˌsæn frənˈsɪskəʊ]
Sanaa [səˈnɑː]
the Seychelles [ðə seɪˈʃelz]
Sierra Leone [siˌerəˈliˈəʊn]
Singapore [ˌsɪŋəˈpɔː]
the Solomon Islands [ðə ˈsɒləmən ˌaɪləndz]
Somalia [səˈmɑːliə]
South Africa [saʊθ ˈæfrɪkə]
South Yorkshire [ˌsaʊθ ˈjɔːkʃə]
Sri Lanka [srɪ ˈlæŋkə]
St. Andrews [sənt ˈændruːz]
St. Kitts-Nevis [sənt ˌkɪts ˈniːvɪs]
St. Lucia [sənt ˈluːʃə]
St. Vincent and the Grenadines [sənt ˌvɪnsənt ænd ðə ˈɡrenədiːnz]
Staten Island [ˌstætn ˈaɪlənd]
Sudan [suˈdɑːn]
Swaziland [ˈswɑːzilænd]
Sweden [ˈswiːdn]
Sydney [ˈsɪdni]
Tanzania [ˌtænzəˈniːə]
Texas [ˈteksəs]

Thailand [ˈtaɪlænd]
the Philippines [ðə ˈfɪləpiːnz]
Tonga [ˈtɒŋɡə]
Toronto [təˈrɒntəʊ]
Torres Strait [ˌtɒrɪs ˈstreɪt]
Trinidad and Tobago [ˌtrɪnɪdæd ænd təˈbeɪɡəʊ]
Tuvalu [tuˈvɑːluː]
U.A.E. (= United Arab Emirates) [juːˈeiˈiː, juˌnaɪtɪdˈærəb ˈemərəts]
Uganda [juˈɡændə]
Uluru [ˌuːləˈruː]
Vancouver [vænˈkuːvə]
Vanuatu [ˌvænuˈɑːtuː]
Vietnam [ˌviːetˈnæm]
Wales [weɪlz]
Washington, D.C. [ˌwɒʃɪŋtən diːˈsiː]
Wellington [ˈwelɪŋtən]
Western Australia [ˌwestən ɒˈstreɪliˈə]
Windhoek [ˈwɪndhʊk]
Winnipeg [ˈwɪnipeg]
Yaoundé [jɑːˈʊndeɪ]
Yemen [ˈjemən]
York [jɔːk]
Zambia [ˈzæmbiə]
Zimbabwe [zɪmˈbɑːbwi]

NUMBERS / MONTHS

Numbers

0	oh, zero, nil [əʊ, ˈzɪərəʊ, nɪl]	21	twenty-one [ˌtwenti ˈwʌn]	1st	first [fɜːst]	
1	one [wʌn]	22	twenty-two [ˌtwenti ˈtuː]	2nd	second [ˈsekənd]	
2	two [tuː]	⤋	⤋	3rd	third [θɜːd]	
3	three [θriː]	30	thirty [ˈθɜːti]	4th	fourth [fɔːθ]	
4	four [fɔː]	40	forty [ˈfɔːti]	5th	fifth [fɪfθ]	
5	five [faɪv]	50	fifty [ˈfɪfti]	6th	sixth [sɪksθ]	
6	six [sɪks]	60	sixty [ˈsɪksti]	7th	seventh [ˈsevnθ]	
7	seven [ˈsevn]	70	seventy [ˈsevnti]	8th	eighth [eɪtθ]	
8	eight [eɪt]	80	eighty [ˈeɪti]	9th	ninth [naɪnθ]	
9	nine [naɪn]	90	ninety [ˈnaɪnti]	10th	tenth [tenθ]	
10	ten [ten]	100	a/one hundred [ə/wʌn ˈhʌndrəd]	11th	eleventh [ɪˈlevnθ]	
11	eleven [ɪˈlevn]	101	one hundred and one [wʌn ˌhʌndrəd ən ˈwʌn]	12th	twelfth [twelfθ]	
12	twelve [twelv]			13th	thirteenth [ˌθɜːˈtiːnθ]	
13	thirteen [ˌθɜːˈtiːn]	102	one hundred and two [wʌn ˌhʌndrəd ən ˈtuː]	⤋	⤋	
14	fourteen [ˌfɔːˈtiːn]			20th	twentieth [ˈtwentiəθ]	
15	fifteen [ˌfɪfˈtiːn]	⤋	⤋	21st	twenty-first [ˌtwenti ˈfɜːst]	
16	sixteen [ˌsɪksˈtiːn]	1,000	a/one thousand [ə/wʌn ˈθaʊznd]	22nd	twenty-second [ˌtwenti ˈsekənd]	
17	seventeen [ˌsevnˈtiːn]	⤋	⤋			
18	eighteen [ˌeɪˈtiːn]	100,000	a/one hundred thousand [ə/wʌn ˌhʌndrəd ˈθaʊznd]	30th	thirtieth [ˈθɜːtiəθ]	
19	nineteen [ˌnaɪnˈtiːn]			40th	fortieth [ˈfɔːtiəθ]	
20	twenty [ˈtwenti]			50th	fiftieth [ˈfɪftiəθ]	
		⤋	⤋	60th	sixtieth [ˈsɪkstiəθ]	
		1,000,000	a/one million [ə/wʌn ˈmɪljən]	70th	seventieth [ˈsevntiəθ]	
				80th	eightieth [ˈeɪtiəθ]	
		⤋	⤋	90th	ninetieth [ˈnaɪntiəθ]	
		1,000,000,000	a/one billion [ə/wʌn ˈbɪljən]	100th	hundredth [ˈhʌndrədθ]	

1/2	a/one half [ə/wʌn ˈhɑːf]
1/3	a/one third [ə/wʌn ˈθɜːd]
1/4	a/one quarter [ə/wʌn ˈkwɔːtə]
1/8	a/one eighth [ən/wʌn ˈeɪtθ]
3/4	three quarters [θriː ˈkwɔːtəz]

Months

January [ˈdʒænjuəri]	May [meɪ]	September [sepˈtembə]
February [ˈfebruəri]	June [dʒuːn]	October [ɒkˈtəʊbə]
March [mɑːtʃ]	July [dʒʊˈlai]	November [nəʊˈvembə]
April [ˈeɪprəl]	August [ˈɔːgəst]	December [dɪˈsembə]

infinitive	simple past	participle	
awake [əˈweɪk]	awoke [əˈwəʊk]	awoken [əˈwəʊkən]	aufwachen, erwachen
be [biː]	was/were [wɒz/wɜː]	been [biːn]	sein
beat [biːt]	beat [biːt]	beaten [biːtən]	schlagen; besiegen
become [bɪˈkʌm]	became [bɪˈkeɪm]	become [bɪˈkʌm]	werden
begin [bɪˈgɪn]	began [bɪˈgæn]	begun [bɪˈgʌn]	anfangen, beginnen
bend [bend]	bent [bent]	bent [bent]	(sich) biegen, beugen
bet [bet]	bet/betted [bet/ˈbetɪd]	bet/betted [bet/ˈbetɪd]	wetten
bite [baɪt]	bit [bɪt]	bit/bitten [bɪt/ˈbɪtən]	beißen
break [breɪk]	broke [brəʊk]	broken [ˈbrəʊkən]	(zer)brechen
bring [brɪŋ]	brought [brɔːt]	brought [brɔːt]	(mit)bringen
build [bɪld]	built [bɪlt]	built [bɪlt]	bauen
burn [bɜːn]	burnt/burned [bɜːnt/bɜːnd]	burnt/burned [bɜːnt/bɜːnd]	(ver)brennen
buy [baɪ]	bought [bɔːt]	bought [bɔːt]	kaufen
catch [kætʃ]	caught [kɔːt]	caught [kɔːt]	fangen; kriegen; festnehmen
choose [tʃuːz]	chose [tʃəʊz]	chosen [ˈtʃəʊzən]	auswählen
come [kʌm]	came [keɪm]	come [kʌm]	kommen
cost [kɒst]	cost [kɒst]	cost [kɒst]	kosten
cut [kʌt]	cut [kʌt]	cut [kʌt]	schneiden; mähen
deal with [ˈdiːl wɪð]	dealt with [ˈdelt wɪð]	dealt with [ˈdelt wɪð]	sich befassen mit, sich kümmern um
do [duː]	did [dɪd]	done [dʌn]	machen, tun
draw [drɔː]	drew [druː]	drawn [drɔːn]	zeichnen
dream [driːm]	dreamt/dreamed [dremt/driːmd]	dreamt/dreamed [dremt/driːmd]	träumen
drink [drɪŋk]	drank [dræŋk]	drunk [drʌŋk]	trinken
drive [draɪv]	drove [drəʊv]	driven [ˈdrɪvən]	fahren
eat [iːt]	ate [eɪt]	eaten [ˈiːtən]	essen
fall [fɔːl]	fell [fel]	fallen [ˈfɔːlən]	fallen; stürzen
feed [fiːd]	fed [fed]	fed [fed]	zu essen geben, füttern
feel [fiːl]	felt [felt]	felt [felt]	(sich) fühlen
fight [faɪt]	fought [fɔːt]	fought [fɔːt]	kämpfen, streiten
find [faɪnd]	found [faʊnd]	found [faʊnd]	finden
fit [fɪt]	fit/fitted [fɪt/ˈfɪtɪd]	fit/fitted [fɪt/ˈfɪtɪd]	sich eignen; passen
flee [fliː]	fled [fled]	fled [fled]	fliehen
fly [flaɪ]	flew [fluː]	flown [fləʊn]	fliegen
forget [fəˈget]	forgot [fəˈgɒt]	forgotten [fəˈgɒtən]	vergessen
freeze [friːz]	froze [frəʊz]	frozen [ˈfrəʊzən]	gefrieren, einfrieren, zufrieren
get [get]	got [gɒt]	got/gotten (AE) [gɒt/ˈgɒtən]	erhalten, bekommen; gelangen; werden; holen; verstehen
give [gɪv]	gave [geɪv]	given [ˈgɪvən]	geben
go [gəʊ]	went [went]	gone [gɒn]	gehen; werden
grow [grəʊ]	grew [gruː]	grown [grəʊn]	wachsen
hang [hæŋ]	hung [hʌŋ]	hung [hʌŋ]	hängen
have [hæv]	had [hæd]	had [hæd]	haben; essen
hear [hɪə]	heard [hɜːd]	heard [hɜːd]	hören
hide [haɪd]	hid [hɪd]	hid/hidden [hɪd/ˈhɪdən]	(sich) verstecken
hit [hɪt]	hit [hɪt]	hit [hɪt]	schlagen (auf); treffen, erschüttern; anfahren
hold [həʊld]	held [held]	held [held]	(fest)halten; besitzen
hurt [hɜːt]	hurt [hɜːt]	hurt [hɜːt]	wehtun, schmerzen; schaden
keep [kiːp]	kept [kept]	kept [kept]	(be)halten
know [nəʊ]	knew [njuː]	known [nəʊn]	wissen; kennen

IRREGULAR VERBS

infinitive	simple past	participle	
lay [leɪ]	laid [leɪd]	laid [leɪd]	legen
lead [liːd]	led [led]	led [led]	(an)führen, leiten
learn [lɜːn]	learnt/learned [lɜːnt/lɜːnd]	learnt/learned [lɜːnt/lɜːnd]	lernen
leave [liːv]	left [left]	left [left]	verlassen; da lassen; hinterlassen; abfahren; weggehen
let [let]	let [let]	let [let]	lassen
lose [luːz]	lost [lɒst]	lost [lɒst]	verlieren
make [meɪk]	made [meɪd]	made [meɪd]	machen
mean [miːn]	meant [ment]	meant [ment]	bedeuten; meinen
meet [miːt]	met [met]	met [met]	(sich) treffen
pay [peɪ]	paid [peɪd]	paid [peɪd]	bezahlen
put [pʊt]	put [pʊt]	put [pʊt]	setzen, legen, stellen; eingeben
read [riːd]	read [red]	read [red]	lesen
ride [raɪd]	rode [rəʊd]	ridden ['rɪdən]	fahren; reiten
ring [rɪŋ]	rang [ræŋ]	rung [rʌŋ]	klingeln, läuten
rise [raɪz]	rose [rəʊz]	risen ['rɪzn]	(auf)steigen
run [rʌn]	ran [ræn]	run [rʌn]	laufen, rennen
say [seɪ]	said [sed]	said [sed]	sagen
see [siː]	saw [sɔː]	seen [siːn]	sehen; einsehen, verstehen
sell [sel]	sold [səʊld]	sold [səʊld]	verkaufen
send [send]	sent [sent]	sent [sent]	(zu)schicken
set [set]	set [set]	set [set]	setzen
shake (out) ['ʃeɪk ('aʊt)]	shook (out) ['ʃʊk ('aʊt)]	shaken (out) ['ʃeɪkən ('aʊt)]	(aus)schütteln
shine [ʃaɪn]	shone [ʃɒn]	shone [ʃɒn]	scheinen (Sonne)
show [ʃəʊ]	showed [ʃəʊd]	shown [ʃəʊn]	zeigen
sing [sɪŋ]	sang [sæŋ]	sung [sʌŋ]	singen
sink [sɪŋk]	sank [sæŋk]	sunk [sʌŋk]	untergehen, sinken
sit [sɪt]	sat [sæt]	sat [sæt]	sitzen
sleep [sliːp]	slept [slept]	slept [slept]	schlafen
smell [smel]	smelt/smelled [smelt/smeld]	smelt/smelled [smelt/smeld]	riechen
speak [spiːk]	spoke [spəʊk]	spoken ['spəʊkən]	sprechen
spell [spel]	spelt/spelled [spelt/speld]	spelt/spelled [spelt/speld]	buchstabieren
spend [spend]	spent [spent]	spent [spent]	ausgeben (Geld); verbringen (Zeit)
split up [splɪt‿'ʌp]	split up [splɪt‿'ʌp]	split up [splɪt‿'ʌp]	sich teilen; sich trennen
stand [stænd]	stood [stʊd]	stood [stʊd]	stehen; ertragen, aushalten
steal [stiːl]	stole [stəʊl]	stolen ['stəʊlən]	stehlen
stick [stɪk]	stuck [stʌk]	stuck [stʌk]	kleben
swim [swɪm]	swam [swæm]	swum [swʌm]	schwimmen
take [teɪk]	took [tʊk]	taken ['teɪkən]	(mit)nehmen; brauchen; dauern
teach [tiːtʃ]	taught [tɔːt]	taught [tɔːt]	unterrichten, beibringen
tell [tel]	told [təʊld]	told [təʊld]	erzählen; sagen
think [θɪŋk]	thought [θɔːt]	thought [θɔːt]	denken, glauben, meinen; nachdenken
throw [θrəʊ]	threw [θruː]	thrown [θrəʊn]	werfen
understand [ˌʌndə'stænd]	understood [ˌʌndə'stʊd]	understood [ˌʌndə'stʊd]	verstehen
wake up [weɪk‿'ʌp]	woke up [wəʊk‿'ʌp]	woken up [ˌwəʊkən‿'ʌp]	aufwecken; aufwachen
wear [weə]	wore [wɔː]	worn [wɔːn]	tragen (Kleidung)
win [wɪn]	won [wʌn]	won [wʌn]	gewinnen
write [raɪt]	wrote [rəʊt]	written ['rɪtən]	schreiben

QUELLENVERZEICHNIS

BILDQUELLEN

Umschlag außen: blum DESIGN & KOMMUNIKATION, Hamburg; Mauritius, Mittenwald (Skateboarder); © Juniors Bildarchiv, Ruhpolding (Känguru); © Picture Press, Hamburg/Frank P. Wartenberg (Jugendlicher im Overall); Caro Fotoagentur/ Rupert Oberhäuser (Pub); Mauritius, Mittenwald/Dirk v. Mallinckrodit (Uluru)

3 Alamy Limited, Oxfordshire/Life File Photo Library Ltd.

10 AGE Fotostock, New York (Jamaicaner); Strandperle Medienservices, Hamburg/Corbis (junger Afrikaner); AGE Fotostock, New York (Waliserin)

11 Strandperle Medienservices, Hamburg/PhotoAlto (Chinesin); F1online digitale Bildagentur GmbH, Frankfurt/Main/Eyecandy (Australier); Alamy Limited, Oxfordshire/© Chris Rout (Inderin); Technisch-Grafische Abteilung Westermann

12 fotolia.com, New York/© Stihlo24 (Flaggen); Deutsche Gesellschaft für Luft- und Raumfahrt, Oberpfaffenhofen (Erde)

13 Mediacolor's Bildagentur, CH-Zürich/Senff/cmi (Aborigines); Getty Images, München/Handout (Wellenreiterin)

14 actionplus sports images, London/Neil Tingle (Rugby Spieler); Visum Foto GmbH, Hamburg/Wildlight (Schafscherer); Australia Post, Melbourne/National Philatelic Collection (Briefmarke); fotolia.com, New York/© picture-optimize (Flagge); Colditz, Margit, Halle (Aborigine); MEV Verlag GmbH, Augsburg (Koalas)

15 allover, Kleve (Opernhaus Sydney); images.de, Berlin/ © IPN/Kevin Taylor (Reisepass); Corbis, Düsseldorf/ © Jose Fuste Raga (Känguru Schild); Getty Images, München/Axiom Photographic Agency/Michael Coyne (Aborigine malt); Wildlife Bildagentur GmbH, Hamburg/ D.J. Cox (Schlange); Bridgeman Berlin, Berlin/© Heini Schneebeli, Australien (dot painting); picture-alliance/ dpa, Frankfurt/Main (Weihnachten am Strand); Roberts, G. R., Nelson, Neuseeland (Truck)

16 National Archives of Australia (ital. Einwanderer); Getty Images, München/Hulton Archives (Captain Cook); Getty Images, München/Taxi/Gary Bell (Great Barrier Reef); Associated Press GmbH, Frankfurt am Main/© 2008 Discovery Networks U.S. (Mann mit Krokodil); The Image Bank, München/Rossi (Ayers Rock); Alamy Limited, Oxfordshire/Bachmann (Outback)

17 Technisch-Grafische Abteilung Westermann

18 Picture-Alliance GmbH, Frankfurt/Main/dpa/AAP Image/ Kylie Walker (Flying Doctors); Picture-Alliance GmbH, Frankfurt/Main/dpa/Grab (Outback); Getty Images, München/Bec Parsons (Weihnachten)

20 Alamy Limited, Oxfordshire/Bill Bachman (Dingo); Alamy Limited, Oxfordshire/Gerry Pearce (Wombat); Jung, Manfred, Bad Vilbel (Emu); OKAPIA KG Michael Grzimek & Co, Frankfurt/Main/BIOS/D. Heuclin (Känguru)

21 Franken, Britta, Rothemühle (Aborigine); action press, Hamburg/Franziska Krug (austral. Band); Heinemann, Rigby, Port Melbourne (Dot painting)

24 Getty Images, München/Jeff Hunter (Meeresschildkröte); Corbis, Düsseldorf/© Mark Karrass (Great Barrier Reef); Getty Images, München/Stephen Frink (Clownfische)

25 plainpicture GmbH & Co. KG, Hamburg/T. Reutter (Junge); Sea Tops, Karlsruhe/Mark Conlin (tote Koralle); Corbis, Düsseldorf/© Amos Nachoum (rote Koralle)

26 mauritius images, Mittenwald/World Pictures

27 Picture-Alliance GmbH, Frankfurt/Main/dpa/Film Arsenal, Hamburg

29 Getty Images, München/Andrew Sheargold (Kevin Rudd); Getty Images, München/AFP/Torsten Blackwood (Australier gerührt); Picture-Alliance GmbH, Frankfurt/ Main/dpa/epa AAP/Andrea Hayward (Aborigines)

31 Tom Oldham Photography, London (Sam Kilcoyne); Masterfile Deutschland GmbH, Düsseldorf (Frau mit Kopftuch); Picture-Alliance GmbH, Frankfurt/Main (Feuer); Strandperle Medienservices, Hamburg/ Photodisc (Skater); Masterfile Deutschland GmbH, Düsseldorf (Trösten); Associated Press GmbH, Frankfurt am Main/The Daily Reflector/Jenni Farrow (Teen Court)

32 Strandperle Medienservices, Hamburg/Comstock (Jungen auf Sofa); Jupiterimages GmbH-Creativ Center, Düsseldorf/© POLKA DOT (High Five); F1online digitale Bildagentur GmbH, Frankfurt/Main (Mädchen telefonieren); Alamy Limited, Oxfordshire (Jungengruppe)

36 CartoonStock Ltd, GB-Bath

37 Getty Images, München/Matt Cardy

38 Fotostudio Druwe & Polastri, Cremlingen/Weddel

40 Picture-Alliance GmbH, Frankfurt/Main/dpa/Phil Noble (ausgebranntes Auto); Masterfile Deutschland GmbH, Düsseldorf/© Marnie Burkhart (Junge)

42 Associated Press GmbH, Frankfurt am Main

43 InGestalt, Leipzig

46 Getty Images, München/Mike Powell (Boxen); Alamy Limited, Oxfordshire/© Carole Edrich Extreme and Endurance Photography (Parkour); Capps, Krista, Department of Ecology and Evolutionary Biology, NY 14853-2701 (Höhlenklettern); Corbis, Düsseldorf/MaXx Images Inc./zefa (Bungee Jumping); Picture-Alliance GmbH, Frankfurt/Main (Freeclimber); mauritius images, Mittenwald (Rafting)

47 Getty Images, München/Peter Lilja (Hundeschlitten); www.outwardbound.de (Logo)

48 Corbis, Düsseldorf /ZEFA visual media/M. Martin

49 Alamy Limited, Oxfordshire/© S.I.N

50 Masterfile Deutschland GmbH, Düsseldorf/ WirelmageStock (Motorradfahrer); Konovalenko, Alexander, Jerusalem © 2005 (Hippie); Sodapix, Zürich/© Pymca/Marc Vallee (Rasta); transit - Fotografie und Archiv, Leipzig/Peter Hirth (Gothicfrau); mauritius images, Mittenwald (Punk)

51 iStockphoto, CAN-Calgary/© Camilla Wisbauer (Mädchen); Getty Images, München/Ethan Miller (Hip-Hopper); Jupiterimages GmbH, Ottobrunn/© PYMCA (Emos)

52 Picture-Alliance GmbH, Frankfurt/Main/EPA/Ali Haider

53 Getty Images, München/David Sacks (Junge); iStockphoto, CAN-Calgary/© Mark Hayes (Mädchen); Corbis/Bettmann (Gruppe Hippies); ullstein bild, Berlin (Hippies auf Bus); Corbis/Hulton Deutsch Collection (drei Hippies)

54 Technisch-Grafische Abteilung Westermann

55 Expedition 360 Productions, London

56 Expedition 360 Productions, London

57 Jupiterimages GmbH, Ottobrunn/© DYNAMIC GRAPHIC (Ballon); Getty Images, München/Sergio Pitamitz (Jeeps); Outdoor Archiv, Hamburg (Floß); argus Fotoarchiv GmbH, Hamburg (Kamele)

58 Picture-Alliance GmbH, Frankfurt/Main/Abaca Lionel Hahn (Christina Aguilera, platinblond); Keystone Pressedienst, Hamburg/Topham Picturepoint (Christina Aguilera, Zöpfe); Picture-Alliance GmbH, Frankfurt/

TEXTQUELLEN

North Sea

Great Britain

Shetland
Islands

Orkney
Islands

John o'Groats

● Aberdeen

Balmoral

Dundee ●

Edinburgh ●

Ben Nevis
1344 m

Loch Ness

Scotland

Forth

Glasgow ●

Clyde

Tweed

Newcastle ●

Hadrian's Wall

Tyne

Carlisle ○

Isle of
Lewis

Isle of
Skye

Outer Hebrides

(London) Derry ○

Belfast

Ocean

Atlantic